Media Policy in CANADA
Sources for Critical Analysis

Marian Bredin
Brock University

Kendall Hunt
publishing company

Cover image © Shutterstock, Inc.

Kendall Hunt
publishing company

www.kendallhunt.com
Send all inquiries to:
4050 Westmark Drive
Dubuque, IA 52004-1840

Printed in the United States of America
10 9 8 7 6 5 4 3

Table of Contents

Preface

This book combines a series of critical and analytical readings on media policy in Canada with a selection of primary policy sources drawn from interest groups, media institutions, and government agencies. Each chapter begins with a critical analysis reflecting a range of methodologies and approaches to media policy research. Selected from recent books, research studies, and journal articles, these analyses have been chosen for their comprehensive view of key areas of media policy while presenting research findings in an accessible and engaging manner. These readings cover a range of essential topics in media policy, including rationales and objectives for media policy, the impact of interest groups and social movements, the evolving role of public broadcasting, critical perspectives on regulation, subsidies and cultural protectionism, assessments of policy outcomes, and the impact of international trade agreements on domestic media policies.

In most chapters, two selections from primary policy documents are also presented to give readers a concrete example of how different policy objectives, interests, instruments, and outcomes are reflected and addressed in the policymaking process. These primary documents pick up on themes and topics raised in the critical analysis that opens each chapter. They are organized around a range of different policy approaches and tools that have been applied to Canadian media. The primary policy sources are drawn from documents produced by such agencies and institutions as the Massey Commission, the House of Commons Standing Committee on Canadian Heritage, the federal Department of Canadian Heritage, the Canadian Media Producers Association, the Canadian Broadcasting Corporation (CBC), the National Film Board (NFB), the Canadian Radio-Television and Telecommunications Commission (CRTC), among others. These primary policy documents capture the complexity of media policy by providing a series of 'snapshots' of policies and programs for a variety of Canadian media industries, including radio, television, film production, book publishing, magazines and periodicals, recorded music, and new digital media. Each primary source allows readers to engage with media policy in action and to understand its impact on both creators and consumers of media culture.

This book is intended for undergraduates and graduate students, as well as researchers and scholars in Communication and Media Studies with interests in cultural and media policy and media industries. While this collection has a distinctively Canadian perspective, it provides a broader context for understanding the practices and processes of media policymaking. It serves as a rich resource for comparative perspectives on media policy and also has a place within the interdisciplinary field of Canadian Studies. Opening with a detailed chapter that surveys approaches to media policy, the book establishes the central link between the characteristics of media industries and the impetus for government interventions. Chapter 1 outlines the main rationales and objectives for media policy, while describing the features of the most common policy tools as they are implemented in the Canadian context. The first chapter also explores the tension between public interest and private profit, and the contradictions within contemporary media as both culture and commerce. This central conflict can be traced throughout the history of Canadian media policy and Chapter 2 explores recurring themes and discourses by examining the evolution of policy over the past five decades. Each subsequent chapter is focused around specific policy instruments as they are currently being applied to individual Canadian media institutions and industries.

This collection will work well as an introductory text to media policy in Canada. It has been designed to organize relevant readings for large classes and lectures, while the primary sources make excellent material for discussion and analysis in smaller groups and seminars. The framework for policy analysis developed in Chapter 1 is summarized in table format, a feature that can be used to guide students through oral discussion of primary policy material, or to help structure written policy analyses. Each chapter also concludes with a list of questions for discussion that pinpoint key arguments in the research and scholarly contributions, while directing readers to the most salient aspects of each primary policy source. This book is the first of its kind to present both critical perspectives on policy and primary documents in a single collection. The primary material has been culled from thousands of pages of on-line government documents to foreground those which most clearly demonstrate how the policy process is actually undertaken. Reading and evaluating primary policy sources such as the ones presented here helps students develop valuable critical and analytical skills and move beyond elementary knowledge of policy facts and figures to a deeper engagement with its public origins, political interests, and its social and cultural impact.

Rationales for Media Policy: Culture or Commerce?

MEDIA POLICY AND MEDIA INDUSTRIES

The media in Canada today are primarily commercial enterprises, designed to make a profit for their shareholders and, in the case of publicly owned media like the Canadian Broadcasting Corporation (CBC), to compete successfully in a commercial environment while returning value to taxpayers for their 'investment.' Yet, unlike most other businesses or industries that we might think of, the mass media are the main means by which people today create and experience their culture, communicate their values, and understand the social and political contexts within which they live. The study of media policy in Canada explores the tension between these creative and commercial roles for media and considers how and why governments might intervene to further social and cultural goals in the commercial media environment. This book will help you think critically about how media combine these dual commercial and cultural or social functions and how governments in Canada have tried to balance these roles. The scholarly research and primary policy sources presented here explore how Canadian media, as both industries and cultural entities, are in a state of constant tension and often show evidence of profound contradictions in our society.

As institutions and industries, the media involve processes of mass communication from a centralized point of production to a large and complex audience. The technologies of mass media have evolved from the original forms of simple mechanical reproduction (print, photography, and film), to electronic production and distribution (music recording, radio, television, and telecommunications), to the present era of digital technologies in which earlier types of media content are converted to digital form and circulated via networked computers and mobile communication devices. Even though digital technologies are currently reshaping the media environment, we still refer to each industry with reference to its original technological form. The print industry includes books, newspapers, and magazines. The Canadian film industry produces hundreds of feature and documentary films every year. Broadcasting includes radio stations and television channels, as well as cable and satellite distribution. Canada's music industry produces many different genres of music, though recorded music is now distributed almost exclusively in digital format. This book explores the evolution of policy instruments and government strategies for each of these different industries.

To understand why Canadian governments are involved in creating regulations and policy for media, it is important to review some key features of the media industries. We can organize our thinking on media industries and institutions by distinguishing between:

- Media content as **products.**
- Practices and processes of media **production.**
- The social and economic **environment** within which media products circulate and media production occurs.

Media **products** can be divided into those which rely primarily on revenue from advertising (magazines, newspapers, television, and radio, for example) and those which derive their profits mainly from direct sales to consumers (books, film, and recorded music). The main financial challenge facing all Canadian media products, whether supported by advertising revenue or consumer revenue, is the initial high cost of production and the large investment required for creation of the content. These high production costs are complicated by the potentially high risk of failure in the Canadian marketplace. In the global context, media industries are always seeking major hit series, blockbuster films, or top-selling songs and albums to recover losses on the many other products that are not commercially successful. The 'misses' are more easily balanced against 'hits' when media companies can establish a vast catalogue or repertoire of content and attract audiences through the use of popular genres and star talent. Canadian media industries are constrained because they cannot always easily compete with their US and European counterparts in creating large inventories and attracting star talent. Yet they must take the same financial risks of investing in media content without being able to predict its success in the marketplace. These risks are compounded by the fact that Canadian markets and audiences are already many times smaller than those in the US and many other countries. Media policy in Canada works to protect Canadian media industries from some of the economic risks and disadvantages they face in the creation of domestic media content.

Media profits can be maximized by concentration of ownership in the industry and forms of corporate integration that control distribution and access to markets by competitors. Researchers study processes of media **production** by examining these patterns of ownership and the emergence of media conglomerates as responses to the risks inherent in the creation of media content. The theoretical perspective of critical political economy can be used to analyze the effects of media industry structures on content and on producers. In Canada, political economists who study media industries are particularly interested in how the creation of media content is shaped by the commercial influences of media industries. Policy analysts are similarly interested in how ownership, competition, and concentration in media industries influence the amount and type of Canadian media content produced and circulated.

If we consider media as social and cultural institutions, we also need to focus on the larger **environments** within which they operate. We need to understand the shifting environment of technological change, the emergence of high-speed digital networks, the rise of global media culture, and the constantly changing dynamics of Canada's multicultural and multiracial society. In the development of media policy, governments regulate the balance between commerce and culture, and between private profit and public responsibilities, within these wider environmental transformations. As this brief overview suggests, Canadian media policy must grapple with the complexities of media products, challenges of media production, and transformations in media environments. The next part of this chapter introduces some critical concepts and analytical approaches for the study of media policy and explores some of the rationales and objectives for media policy in the Canadian context.

CONSUMERS AND CITIZENS IN THE PUBLIC SPHERE

Political economists of the media argue that we are not merely consumers of products and of media content, but we are also citizens and members of the public. To really understand media's political and social role, and the link between media policy and media industries, we need to take a brief detour through the theoretical concept of the public sphere. The notion of the public sphere originates with German social theorist Jurgen Habermas (2001). Habermas was interested in the historical development of a realm of public debate and discussion that resisted church and state control of ideas during the eighteenth century in Europe. Later, Habermas saw a positive role for the mass media in society, one that was not entirely taken over by capitalism and commercial culture. According to Habermas (2001), publics are formed in different historical contexts under different social conditions, but share the common practice of open debate and exchange of views about social issues. He viewed these publics as places where reason, debate, and dialogue could be freely exercised without fear or threat of domination. Following Habermas, we might define the public sphere as the realm of social life in which public opinion is formed and to which all citizens have access. Citizens act as a public body whenever they freely express ideas and opinions, and the public sphere depends on communication as a means of sharing these ideas and influencing opinion.

Habermas' work is concerned with communication as the process of rational dialogue and the foundation of democratic society. We take the idea of the public for granted now, but it is important to recognize that public debate and a public sphere as we understand it now did not always exist. The significance of mass media in this process is that media helped create specific publics throughout history. For example:

- The early periodical press in Europe created a relatively elite public of readers and writers who would debate newspaper and journal articles in coffee houses and other public spaces.
- Broadcasting created a different kind of public in North America and Europe beginning in the 1930s with radio and the 1950s with TV.

- The internet, the web, and social media created both global and local publics at the turn of the twentieth century and into the present.

Today, the media are the primary forms of communication in the public sphere. Media policy can thus be seen as articulating objectives and implementing tools for these central forms of public communication.

Habermas and other analysts of media and the public sphere see a central need for non-commercial media that have an arms-length relationship to the state. In this view, public service broadcasting like the CBC in Canada, although flawed in some respects, allows for the expression of oppositional and critical points of view more effectively than do privately owned and heavily commercial media. Public service media are distinctive in their forms of public ownership and control. Public service broadcasters often create non-commercial, non-profit programming based on a mandate that provides access for all tastes, interests, and needs, even those minority groups and audiences for whom the creation of media content would not be profitable (see Chapter 5). Political economists of media also look to state intervention and regulation as a means of ensuring public accountability in media industries. Ideally, media policy encourages media owners to address the public interest and strike a balance between the desires of the consumer and the needs of the citizen. The ideals of the public sphere help explain why most countries have some kind of publicly owned or public service media like the CBC in Canada or the British Broadcasting Corporation (BBC) in Britain. Public ownership of media in Canada occurs mainly through the CBC, but we also have a publicly owned and funded film producer, the National Film Board (NFB), publicly supported provincial educational television broadcasters (TV Ontario, British Columbia's Knowledge Network, and Access Alberta for example), and community owned and operated radio and television in many towns and cities. Though these media outlets are part of the wider media industries and face many of the same risks and constraints, their public ownership and state support help protect their function of informing and educating people as citizens from being overwhelmed by market forces. This book explores key questions about the role played by public service goals and publicly owned media in Canadian society. The sources collected here explore questions about how media policy protects, or sometimes undermines, the place of the media in the public sphere.

APPROACHES TO POLICY ANALYSIS

Governments intervene in the media industries to ensure that public needs and cultural objectives can be addressed by media in their role as social institutions. Canadian policy-making for media, as in other sectors, is a process of defining ends, choosing means, carrying out decisions, and evaluating results. Policy analysis highlights the 'normative intent' or value assumptions of policy making, and shows how policy is determined by the exercise of power, influence, and legitimate coercion. Before governments make choices about policy tools and their implementation, there is usually some form of public and political debate about policy objectives. In public debates, the purposes of particular policies must be made explicit, conflicts negotiated and compromises achieved in order for these stated objectives to be implemented.

As Des Freedman (2008, 1) argues, media systems and therefore media policy, are shaped by competing political interests within any given country or region. All forms of

POLICY GOALS FOR CANADIAN MEDIA

Policy **rationales** are the underlying political and social motivations for policy, while **objectives** are the specific and concrete goals which governments hope to achieve through policy. In his article on the features of federal cultural policy that follows, John Foote identifies four key rationales for Canadian media policy:

- Media are a **public good** with broad social and cultural value. Media policy should ensure access for all while generating positive benefits for Canadian society.
- Media should operate in the **national interest,** support Canadian cultural sovereignty, and be protected from undue foreign influence and control.
- Media should foster **national unity** and enhance Canadian identity, internal social linkages, inclusion, and participation for all Canadians.
- Media should encourage **economic growth** by generating jobs in the media and cultural industries, addressing weaknesses in Canadian media markets and promoting exports of Canadian media products.

Beyond these four broad rationales for media policy, Foote identifies three concrete objectives against which the outcomes of government policy can be assessed. First of all, Canadian media policy should focus on the creation of Canadian media **content.** Secondly, media policy should work to ensure that Canadians citizens have **access** to Canadian media content, through profitable and stable Canadian-owned media channels. Finally Canadians should have freedom of **choice** from among the wide range of global media available today, while still preserving 'shelf space' for Canadian media content.

Debates about the rationales and objectives of media policy take place among various stakeholders at the 'input' stage of the policy process. Governments and bureaucracies then act to design and implement policies by choosing from among various possible policy tools and instruments. In Canada, media and communications policy is mainly a federal rather than provincial jurisdiction under the constitutional division of powers. Federal agencies and institutions that are directly involved in media policy include the Department of Canadian Heritage, which oversees media institutions like the CBC, the NFB, and Telefilm Canada; the House of Commons Standing Committee on Canadian Heritage; and the Senate Committee on Transport and Communication, both of which hold Parliamentary hearings and produce reports on aspects of media policy; and the CRTC which licences all forms of radio, television, and telecommunications in Canada as well as regulating media ownership and Canadian content in broadcasting.

THE MEDIA POLICY TOOL KIT

Various instruments or items in the policy 'tool kit' described in the previous section have been applied to Canadian broadcasting and other media since the first government intervention in the licencing of radio stations in the 1920s. These various media policy tools are described in detail in the following, but the schematic diagram in Figure 1 shows how each of these tools has been applied in the field of Canadian media policy and how they are interrelated.

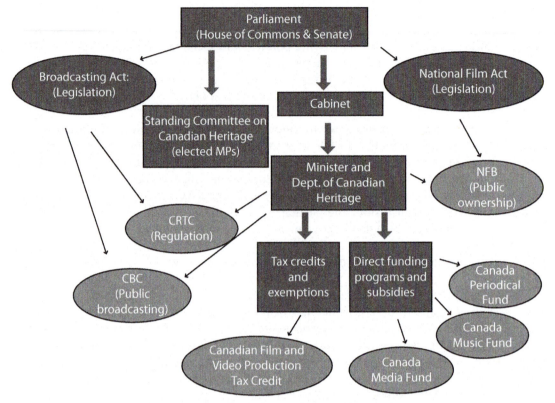

FIGURE 1   Canadian media policy tools

a. Indirect government pressure, negotiation, and persuasion

This is the least formal of tools in the kit, one that involves achieving objectives for media by indirect means. It would include public hearings held by Parliamentary Committees or the Canadian Radio-television Telecommunications Commission (CRTC) in which legislators and regulators make their goals known and seek the voluntary participation and support of media owners and producers. One example is the 2003 hearings into the Canadian broadcasting system held by the House of Commons Standing Committee on Canadian Heritage. These hearings, including the background research and the final report, *Our Cultural Sovereignty,* produced by then Committee chair MP Clifford Lincoln, laid out clear goals and recommendations for the future development of Canadian media. Part of this report describing Canada's broadcast regulatory history is included in Chapter 2 of this book. Although no new legislation or regulation was drafted as a result of these hearings, they presented an opportunity for the government to articulate its goals for media policy while consulting with members of the industry.

b. Legislation

The most formal and complex form of government intervention in media is the creation and passing of legislation. Parliament has passed a series of laws to direct the development of film, radio, and television in particular. Canada's first contemporary media legislation was the *Canadian Radio Broadcasting Act* passed in 1932 and amended in 1936. It created the Canadian Radio Broadcasting Commission, later to become the CBC. Another *Broadcasting Act* was passed in 1958 after the introduction of television in Canada. The Act was revised again in 1968 and this version emphasized the new role of regulation and ultimately led to the creation of the CRTC in 1976. The *Broadcasting Act,* last revised and amended in 1991, still determines the role and function of Canada's broadcasting system (see Chapter 3 for a selection from the 1991 *Act*). The NFB (originally the National Film Commission) was also created by an Act of Parliament in 1939 and takes its current mandate "to produce and distribute and to promote the production and distribution of films designed to interpret Canada to Canadians and to other nations" from *The National Film Act* of 1950 (NFB, 2010).

c. Public ownership

Public ownership of media in Canada includes the operation and funding of CBC Radio, CBC Television and the internet service cbc.ca in English Canada, Société Radio Canada (SRC) radio, television, and internet in Quebec and in French-speaking communities in the rest of the country, as well as the National Film Board. These federal agencies operate with parliamentary grants but at arm's length from direct government control. Public ownership of the CBC is defined and described in the *Broadcasting Act* (1991), and in Section 3(1)(m) of the Act, CBC programming is mandated to:

   i. be predominantly and distinctively Canadian, reflect Canada and its regions to national and regional audiences, while serving the special needs of those regions,
   ii. actively contribute to the flow and exchange of cultural expression,
   iii. be in English and in French, reflecting the different needs and circumstances of each official language community, including the particular needs and circumstances of English and French linguistic minorities,
   iv. strive to be of equivalent quality in English and French,
   v. contribute to shared national consciousness and identity,
   vi. be made available throughout Canada by the most appropriate and efficient means and as resources become available for the purpose, and
   vii. reflect the multicultural and multiracial nature of Canada.

d. Direct expenditures, grants, subsidies, and transfer payments

Many people think of direct government spending on programs and infrastructure when they think of media policy. This policy tool includes federal government support for Canadian publishing and magazines, music recording, film and television production under various programs such as the Canada Periodical Fund, Canada Book Fund, Canada Music Fund, or Canada Media Fund, all administered by the Department of Canadian Heritage (see Chapters 7–10 for primary policy sources in each of these areas). These different grants and subsidies for Canadian media content have been developed as a means of ensuring the 'shelf space' that Foote describes, especially since Canadian media producers face significant competition from American and multinational media conglomerates. The federal government spent $3.74 billion on culture in 2007–08 and concentrated its spending on the cultural industries, including broadcasting, the film and video industry, book and periodical publishing, and the sound recording industry. Spending on these industries represented $2.22 billion or 59.4 percent of total federal expenditures on culture (Statistics Canada, 2010, 1). Thus, direct expenditures by the Canadian government play a substantial role in the survival and success of the media industries.

e. Tax expenditures, deductions, or credits

Using tax deductions and tax credits as a policy tool helps attract investment to the media industries without requiring that governments spend money directly on programs or subsidies. However, the tax credit must be accounted for as potential government tax revenue that is forfeited. Examples of tax credit programs in Canada include the Canadian Film and Video Production Tax Credit (CPTC), a program that allows companies to claim tax refunds for the labour and production costs of Canadian film or television productions as long as they are shot in Canada using Canadians in key production roles (see Chapter 10 for discussion of the CPTC). The CPTC program allows for a tax refund of up to 15 percent of the cost of production (Department of Canadian Heritage, 2010a). Federal and provincial tax credit programs are responsible for attracting foreign film and TV producers to shoot on location in Canada. Canadian cities like Vancouver actively work to attract foreign film production especially from Los Angeles and Hollywood (these are sometimes referred to in the US as 'runaway' productions). A tax expenditure program also applies to magazines and periodicals. As long as a minimum of 80 percent of a magazine is original Canadian editorial content, advertisers may count the full cost of their advertising in magazines as a business expense for an income tax deduction, (see Chapter 7 for detailed discussion of how tax deductions work for magazines in Canada).

f. Taxation

As with most products and services in Canada, media products and services are subject to the federal Goods and Services Tax (GST) and provincial sales tax as well. However, the revenue from these taxes is not channelled back to government expenditures on media industries in any explicitly correlated manner as, for instance, taxes on cinema tickets in France go back to the production of new French films. One case where taxes are channelled back to media production in Canada is the case of the import levy on blank CDs. This levy is charged under the terms of the *Copyright Act* and is collected by the Copyright Board of Canada. It is meant to address the loss of income to music producers triggered by downloading and copying music from the internet. The revenue from this levy is then distributed to music rights holders in Canada by the Canadian Private Copying Collective (CPCC). CPCC describes the levy as a 'royalty' rather than a tax, since the policy objective is to compensate music producers for the circulation of their work on individual copies (CPCC, 2011). The policy tool of taxation is also used in Canadian media through compulsory industry contributions to joint public/private funds such as the Canada Media Fund and the Foundation to Assist Canadian Talent on Recordings (FACTOR). In this case Canadian cable and satellite television companies must contribute to the Canada Media Fund and radio broadcasters support FACTOR under

CRTC requirements that these media producers use part of their profits to help fund the creation of more Canadian music and media content (see Chapter 9 for examples of media industry support for Canadian content).

g. Regulation

The CRTC, created in 1968, is the main regulator of broadcasting in Canada but does not play a role in the operation of other media industries. The Commission controls levels of radio and television ownership, ensuring that stations and networks are majority Canadian-owned (no less than 80 percent Canadian control) and it ensures that mergers, cross-ownership, and horizontal integration do not limit the number of media outlets operating in any one market. The CRTC also issues licences for radio and television stations, renewable every seven years. These licences come with certain expectations about programming, both in terms of format and genre and in relation to Canadian content. The CRTC sets minimum levels of Canadian content for radio and television. Radio stations must play 35 percent Canadian music during the broadcast day. Canadian music is defined as satisfying at least two of the following MAPL criteria:

M (music): the music is composed entirely by a Canadian
A (artist): the music is, or the lyrics are, performed principally by a Canadian
P (performance): the musical selection consists of a live performance that is
  ▪ recorded wholly in Canada, or
  ▪ performed wholly in Canada and broadcast live in Canada
L (lyrics): the lyrics are written entirely by a Canadian (CRTC, 2010c)

In television, the CRTC requires that conventional television licensees devote no less than 55 percent of the broadcast year and not less than 50 percent of the evening broadcast period (6 P.M. to midnight) to Canadian programs (CRTC, 2010a). Canadian content requirements for the various specialty television channels like YTV, TSN or the Food Network are set individually as conditions of their licences. Chapter 6 explores the CRTC's radio and television policies in more detail. CRTC content quotas should not be confused with censorship of Canadian media. Canadians have access to one of the most varied and diverse range of choices in media in the world and there are very few types of media content that are not available here. The CRTC does not prevent broadcasters from carrying highly popular US programs; it only requires that some of the advertising revenue and profits generated by top rated foreign programs like *House, Survivor,* or *CSI* be directed into supporting the creation of Canadian programming.

POLICY OUTCOMES

To understand why Canadian governments have been so heavily involved in the direction and regulation of broadcasting and other media we need to look back to the economic influences of the media industries. Much Canadian media policy is organized around the idea of **market failure,** or the notion that in Canada our small markets cannot support enough of our own domestic media products to generate adequate profits. As we have seen from the discussion of both advertising revenue and consumer revenue earlier in this chapter, profitable media products depend on maximizing both audiences and the rate of consumption. Canadian audiences simply are not large enough to generate an adequate return on the initial investment in media production. Canadian media products are not always profitable, even though they may be both popular and of high quality. The problem of Canada's small domestic media market is made more complicated by the ready access to US media products, most of which are already generating profits from much larger American audiences and consumers before they ever even cross the border. These media products can be sold in Canada for much lower prices than the equivalent Canadian-made media content. This is especially true in television, as discussed by Grant and Wood and several other authors in this book, where Canadian television networks can re-broadcast an American television program for far less than it costs to purchase a Canadian program.

Most Canadians accept that culture and media are **public goods** with social and cultural value, even though they also have attributes of private consumption. But in a country with a small population like Canada's, the market cannot provide guaranteed access to domestic cultural content for everyone who might wish to consume it. Media economists define **market failure** not as the lack of commercial success of media content, but in a larger sense as "the failure of the market as a whole to do what markets are presumed to best that is, to lead to the best possible outcome for the greatest possible number of participants" (Grant and Wood, 2004, 58). Thus the main rationale for media policy is to address the limits of the market in order to enhance the social and cultural benefits of Canadian media content.

From the 1920s to the 1960s, cultural and media policy focussed on the development of public broadcasting and publicly funded media outlets like CBC and NFB as a means of addressing social and cultural rationales for government intervention in media production. Since the 1970s, Canada's media policy has gradually shifted toward manipulating media markets and the media industry to help achieve policy goals. Government grants, subsidies, and tax credits for film and television production in Canada, using Canadian crews, act as incentives for independent media producers to create Canadian content. These incentives are targeted at increasing local **supply** of Canadian content and protecting the domestic industry. An example of a company that benefits from these policies is Epitome Pictures, the creators of the TV series *Degrassi: The Next Generation*. The company benefits from tax breaks, making it easier to attract investment in its productions and also gets direct grants from the Canada Media Fund that go toward production costs. With this financial assistance, Epitome is also able to sell its television series in the US and around the world. Canadian government policy helps make the company more competitive in a global market.

CRTC content regulations requiring minimum amounts of Canadian content on radio and television are targeted at raising the **demand** for Canadian content in the market. To meet CRTC requirements, broadcasters seek out Canadian music and Canadian television programming and, when given some access to air time, this content is often popular with Canadian audiences. Canadian musicians from Bruce Cockburn to Nickelback, from Feist to K'naan, have gained exposure to national and international audiences with a little help from Canadian content requirements. The combined policy strategy of increasing supply and boosting demand has undeniably resulted in the outcome of more profitable media industries and more widely available domestic media content in Canada. However the focus on using government regulations and incentives to support commercial media production tends to favour commercial interests over purely cultural and social interests. At the same time, these industry-oriented policies don't really further the objectives of the public sector media and as a result well-established institutions like the CBC and the NFB suffer from declining political and popular support, as well as a real decrease in access to government resources.

CONCLUSION

From this chapter you can see that media content and its cultural meaning are intricately caught up in economic and political aspects of media policy. Media industries have become big business, and the creation and circulation of media products is partly determined by their successes and failures in the marketplace. When vertical and horizontal integration of media industries inevitably leads to a concentration of ownership, the range and diversity of points of view available in the media are affected. As Habermas (2001) suggests, media are essential to the maintenance of the public sphere and the circulation of public opinion, and this is why governments get involved in the regulation of media. In Canada the creation of the CBC and public service broadcasting and CRTC quotas for Canadian content in radio and television are a means of asserting the public responsibilities of media institutions. But Canadian media policy also addresses the economic realities of sharing a border with the world's largest producer of popular culture and entertainment. One rationale for Canadian media policy is to support and provide access to Canadian content, because economic conditions of our small domestic market and competition with US media make it nearly impossible for domestic programming to be profitable.

The connection between media industries and media policies has become even closer in recent years as the CRTC and successive Canadian governments have used economic interventions and market tools to foster investment and competition in Canadian media. At the same time, government support for public broadcasting and public media institutions like the CBC and NFB has been eroded. It remains to be seen whether the positive policy outcomes for the privately owned commercial media in Canada can be maintained without some equal attention to the different needs and priorities of public sector media.

Critical Analysis

Foote, J. A. (2000). *Federal cultural policy in Canada.* Unpublished manuscript. Published in French as 'La politique culturelle fédérale au Canada.' *Loisir et Société 22*(2).

Federal Cultural Policy in Canada

John A. Foote, Ph.D
Department of Canadian Heritage
1 February 2000

EXECUTIVE SUMMARY

This article provides an overview of the federal government's cultural policy in Canada and is intended to contribute to the growing body of literature and public discussion of the federal role in culture. A limited number of recent historical references are cited in support of the principal themes covered in the article.

The author discusses some definitions and general approaches to culture and describes the complex factors and linkages involved in defining the scope of federal cultural policy involvement. The article includes a descriptive synthesis of key rationales of federal cultural policy—public good, national interest, identity and social linkages, economic growth and the cultural influence of the United States—along with examples provided for the reader desiring more information. These factors have helped shape the principles, objectives and policy instruments that have shaped federal cultural intervention in Canada since its inception.

Several improvements to the study of culture and cultural policy research are explored in the second half of the paper. Changes in the cultural environment—new technologies, globalization, cultural diversity—are described as important forces pushing and pulling cultural creativity, output and consumption. The author recommends a more critical analysis of the assumptions underlying federal cultural policy, the results of policies over time and the identification of major cultural research gaps and emerging policy research issues.

*The views represented in this article are those of the author and do not necessarily represent those of the Department of Canadian Heritage.

I. DEFINITIONS AND APPROACHES TO CULTURE

Culture has been defined broadly as "an expression of ways of life" that is "central to everything we do and think." **(1 Ostry 1978)** This inclusive "anthropological/sociological" definition is similar to UNESCO's Mexico City vision of culture as the "whole collection of distinctive traits, spiritual and material, intellectual and affective, which characterize a society or a social group. It comprises, besides arts and letters, modes of life, human rights, value systems, traditions and beliefs." **(UNESCO 1982)** Defined broadly, culture gives meaning to individual and collective lives, sets the context for communications by creating shared understandings and contributes to the knowledge-based economy and society, quality of life and a diverse society.

Culture has also been defined in terms of a typology of economic organizations and industries, professional and amateur practitioners, and related academic disciplines. However, unless individual measures of culture are aggregated in a single framework, a narrow approach to culture tends to ignore its broader economic, social and political effects. For example, through the many voices and works of artistic creators distributed to audiences and consumers, culture reflects and helps shape society by inculcating values and traditions and educating, informing and entertaining the attentive public. A more complete description of the definition of culture is provided in **Cuche 1996.**

While there are many definitions attributed to it, culture includes, at a minimum, carriage infrastructure (equipment and networks), human resources (cultural labour force) and cultural content (intellectual property). Culture is an inter-disciplinary activity and field of study that encompasses aesthetic (creation, performance, criticism), social (consumption, participation), economic (technology-driven, consumer-fed) and political (state intervention) dimensions. Cultural content moves along a continuum from creation and production, at one end of the cultural chain, to distribution, participation/consumption and conservation, at the other. A successful and lasting culture operates optimally at each stage of the continuum.

Opting for a broad definition of culture, or a more narrow one, has obvious implications in defining the role of the state, measuring the economic and social impacts of the sector and identifying linkages between otherwise unconnected industries. While this article focuses principally on culture as "content", it is important to recognize the power of people, values, customs and technology in shaping cultural expression and reception. For example, technology change and digital convergence give rise to new players and new media forms (multi-media, Internet) and expand the role in culture of traditionally separated interests such as telecommunication companies, the computer industry and broadcasters. Although the linkage between the information sector and the cultural sector—how much information is cultural and how much non-cultural?—is not yet clearly spelled out, their combined direct economic impact in Canada was estimated at $65 billion, or 8% of the GDP in 1995. **(Statistics Canada 1996)**

The implications of converging content and communications are only now starting to be felt throughout the economy. The combined culture and information sectors act as engines or catalysts for growth in the knowledge-based economy and society. This growth is fueled by digitization and enhanced competition among traditional and new players and globalization. Results include an ever-increasing volume and diversity of mass- and specialized-appeal content, speed of access and manipulation, and interactivity, which together promise to bring much broader consumer choice to the cultural and information marketplace. The emerging culture and information sector holds out the promise of significantly empowering individuals, organizations, communities and societies.

II. CANADA'S FEDERAL CULTURAL POLICY APPROACH

1. Phases of Intervention

The federal government's involvement in culture is neither accidental nor unplanned. Cultural policy is deliberately grounded in the perception that Canada's cultural sovereignty is an indispensable element of independence required in the face of the country's long common border and close economic and social ties with the much more powerful and populous United States of America.

Successive federal governments in Canada have demonstrated a growing appreciation of the significance of culture in helping to resolve many political, social and economic issues. They have done this through the development and implementation of cultural policies, programs and initiatives that connect Canadians to the diversity of their experiences—their history, values, and voices—and to each other, the world at large and future generations. Cultural communities, the Press, academia and the attentive public have exerted pressure on governments to ensure that culture is put to broadly beneficial social and economic uses. Canada is certainly not alone in showing growing interest and involvement in culture. As the Report of the UNESCO World Commission on Culture and Development states, "The range of manifestations that governments choose to see as relevant for their cultural policies has broadened in recent years, as the production of and the demand for artistic goods for mass consumption has expanded, together with awareness that cultural identity is shaped by many different forms of cultural expression." **(233 UNESCO 1995)**

As new technologies emerged and Canada's economy modernized, federal involvement in culture broadened beyond the operations and funding of public institutions, such as CBC Radio, the National Film Board, the National Gallery of Art and the Public Archives, all established during the first phase of federal intervention from 1867 to 1950. A second, more active period of federal intervention marked the 1951 release of the Report of the Royal Commission on National Development in the Arts, Letters and Sciences, co-chaired by Vincent Massey and Georges-Henri Lévesque. Over the next twenty years, the federal government created still more national cultural institutions including the National Library (1953), the Canada Council (1957), the Canadian Film Development Corporation (1968), the Department of Communications (1969) and the Canadian Radio and Television Commission (1969). This period of institution building was followed in the 1980s and 1990s with the passage of major pieces of cultural legislation (Broadcasting Act, Copyright Act), the establishment of Telefilm Canada (1983) and several heritage institutions, and the development of policies, programs and other forms of intervention to assist in the development of film, sound recording, publishing, the arts and heritage. Federal spending in culture reached its zenith with $2.8 billion in 1990–91.

During the mid- to late 1990s, federal cultural spending was cut back pursuant to a policy of general spending restraint applied throughout the federal government. In 1997–98, total federal cultural spending including both operating expenditures and grants and transfers had dropped to $2.66 billion (1997–98). **(Statistics Canada**

1999) Since then, however, significant new investments have been made for new or expanded funding in sound recording, book publishing, film and broadcasting, multimedia and the arts. The current period of federal cultural policy features the consolidation of functions within the Department of Canadian Heritage including, culture, citizenship and identity, Sport Canada and until recently, Parks Canada. More generally, the federal role in cultural policy is shifting from "doer" or "sole financer" to "facilitator", "referee" and "partner" with other governments and the private sector. The federal government is also acting proactively in protecting digital copyright, assisting in the provision of new skills and training in the knowledge economy, ensuring post-convergence competition, promoting social connectedness and reflecting cultural diversity.

The federal government is certainly not the only jurisdiction in Canada to develop and administer policies and programs in culture. Provincial and municipal governments also intervene directly and indirectly in the cultural sector within their respective boundaries. The federal share of total spending has declined slightly from 45.9% in 1989 to 45.5% in 1997. The provincial share has decreased from 31.2% in 1989 to 29.3% in 1997. The municipal level increased from 22.9% in 1989 to 25.2% in 1997. By allowing for national, provincial, regional and municipal policies and activities, shared or concurrent jurisdiction has proven an effective tool in promoting culture in all parts of Canada.

2. Rationale

Canada's federal cultural policies are designed to foster the viability of the country's cultural sector and to protect it from drowning in a sea of global entertainment. The challenge for cultural policy in Canada is to help create both the infrastructure and international rules needed to ensure that Canadians have a "real" choice in accessing both domestic and foreign content and are able to take full advantage of emerging global market opportunities through enhanced exports. To some extent, the rationales for cultural policy in Europe—moral improvement, economic benefits and national identity and prestige—are also present in Canada. **(70 Bennett 1997)**

Federal intervention in culture in Canada is based on perceptions of the public good, the national interest, economic growth, social linkages and foreign influence and control. Canada's cultural fabric has been shaped by a small and geographically dispersed population, limited economies of scale and high costs of production, the ubiquitous proximity and presence of the USA—the world's largest and most influential cultural super-power—and a unique blend of multicultural demographics and linguistic duality. A succinct description of the federal cultural policy rationale states, "Culture has come to be recognized as being at the heart of a nation-state's will to survive and flourish. . . . Canada's domestic cultural base is critical to its future as a united and distinct country. Successive national governments have sought to ensure that Canadians have access to all forms of cultural expression and have recognized that cultural expression would need many types of support." **(25–26 Rabinovitch 1998)**

A. Public Good

The concept of culture as a public good is based on the premise that the existence of many types of cultural products, such as not-for-profit arts and heritage "merit goods" and a significant part of the cultural industries and broadcasting sector in Canada, can not be funded solely by the consumer. Nor can they be provided by the private sector alone, given the weak economies of scale facing both English- and French-language content providers in Canada. Most countries, even the USA, maintain some kinds of government support to culture on the basis that much of it constitutes a public good.

While most cultural industries and broadcasting also produce and distribute "private" goods and services, paid for by the consumer, these same goods and services carry high positive externalities throughout society and the economy. The consumer alone does not capture all the benefits from their consumption. Society at large benefits directly from the contribution of publishing, broadcasting, film and sound recording to the quality of life enjoyed by its members. This argument also applies to new media, the knowledge-based economy and society and the information highway, where government intervention is also required to generate critical mass and to even out the emerging international competitive playing field.

Canada's cultural policies are designed to further the public good by nurturing the creativity of Canadian artists and professionals and facilitating the dissemination of Canadian content. The latter can be defined as "cultural works that are created, produced, distributed, consumed or preserved in Canada and that reflect the values and images of Canadians and the vision and professional skills of their creators and providers." **(19 Foote 1998)** However it is defined, Canadian content is critical to many issues that exist at each stage of the cultural continuum: creation (Canadian artists' training and talent and economic revenues), production (domestic market share), distribution (foreign product dominance), consumption and attendance (retail shelf space, cultural curricula in education, participation levels), and preservation (digitization). Canadian content is also closely linked to associated cultural policy issues and rationales such as social linkages, identity and attachment, competition, program efficacy, export development and the harmonization of international trade and investment positions and responsibilities with domestic policy objectives and guidelines.

B. National Interest

Some of the literature on cultural policy in Canada has referred to the need to preserve Canadian culture in "the national interest." One such view is that governments in Canada need to connect institutionalized support for domestic culture in Canada with a sense of Canada's culture sovereignty which is, in turn, imbedded in the national interest. According to this view, culture is a central part of the unique make-up of the Canadian character and range of identities, notably through the accommodation of the cultural interests and needs of its diverse population. **(Goodenough 1998)** According to this rationale, culture is like other social goods and associated national goals such as defense, health and higher education. Under this argument, "cultural security" is a form of "national security." The Massey Report noted that while Canada's military defences must be made secure, its "cultural defences equally demand national attention . . ." **(275 Report of the Royal Commission on the Arts and Letters 1951).** More recently, Kevin Dowler concluded that "the rationale for a Canadian cultural policy is to be found in the security interests of the state." **(330 Dorland 1996)**

C. Identity and Social Linkages

Culture is an important factor in the formation and reinforcement of political and social identities, attitudes and linkages. The contrasting paired variables included in Jenson's map of "social cohesion"—belonging/isolation, inclusion/exclusion, participation/non-involvement, recognition/rejection, legitimacy/illegitimacy—have clear cultural policy application. **(Jenson 1998)** While some observers believe the term, "social cohesion" is too centrist and potentially homogeneous when applied to the Canadian reality with its two official languages and multiple identities, "social linkages" are an important rationale for federal cultural policy that helps ensure that domestic content is relevant and meaningful to audiences and bolsters their sense of identification with Canada and its constituent parts.

Culture is central to "social connectedness" at all levels of political association, federal, provincial or municipal. It is promoted through shared information and cultural expression. The capacity of national, regional, provincial and local cultures to communicate within and without their geographic or political boundaries could be placed in jeopardy by the absence of creative, production and distribution capacity at each level. In order that Canadians have adequate levels of information and creative works that reflect their country's values and stories, the supply of cultural content must be competitive and accessible to consumers in the language of their choice.

Culture and cultural policy in Canada are strongly affected by the laws on bilingualism and multiculturalism. Language and ethno-cultural heritage shape the profile of the cultural sector in important ways. Two distinct linguistic cultural markets in Canada operate across the country, especially through federal broadcasting services, but also through the auspices of other federal cultural support programs. The growing numerical force of multiculturalism is also gradually changing the cultural landscape through the creation, circulation and reception of programming and other works that reflect the backgrounds of their creators and consumers. The impact of official bilingualism and multiculturalism on culture is one among several manifestations of "cultural diversity" in Canada.

D. Economic Growth

While it is not the core rationale motivating federal cultural policy, economic growth is an important by-product of concerted federal intervention in the cultural economy. The creation, production and distribution (including wholesale and retail) of culture in Canada contributed more than $20 billion to the country's Gross Domestic Product in 1994–95. An estimated 610,000 direct jobs were sustained by the cultural sector and the cultural labor force grew approximately 32% from 1981 to 1995, compared with 12% growth in the general population and 15% in the experienced labor force. **(Statistics Canada 1995)** These and other indices of culture's economic impact are likely to be significantly higher today. For example, tourism is directly affected by cultural attractions and the economic impact of spending on the part of incoming international tourists taking part in cultural events is estimated at more than $1 billion.

E. United States' Cultural Influence

Federal cultural intervention in culture, or the perceived need to do so, is also a rational response to the high levels of foreign, mostly American cultural content in the Canadian system. The structure of Canada's cultural marketplace and the role of government policy in helping shape that marketplace are strongly affected by foreign content. Foreign content accounts for:

- 45% of book sales in Canada
- 81% of English-language consumer magazines on Canadian newsstands and over 63% of magazine circulation revenue
- 79% of the retail sales of tapes, CDs, concerts, merchandise and sheet music in Canada
- 85% of the revenues from film distribution in Canada
- 95% of the feature films screened in theatres in Canada **(4 Cultural Industries SAGIT 1999)**

While the great majority of Canadian content works are produced by Canadian-owned and -controlled cultural undertakings, most such undertakings are under-capitalized, have limited access to their own domestic market and earn only a small portion of the total cultural revenues generated on Canadian soil. Canadian cultural producers are often vulnerable to foreign competition with strong comparative advantages of lower costs per unit amortized in much larger markets.

Canada's cultural system has always been an amalgam of public and private sector structures and players. The mixed system is a rational response to the reality of US economic influence and control in much of Canada's cultural economy, especially its cultural industries. For this reason, Canada's public-private cultural system is unlikely to disappear despite the recent decline of state involvement in many other areas of society and the economy.

3. Cultural Policy Objectives

Over the course of the last century, Canadian federal government has intervened in the cultural sector to achieve two fundamental cultural objectives: the creation and development of cultural content and the provision of access to cultural content. Cultural development (or content) and the open cultural economy (or access) have been the focus of Canadian cultural policy since its inception. **(Audley 1997)**

The longest-standing federal objective in cultural policy has been the creation of supply through the subsidization of Canadian cultural content. Several cultural institutions, such as the Canadian Broadcasting Corporation/Radio-Canada and the National Film Board, produce much of their own programming. Granting agencies, such as the Canada Council for the Arts and Telefilm Canada, facilitate the development of cultural content by the private sector. Canada's open cultural economy has allowed for both public and private sector institutions, thus increasing the viability of assets and experience in a small scale market.

A second core cultural policy objective is access by consumers and audiences and by content creators and providers to approved distribution vehicles. Access receives federal program and policy support through such instruments as marketing support, broadcasting regulations on simultaneous substitution and cable carriage priorities, and foreign ownership regulations and guidelines. Internet and satellite-delivered services make universal access possible, although viable pricing models would have to be in place before this objective is ever fully achieved.

Principles flowing from these two federal objectives include freedom of choice, a domestic market open to the world, diversity of content and content providers, the reservation of cultural shelf-space for Canadian content, the availability of new technologies to artists, producers, distributors and consumers, and combined public/private sector roles and involvement. The objective and letter of Canadian cultural policies and regulations are not to keep foreign products out of the country but rather to ensure that Canadian content has appropriate "shelf space" and media outlets in Canada. The federal government's cultural objectives are intended to ensure real choice from among the wide range of domestic and foreign content. They also constitute a response to the high levels of foreign content and control in Canada's domestic cultural market and attract broad public support as part of a federal commitment to maintain an active presence in culture.

4. Cultural Policy Instruments

Federal cultural institutions, policies, programs and legislation are examples of public sector instruments designed to ensure that Canadian voices share Canadian spaces and safeguard the collective memories of its citizens. Selected examples of federal cultural policy instruments include tax incentives (the Canadian Film and Video Production Tax Credit and federal tax write-offs for donations to not-for-profit cultural organizations), direct grants and contributions ($460 million in direct federal subsidies in 1997–98), direct spending by national cultural institutions ($750 million in CBC Parliamentary appropriations in 1998–99), mandated contributions by distributors of audio-visual content to production funds, regulations and licensing (CRTC), foreign investment guidelines applied to the cultural industries and broadcasting (now the responsibility of the Department of Canadian Heritage), legislation *(Broadcasting Act, Copyright Act)* and inter-governmental agreements (North American Free Trade Agreement cultural exemption, film co-productions).

The federal challenge is to examine what works in existing cultural support instruments and how the latter might be improved or replaced by alternative measures to achieve policy objectives. Government instruments in support of culture periodically need renewal and affirmation especially during a period of rapid environmental change. Governments are now expected to handle a wide range of new issues such as raising domestic market share in the cultural industries and new media, improving the remuneration and working conditions of artists and cultural technicians, ensuring equitable access to the cultural system by Canadians, facilitating growth of a steady stream of Canadian content that tell Canadian stories and embody the voices of Canadian talent and creators in both official languages, reflecting changes in the demographic and ethno-cultural diversity in programming, access and employment policies of federal cultural institutions, and supporting viable cultural output through enhanced consumption, marketing and distribution.

Daniel Schwanen concluded that of the principal tools of cultural policy which have been gradually put in place since the 1930s—the establishment of foreign ownership rules in broadcasting and the creation of a public broadcaster, the enhanced public financial support for the cultural industries, the imposition of fiscal disincentives for business to advertise outside Canadian media, the formulation of Canadian content rules for broadcasting, the extension of effective Canadian ownership restrictions to most of the cultural industries, and the extension of the reach of Canadian-owned firms in the distribution of foreign and domestic cultural products in Canada—many are now challenged by technology, budgetary pressures and the increasing scrutiny of its trading partners. **(Schwanen 1998)** Schwanen's analysis suggests that each federal cultural instrument must be carefully examined to ensure that it can stand the test of efficiency, economy and public support.

III. CHANGING CULTURAL ENVIRONMENT

1. New Technologies

Cultural policies are heavily influenced by constant technological change, although some instruments such as the technologically-neutral *Broadcasting Act* (1991) are inherently flexible. Technological innovations provide significant potential for broader content diversity and consumer access. Such improvements are stimulated by inter-modal carriage competition (cable and telephony) while consumers benefit from enhanced presentation capacity such as large screen digital and high definition television. Technological innovation has also led to fragmented audiences and the growth of specialized content, formerly called "narrowcasting" and now, "specialty services" in contrast to mass appeal "broadcasting".

The rapid succession of new technologies for the creation, transmission and reception of cultural content is both destabilizing and invigorating. New technologies allow new players to enter the cultural marketplace, increase competition among traditional players and expose vast amounts of digital content to interested consumers. In order to remain competitive, cultural industries face the challenge of using new technologies to develop new products and to maintain overall corporate market share in both traditional and new media modes. The introduction of new communication technologies tends to complement rather than displace existing media and cultural formats.

The information highway Internet creates new opportunities for the dissemination of cultural and other forms of content. Creators, producers and distributers of Canadian content are pressed to secure prominent places on the electronic systems accessed by Canadians in the face of rapid, massive and global information flows. Governments, like the private sector and consumers, ignore new technologies at their peril. In 1989, then Minister of Communications, the Honorable Flora Macdonald said, "We have been driven for over twenty years by technology—by the art of what is technically possible. What we must try to ensure in our legislative framework is that programming goals play an equally large role in shaping the broadcast system and that the appropriate technology is harnessed, or at least anticipated and controlled, as an adjunct to or in facilitation of those programming objectives." **(40 Rabinovitch 1998)**

2. Globalization

Global economic restructuring and trade and investment ties touch all parts of the Canadian economy, including the cultural sector. Economic restructuring and globalization have triggered a resurgence in inter- and intra-media concentration of ownership in the culture and information sector, technological convergence that will ultimately drive the cultural and information sector, a growing proliferation of new media that will enrich the diverse range of cultural and information products as well as the fusion of many information, entertainment and educational goods and services.

Global cultural investment and trade accentuates Canada's traditional concerns with foreign content levels in light of constantly growing cultural imports and existing levels of foreign influence and control in the domestic market. At the same time, globalization is opening up cultural export prospects especially in those areas where Canada is competitive, such as animation, children's programming, documentaries, some sound recordings and certain genres of literature. Cultural exports (excluding cultural equipment) totaled $2.8 billion in 1997, a 140% increase since 1991. **(Statistics Canada 1999)** However, it is also true that exports of works containing purely Canadian content were probably in the range of $550 million to $600 million. **(30 Audley 1996)**

The liberalization of international trade and investment rules poses a particular challenge to some of Canada's domestic regulations and measures developed to ensure the availability of Canadian television programming, films, records and tapes, books and magazines and access to them by Canadians. While the general objective of these international agreements is to eliminate trade-distorting regulations and national measures, Canada has taken the position that culture should be excluded or exempted from such agreements. However, neither the "cultural exemption" in the bilateral Free Trade Agreement and its successor, NAFTA, nor Canada's refusal to grant national treatment in the cultural industries sector in the GATT have prevented the USA from exerting persistent pressure on Canada to grant "national treatment" to foreign cultural products, services and firms. Unless Canada succeeds in securing international support for the introduction of a "cultural exception" in future instruments, such as a revived multilateral agreement on investment and a World Trade Organization agreement on services, there will be considerable pressure to put culture on the table in future trade negotiations.

Globalization, along with WTO rules and rulings, is straining the capacity to maintain existing cultural support instruments and to create new ones where required. There is some concern that a nascent global culture might eventually overwhelm the output of domestic creators and distributors of cultural content. Cameron and Stein state, "As global processes promote cultural homogenization and fragmentation, cultural boundaries—historically an essential component of national identity—are beginning to diverge even more than economic boundaries from national political spaces." **(16 Cameron and Stein 1999)**

For Canada to take full advantage of global opportunities, it must first ensure that competitive Canadian cultural content and the means of distributing it are fully available at home. Economic restructuring and globalization place a premium on securing detailed information on market demand and better-funded marketing strategies for selling Canadian cultural content inside and outside the country. Canadian cultural enterprises need adequate financial resources to produce and sell works that will satisfy the growing global and domestic demand for cultural products.

3. Cultural Diversity

Cultural diversity is an important part of the Canadian cultural sector. Culture at every stage of its development and expression is affected by provisions in the *Multiculturalism Act* and the *Official Languages Act,* which are applied in federal cultural policies, regulations and institutions. Another sense of diversity extends to programming or content that reflects the interests, values and histories of francophones, anglophones and allophones in Canada. Diversity reflects the evolving Canadian cultural workforce, educational curricula, national cultural training institutions, program mandates, marketing strategies, and consumers' viewing/participation patterns.

Diversity is also embodied in cultural content objectives. Canada's cultural mosaic is showcased by the creation, production, distribution and consumption of many forms and formats of audiovisual programming, literature and sound recording. This content-based definition of diversity includes both domestic and foreign content. Demographics are important to the production of cultural goods and services and their consumption. While various ethno-cultural communities, or age cohorts, support their own unique forms of cultural expression, they also participate in established forms.

Since one of the cultural policy goals is for each Canadian to have maximum access to a board range of cultural products and means of cultural expression, avenues of access to cultural content must be made widely available to all parts of the population, particularly as new delivery modes come on stream, e.g. Internet. While Canada's demographic profile is diversifying rapidly, the cultural marketplace is fragmenting through the extensive proliferation of domestic and global content and new delivery mechanisms. Segmentation owes its origin not only to enhanced technological capacity and globalization but also to the changing face of Canadian audiences and consumers and their interest in specialized content. It is anticipated that a fragmented cultural marketplace will not erode the financial viability of new and traditional content and service providers to reach a diverse range of end-users.

Growth in the capacity to interact technologically should help lower the cost of preserving cultural and linguistic diversity, slow the push towards cultural standardization, develop new cultural development programs, reinforce local cultures, build inter-cultural bridges and increase access to natural and built cultural heritage through virtual reality. **(Council of Europe 1996)** Canada's demographic diversity adds to the competitiveness of domestic culture at home and abroad through the creative forces of its artists who form the human backdrop and talent pool of cultural organizations. Canada's two official languages and cultures are reflected in French- and English-language networks that extend across the country. Minority languages other than the two official languages are also making considerable inroads in most cultural disciplines. These accomplishments, achieved in the face of tough economic odds and unrelenting foreign competition, have expanded the opportunity for international cultural trade and exposure. Canada's core values—democracy, the rule of law, internationalism, persuasion and compromise—are reflected in its cultural output which has become an important asset in the development and implementation of Canada's image abroad.

🍁 🍁 🍁

V. CONCLUSIONS

Federal cultural policy in Canada has been deliberate, flexible and always evolving. The best measure of its performance is the degree to which it reflects and responds to the cultural interests of Canadians in a high risk and very competitive domestic and global setting. Culture is likely to become increasingly important and relevant to Canadians as the global information revolution unfolds to which the growing interest in an enhanced public dialogue on changes in the cultural system attests. This interest extends to changes in the role of the federal government through sectoral review and the possible enunciation of a federal cultural policy framework and vision of culture in Canada in the years to come.

It is especially important that dialogue among governments at each level and the private sector—the users and providers of content—is inclusive and transparent. Publicly debated issues such as a national cultural policy and the impact of globalization on cultural policies complement the need for analytical work in identifying the problems and opportunities facing culture in Canada. These challenges include, **inter alia,** the linkage between domestic and international cultural policies and practices, the increasing value of partnerships and cooperation between private and public sectors, and improved efficiencies and evaluations of cultural policies, i.e. more precise measurement and frequent assessment of policy and program results juxtaposed with objectives.

This article has identified a number of research gaps that, if not addressed, could hold back policy development and review. Many of these research lacunae have to do with the major environmental forces transforming much of culture as we know it, i.e. technological innovation, convergence and digitization, economic restructuring and demographic diversity. Technological inventiveness is relentless, the creativity of artists and other content providers is constantly expanding, and the public's appetite for cultural content appears insatiable. While the future of culture can never be known definitively, all countries, nations and individuals have an opportunity to use new tools and content forms to forge their own cultural presence and yet stay connected with the world.

VII. BIBLIOGRAPHY

Acheson, K. and C. Maule (1994). Understanding Hollywood's organization and continuing success. *Journal of Cultural Economics* 18.

Audley, P. (1983). *Canada's Cultural Industries: Broadcasting, Publishing, Records and Film*. Toronto, James Lorimer and Company, Publishers.

Audley, P. (1994). Cultural industries policy: Objectives, formulation and evaluation. *Canadian Journal of Communication* 19, 317–352.

Audley, P. (1997). *The Export of Canadian Cultural Goods and Services: a Reassessment*. Ottawa, a Report to the Department of Canadian Heritage.

Banting, K., G. Hoberg and R. Simeon, ed. (1999). *North American Integration and the Scope for Domestic Choice: Canada and Policy Sovereignty in a Globalized World*. Ottawa, a Paper for the Policy Research Initiative Secretariat.

Bennett, O. (1997). Cultural policy, cultural pessimism and postmodernity. *International Journal of Cultural Policy,* 4 (1), 67–84.

Bennett, T. and C. Mercer (1998). *Improving Research and International Cooperation for Cultural Policy*. Paris: a Paper for the UNESCO Intergovernmental Conference on Cultural Policies for Development.

Browne, D. (1998). *The Culture/Trade Quandary: Canada's Policy Options*. Ottawa, Centre for Trade Policy and Law.

Browne, D. (1999). Canada's Cultural Trade Quandary. *International Journal LIV* (3), 363–374.

Bumsted, J. (1999). *North American Integration and Canadian Culture.* Ottawa, a Paper for the Policy Research Initiative Secretariat.

Cameron, D. and J. Stein (1999). *Globalization, Culture and Society: the State as Place Amidst Shifting Spaces.* Ottawa, a Paper for the Policy Research Initiative Secretariat.

Canadian Radio-television and Telecommunications Commission (1999). *Building on Success—a Policy Framework for Canadian Television.* Hull, CRTC Public Notice 1999–97.

Comer, E. (1991). The Department of Communications under a free trade regime. *Canadian Journal of Communication.* 16 (2), 239–261.

Council of Europe (1996). *In From the Margins: a Contribution to the debate* on Culture and Development in Europe. *Strasbourg, European Task Force on Culture and Development.*

Cuche, D. (1996). *La notion de la culture dans les sciences sociales.* Paris, Découverte.

Department of Communications (1987). *Vital Links: Canadian Cultural Industries.* Ottawa, Queen's Printer.

Department of Foreign Affairs and International Trade (1999). *Canadian Culture in a Global World: New Strategies for Culture and Trade.* Ottawa, Cultural Industries Sectoral Advisory Group on International Trade.

Doern, G. B., L. Pal and B. Tomlin, eds. (1996). *Border Crossings, The Internationalization of Canadian Public Policy.* Toronto, Oxford University Press.

Dorland, M., ed. (1996). *The Cultural Industries in Canada, Problems, Policies and Prospects.* Toronto, James Lorimer and Company.

Federal Cultural Policy Review Committee (1982). *Report of the Federal Cultural Policy Review Committee.* Ottawa, Supply and Services Canada.

Flaherty, D. and F. Manning, eds. (1993). *The Beaver Bites Back, American Popular Culture in Canada.* Montreal and Kingston, McGill-Queen's University Press.

Foote, J. (1998). *Canada's Cultural Policy.* Ottawa, a Paper for the Canadian Cultural Research Network Conference.

Fortier, A. (1992). Le pouvoir fédéral-des actions culturelles dont la somme forme peut-être une politique. *Actes du Colloque: Pouvoirs publics et politiques culturelles: enjeux nationaux* Chaire de gestion des arts, École des Hautes Études Commerciales de Montréal.

Globerman, S. (1987). *Culture, Governments and Markets: Public Policy and the Cultural Industries.* Vancouver, The Fraser Institute.

Goodenough, O. (1998). Defending the imaginary to the death? Free trade, national identity and Canada's cultural preoccupation. *Arizona Journal of International and Comparative Law.* 15 (1).

Government of Canada (1999). *Canada and the Future of the World Trade Organization—Response to the Report of the Standing House Committee on Foreign Affairs and International Trade.* Ottawa, Public Works and Government Services Canada, Cat. No. E2–195.

Government of Canada (1999). *Connecting to the Canadian Experience: Diversity, Creativity and Choice—Response to the Ninth Report of the Standing House Committee on Canadian Heritage.* Ottawa, Public Works and Government Services Canada, No. CH4–44/1999E.

Griffiths, F. (1996). *Strong and Free: Canada and the New Sovereignty.* Toronto, Stoddart Publishing Co. Ltd.

Griffiths, F. (1999). *The Culture of Change.* Ottawa, a Paper for the National Policy Research Conference (PRI).

Hannigan, J. (1999). *The Global Entertainment Economy: a Critical Essay.* Ottawa, a Paper for the National Policy Conference (PRI).

Helliwell, J. (1999). *Checking the Brain Drain: Evidence and Implications.* Ottawa, a Paper for the Policy Research Initiative Secretariat.

Henighan, T. (1996). *The Presumption of Culture, Structure, Strategy and Survival in the Canadian Cultural Landscape.* Vancouver, Raincoast Books.

Hoskins, C., S. MacFayden, A. Finn (1994). The environment in which cultural industries operate. *Canadian Journal of Communication.* 19 (3/4), 99–122.

Hoskins, C., S. MacFayden, A. Finn (1997). *Global Television and Film: an Introduction to the Economics of the Business.* Oxford, Clarendon Press.

Houle, M. (1996). *Statistical Analysis on the Relevancy of the Canadian Cultural Policy Regarding Film Distribution.* Ottawa, a Report for the Department of Canadian Heritage.

House Standing Committee on Canadian Heritage (1999). *A Sense of Place, a Sense of Being: the Evolving Role of the Federal Government in Support of Culture in Canada.* Ottawa, Public Works and Government Services Canada.

Jeannotte, S. (1999). *Tango Romantica or Liaisons Dangereuses: Cultural Policies and Social Cohesion.* Bergen, a Paper for the International Conference on Cultural Policy Research.

Jenson, J. (1998). *Mapping Social Cohesion: the State of Canadian Research.* Ottawa, Canadian Policy Research Networks Study No. FO3.

KPMG Consulting (1997). *The Economics of Culture and Canadian Content in the Information Society—an Overview of the Numbers and the Issues.* Ottawa, a Report to the Department of Canadian Heritage and the Information Highway Advisory Council.

Kresl, P. K. (1997). The Political Economy of Canada's Cultural Policy in the 1990s. *Language, Culture and Values in Canada at the Dawn of the 21st Century.*

Mandate Review Committee (1996). *Making Our Voices Heard—Canadian Broadcasting and Film for the 21st Century—CBC, NFB, Telefilm,* Ottawa, Supply and Services Canada, Cat. No. CH4–15/96E.

Meisel, J. (1998). Cultural Research Priorities in Murray, C. ed. *Cultural Policies and Cultural Practices: Exploring the Links Between Culture and Social Change: a Report of the Founding Colloquium of the Canadian Cultural Research Network.* Hull, a Report for the Department of Canadian Heritage.

Ministère de la Culture et des Communications, Gouvernement du Québec (1999). *De la démocratisation de la culture à la démocratie culturelle.* Québec, ISBN No. 2-550-35323-4.

Murray, C. (1999). *Cultural Populism and Policy Practice: Canadian Perspectives on the Agenda for Audience Research.* Vancouver, a Paper presented at UNESCO Conference, Florence, Italy.

Murray, C. (1999). *Rethinking Cultural Policy.* Hull, Notes for an address to the Social Cohesion Workshop, Department of Canadian Heritage.

Murray, C., ed. (1998). *Cultural Policies and Cultural Practices: Exploring the Links Between Culture and Social Change: a Report of the Founding Colloquium of the Canadian Cultural Research Network*. Hull, a Report for the Department of Canadian Heritage.

Ostry, B. (1978). *The Cultural Connection: an Essay on Culture and Government Policy in Canada*. Toronto, McClelland and Stewart Limited.

Policy Research Initiative Secretariat (1998). *Sustaining Growth, Human Development and Social Cohesion in a Global World*. Ottawa, Public Works Canada.

Policy Review Panel (1995). *Direct-to-Home Satellite Broadcasting*. Ottawa, a Report to the Ministers of Canadian Heritage and Industry.

Rabinovitch, V. (1998). The Social and Economic Rationales for Domestic Cultural Policies. *The Culture/Trade Quandary*. Ottawa, Centre for Trade Policy and Law, 25–47.

Royal Commission on National Development in the Arts, Letters and Sciences (1951). *Report of the Royal Commission on National Development in the Arts, Letters and Sciences, 1949–1951*. Ottawa, Queen's Printer.

Royal Commission on Radio Broadcasting (1929). *Report of the Royal Commission on Radio Broadcasting*. Ottawa, King's Printer.

Schafer, D. P. (1995). *Canadian Culture: Key to Canada's Future Development*. Markham, Ontario, World Culture Project.

Schafer, D. P. and A. Fortier (1989). *Review of Federal Policies for the Arts in Canada—1944–1988*. Ottawa, Canadian Conference of the Arts.

Schwanen, D. (1997). *A Matter of Choice: Toward a More Creative Canadian Policy on Culture*. Toronto, Comentary 91, C. D. Howe Institute.

Smith, J., ed. (1998). *Media Policy, National Identity and Citizenry in Changing Democratic Societies: the Case of Canada*. Washington, Embassy of Canada.

Standing Senate Committee on Social Affairs, Science and Technology (1999). *Final Report on Social Cohesion*. Ottawa, Public Works and Government Services Canada.

Standing House Committee on Foreign Affairs and International Trade (1999). *Canada and the Future of the World Trade Organization: Advancing a Millenium Agenda in the Public Interest*. Ottawa, Public Works and Government Services Canada.

Statistics Canada (1996). The Economic Impact of the Arts and Culture Sector, 1994–1995. Ottawa, *Focus on Culture* 8 (2), Cat. No. 87–004–XYB.

Statistics Canada (1997). Towards a cultural statistics framework for Canada. *Focus on Culture* 9 (3). Ottawa, Cat. No. 87–004–XYB.

Statistics Canada (1996). International Trade in the Arts and Culture Sector. Ottawa, *Focus on Culture* 8 (3), Cat. No. 87–004–XYB.

Statistics Canada (1999). *Survey of Government Expenditures on Culture, 1997–98*. Ottawa, Cat. No. 87-004-XPB.

Statistics Canada (1999). *Cultural Trade and Investment Report*. Ottawa, a Report to the Culture Trade and Investment Working Group.

Statistics Canada (1996). *The Economic Impact of the Cultural and Information Services Industries in Canada*. Ottawa, a Report to the Department of Canadian Heritage.

Subcommittee on Communications of the Standing Senate Committee on Transport and Communications (1999). *Wired to Win—Canada's Positioning Within the*

World's Technological Revolution. Ottawa, Public Works and Government Services Canada.

Task Force on the Future of the Canadian Music Industry (1996). *A Time for Action—a Report to the Minister of Canadian Heritage*. Ottawa, a Report to the Department of Canadian Heritage.

Throsby, D. (1997). Sustainability and Culture: Some Theoretical Issues. *Cultural Policy*, 1 (1), 7–19.

United Nations Education, Science and Culture Organization (1982). Mexico City Declaration on Cultural Policies. Paris, UNESCO.

United Nations Education, Science and Culture Organization (1995). *Our Creative Diversity—Report of the World Commission on Culture and Development*. Paris, UNESCO.

United Nations Education, Science and Culture Organization (1998). *Stockholm Action Plan on Cultural Policies for Development*. Paris, UNESCO.

Wall Communications, Inc. (1996). *Canadian Independent Film and Video Industry: Economic Features and Foreign Investment Related to the Distribution Sector*. Ottawa, a Report to the Department of Canadian Heritage.

Wolf, M. (1999). *The Entertainment Economy*. New York, Times Books.

DISCUSSION

John A. Foote, 'Federal Cultural Policy in Canada.'

1. Foote describes media as a 'public good.' What is a public good and why does media policy need to take this characteristic of media into account?
2. Foote lists several different phases of federal government involvement in culture and media in Canada. Describe these phases in your own words and explain how he characterizes the main shift in the government's role between the 1950s and the present.
3. What three features of the changing cultural environment does Foote discuss? What are the potential impacts on policy objectives and rationales of each of these three changes?

Historical Perspectives on Canada's Media Policy

INTRODUCTION

The history of Canadian media policy includes several recurring themes and important moments that continue to shape the interest groups involved, instruments chosen, and outcomes today. As indicated in the previous chapter, most forms of broadcasting policy and media policy are developed at the federal level in Canada. Parliament passes legislation that affects radio, television, and telecommunications. This is because the radio frequency spectrum through which signals pass is a finite resource and is managed by the government as a form of 'public property' much the same as waterways, air space, and other shared resources that cross provincial and national boundaries. In the early days of broadcasting, tensions developed between Quebec and the federal government over the control of radio licencing and the balance between public and private ownership. In 1931, the Supreme Court of Canada ruled that broadcasting was principally a federal jurisdiction under the *British North America Act,* a decision that was later upheld by the Judicial Committee of the Privy Council in Britain (Canada's court of last appeal at that time). Since then, the constitutional division of powers has given the Parliament of Canada exclusive power to regulate and control radio communication in Canada (Raboy, 1990, 35). We can review various federal government commissions, committees, reviews, task forces, legislation, and other policy statements from 1928 to the present to trace common themes that have shaped the media environment in Canada today. These themes include tensions between economic and social policy goals, the role of internal conflicts and external threats to Canadian sovereignty, and contrasting conceptions of public, markets, and technologies in media policy discourses.

ECONOMIC OR SOCIO-CULTURAL POLICY GOALS?

Media policy-making in Canada illustrates the interaction of different public and private institutions, actors, processes, and ways of understanding culture and society. Policy processes involve the circulation of ideas and discourses about media, as well as practical political strategies to manage the elements of policy-making introduced in the previous chapter. The history of Canadian media policy revolves around a central conflict— whether the rationales for communication and media policy should be primarily social and cultural, or economic. Policy debates throughout the twentieth and early twenty-first centuries have placed varying degrees of emphasis on these contrasting purposes. As different policy paradigms have prevailed, they have shaped outcomes in the development of both public and private media institutions and in the media content ultimately made available to Canadians. The tensions between economic goals for media and cultural goals for media are evident from the first public debates about the roles of radio in Canada to current policy developments related to the emergence of digital media platforms. Within these policy debates, 'culture' has been defined in a wide range of ways: as elite culture and the arts, as a distinctively Canadian national culture, as popular culture produced and distributed by mass media, or as local, regional, or minority cultures throughout Canada. Policy debates also often include widely different views on how cultural expression, production, and distribution should be understood. Some politicians and policy-makers have strongly argued that communication needs are social needs, that decisions about media and cultural production have social consequences, and that media policy should therefore be considered a form of social policy rather than economic policy. If the goals of media policy are social goals, then the important questions do not concern what culture is, or how it should be distributed or consumed, but might instead consider who creates culture and media content, and what skills and supports they require. This perspective most clearly recognizes the social and interactive nature of media and situates media policy within broader relations of power in society. However the tension between conflicting economic and cultural objectives for media policy can be traced throughout its history in Canada.

MEDIA POLICY'S RESPONSE TO EXTERNAL THREATS AND INTERNAL CONFLICTS

The history of media policy in Canada is also marked by a conflict between the goals of 'national unity' and 'cultural sovereignty,' and the existence of local and regional identities, linguistic divides, and cultural diversities. Canadian media policy often tries to create homogenizing and unifying notions of national identity. These notions are challenged by the rise of audience fragmentation and diverse, and often competing, public demands for media institutions and media content. Media policy-making reflects tensions between Quebec and English Canada, between urban and rural communities, between central Canada and other regions, and between Euro-Canadians and Aboriginal or ethnic minorities. Policy discourses also engage the recurring theme of the role of media in fostering Canadian 'cultural sovereignty' against the threat of American cultural imports. However, this protectionist impulse against external threats often obscures the various internal conflicts and tensions that characterize Canadian society. The history of broadcasting legislation, for example, has shaped the CBC and the CRTC in response to the federal government's definition of Canadian interests. These interests, as Richard Collins (1986, 156) has argued, tend to be those of the most populous region of Central Canada. Marc Raboy (1990, 8) has suggested that definitions of Canadian cultural sovereignty in opposition to American popular culture often disguise the degree to which media policy protects the economic interests of a small number of powerful private broadcasters and media conglomerates. The spectre of foreign cultural influences has more recently prevented policy debates from fully addressing the positive role of public broadcasting in the increasingly commercialized media environment. Too often the equation of 'cultural sovereignty' with the economic protection of Canadian media industries has closed off other voices and interests in the creation of a truly diverse and dynamic expression of Canadian identity through media policy.

PUBLICS, MARKETS, AND TECHNOLOGIES

A historical survey of media policy debates traces three other key themes: the place of the public, the role of the market, and the ever changing imperatives of technological change. The 'public' element of media policy in Canada has been founded on the assumption that broadcasting frequencies—the media of radio and television—are public property, protected from unrestrained private or commercial exploitation. This concept appears in many key moments in Canadian examinations of and legislation on broadcasting, including the Aird Commission of 1928, the *Radio Broadcasting Acts* of 1932 and 1936, the Massey Commission in 1951, and the *Broadcasting Acts* of 1968 and 1991. This basic assumption supports the notion of a 'single' broadcasting system composed of public and private sectors. Within this single system the state itself has certain interests, some of which have historically been projected onto the role of the CBC. In turn, the CBC has become the primary location of the public interest in broadcasting, the dominant force in public broadcasting, and the major beneficiary of public funds. But the definition of public interest is a shifting one. As already suggested, it is often associated with the political and economic strategies of the state in its attempts to foster national unity and cultural sovereignty. However, the public interest in media policy is broader than just the needs of the federal government and its agencies. More recently 'public interest' has come to stand for the 'special interests' of those audiences or social groups whose needs are not met by imported American programming or national public broadcasting. This equation of public interest with special interests relies on a concept of 'access' and promotes the idea that public broadcasting, again mainly through the CBC, should try to reflect the tastes and interests of a wide range of marginal or minority groups in Canadian society. This is the 'something for everyone' model for national public broadcasting. At the same time, Canada has a variety of non-commercial public broadcasters that are not the CBC, including local campus or community radio and television, Aboriginal media, and educational networks in many provinces. The debate about definitions of the public interest in media policy continues to evolve, but it might be helpful to move beyond the idea of a monolithic 'national public' to think about how various Canadian 'publics' have an interest in media policy. We also need to think critically about the balance between public and private interests in Canadian media policy. There is considerable evidence that governments increasingly work to support profits in private sector commercial media, without any explicit plan for funding or developing a public media sector, whether through the CBC or other forms.

Two other themes that shape the media policy-making process are the roles of 'markets' and 'technology.' These are often represented as anonymous forces outside of human construction. It is difficult for policy-makers to establish the social and cultural objectives of media policy when markets and technologies are represented as unseen forces beyond political control. If the goals of media policy are social and cultural, then policy-makers need to find concrete ways of channelling media technologies for cultural purposes while ensuring that the demands of the marketplace do not outweigh social needs. A historical reading of media policy demonstrates that the balance has shifted substantially away from social goals toward greater intervention in media markets. Policy support for the profitability of private broadcasting became more apparent in the 1980s. Prior to that point the government had concerned itself mainly with supporting public broadcasting, but in 1980 the transfer of jurisdiction over cultural agencies to the newly created Department of Communication marked the merging of goals for broadcasting with those for industrial development. Throughout the 1980s and 90s successive federal governments developed a model of 'cultural industries' and launched new policies that would allow privately-owned media companies to access public funds and use these to gain competitive advantages over foreign media outlets in Canadian markets. The rationale for state intervention in media industries was grounded in the idea of 'market failure' as explained in Chapter 1. According to this concept, cultural expression was seen to have intrinsic merit, thus Canadian industries engaged in its production and distribution should be protected, because domestic markets were too small to support them otherwise. The growing emphasis on producing media content for Canadian companies to export, as a way of making Canadian content more affordable, further illustrates how culture is viewed as a commodity to be produced and consumed in local or global markets. In summary, the government has tried to strengthen Canada's media industries, not by supporting and diversifying the public sector, but by regulating and protecting the private sector, especially in the television and cable industries. Ironically, these industries have benefited from various supportive media policies by importing greater volumes of American content, while directing as little revenue as possible to the creation of Canadian content. Relying on the language of markets in the formulation of media policy has the further disadvantage of casting Canadian citizens primarily as 'consumers' and creators as 'producers.' This language distracts us from the fact that attention to market forces clearly favours some interests over others. The needs of citizens as members of a broader public are not identical to those of producers and consumers.

The idea of a 'technological imperative' in the history of media policy must be similarly understood. Technological change is often represented as a force that must be adapted to at any cost. Just as Canadian media outlets must become competitive in national and international markets, they must adapt to and make use of emerging technologies to protect our cultural sovereignty. However media technologies are not neutral or disinterested objects, they are already designed to meet certain needs and promote certain economic and political interests. Satellites, for instance, were first launched in the

1970s as a way of carrying communication and media channels across Canada more quickly and efficiently. They were used by telecommunications companies and broadcasters, with the economic support of the government, as a means of reaching remote areas of the country and expanding the reach of radio and television networks. Satellites allowed the multiplication of channels in major cities and in rural and remote areas even though there was insufficient Canadian programming to fill these channels. Satellites brought an influx of foreign and Southern programming into remote Northern Aboriginal communities with a negative impact on Native language use and cultural traditions. With each new wave of technological change, from the cross-border radio transmissions of the 1920s, to the growth of television in the 1940s, to the explosion of on-line media today, we can see these technological shifts as part of larger networks of economic and political power. Policy-makers are forced to respond to economic priorities and technological designs that undermine social and cultural goals and the public interest in media. Technological and market forces are perceived as more difficult to challenge, and so media policy is increasingly reactive, driven by response to these outside forces, rather than proactive engagement with cultural change.

The two primary policy sources selected for this chapter come from the 1951 Report of the Royal Commission on National Development in the Arts, Letters, and Sciences (Massey Commission), and from the 2003 Report of the Parliamentary Standing Committee on Canadian Heritage chaired by MP Clifford Lincoln and titled 'Our Cultural Sovereignty' (Lincoln Report). These two selections represent a span of fifty years of Canadian media policy, but they are linked by many common themes and issues as outlined in this chapter. Consider how each of the two reports articulates the ideas of national unity, cultural sovereignty, public interest, market forces and technological change. Review the Policy Analysis Framework in Chapter 1 on page 6 before you begin reading these selections and locate as many of the rationales and objectives for media policy listed in the table as you can while reading each of the two reports.

Primary Sources: Fifty Years of Cultural and Media Policy
Policy Source 1
Canada. Royal Commission on National Development in the Arts Letters and Sciences.
(1951). *Report of the Royal Commission on National Development in the Arts, Letters, and Sciences 1949–1951 (Massey Commission). Radio Broadcasting* (Chapter 18).

Report of the Royal Commission on National Development in the Arts, Letters, and Sciences 1949–1951. (Massey Commission) Radio Broadcasting (Chapter 18)

Chapter XVIII
Broadcasting*

RADIO BROADCASTING

Our Terms of Reference instruct us to consider the principles upon which the policies of radio and television broadcasting in Canada should be based. In Part I we have spoken in some detail of the the [*sic*] development of national radio in Canada and of the views both of the public and of the expert on the nature and quality of programmes from national networks and from local stations. We must now consider and recommend a public policy on radio broadcasting designed to ensure for Canadian listeners the best and most appropriate programmes from every point of view.

2. Radio broadcasting is akin to a monopoly. Any man who has the impulse and the means may produce a book, may publish a newspaper or may operate a motion picture theatre, but he may not in the same way operate a radio station. The air-channels are limited in number and normal competition in any air-channel is impossible. Throughout the world these channels are recognized as part of the public domain; and radio stations may operate only with the permission of the state.

3. The state, having the right and the duty of issuing licences, must impose certain conditions on radio broadcasting. There are, it seems to us, two alternative views between which every country must choose. First, radio may be regarded primarily as a means of entertainment, a by-product of the advertising business. Such a view does not imply that it may not be used for education, for enlightenment and for the cultivation of taste; all these bring entertainment to many people. On the other hand, radio, as one of the most powerful means of

---

*From: *Canada. Royal Commission on National Development in the Arts, Letters, and Sciences. Report. Ottawa: King's Printer, 1951.* By permission of the Privy Council Office.

education, may be regarded as a social influence too potent and too perilous to be ignored by the state which, in modern times, increasingly has assumed responsibility for the welfare of its citizens. This second view of radio operation assumes that this medium of communication is a public trust to be used for the benefit of society, in the education and the enlightenment as well as for the entertainment of its members.

4. The experience of other nations in the western world in choosing between these views, or in attempting to reconcile them, may be helpful; although the peculiarities of our radio problem, as explained in Part I, seem to preclude any ready-made solution for Canada.

5. The United States has accepted the first view mentioned above and has treated radio primarily as a means of entertainment open to commercial exploitation, limited by the public controls found necessary in all countries. Radio broadcasting in the United States is carried on entirely by private stations. More than half of these are allied with one or other of the four principal national networks. Radio broadcasting, maintained almost entirely by advertising revenue, has become an important industry supporting in 1950 more than three thousand stations and receiving more than $445 million in gross revenues from the sale of advertising time.

6. The Government of the United States, accepting the general principle that radio frequencies are within the public domain, in 1934 created the Federal Communications Commission, (F.C.C.), appointed by the President and responsible to Congress. The F.C.C. exercises control through its power to license which must be exercised with a view to the "public interest, convenience or necessity". It is specifically prevented from exercising any powers of censorship. A number of policies of the F.C.C. has provoked discussion and opposition in the United States. One consists of regulations designed to control network monopolies. These regulations were upheld by the United States Supreme Court in 1943. Another, at present a subject of controversy, lies in an effort to secure better programmes through the admonitions of the *F.C.C. Bluebook*. The *Bluebook* states in effect that the maintenance of balance through sustaining programmes, the use of local live talent, the discussion of public issues, and the elimination of advertising excesses are important factors in the public service, and that these will be considered when a licence to broadcast is to be issued or renewed. Stations and networks oppose this advice as a form of indirect programme control. The issue has yet to be decided by the Supreme Court of the United States, but it is reported that the *Bluebook* has had a salutary effect on certain radio programmes.

7. Broadcasting in Great Britain is not an advertising industry but a service provided by the British Broadcasting Corporation, a corporation of the state. "The purpose of the B.B.C. is to give the listener a great deal of what he wants and to give him a chance to want other things as well".[1] This Public corporation operates under a licence from the Postmaster-General and is supported by licence fees which in 1949 yielded well over £12 million. Its publications provide an additional revenue of over £1 million. In practice there is no ministerial or governmental interference with programmes. The Charter of the Corporation is reviewed by a Special Committee appointed for this purpose, and is granted for five year periods; the present Charter comes up for revision in 1951. As this Report goes to press, we have been interested to note that the Broadcasting Committee appointed by the British House of Commons in June of 1949 has in its Report which was made public in January of 1951 recommended in general a continuance of the existing system of broadcasting in Great Britain.

8. France, like Great Britain, has a state system of radio broadcasting. This system, however, is not conducted by a corporation but is directed by a General Manager under the authority of the Premier's office. The private stations in existence before the second world war were requisitioned after the liberation. The ultimate aim, apparently [*sic*] not yet entirely practicable, is to provide alternative programmes over the whole of France, and an additional programme in Paris. There is no advertising over the French broadcasting system, and listeners pay licence fees, as in Great Britain.

9. The Australian system bears some resemblance to the Canadian in that there are both public and private stations. The Australian radio broadcasting system was initiated about 1924 when two types of stations were licensed, "B" stations which were purely commercial, and "A" stations which permitted only limited advertising but received support from licence fees. Since then the Postmaster General's Department has taken over all "A" stations. These do not now accept advertising, and broadcast programmes are prepared under the Australian Broadcasting Commission, a board of seven members appointed by the Governor-General. The Commission is supported by a parliamentary grant which is partially recovered through licence fees. Technical services are provided by the Postmaster-General's Department.

10. In 1948 there were in Australia thirty-nine public and one hundred and two private stations. The public stations have adequate service in the well-populated areas, but achieve only a partial coverage inland. In 1948 legislation was passed setting up the Australian Broadcasting Control Board which began its work in the following year. Operating within the Postmaster-General's Department the Board controls, under the Minister, all broadcasting, both programmes and technical matters. Its intended function appears to be to ensure adequate coverage and better programmes throughout the country. It may even, subject to the approval of the Minister, offer financial assistance to commercial stations for the improvement of their programmes. One of the methods by which this is to be done, it seems, is to arrange for programmes of the Australian Broadcasting Commission to be carried by private stations. So far as we have been able to determine, the Australian Broadcasting Control Board has not yet found it possible to exercise that measure of control over radio programmes in Australia for which it was originally established. It seems correct to say that the present Australian system is still in an experimental stage.

11. Thus, of four leading countries in the western world, the United States alone follows the view that radio broadcasting is primarily an industry; in Great Britain and France it is a public trust; Australia has hesitated between the two views and there the matter has been the occasion of considerable controversy.

12. In Canada, we conceive, the principle that radio broadcasting is a public trust has been followed consistently for twenty years. We have mentioned in Part I the principle advocated by the Aird Report of 1929, which, starting with the proposition that "Canadian radio listeners want Canadian broadcasting", stated that although the enterprise of private broadcasters was providing free entertainment for the benefit of the public, Canadian broadcasting showed an increasing tendency to excessive advertising, importing most of its programmes from outside the country and catering mainly to urban centres. The authors of the Report stressed the importance of complete coverage, of varied programmes including information and education as well as entertainment, of an exchange of programmes between different parts of the country, and, in general,

emphasized the necessity of carrying on broadcasting "in the interests of Canadian listeners, and in the national interests of Canada".

13. This analysis of the situation and this statement of principle were followed by recommendations for a broadcasting system owned and controlled by the nation. These recommendations were adopted in the main, and the principles of Canada's system, established by legislation, have been confirmed year after year by ten Special Committees of the House of Commons and by the opinion of disinterested radio listeners. The system recommended by the Aird Commission to the nation has developed into the greatest single agency for national unity, understanding and enlightenment. But, after twenty years, the time has now come for a restatement of the principles of Canadian broadcasting, tacitly accepted for so many years, and also for some account of what it has done for the country.

14. We have already spoken in Part I of the very great importance of radio broadcasting in Canada and we have pointed out that the isolated areas of the country which need it most would not enjoy its benefits except under a national system. As we have suggested in Part I, we believe that the national system has fulfilled the expectations of those who planned it. We think that, despite the inevitable limitations and deficiencies of which we shall have something to say later, it has exceeded all reasonable expectations; it has become, we have found, a source of pride and gratification to the groups most representative of Canadian listeners; and we can state here that we fully share their feelings.

15. In the early days of broadcasting, Canada was in real danger of cultural annexation to the United States. Action taken on radio broadcasting by governments representing all parties made it possible for her to maintain her cultural identity. Through Canadian radio, however, much more than this has been done. Radio has opened the way to a mutual knowledge and understanding which would have seemed impossible a few years before. Canadians as a people have listened to news of their own country and of the world, have heard public topics discussed by national authorities, have listened to and have participated in discussions of Canadian problems, and have, through radio, been present at great national events. All these things are so obvious today that it is easy to forget what they have meant especially to the many Canadians who live in relative isolation, lacking a daily newspaper and enjoying little contact with the outside world.

16. Canadian sectionalism is not yet a thing of the past, but it is certain that the energetic efforts of the Canadian Broadcasting Corporation in providing special regional programmes and informative talks, and in introducing a great variety of Canadians to their fellow-citizens, have done much to bring us nearer together. From Vancouver Island to Newfoundland and from the Mackenzie River to the border, Canadians have been given a new consciousness of their unity and of their diversity.

17. But national unity and knowledge of our country are not the only ends to be served. These important purposes are also a means to that "peaceful sharing of the things we cherish", in St. Augustine's phrase cited at the beginning of this volume. We are thus further concerned with radio broadcasting in that it can open to all Canadians new sources of delight in arts, letters, music and the drama. Through a fuller understanding and a heightened enjoyment of these things Canadians become better Canadians because their interests are broadened; they achieve greater unity because they enjoy in common more things, and worthier things.

18. This view of the principle or purpose of Canadian radio broadcasting, as we see it, dictates Canadian policy. Other countries may adopt the policy of licensing privately-owned radio stations which depend for revenue on advertising. That such a system may produce excellent programmes is undeniable and many of these from the United States are received and enjoyed by Canadians. But such a system may also produce many programmes which are trivial and commonplace and which debase public taste. In Canada, although not wishing to dispense with plenty of light entertainment, including American entertainment which we import freely, we have been forced by geography and by social and economic conditions to exploit deliberately the more serious possibilities of radio broadcasting in the interests of Canadian listeners and of the Canadian nation. For this purpose we have developed our own national system, which is different from that of the United States, or of any other country, and which this Commission believes to be admirably suited to our special needs.

19. This system has, however, a striking peculiarity in that it continues the existence within the national system of "private", "commercial" or "community" stations as they are variously styled. The C.B.C. had and still has the right to take over all private stations, and for a time these led a somewhat uneasy existence. It soon appeared, however, that these pioneers in the field of radio broadcasting had made a place for themselves in their own communities and that they could perform important national services. It seemed therefore in the national interest that the C.B.C. should recommend the continuance of their licences and that they should be regarded as an integral part of the national system.

20. We have in Part I described in detail the intricacies of the "Basic" and "Supplementary" stations and the complications of "commercial" and "sustaining" programmes. It is necessary here only to refer to the functions of the privately-owned station. In this broad country we still have inadequate radio coverage; without the supplementary outlets of the private stations many more areas would be deprived of the national programmes of the C.B.C., and could be reached only at great additional public expenditure. Apart from this direct national service, the private stations perform community services which, as they rightly point out, are important to the nation: local advertising is in itself a service of value to the community; local news, information and the promotion of worthy causes are essential services, as many individuals and groups have testified. A third proper function of the local station is the encouragement and development of local talent. As we have stated in Part I, this third function has in general been neglected.

21. Most private stations have prospered within the national system. In addition to their private business many of them have benefited from C.B.C. programmes, both commercial and sustaining. That all have not benefited equally is certainly true. But that private stations have increased greatly in numbers, size and wealth since 1932 is undeniable; and that this increase is at least partly due to their incorporation in the national broadcasting system many of them are prepared to admit.

22. It is perhaps in part the growth in numbers and prosperity of the private stations which has led to their increasing protest about their status. During three years, 1946–48, the total operating revenues of the private stations increased from nearly ten to over fourteen million dollars; during the same period C.B.C. operating revenues rose from nearly six millions to seven and a half millions, little more than half the revenues of the private broadcasters. The total assets of the latter at the end of 1948 were twenty-seven millions. In three years the number of private stations rose from

88 to 109, and the total capital increased by seven millions, a large part of which appears to have been fresh investment. The assets of the private investors in 1948 were three times as great as the assets of the C.B.C.

23. A similarly increased prosperity no doubt was to some degree responsible for the representations made by the Canadian Association of Broadcasters (C.A.B.) in 1943, 1944, 1946 and 1947, which asked for changes in the broadcasting regulations to recognize the position which the private broadcasters thought to be appropriate to their current role in Canadian radio broadcasting.

24. Later, in September 1949, and again in April 1950, representatives of the C.A.B., which then comprised ninety-three of the one hundred and nineteen private stations, appeared before this Commission to explain their views on Canadian radio broadcasting and on the status of the private stations. Their case briefly is as follows: seventy private stations existed before the establishment of a public system in 1932. They were not specifically abolished by that system; and many new stations have been licensed since. The representatives of the C.A.B. consider, therefore, that the Act may now fairly be interpreted as having established not one exclusive national system, but a new public system, while permitting the continued existence of the private one.

25. The C.A.B., on the basis of this interpretation, protests against the regulation of the private broadcasters by the Board of Governors of the C.B.C., a public corporation which is their commercial rival. Examples of competition were given: on one occasion cited, the C.B.C. is accused of spending $22,000 in a period of six months to secure local advertising in the district of Toronto. This aggressive competition, it is stated, is evidence at once of the existence in practice of two systems and of the injustice of allowing one of them to control and regulate the other.

26. Regulation of radio broadcasting is carried out chiefly through rules drawn up and enforced by the Board of Governors of the C.B.C. The regulations complained of include the control of network broadcasting, the right to require private station affiliates to reserve time for national programmes, the regulation of advertising practices, and limitations on the use of records and transcriptions. Exception is also taken to rules governing political broadcasts as prescribed by existing legislation. The principal complaint is that the C.B.C., ". . . is at one and the same time competitor, regulator, prosecutor, jury and judge". Even the benefits derived from C.B.C. commercial and sustaining programmes may be abruptly lost if the C.B.C. chooses to open a high power station in the vicinity.

27. The Canadian Association of Broadcasters states that its members do not complain of unjust or inconsiderate treatment, but on the contrary acknowledges cordial relations with the Board of Governors and with the officials of the C.B.C.; but, they add, "a generous and benign master can scarcely take the place of equal or properly established right". They therefore express the wish that as the Broadcasting Act, in their view, lends itself to two conflicting interpretations (one national system of radio, as distinguished from a public system operating together with a number of privately-owned broadcasting stations) the Act should be clarified; further, that it should be re-written "to provide for the regulation of all radio broadcasting stations, whether C.B.C. owned or privately-owned, by a separate and completely impartial authority not associated in any way with the operation of the Canadian Broadcasting Corporation".

28. This general representation of ninety-three associated stations was supported by operators of twenty stations who appeared individually. Seven other private radio

broadcasters supported the present system and advocated no change in principle, one of them remarking, "I am less afraid of the C.B.C. as it exists today than of an unbridled private radio—much less".

29. We wish to acknowledge here the frankness and clarity with which the private broadcasters have presented their views. It must, however, be obvious, from what has already been said, that we cannot agree with their conclusions. We believe that Canadian radio broadcasting legislation contemplates and effectively provides for one national system; that the private stations have been licensed only because they can play a useful part within that system; and that the C.B.C. control of network broadcasting, of the issue and renewal of licences, of advertising and of other matters related to radio broadcasting, is a proper expression of the power of the C.B.C. to exercise control over all radio broadcasting policies and programmes in Canada.

30. The principal grievance of the private broadcasters is based, it seems to us, on a false assumption that broadcasting in Canada is an industry. Broadcasting in Canada, in our view, is a public service directed and controlled in the public interest by a body responsible to Parliament. Private citizens are permitted to engage their capital and their energies in this service, subject to the regulations of this body. That these citizens should be assured of just and equal treatment, that they should enjoy adequate security or compensation for the actual monetary investments they are permitted to make, is apparent. We shall have recommendations to make on this matter later. But that they enjoy any vested right to engage in broadcasting as an industry, or that they have any status except as part of the national broadcasting system, is to us inadmissible.

31. Before 1919, there was in Canada no property interest in any aspect of radio broadcasting and no citizen's right with regard to broadcasting. From 1919 to 1932, some citizens enjoyed, under licence, the privilege of radio broadcasting. In 1932, the Parliament of Canada, with full jurisdiction over the whole legislative field of radio broadcasting communication, established a commission "to carry on the business of broadcasting" in Canada by a system which contemplated the subordination and final absorption of private stations. In 1936, the C.B.C. was constituted to "carry on a national broadcasting service within the Dominion of Canada". It was given for that purpose the very powers over private stations which are now the subject of complaint. The only status of private broadcasters is as part of the national broadcasting system. They have no civil right to broadcast or any property rights in broadcasting. They have been granted in the national interest a privilege over their fellow-citizens, and they now base their claim for equality with their "business rivals" on the abundant material rewards which they have been able to reap from this privilege. The statement that the Board of Governors of the Canadian Broadcasting Corporation is at once their judge and their business rival implies a view of the national system which has no foundation in law, and which has never been accepted by parliamentary committees or by the general public. The Board of Governors is the national authority under whose direction the private stations exercise their privileges and with whom their arrangements are made.

32. We wish to recognize fully the private stations as important elements within the framework of our national system. We shall be making recommendations designed to remove certain inconsistencies of which they have reasonably complained. But we are resolutely opposed to any compromise of the principle on which the system rests and should rest. Radio has been the greatest single factor in creating and in fostering a

sense of national unity. It has enormous powers to debase and to elevate public under-standing and public taste. Believing as we do that it is an essential instrument for the promotion of unity and of general education in the nation, we cannot accept any sug-gestions which would impair the principles on which our present national system is based.

33. This does not mean that we claim perfection for the system or that we are not impressed with the importance of taking every possible measure for the further im-provement of programmes. We have had this matter in mind in framing the financial rec-ommendations which follow, and in certain recommendations on programme produc-tion. We are, however, convinced that the policies advocated by the private stations must lead to an extension of the commercial tendencies in radio programmes which are already too strong, and which have been the subject of much complaint. We were par-ticularly impressed by the fact that few of the representatives of private stations who appeared before us recognized any public responsibility beyond the provision of ac-ceptable entertainment and community services. The general attitude was that the gov-ernment might, if it chose, subsidize "cultural programmes" but that the private sta-tions must be left free to pursue their business enterprise subject only to limitations imposed by decency and good taste. We offer no criticism of this frankly commercial at-titude; we cite it only as evidence that those who honestly hold these views are not pri-marily concerned with the national function of radio. Indeed the improvement of na-tional programmes was not urged by the Canadian Association of Broadcasters as a reason for the reorganization of the national system or for any concessions to commer-cial groups.

34. We have received representations on three important aspects of Canadian ra-dio, and on each of these we have recommendations to make. The first is the manner in which broadcasting in Canada should be controlled and directed. The second is the pro-vision of adequate funds for the operations of the Canadian Broadcasting Corporation. The third is the production of programmes in the national interest and the means by which radio may best serve its national purpose in Canada.

CONTROL AND DIRECTION OF BROADCASTING IN CANADA

A Separate Regulatory Body

35. The chief demand of private broadcasters is that in place of the present system of control exercised by the Board of Governors of the C.B.C., a new and separate body should be set up to regulate all broadcasting in Canada. There is a difference of opin-ion on the powers which it should exercise. Some suggest that it should have powers equivalent to those of the present Board of Governors; others have in mind something like the Federal Communications Commission of the United States. Others again think that such control might be too irksome, an opinion shared by some American broad-casters.

36. We have considered these proposals and find that they would either divide and destroy, or merely duplicate the present system of national control. Legislation to set up a separate regulatory body would alter the present national system and would result

in two independent groups of radio broadcasting stations, one public and one private. The C.B.C. would no longer have the control over all clear channels considered necessary to ensure national coverage. This matter might be arranged but the C.B.C. would still lose the outlets through private stations which are equally necessary for national coverage under existing conditions. Moreover, if the two groups of stations were to be considered as on a parity it would be impossible to refuse network privileges to private broadcasters, with consequences which we shall mention later. A completely separate body treating public and private radio broadcasting with judicial impartiality could not fail to destroy the present system upon which we depend for national coverage with national programmes.

37. But, it may be argued, such a body would have the power to improve, but not to destroy. It could concern itself with the programmes of public and of private stations and strive for the improvement of both in the public interest. The theory may sound plausible, but we doubt whether it would be effective in practice.

38. It is true, as we have observed, that the Federal Communications Commission in the United States is trying to raise the level of programmes by promulgating principles of good broadcasting. Three facts, however, should be noticed. First, the principles themselves are fairly obvious and reflect the prevailing standards. Second, pressure is brought on stations to improve their own programmes, not by detailed instructions but by the implied threat of the non-renewal of their licence if the programmes do not reach a certain unspecified standard. Such a sanction obviously can be applied only in rather glaring cases. The present Canadian system allows and even encourages a House of Commons Committee to bring much more direct and effective pressure to bear on the C.B.C. every year or two. Third, the enforcement of minimum standards in the manner just explained, although it might improve the less desirable programmes of private stations, could do nothing for those of the C.B.C. The public quite properly requires a higher standard for public than for private programmes. But as the completely separate regulatory body contemplated must treat all alike, its activities might well have the effect of reconciling the C.B.C. to relatively low commercial standards rather than of raising the programmes of both the C.B.C. and of private stations to a higher level.

39. It is conceivable that some who might favour a separate regulatory body assume that such an authority would have the duty of securing the necessary channels and sufficient outlets for national sustaining programmes. Such an arrangement would be completely inconsistent with the notion of a separate regulatory body holding the balance between public and private stations. The regulatory power would then become merely an agent for the C.B.C. in securing coverage for national programmes. It would, in fact, parallel in power and responsibility the present Board of Governors of the C.B.C.

40. We must return then to the statement that a new regulatory body would either destroy or duplicate the present national system of control. If the national system were not to be destroyed, a separate body could do only what the present Board of Governors is supposed to do. If it did not mark the end of the national system it could not possibly be "the separate and completely impartial body not connected in any way with the C.B.C." which the C.A.B. has requested.

41. We have no evidence that the present Board of Governors has used its powers harshly or unjustly. If it had done so, the proper remedy would be an improved Board rather than a second one. However, we are strongly of the opinion that in view of the

place occupied by radio broadcasting in the life of the nation, and particularly because of the new and even disturbing possibilities of television broadcasting, no effort should be spared to make the Board of Governors of the C.B.C. as effective as possible. It should be large enough to be fully representative of the country as a whole; and it should be composed of persons fully qualified by knowledge, experience and interests not only to maintain but to advance the present standards of radio broadcasting in Canada whether national or local. We feel very strongly the importance of retaining for the Board the services of qualified persons who are free to devote the necessary time and thought to these grave responsibilities.

We therefore recommend:

a. *That the grant of the privilege of radio broadcasting in Canada continue to be under the control of the National Government; that the control of the national broadcasting system continue to be vested in a single body responsible to Parliament; that the Canadian Broadcasting Corporation as now constituted be that authority and continue to provide directly by its operations and indirectly by its control of the operations of others a national radio broadcasting service free from partisan influence.*

b. *That the present Board of Governors be enlarged in order to make it more widely representative.*

THE FINANCIAL PROBLEM

60. The Board of Governors of the C.B.C. have told us that they are faced with a financial crisis which threatens to disrupt the national broadcasting service. The only way to reconcile rising costs and a stationary income is to reduce expenditures through a reduction in the quantity or quality of service, or both. But the national radio broadcasting service needs expansion and improvement, as we have been informed not only by the C.B.C. but by Canadians everywhere. There is need for more adequate coverage in several parts of the country, for a second French network and for a French station in the Maritimes, for a greater use of Canadian talent, for improved programmes, and, as we have recommended, for the elimination of local advertising and a more selective policy in national advertising.

61. The C.B.C. has stated that in order to maintain services even at their present level it requires about $3,000,000 a year in addition to its current income of approximately $7,500,000. For the improvement and extension of its services, it requires another $2,200,000, making a total annual budget of about $12,700,000. If all the local and the less desirable national commercial programmes are dropped, the Corporation will require an additional $1,500,000—some $14,200,000 in all. This may seem to be a very large annual expenditure, but it represents less than a dollar a year for each Canadian, less than what is paid yearly in Canada for chewing gum. Canadians on an average spend $7 each year on moving pictures. We see no reason therefore to suppose that they will think that one dollar a year each is an excessive sum to pay for a national

service which they greatly value; on the contrary, we have had many demands from listeners that the C.B.C. be granted all necessary funds to develop and improve its programmes and to increase their Canadian content.

62. We have received a number of specific suggestions on how this should be done. The C.B.C.'s own proposal to raise the licence fee to $5 is generally unpopular. It was claimed in our sessions that this increased fee would be a hardship to many listeners, and that it would not be readily accepted since there is a widespread impression that the present licence fee is not effectively collected.

63. Many witnesses and correspondents have suggested to us that an improved method of collecting the license fee would provide an immediate, if partial, method of financial relief. The Department of Transport considers that the present method of collection is reasonably effective and thorough. However, if the figures of the Dominion Bureau of Statistics are to be accepted, Canada's three and a half million private receiving sets which should be licensed ought to yield over eight and a half millions a year in licence fees instead of something over five million.

64. Even this sum, however, would clearly fall short of what is needed. We see no solution to the financial problem of the C.B.C. except in additional support from public funds. Some witnesses have even proposed that because all Canadians benefit from the national radio system directly or indirectly, the licence fee be abolished and the entire cost be borne by the taxpayer. This proposal we cannot accept, since we think it proper for the listener to make a direct payment for services received and we believe that he appreciates these services the more for doing so. But we have come to the conclusion that because the C.B.C. serves the nation as a whole, it is reasonable that the revenue required over and above a moderate licence fee be provided from general taxation.

65. There are, however, serious objections to an annual grant to be voted by Parliament. Although other essential government services depend on an annual vote, it is so important to keep the national radio free from the possibility of political influence that its income should not depend annually on direct action by the government of the day. A statutory grant seems to us a more satisfactory method, because it enables the C.B.C. to formulate reasonably long range plans with the confidence that its income will not be decreased over a period of years. A convenient way of providing adequate revenue for the C.B.C. might be to set the necessary revenue for the C.B.C. at a total amount equal to one dollar per head of the Canadian population as determined decennially by the census and estimated each year by the Dominion Bureau of Statistics. This amount, which could be calculated annually, would be the total revenue of the C.B.C. for the year. It would be made up first of net receipts from licence fees, and of commercial and miscellaneous revenue. The balance would be paid to the C.B.C. by the Federal Government out of public money on the authority of the statute. For example, in 1947–48 the statutory revenue on the basis of the population estimate would have been $13,549,000. This would have been received by the C.B.C. as follows:

Net Licence Fees	**$5,135,374.65**
Commercial Broadcasting	2,217,129.91
Miscellaneous	200,709.24
	7,553,213.80
Statutory Grant	5,995,786.20
	13,549,000.00

We therefore recommend:

k. *That the annual licence fee for radio receiving sets be maintained at its present level, but that a more efficient method of collection be devised.*

l. *That the total annual income of the Canadian Broadcasting Corporation for all radio broadcasting purposes other than its International Service be set by statute for five years, and that this income be found from licence fees, from commercial and miscellaneous revenue, and from a payment out of public money sufficient to make up the total statutory income.*

PROGRAMMES

Programmes in the National Interest

66. We have in our hearings and in our deliberations spent many hours in discussing the proper methods of governing and of financing the national broadcasting system. These methods, however, are only the administrative and material basis for one of the great forces in our country in promoting Canadian unity and Canadian cultural life. Herein lies, as we see it, our main responsibility as a Royal Commission. We have received in our public hearings many and differing opinions and views on Canadian radio. We think it a particularly successful and useful part of our work that we have been able to elicit these comments on Canadian radio from so many of our fellow citizens.

67. We cannot state too forcefully that our primary interest in broadcasting lies in the kind and quality of programmes broadcast in Canada and in their influence on Canadian life. Our study of problems of control and of finance has been guided by our desire to see maintained and improved the standards of our national programmes. We have recommended that the present national system be continued because of its achievements in the past and its promise for the future. We do not take it to be our duty to make detailed recommendations for the development and improvement of programmes. Nevertheless it seems to us important to say something of the view suggested in Part I that the distinguished work of the C.B.C. in music and drama does not appear to be equalled in what are known as "talks". This is not surprising. Talks are as a rule less popular than music, drama, news reports and variety entertainment. They occupy a relatively small proportion of programme time, and may easily be dismissed as comparatively unimportant. This attitude, if it exists, seems to us regrettable.

68. Our concern with the radio as a means of national unity and general education has led us to make a somewhat detailed examination of the content of radio talks. We find that a number, including those on the *Wednesday Night* programmes given by distinguished Canadian authorities in their fields, fufils what seems to us the proper function of the talk on a national network. Of such programmes every Canadian may be proud. Other talks, even some given during important Sunday listening hours, seem to us to fall short of this high standard. On inquiry we learn that speakers with no special knowledge or reputation in their fields may be engaged because they have a natural facility for broadcasting and also, apparently, because the popular approach of the amateur is thought to have a special appeal to the average listener.

69. We think it important to express our dissent from this policy. Through the services of the C.B.C., Canadians have been privileged to listen to speakers on the B.B.C. distinguished in many fields of thought. It is the principle of the B.B.C. that the popular talk should be in quality and authority comparable to the scholarly. In this matter Britain shares the fine tradition of France where even philosophers are expected to make themselves comprehensible to *l'homme moyen raisonnable*. We cannot believe that it is impossible to find in Canada authorities in every field who are capable of living up to this great tradition. It should be a set principle with the C.B.C. that all its talks, even the most popular, should if published be acceptable to the expert and enjoyed by the layman. We see no reason why there should not be ultimately a Canadian equivalent to *The Listener* in Great Britain.

70. We have given serious consideration to possible measures for improvement. We realize that financial stringency may be responsible for the deficiencies which we have noticed. We cannot, however, accept the assumption already mentioned that a natural facility for broadcasting is more important to a radio speaker than recognized competence in his subject. It is possible that the C.B.C. might add to its staff more officials of experience and authority in intellectual matters to assume some direct responsibility for the planning of talks. Also, there should be, we think, a closer contact between C.B.C. officials and leading Canadians in all fields of intellectual interest.

We therefore recommend:

m. *That the Canadian Broadcasting Corporation provide more adequately in its budget for the department or departments responsible for the talks programmes.*

n. *That the officials of the Canadian Broadcasting Corporation make greater efforts to secure for its talks programmes, popular as well as serious, representative persons of proven ability, knowledge and experience in the subject matter of the talk.*

o. *That the Board of Governors of the Canadian Broadcasting Corporation take into consideration the advisability of appointing national advisory councils on talks, in order that its officials may receive advice on programme policy, and information on programme material.*

Coverage and Programmes of French-Language Stations

71. It has been pointed out to us repeatedly in different parts of Canada that the French-speaking Canadian listener does not receive a broadcasting service equal to that intended for his English-speaking neighbour. Officials of the C.B.C. are aware of this fact and regret it, but they have explained that it is one of the consequences of their financial dilemma. One of the reasons prompting us to recommend greater financial resources for the C.B.C. is the desirability of removing this inequality which is inconsistent with the conception of a national service.

We therefore recommend:

p. *That the Canadian Broadcasting Corporation, as soon as funds are available, proceed with the organization of a second French network and the establishment of a French-speaking broadcasting station to serve French-speaking people in the Maritime Provinces; that it also initiate and carry out plans for a special pro-*

gramme on a French network comparable to the Wednesday Night programme of the Trans-Canada network.

q. *That the Canadian Broadcasting Corporation take into serious consideration the use of existing French language stations in Western Canada as outlets for national French programmes, by transcription or by some other means.*

Development of Canadian Talent

72. We have already shown in Part I the important part which the national broadcasting system has played and can play in the development of Canadian talent and in the encouragement of Canadian artists. We received many appreciative comments on the consistent work of the C.B.C. in this field. We received also, however, protests against what was described as over-centralization of programme production. In 1948–49 expenditure on artists' fees for programmes produced in Toronto and Montreal amounted to $1,302,595. In all the rest of Canada it amounted to $593,236 of which $261,704 was spent in Vancouver. We are aware that this centralization may be dictated by motives of economy, and therefore, on a limited budget, of good programming. We consider, however, that a national system must keep in mind considerations other than those of convenience or even of financial economy and might well give its own interpretation to the expression "good programming". We have heard with concern the representations of smaller centres that although help may be given to their local talent by invitations to appear on the national network, this aid hardly compensates for the continuous loss of their most promising performers to the two large cities of central Canada. It is presumed that the C.B.C.'s demands for television performers will accentuate this concentration of talent.

73. We have already shown that the development of local talent, which can be undertaken only very partially by the C.B.C., lies decidedly within the responsibilities of private broadcasters who have largely neglected it.

We therefore recommend:

r. *That the Board of Governors of the Canadian Broadcasting Corporation take into serious consideration the further development of radio programmes in points of origination other than Toronto and Montreal.*

s. *That the Board of Governors of the Canadian Broadcasting Corporation investigate ways of ensuring that private radio broadcasters employ more Canadian talent.*

78. In Canada radio has a particularly important task. It must offer information, education and entertainment to a diverse and scattered population. It must also develop a sense of national unity between our two main races, and among our various ethnic groups, in spite of a strongly developed regional sense and of the attractions of our engaging and influential southern neighbour.

79. Has our national system performed this function? It has done much; much yet remains to be done. We have already spoken of its contributions to national unity and understanding. We cannot praise too highly its clear, complete and impartial news and

information services. We have reported and we agree with the praise given to its school broadcasts. In music and drama and particularly in the *Wednesday Night* experiments, we think that it has shown what may be done in developing new tastes and interests.

80. Obviously, Canadian radio has not yet achieved all that we hope for in a national system. It is still young. It has had to struggle against poverty, inexperience, and the physical obstacles of this difficult country. But, as we have suggested in Part I and have stated here in language as clear and unambiguous as we can command, we are convinced that the existing Canadian system of broadcasting has served the country well in the past and offers the greatest hope of national unity and enlightenment in the future. We urge that the national broadcasting system be given the power and resources sufficient for its great national responsibilities.

Endnotes

1. Crosby, John. (1951). Radio and television. *New York Herald Tribune.*

DISCUSSION

Report of the Royal Commission on National Development in the Arts, Letters, and Sciences 1949–1951 (Massey Commission), Chapter 18 'Radio Broadcasting.'

1. What two common views of the place of radio in society does the Massey Commission review? What type of international models of radio broadcasting does the report outline?
2. Read through the discussion of radio broadcasting and the specific recommendations made in this chapter and find one example of each of the different media policy rationales and objectives outlined in the Policy Analysis Framework in Chapter 1 on page 6 Which rationale do you think is most predominant in this chapter of the Massey report?
3. The Canadian Association of Broadcasters is a long-standing example of a 'stakeholder' in the media policy process. What type of interests does the CAB represent and what demands has it put forward to the Massey Commission?
4. What reasons does the Commission give for rejecting the CAB's demand for a 'separate regulatory body' to oversee radio broadcasting? Which side of this debate do you find most convincing and why?
5. The Massey Commission recommended a combination of licence fees and a five-year Parliamentary statutory grant to fund CBC radio. Using the list of policy tools and instruments outlined in the Policy Analysis Framework in Chapter 1 on page 6 explain which two different types of tools are represented by these options. What are some of the strengths and limitations of each choice for funding public broadcasting?

Policy Source 2
Canada. Parliament. House of Commons. Standing Committee on Canadian Heritage.
(2003). *Our cultural sovereignty: The second century of Canadian broadcasting.*
(Lincoln Report). Retrieved from http://www.parl.gc.ca/content/hoc/Committee/372/
HERI/Reports/RP1032284/herirp02/herirp02-e.pdf *Regulatory History* (Chapter 2).

Our Cultural Sovereignty (Lincoln Report), Chapter 2, Regulatory History

Since the earliest days of Confederation, Canada's vast size, long winters and fragmented population have necessitated a well-developed communications network. At first it was the printed word and the railways that helped serve this function. Later, the telegraph and the telephone were added. In the early years of the twentieth century it was radio, followed in the 1950s by television, and since the mid-1990s, the Internet. Over time, Canada's broadcasting system has become one of the principal ways through which Canadians have developed a sense of community and identity. In parallel, Canada's broadcasting infrastructure has become a multi-billion dollar industry, offering valuable opportunities for tens of thousands of Canadians in countless areas of the broadcasting, telecommunications and technology sectors.

A strong point of the Canadian broadcasting system is the elaborate physical infrastructure its trustees have developed to deliver radio and television services to potential audiences. Its weakness has always been the amount of original Canadian programming written and produced by Canadians, for Canadians.

Some have argued that the absence of adequate Canadian programming combined with the pervasiveness of the popular American variety represents a force that undermines Canadians' social, cultural, economic, public and national interests. This is why successive governments for more than 70 years have developed and funded a national public broadcaster, an independent production industry and an arm's-length regulator to oversee the practices and activities of those who deliver our programming services.

The introduction of radio created at least as much and perhaps more excitement than the development of railroads. It was now possible for communities to share information across vast distances without having to worry about the state of the roads, the railroads or the weather. All that was needed was electricity—a crystal in the early days—and, later on, a four or five tube radio set.

From the beginning, the benefits of broadcast programming were imagined to be considerable. Indeed, the Aird Commission of 1928–29 believed that:

. . . broadcasting should be considered of such importance in promoting the unity of the nation that a subsidy by the Dominion Government should be regarded as an essential aid to the general advantage of

Canada rather than as an expedient to meet any deficit in the cost of maintenance of the service.[1]

It also observed that:

> ... the potentialities of broadcasting as an instrument of education have been
> impressed upon us; education in the broad sense, not only as it is conducted in
> the schools and colleges, but in providing entertainment and in informing the
> public on questions of national interest.[2]

Thus, education, information, entertainment and national unity were the core reasons
why Aird's Commission recommended the creation of a national public broadcaster.
And it is these same motivations that have informed every Canadian review that has
considered broadcasting since that time.

For example, in 1932, Prime Minister R. B. Bennett spoke of an:

> ... enduring fellowship ... founded on the clear and sympathetic understanding
> which grow out of closer mutual knowledge. In this stage of our national devel-
> opment, we have problems peculiar to ourselves and we must reach a solution .
> .. through the employment of all available means. The radio has a place in the
> solution ... It becomes, then, the duty of Parliament to safeguard in such a way
> that its fullest benefits may be assured to the people as a whole.[3]

Similarly, in 1951, the Royal Commission on National Development in the Arts, Letters
and Sciences (known as Massey-Lévesque) concluded that:

> In Canada ... the principle that radio broadcasting is a public trust has been fol-
> lowed consistently for twenty years [therefore] broadcasting in Canada, in our
> view, is a public service directed and controlled in the public interest by a body
> responsible to Parliament.[4]

Nearly 20 years later, in 1970, the Special Senate Committee Report on Mass Media
agreed that:

> ... broadcasters [use] public property in transmitting their signals through the
> air, and ... Canadians [have] a right to expect that broadcasters [will use] that
> public property to strengthen our culture, rather than dilute it.[5]

This view was reaffirmed by the 1986 Task Force on Canadian Broadcasting when it
stated that:

> Those who are granted the right to use radio frequencies are given an impor-
> tant responsibility. Contributing to the dissemination of Canadian culture is a
> duty inherent in the privilege they are granted as a public trust on behalf of
> Canadians.[6]

Ten years later, the report of the Mandate Review Committee arrived at a similar conclusion when it argued that:

> We need Canadian programs and films to enable our citizens to understand one another, to develop a national and community consciousness, to help us shape our solutions to social and political problems, and to inspire the imagination of our children and express their hope.[7]

Remarkably, the Aird Commission made much the same point—albeit more provocatively—in 1929 when it noted that:

> ... the majority of the programs heard are from sources outside of Canada. It has been emphasized to us that the continued reception of these has a tendency to mould the minds of young people in the home to ideals and opinions that are not Canadian.[8]

Thus, while not all studies of broadcasting have necessarily used the expression "public trust," it is clear that they have consistently embraced a vision of a broadcasting system that serves the public interests of all Canadians. For this reason, it is both fitting, not to mention somewhat troubling, that the 1929 Report of the Royal Commission on Radio Broadcasting—which is a mere nine pages, with 19 pages of appendices—seems as timely today, more than 70 years after it was written.

That said, the Standing Committee on Canadian Heritage Committee faces a far more complex world than any of our predecessors could possibly have imagined. This makes it inevitable that this Committee's report cannot be as concise as Aird's was in 1929, but in no way precludes it from being as daring and provocative.

The following sections briefly describe the circumstances underlying the legislation that has entrenched broadcasting in Canada as a public trust.[9] As will be seen, this evolution can best be described as a series of stages triggered by government studies and successive Acts of Parliament.

The Beginnings: 1913–28

Under the *Radiotelegraph Act* of 1913, a government minister was authorized to licence radio broadcasters and to charge a small licence fee for each receiving set. Starting in 1922, radio administration became the sole responsibility of the Radio Branch of the Department of Marine and Fisheries. At this time, most broadcasting, except for the military, was in the private sector and was used by hobbyists, commercial broadcasters and non-profit groups. Popular programming included: music, news, weather, sports, entertainment and live events. A radio network operated by the Canadian National Railways (CNR) provided the only national programming during this time.

By 1928 about 68 radio stations and some 400,000 battery-operated radio receivers were in operation across Canada, including CKUA, Canada's first educational broadcaster. Radio set licence fees were one dollar and regulations restricting content were minimal.

PUBLIC OWNERSHIP AND GOVERNMENT REGULATION: 1928–36

As already noted, the federal government launched the Royal Commission on Radio Broadcasting in 1928 to study the state of the Canadian broadcasting system. Chaired by Sir John Aird, the Commission's stated purpose was to "determine how radio broadcasting in Canada could be most effectively carried on in the interest of Canadian listeners and the national interests of Canada."[11] It was also expected to "make recommendations to the Government as to the future administration, management, control and financing thereof."[12]

Signal interference and overcrowded airwaves due to a relative lack of spectrum management was one reason for the launch of the Aird Commission study. Of paramount concern, however, was the disproportionate number of Canadians who were receiving and listening to American radio signals, a phenomenon which was not only slowing the growth of Canadian radio but was, as noted above, having "a tendency to mould the minds of young people in the home to ideals and opinions that are not Canadian."[13]

Another issue for many during this era was the uneven availability of Canadian services and programming in different parts of the country. The Aird Commission recognized this problem and observed that: "In a country of the vast geographical dimensions of Canada, broadcasting will undoubtedly become a great force in fostering a national spirit and interpreting national citizenship."[14] For this reason, the report proposed the creation of a publicly owned national broadcaster not unlike the BBC. Only by doing so, it explained, would "the interests of the listening public and the nation . . . be adequately served."[15]

In parallel with the Aird Commission's efforts, the Quebec government took an active part in establishing a provincial role in broadcasting. It passed the first radio legislation in 1929, while the Aird Commission was still sitting, and strengthened it in 1931 with legislation concerning licencing and civil responsibility for broadcasting.[16]

The next year, in 1932, following judgments by the Supreme Court of Canada as well as the Judicial Committee of the Privy Council in London, it was confirmed that federal jurisdiction over the airwaves and programming content made it feasible to proceed with a national public radio broadcaster. Thereafter, a special parliamentary committee was created to implement the Aird Commission's recommendations, culminating with all-party support that same year for the passage of the *Canadian Radio Broadcasting Act,* an Act creating the Canadian Radio Broadcasting Commission (CRBC).

In keeping with the Aird Commission's vision of a "national company which will own and operate all radio stations located in . . . Canada"[17], the CRBC was conceived as a three-man commission empowered to regulate, control and carry on broadcasting activities in Canada in the public interest. The CRBC was mandated to originate and transmit programs; lease, buy or build facilities; and, over time, assume complete control over all aspects of Canadian broadcasting. In other words, it was expected to create a monopoly situation similar to that enjoyed by the BBC in the United Kingdom.

The creation of the CRBC coincided, however, with the economic Depression of the 1930s, meaning that Prime Minister Bennett's government could not fund the CRBC as required. As a result, the Commission established stations in just five cities, and relied on private broadcasters to rebroadcast its network programming in other cities and regions. This had the effect of entrenching a public-private system, a mix that characterizes the Canadian broadcasting system to this day.

The CBC as Regulator and Operator: 1936–58

By the early 1930s, more than one million Canadian homes had radio licences and listeners were accustomed to receiving several hours of CRBC network programming each day, not to mention a handful of private stations that offered music, local news, sports and rebroadcasts of popular American entertainment shows. At the same time, Canadians in border regions were continuing to enjoy over-the-air broadcasts from the United States.

Following the election of a new government in 1935, Prime Minister Mackenzie King decided that the *Canadian Radio Broadcasting Act* of 1932 should be revised to more fully capture the essence of the Aird Report and to address concerns that the CRBC was not sufficiently arm's-length in its functioning. Soon thereafter, in 1936, a considerably revised Act was adopted by Parliament, which enshrined the principle that the public broadcaster was a public, not a state broadcaster. It also created a more autonomous body, the Canadian Broadcasting Corporation (CBC), as a replacement for the CRBC.

The new Act gave CBC the mandate to licence and regulate all parts of the national broadcasting system, including those private stations that it did not directly own or operate. Funded by an increased licence fee, it was therefore able to take swift action to enlarge its reach through the construction of a network of regional transmitters. It also increased its programming hours by importing American shows. As a result, within eight years, the CBC was operating two English networks (TransCanada and Dominion) and one French network. At the same time, despite not being allowed to form national networks, private radio stations were flourishing.

As already noted, the Massey-Lévesque Commission identified and affirmed the public trust characteristics of Canadian broadcasting activities in 1951. This report—which was issued just months before the introduction of television to Canadians—did not and perhaps could not have foreseen the speed with which this new technology would make the CBC's dual role as a broadcasting monopoly and broadcast regulator untenable.

In September 1952, CBC television went on the air in Montréal and Toronto. At first, each Canadian market was limited by CBC broadcast regulators to one television station (typically a private-station licensee) that was expected to carry the CBC's national programming. It soon became clear, however, that the public thirst for more choice and content could not be fulfilled under a policy regime in which the system's sole public broadcasting trustee was also its regulator. This issue was so contentious that a Royal Commission on Broadcasting, to be chaired by Robert M. Fowler, was established in 1955 with a view to recommending new broadcasting legislation.

Regulation by the Board of Broadcast Governors: 1958–68

The Fowler Commission's 1957 report on Canadian Broadcasting recognized the inherent conflict underlying the CBC's dual role as operator and regulator and recommended that its statutory broadcasting functions be separated from its broadcast regulation duties and that a separate and independent body be established to regulate broadcasting in the public interest. Its authors explained:

> We think there have in fact been two public elements involved in radio and television broadcasting. This factual separation of powers should be more precisely defined in law. One of these elements should be an operating agency, engaged in the operation of publicly owned stations and national networks and in the production and distribution of a national programme service throughout Canada. . . .
>
> The other public agency in the Canadian broadcasting field should be a board created and authorized to act for Parliament, and responsible to Parliament, for the direction and supervision of the Canadian broadcasting system. This board should have responsibility for all elements in Canadian broadcasting. It should not, we suggest, be part of the Canadian Broadcasting Corporation and its members should not . . . comprise the Corporation.[18]

Convinced by this argument, the government of Prime Minister Diefenbaker moved quickly to introduce and adopt the *Broadcasting Act* of 1958, which created a new policy framework for Canada's broadcasting system.

The *Broadcasting Act* of 1958 created a 15-member Board of Broadcast Governors (BBG) that was responsible for regulating the activities, and relationships between Canada's public and private broadcasters and to ensure the efficient operation of national radio and television broadcasting. The BBG was to consider applications for new stations and make licencing recommendations to the minister responsible. The Act also created a board of governors to oversee CBC operations that would report separately to Parliament.

Under the BBG, Canadian television expanded quickly while radio, for the most part, became a local or community service, with the exception of the CBC, which continued to maintain and expand its national network. Meanwhile, a private television network, the Independent Television Organization—soon to be known as CTV—began broadcasting in larger centres in the early 1960s. Around this time, broadcasting (both television and radio) ranked third in profitability among Canada's top 140 industries.

In 1964, the federal government created the Fowler Broadcasting Committee to study the increasing dominance and availability of American programming in Canada. Fowler's Committee was also asked to address and fine-tune some of the ambiguities in the *Broadcasting Act* that were causing disputes between the BBG and the CBC.

The Fowler Committee made its report to Parliament in 1965. The Committee roundly criticized the performance of the BBG, the CBC and private broadcasters and declared that Parliament should state broadcasting policy in firm and clear terms. That said, it was of the view that neither the government nor Parliament should be involved in the details of administration, finance and programming. For this reason, it proposed that a new broadcasting authority—which would be held accountable to Parliament for the achievement of stipulated goals—be formed.

In response, the government issued a White Paper on Broadcasting in 1966 and referred it to the Standing Committee on Broadcasting, Film and Assistance to the Arts. In it, the government declared that Parliament would be asked to enact new broadcasting policy and legislation that would establish the authorities and responsibilities for management of the CBC and the regulation of public and private broadcasting in Canada.

In March 1967, the Standing Committee issued its Report. It declared that:

> A distinctly Canadian broadcasting system is essential to our national identity, unity and vitality in our second century . . . The Committee feels strongly that it is not a proper function of Parliament or government to be involved in the programming, or day-to-day operation or supervision of the broadcasting system. It is, however, the responsibility of Parliament to define the public interest to be served by our broadcasting system and to enunciate the national policy. It is also Parliament's duty to create a viable structure within which the service we seek can be assured to the Canadian people.[19]

With this in mind, the Standing Committee made a number of recommendations of lasting significance in the development of policy for the regulation and supervision of the Canadian broadcasting system. These include that: the Canadian Broadcasting Corporation become the prime instrument of public policy in broadcasting; the board of the regulator should not be involved in the day-to-day decision-making or policy-making of the CBC; the regulator should not be empowered to give directions concerning specific programs, other than by generally applicable regulations or in the conditions of licence, to any broadcasters; Canadian talent must be developed; undue concentration of ownership should be investigated by the regulator; and, foreign programming should be welcomed provided Canadians are assured access to Canadian programs of high quality.

Regulation by the CRTC: 1968–91

Based on the policy proposals of the Fowler Report, the White Paper and the Parliamentary Committee, Parliament adopted a new *Broadcasting Act* in 1968. In doing so, it created a new arm's-length regulatory body, the Canadian Radio Television Commission (CRTC),[20] which was empowered to issue broadcast licences and a mandate to ensure that: ownership and control of broadcasting remain in Canadian hands; programming be of high quality with substantial Canadian content; Canadian broadcasting safeguard, enrich and strengthen the nation of Canada from sea to sea. The Act also brought cable television, already well established in some cities, under the authority of the CRTC. The CRTC's first Chair was Pierre Juneau.

From its inception, the CRTC was far more active than the Board Broadcast Governors (BBG) in its efforts to uphold Canadian content quotas. For the CBC, meeting or exceeding the CRTC's Canadian content quotas was not and has never been a significant challenge.[21] For private broadcasters, however, meeting even the barest minimum—especially between the prime-time hours of 7 and 11 PM—was and remains difficult, particularly with the expansion of the television market due to the licencing of new Canadian services and the importation of foreign broadcasting services.

In 1980, the Minister of Communications, the Honourable Francis Fox, launched a Federal Cultural Policy Review Committee, to be chaired by Louis Applebaum and cochaired by Jacques Hébert.

The Applebaum-Hébert Report, which was issued in 1982, studied all areas of relevance to Canadian cultural policy, including broadcasting. In this regard, it made a number of recommendations concerning the Canadian broadcasting system, including that:

- the CBC discontinue all commercial advertising, phase out in-house and local programming, and rededicate itself to regional programming;
- the CRTC require private broadcasters to allocate substantial percentages of their programming time and expenditures on new Canadian programming;
- the CRTC licence new private local stations in markets able to absorb them;
- a new *Broadcasting Act* be enacted by Parliament;
- a new Act give clear authority to the CRTC in matters related to the CBC; and,
- a new Act confirm the total independence of the CRTC from political intrusion, but permit direction by the Minister on the matters of general policy.

In 1984, to address the ongoing challenges the Canadian broadcasting system was facing due to audience fragmentation, changes in technology and ongoing concerns over Canada's cultural sovereignty, the Task Force on Canadian Broadcasting, co-chaired by Florian Sauvageau and Gerald Caplan was created to advise the federal government on changes that should be made to Canada's broadcasting policy.

Echoing Massey's 1951 vision of broadcasting as a public trust, the Task Force delivered a unanimous report in 1986, which as noted earlier stated that: "[c]ontributing to the dissemination of Canadian culture is a duty inherent in the privilege [broadcasters] are granted as a public trust on behalf of Canadians."[22] The Task Force therefore recommended that:

- all broadcasting undertakings be part of a composite system;
- all licensees be regarded as trustees of the Canadian public;
- the CBC play a central role in assuring that Canadians have a truly national broadcasting system, in radio and television, in English and French;
- CBC funding be stable and secure for the duration of its licence period;
- all American programming on CBC television be phased out as soon as possible;
- a new national, public broadcaster, TVCanada, be created.[23]

As for private stations, the Task Force recommended that the CRTC set stricter conditions of licence to ensure that private stations and networks invest more in the creation and production of Canadian programs. The Report also called for some government support and protection for the private sector, in return for which the private sector (in their role as trustees) would contribute to fulfilling the objectives of the Act.

The House of Commons Standing Committee on Communications and Culture examined the Report of the Task Force between 1986 and 1988. Its all-party unanimous report, with more than 140 recommendations, contributed to a revamped Broadcasting Act adopted by the House of Commons in 1991.

Regulation by the CRTC since 1991

As noted above, an Act of Parliament established the CRTC in 1968. Since 1985, the Commission has operated as an independent public authority constituted under the *Canadian Radio-television and Telecommunications Commission Act* and, since 1993, has reported to Parliament through the Minister of Canadian Heritage. Under the Act, the Cabinet may appoint up to 13 full-time and 6 part-time commissioners for renewable terms of up to 5 years. The Commission is also subject to orders from Cabinet and must take into account the needs and concerns of Canadian citizens, industries and various interest groups.

The CRTC's mandate is to ensure that the terms of the *Broadcasting Act*—particularly Canada's broadcasting policy (Section 3)—are fulfilled. The Commission does this by seeking to maintain a balance—in the public interest—between the social, cultural and economic goals of the Act. As the Commission's website explains:

> Our mandate is to ensure that programming in the Canadian broadcasting system reflects Canadian creativity and talent, our linguistic duality, our multicultural diversity, the special place of Aboriginal people within our society and our social values. At the same time, we must ensure that Canadians have access to reasonably priced, high-quality, varied and innovative communications services that are competitive nationally as well as internationally.[24]

With all these interests in mind, the Commission today acts as the regulator for more than 5,900 broadcasters, including: over-the-air television; cable distribution; AM, FM and DAB radio; pay, specialty and digital television; direct-to-home satellite systems (DTH); multipoint distribution systems (MDS); and, subscription television and pay audio.[25] In doing so, it holds regular public hearings, round-table discussions and informal forums to process applications and make decisions regarding broadcasting licences and related requests.[26]

Endnotes

1. Report of the Royal Commission on Radio Broadcasting (Aird Commission) (Ottawa: F. A. Acland, 1929), p. 10.
2. Ibid, p. 6.
3. *Making our Voices Heard: Canadian Broadcasting and Film for the 21st Century,* Report of the Mandate Review Committee, Department of Canadian Heritage, 1996, p. 21.
4. Report of the Royal Commission on National Development in the Arts, Letters and Sciences: 1949–1951 (Massey Commission) (Ottawa: King's Printer, 1951), p. 279, 283.
5. *The Uncertain Mirror,* Report of the Special Senate Committee on Mass Media (Davey Committee) (Ottawa: Queen's Printer, 1970), p. 195.
6. Report of the Task Force on Broadcasting Policy (Caplan-Sauvageau) (Ottawa: Minister of Supply and Services Canada, 1986), p. 147.
7. Mandate Review Committee, p. 23–24.
8. Aird Commission, p. 6.
9. Related to the notion of the "public trust" is "citizenship"; that is, the rights of citizens to have the information that they need to know to make decisions about their lives

and communities; the rights of taxpayers to have money spent on their behalf in a responsible manner; the rights of access; and, the importance of democratic rights.

10. Much of the biographical information in this chapter is adapted from *The Canadian Encyclopedia,* www.thecanadianencyclopedia.com.

11. www.rcc.ryerson.ca.

12. Aird Commission, p. 5.

13. Ibid, p. 6.

14. Ibid.

15. Ibid.

16. In 1945, Maurice Duplessis's government passed an Act to create a provincial broadcasting service, claiming Quebec had constitutional authority. The Act also created Radio-Québec.

17. Aird Commission, p. 7.

18. Report of the Committee on Broadcasting (Fowler Committee) (Ottawa: Queen's Printer, 1965), p. 90–91.

19. Frank Foster, *Broadcasting Policy Development* (Ottawa: Franfost Communications, 1974), p. 229.

20. In 1976, the CRTC was renamed the Canadian Radio-television and Telecommunications Commission to reflect the expansion of its jurisdiction to include common carriers.

21. www.ryerson.ca.

22. Caplan-Sauvageau, p. 147.

23. The TVCanada proposal is also discussed in Chapter 7.

24. www.crtc.gc.ca.

25. The CRTC also regulates over 61 telecommunications carriers, including major Canadian telephone companies.

26. In 1999, for example, the Commission processed 1,754 broadcasting and 1,533 telecommunications applications. It also issued 1,230 orders and granted 90 licences to telephone companies that provide international long distance services. It also responded to 8,900 electronically transmitted documents, as well as over 53,900 telephone calls and 16,000 letters and emails of requests and complaints.

DISCUSSION

Our Cultural Sovereignty (Lincoln Report), Chapter 2 'Regulatory History.'

1. This chapter of the Lincoln Report describes the strength of Canada's broadcasting and media technological infrastructure, but what does the report suggest is one of the historical weaknesses of our system?

2. Using the detailed history of major developments in Canadian broadcasting policy provided in the Lincoln Report, create a time-line of events between 1913 and 2003. Include entries for significant technological changes, major policy processes, and pieces of legislation that have affected Canadian media. If you were to identify one single theme that ties all these events together what would it be?

3. In 1957, in a substantial departure from the Massey Commission's earlier position on this question, the Fowler Commission recommended the creation of an independent regulatory body for broadcasting. What was this proposed regulatory agency called and why did Fowler suggest a 'separation of powers' between public broadcasting and regulation?

4. When the CRTC was created in 1968, in what key area was it more active than the Board of Broadcast Governors that it replaced?

5. Explain how the 1985 federal Task Force on Canadian Broadcasting tried to reinforce the notion of broadcasting as a public trust previously expressed by the Massey Commission?

Policy Objectives and Implementation

INTRODUCTION

In this chapter we further examine primary media policy sources in order to apply the tools of policy analysis outlined in Chapter 1, and to trace the recurring themes in policy discourse as described in Chapter 2. The historical evolution of media policy, traced through the 1952 Massey Commission and the 2003 Lincoln Report, brings us to the contemporary configuration of media policy objectives, implementation, and outcomes in Canada. The first reading in this chapter is taken from Peter Grant and Chris Wood's 2004 book *Blockbusters and Trade Wars: Popular Culture in a Globalized World.* In this selection, Grant and Wood establish an important critical context for understanding media policy by describing the key economic and social forces that shape the contemporary production of media and popular culture. The authors summarize the many reasons why Los Angeles, Hollywood in particular, is the dominant 'creative cluster' in the creation of international film and television content. The reading considers how small countries like Canada can support the creation of domestic popular culture in the face of concentration of financial and creative power in Hollywood. The application of cluster theory to the creative industries has shaped successive Canadian governments' efforts to use media policy tools and instruments to support the development of national creative clusters. Grant and Wood describe the 'carrot and stick' approach to building Canada's media industries, especially film production and broadcasting. This analogy can be used as a shorthand for identifying the different types of incentives and regulations used to help trigger investment in Canadian media industries and to understand the use of broadcasting licences and quotas to encourage distribution of Canadian film and television content.

The first primary policy source provided here is a selection from the current federal *Broadcasting Act* (1991). The use of legislation as a policy instrument is the most formal statement of policy rationales and objectives and the most enduring type of government intervention in media production. Parliament first passed legislation for radio broadcasting in 1932 and the current *Act* rearticulates many of the central policy rationales for government support of Canadian media, dating back to the early days of radio and extending into the present and future world of digital networked media. Part I, Section 3 (1) of the *Act* is a declaration of broadcasting policy for Canada and is a very clear statement of the key policy rationales outlined by Foote, emphasizing the nature of broadcasting as a public good and its use in fostering national unity. This section of the *Act* also clarifies the balance between public and private interests in broadcasting, focussing on the nature of the Canadian media environment as a 'single system' with overarching common goals for both public and private components. Part II, Section 5(1) and (2) lay out the objectives and regulatory powers of the CRTC, which the *Act* refers to as 'the Commission.' In this section, the CRTC is charged with "implementing the broadcasting policy set out in subsection 3(1)" and given the authority in the legislation to enact any regulation required to implement the goals of the *Act* with consideration for the practical characteristics of the Canadian media environment. Finally, Section 10 (1) of the *Broadcasting Act* is very specific about what kinds of regulations the CRTC is able to develop. These regulations are the 'carrots' that Grant and Wood suggest are central to the growth of Canada's creative clusters. The regulatory powers of the CRTC include determining the definition of Canadian programming, the amount of time to be devoted to this Canadian content, the amount and type of advertising, the roles of networks, the relationship between 'distribution undertakings' (such as cable or satellite) and programming, and the information to be provided to the CRTC by all licensees in the system. A close reading of the *Broadcasting Act* helps us understand the very close connection between legislation as a statement of policy objectives, and regulation as a specific tool chosen to implement those objectives.

The second primary policy source in this chapter is *Sharing Canadian Stories,* a 2005 report from the federal Department of Canadian Heritage that details the role of the Department in the creation and implementation of policy for the cultural sector as a whole and the media industries in particular. The report describes the various cultural institutions in the Heritage Canada portfolio and describes how the Department is responsible for implementing many components of Canadian media policy, especially through its jurisdiction over the CBC, CRTC, Telefilm, and the Canada Council for the Arts. The report opens with discussion of key rationales and objectives for media policy and cultural policy with an emphasis on addressing the rationale of national unity through affirming cultural diversity. Each section of the report is explicit in listing concrete, actual outcomes of policy intervention in Canada's cultural and media sectors. Government intervention and support is connected to concrete outcomes such as CBC programming, NFB films, and Canada Council grants to artists. For instance, the report highlights the policy objectives of the creation of Canadian cultural content and developing future Canadian talent and then describes the policy instrument of regulation of radio content by the CRTC. The specific outcome of this policy choice is highlighted in the report's list of the multitude of internationally successful Canadian musicians. *Sharing Canadian Stories* concludes with a review of ways in which the Canadian Heritage portfolio is helping to achieve key policy objectives that corresponds very closely to those identified by Foote and listed on the Policy Analysis Framework on page 6.

Critical Analysis

Grant, P. S., & Wood, C. (2004). Creative Clusters (Chapter 2). In *Blockbusters and trade wars: Popular culture in a globalized world* (25–41). Vancouver: Douglas & McIntyre.

Creative Clusters

More than twenty-five years ago, in July 1976, one of us was visiting the Inuit community of Pangnirtung, on Baffin Island, just below the Arctic Circle. At the local lodge he encountered the least expected of fellow travellers: a film crew working for Eon Productions Ltd.

A documentary for *National Geographic*, perhaps?

No. The crew had just finished shooting the climax of the opening sequence in the tenth James Bond film, *The Spy Who Loved Me,* starring Roger Moore and financed by United Artists.

In this famous sequence, Bond appears to be skiing high in the Alps, chased by a horde of sharpshooting skiers. All appears hopeless as Bond skis along the top of a mountain plateau. But the mountain runs out. Bond skis off a steep cliff into mid-air. He begins falling. There are fully twenty seconds of soundless free fall, during which Bond's skis come off. Suddenly he sprouts a parachute covered with a colourful Union Jack. A close-up shows Bond gently descending, a weary but bemused smile on his face. The opening credits begin to roll over Carly Simon's rendition of "Nobody Does It Better," possibly the best-known of all the Bond themes.

It is an astounding sequence, still ranked among the ten best action stunts ever captured on film. To achieve it, the producers needed a mountain with a long ledge ending in a sharp cliff and a sheer drop of over a mile. One of the few mountains fitting this description is Asgard Peak in Auyuittuq National Park on Baffin Island, just north of Pangnirtung. Stuntman Rick Sylvester received $30,000 to do the stunt, out of a total budget for the film of US$13.7 million. He and the film crew had waited ten days for the wind to die down. When the weather cleared briefly, they shot the footage in a single take with no rehearsal.

The 35 mm film had been airlifted to Los Angeles for processing. The crew stood by in the lodge, waiting for a phone call to tell them whether the shot had been successful or if they would need to go back and do it again. The good news came late in the day. Every camera but one had lost sight of Sylvester shortly after he plunged off the ledge. However, a single second-unit camera had managed to film the whole plunge.

The next day, saying goodbye to Sylvester and the crew, the writer toured the community of Pangnirtung. It is a small place, with barely a thousand inhabitants and only a few hundred buildings, huddled between an icy fjord and a mountain range. One of the buildings is home to a unique centre of cultural production, now called the Uqqurmiut Centre for Arts & Crafts.

Inuit art, sometimes still referred to as Eskimo art, is world famous for its striking soapstone carvings of traditional people, polar bears, walruses, drum dancers and shamans. It is also known for its distinctive prints and drawings and small craft items, displayed in art galleries around the world. The community of Pangnirtung is home to a surprising number of internationally recognized Inuit carvers, graphic artists and tapestry weavers.

Printmaking is a Pangnirtung specialty. Every year the Uqqurmiut Centre publishes a series of limited-edition prints. The designs are captivating and ever-changing. How they come to be is almost equally intriguing as a reflection of Inuit society. Annually, every adult and child in Pangnirtung is invited to submit a design on traditional subjects. They receive a nominal sum for each drawing. Hundreds are submitted. A committee selects a dozen of the most compelling drawings and uses them as the basis for a series of finished images. Limited editions of hand-reproduced prints are sold in galleries round the world; the images also appear in a mass-produced annual calendar.

During the filming that July, Pangnirtung witnessed the production of popular culture from opposite ends of a very wide spectrum. At one end were its own talented printmakers, at the other was the visiting Hollywood-financed film crew—but both groups could be said to be part of the "cultural industries."

Making paper images of Inuit life and legend might seem very far from being an industry. But to succeed, it requires sophisticated production techniques, a financing structure that imposes quality control on the selection of subject matter and a distribution system to market and sell the resulting cultural products worldwide. The same is true for the most expensive form of popular culture, the blockbuster feature film, of which the Bond series is the exemplar. The difference is in degree, not in kind.

But clearly, cultural industries are not evenly distributed around the globe. We start our inquiry into the economics of popular culture, then, by asking why this is so. Why do cultural industries tend to locate in certain places and not in others? Why, in particular, is Hollywood so dominant in the creation of blockbuster movies, and not some other city, like Seattle? Why is a certain sector of the music industry located in Nashville and not Peoria? Why do book publishers congregate not only in particular cities, but on particular streets in cities?

Popular culture, it must be remembered, is a team sport. True, some stages of the modern manufacture of cultural products remain comparatively solitary. The initial creator, whether of prints, books, songs or screenplays, may work alone. But bringing his or her product to its eventual audience requires the input of numerous other specialists and considerable sums of money, in addition to the cash value of whatever time the creator has invested.

Take the oldest and most basic mass-produced cultural good: the book. Once written, it is generally edited by someone skilled in a craft quite different from that of original composition. Whether it is to appear in hardcover or paperback, someone with an eye for visual effect must design the front and back covers; designers devote some thought as well to the appearance of the text. Typesetting is no longer the specialized occupation it was in the days of printers' devils, but even computer-set type profits from a proofreader. Printing and binding are industrial processes that are mainly automated, but the machines that do the work cost millions of dollars and their owners rely on enormous print runs to justify the investment. Once printed, books must be distributed and (authors hope) promoted, tasks that demand further specialized skills.

Much the same process applies to creating a sound recording, with the additional complication that the composer's work must be brought off the page and transformed into actual music. Occasionally since the advent of digital recording, a musician bypasses this necessity by operating a computer to render files that can be transferred directly to a compact disc. But this is the exception. More often it involves actual musicians with warm bodies and real instruments making melodies in a performance hall or recording studio. If the work is choral or symphonic, these performers and instruments may number in the hundreds. Even a studio recording by a nominally solo artist frequently entails the work of a dozen or more sidemen and session musicians. A specialized sound engineer and producer are also part of the team that creates the finished "master"—the equivalent of the author's manuscript. The packaging, mass dubbing, distribution and promotion of a commercially released CD all roughly parallel the requirements of book publishing.

Magazines, because they involve so many contributors, fall closer to the complexity of sound recordings than to books, with the additional challenge of meeting recurring and often very tightly timed production deadlines.

Movies and television increase by at least another order of magnitude the team effort and capital needed to make a finished cultural product. A good sound-recording studio can be contained in a closet, and many an album has been laid down in a musician's basement. Filmed drama or comedies that aspire to commercial release consume vastly greater resources. The staff list for the *Degrassi* series—modest by North American standards—runs to more than seventy people. A mid-sized feature film may have a cast and production crew—not counting extras, outside suppliers and studio overhead—of several hundred.

They include the handful familiar to most moviegoers or couch potatoes: stars and supporting actors, writers and directors. Others belong to crafts that figure further down the credit list: directors of photography, art and set decorators, casting supervisors, props masters, makeup artists and costume designers. Some have curious titles: grips (in charge of camera dollies and anything else that moves on a set) and gaffers (in charge of lighting and whatever plugs in). Then there are trades that few associate primarily with show business at all: carpenters who construct sets and the painters who paint them, electricians, teamsters who drive the vehicles that carry cast and equipment to and from every unionized location shoot, caterers who keep the commissary stocked. Then there are some whose very existence is unknown outside the business. Continuity supervisors make sure the outfit Julia Roberts wears as she enters a motel from the outside matches what she wears inside, in a scene filmed days later. Stand-ins take the place of higher-paid actors when a scene is being blocked out for the purposes of lighting and camera angles. Wranglers keep track of the whereabouts of all the rest of a sprawling production crew.

Then there are the people who may contribute only briefly, but significantly, to a production: day-players on television series, animal handlers, providers of vintage automobiles to period pieces, stuntmen and stuntwomen, voice coaches, special-effects creators. Still others begin their role only when principal photography ends: film editors, composers, post-production supervisors.

For a film or television show to romance an audience and meet its timetable and budget (at least as important to the producers backing it), every one of those many people must perform to at least a minimal standard of competence. To lift a show above the noise, a significant number must perform at a level well above the merely competent. It will not suffice for only the star to sizzle, the director to know her craft or the script to be well constructed. All the parts must work well on their own and, ideally, even better together.

Prints and books are by far the cheapest cultural good to produce; filmed entertainment is by far the most expensive. Books, requiring fewer inputs, are also the easiest to produce to a competitive competence. Scripted film or television drama (even more than comedy) is correspondingly the hardest to "get right."

Access to the many and varied skills required for these team efforts implies a corollary condition: that each specialist enjoys enough work to stay in business and keep in practice. If lighting designers cannot make at least a minimal living, they will eventually be forced to find other work. If they cannot work often enough, their skills will atrophy or at least fail to develop. Their contribution to whatever production they do work on will likely fail to achieve the necessary minimal standard, pulling down the collective result—however skillful the other contributions to the common effort may be.

These multiple skills also cost money—frequently exorbitant amounts of it. Taken together, the subjective requirement for hot talent and the concomitant need for cold cash have a major bearing on where cultural industries locate.

Economists like Michael Porter—who pioneered the notion of "cluster theory"—have articulated the market mechanisms that encourage industries to coalesce in certain places. They would call the locally concentrated critical mass of available work and available crew a "thick market." In thick markets, there is enough regular work to support many providers of each specialty, whether they be book editors, sound engineers or set dressers. As a result, when producers undertake a new project, they have a choice of suitably skilled workers to select from.

Thick markets of specialized suppliers tend to have a wealth of relevant "back and forth linkages"—a broad supply of many specialties. Hence producers of complex creative goods such as filmed entertainment can find not only *all* of the varied specialists they require for a given project—set dressers, grips and gaffers—but also a *choice* of suppliers of any given specialty.

A related mechanism in the formation of industrial clusters further illuminates why many creators congregate in particular places to produce the complex products of commercial culture. This is the effect first noted by the classical economist Alfred Marshall more than as century ago. He suggested that industrial districts arise in part because of "knowledge spillover." Although Marshall was never able to model the phenomenon in mathematical terms, he believed propinquity encouraged an informal but economically significant exchange of trade information. As he put it: "The mysteries of the trade become no mysteries but are, as it were, in the air." A non-economist might think of it as the propensity for people in the same business to talk shop in social situations or the value of networking. Cheekier analysts have identified it as "that constant and necessary industry database known as gossip."

The spillover effect goes beyond the direct participants in creative enterprise. It embraces those satellite activities that, while not strictly necessary to the production of cultural goods, nonetheless support, serve or exploit the producers. They include managers and agents who represent authors, actors, musicians and sometimes other in-demand craft specialists; concert promoters and impresarios; contract publicists who hire on to individual productions or concert tours; book, music and film reviewers; trade journalists and the publications that employ them; celebrity scribes and paparazzi photographers. For this demimonde, proximity is the key to access, and access next to godliness.

The requirement for a sophisticated production infrastructure and the impact of knowledge spillover go far to explain why cultural industries tend to agglomerate in only a few centres. But another factor also contributes powerfully to this result, one unique to the field of cultural industries: the "A-list" effect.

The phenomenon was first observed in the field of performing arts, where it is also referred to as the superstar effect. The emergence of a small number of supernova performers, it is theorized, has less to do with their talent than with other factors. Most consumers have difficulty remembering more than two or three names in any specific performing genre, but thanks to recording media they can select those few from a global talent pool. The social benefits derived from discussing well-known artists with friends may exceed the solitary pleasure of appreciating a less-known performer even if she is more talented. All these factors lead demand to concentrate on a few select artists (the A-list) in each field of popular culture. Thus, very small differences in innate ability may result in very large differences in popularity and incomes.

Over the decades, various cities have been centres of critical mass and cluster economies for different forms of popular culture. Vienna at the end of the nineteenth century was such a centre for classical music and opera. London of the same era was a centre of staged entertainment and book publishing. By the mid-twentieth century, New York had eclipsed London on both counts, and it remains today the English-speaking capital of the musical stage and America's epicenter of publishing and television news media. In its somewhat smaller universe of country music, there is only one Nashville.

But no production capital of any contemporary cultural genre comes close to revalling the dominance that Los Angeles exerts over moviemaking. Los Angeles County (which embraces Hollywood and Burbank as well as the eponymous city) is the undisputed nine-hundred-pound gorilla, the original King Kong (it invented the metaphor) of filmed entertainment. Vienna in its day served Europe. London served the Empire. Nashville serves North America. L.A.'s celluloid fantasies light up the entire planet. "To be on the same playing field with everyone else," Canadian actor Eugene Levy tells aspiring thespians, "you have to do it in L.A., because that's just where it happens."

Although the numbers go up and down, American movies have typically commanded 80 per cent (and often much more) of world big-screen revenue; U.S. television fiction programs a 70 per cent share. Seventy per cent of the filming happens in Los Angeles, ten times the amount done in the next-largest U.S. centre of New York City and *six times* the *combined* production of the next four English-language countries with film industries—Canada, the United Kingdom, Australia and New Zealand.

Why does Hollywood rule the field of blockbuster films? The answer, like movies themselves, turns out to involve a little bit of light, some more luck and a lot of money.

The first moving pictures, like the first audio recordings, came from the prolific laboratory of Thomas Alva Edison. Viewers peeped into a darkened box to watch a few seconds of moving images with limited plot. One snippet showed a mustachioed gent taking a pinch of snuff and sneezing, another a ballerina twirling once. Nonetheless crowds flocked to Edison's first "kinetoscope" parlour, opened in 1894.

A kinetoscope could entertain only one person at a time. Auguste and Louis Lumiere soon overcame that hurdle. The French brothers exhibited the first projection film in 1895. Within a decade, theatres across Europe and North America were showing newsreels and short movies. But lawsuits among competing holders of patents for various aspects of film production hampered the nascent industry's development. The deadlock broke in 1908, when major holders pooled their patent rights—and promptly began buying up film distributors in an attempt to take control of the entire cinematic value chain.

Until then, the critical advances in film had all taken place on the U.S. east coast or in Europe. But the Motion Picture Patents Co.'s predatory attitude produced an unintended consequence. It sent many talented early moviemakers fleeing to California, as far as possible from the company's reach.

That was not the only reason to locate in southern California. The bright, dry weather was good for exterior shooting, and unions had yet to organize local film labour. On such attributes early producers laid the foundations of modern Hollywood. William Fox created 20th Century-Fox; Carl Laemmle founded Universal; Marcus Loew assembled Metro-Goldwyn-Mayer (MGM) and Adolph Zukor became the controlling figure at Paramount.

The introduction of talking pictures, followed by the Great Depression, badly shook the studios. The original moguls were forced to turn to eastern bankers to finance the conversion to sound. In return, the financiers demanded a brutal industry restructuring that left five companies in control of Hollywood: Warner Brothers, RKO, 20th Century-Fox, Paramount and MGM.

It may have hurt, but it also ushered in a golden age of studio profitability. In-house writers, full-time crews and contract players sustained a continuous production line of comedies, dramas and musical spectaculars. Subsidiary distributors fed their output to captive chains of movie theatres. "Stars" had glamour but no freedom: multi-year contracts obliged them to make whatever movies the studios dictated with little liberty to demand higher pay. The handful of theatres the studios did not own had no more leeway: coercive block booking obliged them to exhibit anything the studio sent them, the turkeys along with the hits. Studios could, and did, manipulate every transaction from the conception of a film to the final credit-fade onscreen for maximum return.

It was a picture too perfect to escape challenge for long. In 1938, exhibitor complaints against block booking prompted the U.S. Department of Justice to initiate an anti-trust investigation. Sparring continued for a decade, distracted by war. But in 1948, the U.S. Supreme Court finally heard the case. Its ruling, which came to be known as the Paramount Decree after the lead defendant, ordered the studios to give up ownership of exhibitors and foreswear block booking. Impressively, the decree would hold for five decades.

But like the Great Depression's earlier blow, the Paramount Decree proved a lesser shock than did a concurrent revolution in technology. Once it had been talkies. At mid-century it was television. "The public," as Richard Caves puts it, "could now enjoy B-movie entertainment at home, at no marginal cost and in the company of a six-pack and an undershirt."

Television triggered a transformation in Hollywood far more sweeping than the reorganization of the 1930s. The studios' in-house production model of permanent stars, writers and crews dissolved. Within a decade "the Majors," as they continued to be called, reduced their ongoing activity to the three functions that would most reliably preserve their earnings: financing and distributing new movies, and managing the rights to their libraries of existing ones.

The actual making of films atomized into a freewheeling business of one-off deals. Entrepreneurial producers secured scripts, packaged "talent," hired crews from the pool of newly independent (and frequently unemployed) craft specialists and brought them all together—often on sound stages rented from the majors—just long enough to complete a production. The new model sharply increased the value of personal contacts. Work as an actor or screenwriter or lowly third grip relied more than ever on wide informal networks of personal acquaintance, keeping a close ear to the grapevine and "being there" at the right moment.

But none of this posed a challenge to Hollywood's title as the capital of big-budget moviemaking or as the production centre for the emerging new medium of series television. Indeed, quite the opposite happened.

Martin Dale has described the neural system by which major studios "green light" a project in these terms:

> The Majors directly employ 15,000 people in their film divisions and provide work for another 150,000, but commissioning rests in the hands of the studio chiefs. The "genius of the system" is the wider editorial apparatus that exists in Hollywood. There is constant dialogue between the senior studio executives, the top agents, the leading producers and the star talent which determines which projects feel "right" or not. This is a community of around 200 top "players" . . .
>
> "The business is all about relationships with talent," says one agent. "You learn to quickly form an opinion—is someone still 'in the business' or not. People can disappear overnight" . . . The top 200 players are divided into a series of fiefdoms which coalesce around each studio and the main agencies. But each fiefdom has feelers which stretch throughout the movie colony. There is constant feedback . . .

As a result, "cluster" dynamics, "knowledge spillover" and the A-list effect have all continued to reinforce Hollywood's unique critical mass. So long as the "green light" (financing for particular projects) stayed in Hollywood, then the A-list talent would also hover there, hoping for a positive nod and hiring agents to push for the next deal. The heart of the producers' task is to marry talent and financing, so producers too must go where the green lights are.

In a classic feedback mechanism, the converse also applied. As long as the talent and agents bringing proposals stayed in Hollywood, then the green-light mechanism also had to stay there, so as not to miss out on the next blockbuster package. The networking involved in the new Hollywood was omnipresent and inexorable. To be part of the network, one had to "be there."

The result is that despite the institutional collapse of the studio system in the 1950s, the locus of decision-making never strayed from Los Angeles. The strict corporate camps of the studios may have blurred into the looser affiliations noted above. But, if anything, Hollywood's primacy only increased.

A measure of the forces at work is the insignificance of the changes that occurred when foreign owners bought some Hollywood studios. Even when Japan's Sony bought Columbia, Australia's Murdoch bought Fox, and Canada's Seagram and later France's Vivendi bought Universal, the decision-makers for their film projects stayed firmly in Hollywood. They had no choice; that was where the A-list talent was. As expanding budgets raised the sums at risk and production packages predominated, the pressure to make decisions in Hollywood only increased.

The dominance of Hollywood is not due solely to the cluster effect. A number of other factors also contribute: the majors' control of theatrical distribution, the barriers to entry arising from the unique risk–reward ratio of popular culture and the advantages that arise from wielding price discrimination in different markets. Each of these factors will be explored in later chapters.

What is not in question is that once Hollywood achieved critical mass, it was never eclipsed. It remains the undisputed centre of production and distribution of the blockbuster film. According to figures from the Motion Picture Association of America (MPAA), which represents major studios, 543 movies were made in the United States in 2002. Of those, MPAA members released 220. Significantly, that number included virtually all of the 50 titles that managed to gross more than $20 million in domestic (which, for the MPAA, includes Canadian) box-office receipts that year. Total box-office in 2002 was a record US$9.5 billion.

If these dynamics are real and independent of any magic potency in the southern California water or genetic pool for talent, they should also be observable in other countries.

As, indeed, they are.

Two world wars and an economic depression shattered Europe's moviemaking infrastructure, along with much else. But eventually Europe did rebuild. In the 1950s and 1960s, Rome and Paris became centres of production for directors like Francois Truffaut, Jean-Luc Godard and Federico Fellini, who cast A-list stars like Sophia Loren, Marcello Mastroianni and Catherine Deneuve in movies that drew significant foreign audiences. In the same era, Italy pioneered a production form later to be harshly criticized in Hollywood as the "run-away"—standing in for the American frontier in a series of "spaghetti Westerns." Britain sustained a critical mass of production centred in London.

In the past quarter-century, a handful of additional film and television production clusters have developed. A few emerged organically, mainly where large domestic audiences speaking languages other than English constitute markets that Hollywood is ill-placed to satisfy. Active production centres in India and Hong Kong are examples. By 2000, the almost-800 films made annually in India surpassed the number shot in the United States. Hong Kong makes fewer—133 in 2000—but exports them to audiences in the rest of southeast Asia, Taiwan and South Korea. Japan exports few feature films, but its animated productions are widely viewed abroad. Lesser known is Nigeria as a production centre for direct-to-video feature-length movies that circulate widely in the rest of Africa.

Where large linguistically and culturally distinct domestic audiences have not existed, governments and filmmakers have still sought to create conditions in which film and TV production might coalesce into a critical mass. Screenwriters, directors and actors in many countries, including Canada, Britain and Australia—and, for that matter, in U.S. states such as North Carolina and Texas—have wished to make films on their own physical as well as cultural turf. Policy-makers are lured by the millions of dollars and thousands of jobs that keep the movie-making machine turning over. In Europe, Latin America and the non-U.S. anglosphere, substantial efforts and significant public resources have been invested in various attempts to trigger self-sustaining creative clusters.

That Hollywood remains Hollywood should not be taken as proof that those efforts have failed. The undertaking is a complex one—as is any attempt to assess its success.

To begin with, the critical mass necessary to support a viable cultural industry clearly depends on the product in mind. For some products, like blockbuster films, a large industrial infrastructure may be necessary. But for others, like the production of Inuit prints, sound recordings, or the publishing of books, it is a different story. Authors of literary fiction can live anywhere (although their agents must stay close to the "green lights" at publishing houses). High-quality recording studios can be found in most major cities (and, indeed, in many smaller ones).

Audiovisual products uniquely require an especially elaborate infrastructure. But even there, opportunities may exist to diversify centres of production. To begin with, the talent required to produce films has much in common with that for television drama. Measures to support the accretion of a critical mass in television production may thus also have a positive impact on film.

Moreover, certain categories of audiovisual production can support distinct clusters: documentaries, for instance, or animation. A critical mass of schools, talent, production facilities and access to financing can create a self-sustaining industry in these sub-genres even where large-scale dramatic features may be out of reach.

The Canadian experience here is particularly telling. In the past two decades, government policy has succeeded in creating audiovisual production clusters in three Canadian cities: Toronto, Vancouver and Montreal.

Prior to 1984, independent film and television production essentially did not exist in Canada. State-owned corporations (the Canadian Broadcasting Corporation, the National Film Board and the Canadian Film Development Corporation) dominated the very limited amount of dramatic production. A brief foray into tax-incentive financing for feature films had ended disastrously in the late 1970s. But in the mid-1980s, the government introduced a carrot (a federal subsidy for independent Canadian drama) and a stick (a regulatory requirement that private broadcasters air new Canadian drama). With this combination, an industry gradually came into being.

Over the next fifteen years, thousands of hours of drama were created. A critical mass of audiovisual infrastructure emerged to produce the new programming. And as that programming steadily improved in quality, a fortuitous event occurred. The Canadian dollar declined relative to the U.S. dollar, until by the mid-1990s there was a 35 per cent differential. (In 2003, the Canadian dollar strengthened and reduced the differential to only 25 per cent.)

The result was that Canada suddenly became not only a centre for its own dramatic production but a lure for foreign-location shooting. The major Hollywood studios commissioned and financed productions in Canada for the same reason that Italy had once been a popular location to make spaghetti Westerns: the combination of skilled crews and (comparatively) low costs.

By the mid-1990s, Toronto, Vancouver and Montreal could each claim to have achieved the critical mass of many specialists necessary to modern filmmaking. A trade digest of production service companies and talent agencies in Vancouver runs to 432 glossy pages, covering everything from animatronics to wrap-party venues. The producers, cast, day-players, writers, publicists and suppliers who make *Degrassi* are among more than 46,000 people who work in filmed entertainment production in Toronto (compared with 60,000 in New York).

As moviemaking entered its second new century, Vancouver and Toronto were internationally significant producers of filmed entertainment. In a study by Roger Martin, dean of management at the University of Toronto, that city was identified as the world's second-largest exporter of television programming. Between 1998 and 2000, according to a 2002 report to California's state legislators, Vancouver and Toronto together "produced more MOWs [movies of the week] than the U.S. [and] captured nearly half of all MOWs shot worldwide."

The combined value of audiovisual production in Canada reached c$5.1 billion in 2002, consisting of $3.3 billion in Canadian production and $1.8 billion in foreign-location shooting. Included in the latter total was the 2003 Academy Award winner, *Chicago*, filmed in Toronto.

It is worth putting those numbers in perspective. The combined value of production in all three Canadian centres about equals that of New York City—and was less than one tenth of Hollywood's output. But it was a remarkable achievement nonetheless.

Moreover, it was one for which the tool kit of cultural policies deployed by a succession of Canadian governments could take substantial credit. Researchers who studied Toronto alongside fourteen other media centres in Europe, North America and southeast Asia concluded: "This unusually comprehensive policy framework, enacted by senior levels of government in Canada out of a long-standing concern to promote home-grown culture, has almost single-handedly nurtured the development of Toronto's entertainment, media and publishing cluster."

By the turn of the century, the original city of celluloid dreams had begun to take note of its rivals' success. Even though production spending and employment in Hollywood continued to climb, craft unions in particular seethed at the notion that work that might have been done there was instead going to Toronto and Vancouver. A succession of studies and reports sought to document what many in Los Angeles viewed as predatory Canadian subsidies designed to lure "runaway" productions north. The most exhaustive of those attempts—including the 2002 study done for California—failed to find any evidence that the state was at risk of slipping from the pinnacle of the A-list of filmmaking locations.

Unnoticed in Los Angeles was a fact that to Canadian film and television creators was especially ironic. At the same time that California's unions bemoaned the loss of "runaway" productions, their northern counterparts were experiencing a precipitous decline in the shooting of scripts actually written in or about Canada. Meanwhile the roster of allegedly runaway features and MOWs all had one thing in common. Most creative inputs (the "above the line" talent that includes screenwriters and directors as well as stars) and all of the money still came from only one city—and it was neither Toronto nor Vancouver. For anyone hoping to make a film for $15 million or more (entry level for a commercial feature with a "name" star), only one road led to a green light: Hollywood Boulevard.

The studios may be shooting more projects in lower-cost foreign locations than before. But deciding which films get made is still done where it has always been, where the A-list talent and top film executives who are able to approve such projects live.

This may be entirely acceptable if you are an American filmmaker. But for creators from other countries, the implications are daunting.

Credit where it is due: Hollywood has long been a magnet for the best and the brightest of the world's filmmaking talent. Spokesmen like Motion Picture Association of America chief executive Jack Valenti are found of citing this fact in adopting the language of cultural diversity. As an industry based on ideas and entertainment, Valenti and others claim, Hollywood moviemaking is open to the "best" from every culture.

But this claim is disingenuous. The real Hollywood vision is, rather, to see other countries as farm teams feeding talent to the majors. The talented foreign creators brought to Hollywood rarely make films about their own countries or backgrounds. Rather, they are hired to make the movies that Hollywood's decision-makers believe will do well—first in U.S. theatres and second as products for export. There is a big difference. Simply put, filmmakers who work on Hollywood's dime make Hollywood's movies (and it would take a dedicated filmmaker abroad to resist the dollars Hollywood can offer).

That being said, there is a bright side to the Canadian experience. Despite reverses and disappointments, Canada has shown that once a critical mass of skills, service companies and domestic financing is created, local television drama that speaks to a country's stories and experiences *can* be made successfully. And while it may not be possible to make successful big-ticket films without Hollywood's affirmative nod, it is entirely possible to make successful smaller films that have cultural specificity.

This chapter opened with the contrasts generated when a Hollywood-financed production spent tens of thousands of dollars to film a twenty-second action sequence near Pangnirtung on Baffin Island. Twenty-five years later, a more interesting intersection between the film industry and the world of the Inuit took place just west of there.

It happened over the summer of 1999, in the tiny community of Igloolik. Director Zacharias Kunuk and an all-Inuit cast shot the first feature film ever produced in their own language. Called *Atanarjuat (The Fast Runner)*, the film was a three-hour epic based on Inuit legend, shot in digital video in the High Arctic, then converted to 35 mm film in Vancouver. The story, shown with English subtitles, featured the same themes of nature, shamans and magic that populate the world of Inuit art exemplified in the Pangnirtung prints.

This time, the whole production was conceived, created and produced in the North. Financed in part by the National Film Board of Canada and in part by anticipated licence fees from Canadian pay-television services, the "green lights" for the film came not from Hollywood but from within Canada. The budget for the film was $1.9 million. And because the production used digital video instead of film, there was no need to send the rushes south for processing, as was necessary with *The Spy Who Loved Me*.

Atanarjuat met the same challenge all small-budget films do: its distribution to theatres around the world was problematic. But wherever it did reach the screen, critics raved. The Inuit epic won the Camera d'Or for best first feature at the Cannes film festival in 2001. "Not merely an interesting document from a far-off place," and *The New York Times,* "it is a masterpiece."

It is a masterpiece, however, that proves less about what it is right with Hollywood than about what is necessary in the tool kit of public cultural policy. This will become more evident in the chapters ahead.

DISCUSSION

Peter Grant and Chris Wood, 'Creative Clusters,' from *Blockbusters and Trade Wars.*

1. The authors argue that cultural industries are not evenly distributed in every country around the world. What reasons do they give for this global disparity in cultural production?
2. Explain what Grant and Wood mean when they say 'Popular culture is a team sport?'
3. Cluster theory can be applied to the development of media and cultural industries. In your own words, sum up the authors' explanation of the formation of 'creative clusters' by listing four key elements of creative clusters in the film and television industry.
4. Is there an 'A-list' of Canadian talent in film and television? Can you name any 'stars' in English Canadian creative clusters? Where are most of these people located?
5. Grant and Wood use the analogy of 'carrots and sticks' to describe how Canadian governments have developed policies to trigger the growth of domestic film and television creative clusters. Which media policy tools or instruments do the authors characterize as 'carrots' and which are described as 'sticks?'
6. What do Grant and Wood suggest are some of the weaknesses and limitations in the development of Canada's creative clusters?

Primary Sources: Federal Media Policy Domains
Policy Source 3
Canada. Parliament. (1991). *Broadcasting Act*. Sections 3(1), 5 (1&2), 10(1&2).

Broadcasting Act

S.C. 1991, c. 11

Current to September 14, 2011
Last amended on December 15, 2009
Published by the Minister of Justice at the following address:
http://laws-lois.justice.gc.ca

Broadcasting Policy for Canada

3. (1) It is hereby declared as the broadcasting policy for Canada that

    a. the Canadian broadcasting system shall be effectively owned and controlled by Canadians;

    b. the Canadian broadcasting system, operating primarily in the English and French languages and comprising public, private and community elements, makes use of radio frequencies that are public property and provides, through its programming, a public service essential to the maintenance and enhancement of national identity and cultural sovereignty;

    c. English and French language broadcasting, while sharing common aspects, operate under different conditions and may have different requirements;

    d. the Canadian broadcasting system should

        i. serve to safeguard, enrich and strengthen the cultural, political, social and economic fabric of Canada,

        ii. encourage the development of Canadian expression by providing a wide range of programming that reflects Canadian attitudes, opinions, ideas, values and artistic creativity, by displaying Canadian talent in entertainment programming and by offering information and analysis concerning Canada and other countries from a Canadian point of view,

        iii. through its programming and the employment opportunities arising out of its operations, serve the needs and interests, and reflect the circumstances and aspirations, of Canadian men, women and children, including equal rights, the linguistic duality and multicultural and multiracial nature of Canadian society and the special place of aboriginal peoples within that society, and

    iv. be readily adaptable to scientific and technological change;

e. each element of the Canadian broadcasting system shall contribute in an appropriate manner to the creation and presentation of Canadian programming;

f. each broadcasting undertaking shall make maximum use, and in no case less than predominant use, of Canadian creative and other resources in the creation and presentation of programming, unless the nature of the service provided by the undertaking, such as specialized content or format or the use of languages other than French and English, renders that use impracticable, in which case the undertaking shall make the greatest practicable use of those resources;

g. the programming originated by broadcasting undertakings should be of high standard;

h. all persons who are licensed to carry on broadcasting undertakings have a responsibility for the programs they broadcast;

i. the programming provided by the Canadian broadcasting system should

    i. be varied and comprehensive, providing a balance of information, enlightenment and entertainment for men, women and children of all ages, interests and tastes,

    ii. be drawn from local, regional, national and international sources,

    iii. include educational and community programs,

    iv. provide a reasonable opportunity for the public to be exposed to the expression of differing views on matters of public concern, and

    v. include a significant contribution from the Canadian independent production sector;

j. educational programming, particularly where provided through the facilities of an independent educational authority, is an integral part of the Canadian broadcasting system;

k. a range of broadcasting services in English and in French shall be extended to all Canadians as resources become available;

l. the Canadian Broadcasting Corporation, as the national public broadcaster, should provide radio and television services incorporating a wide range of programming that informs, enlightens and entertains;

m. the programming provided by the Corporation should

    i. be predominantly and distinctively Canadian,

    ii. reflect Canada and its regions to national and regional audiences, while serving the special needs of those regions,

    iii. actively contribute to the flow and exchange of cultural expression,

    iv. be in English and in French, reflecting the different needs and circumstances of each official language community, including the particular needs and circumstances of English and French linguistic minorities,

    v. strive to be of equivalent quality in English and in French,

    vi. contribute to shared national consciousness and identity,

    vii. be made available throughout Canada by the most appropriate and efficient means and as resources become available for the purpose, and

        viii. reflect the multicultural and multiracial nature of Canada;

n. where any conflict arises between the objectives of the Corporation set out in paragraphs *(l)* and *(m)* and the interests of any other broadcasting undertaking of the Canadian broadcasting system, it shall be resolved in the public interest, and where the public interest would be equally served by resolving the conflict in favour of either, it shall be resolved in favour of the objectives set out in paragraphs *(l)* and *(m)*;

o. programming that reflects the aboriginal cultures of Canada should be provided within the Canadian broadcasting system as resources become available for the purpose;

p. programming accessible by disabled persons should be provided within the Canadian broadcasting system as resources become available for the purpose;

q. without limiting any obligation of a broadcasting undertaking to provide the programming contemplated by paragraph *(i)*, alternative television programming services in English and in French should be provided where necessary to ensure that the full range of programming contemplated by that paragraph is made available through the Canadian broadcasting system;

r. the programming provided by alternative television programming services should
    i. be innovative and be complementary to the programming provided for mass audiences,
    ii. cater to tastes and interests not adequately provided for by the programming provided for mass audiences, and include programming devoted to culture and the arts,
    iii. reflect Canada's regions and multicultural nature,
    iv. as far as possible, be acquired rather than produced by those services, and
    v. be made available throughout Canada by the most cost-efficient means;

s. private networks and programming undertakings should, to an extent consistent with the financial and other resources available to them,
    i. contribute significantly to the creation and presentation of Canadian programming, and
    ii. be responsive to the evolving demands of the public; and

t. distribution undertakings
    i. should give priority to the carriage of Canadian programming services and, in particular, to the carriage of local Canadian stations,
    ii. should provide efficient delivery of programming at affordable rates, using the most effective technologies available at reasonable cost,
    iii. should, where programming services are supplied to them by broadcasting undertakings pursuant to contractual arrangements, provide reasonable terms for the carriage, packaging and retailing of those programming services, and
    iv. may, where the Commission considers it appropriate, originate programming, including local programming, on such terms as are conducive to the achievement of the objectives of the broadcasting policy set out in this subsection, and in particular provide access for underserved linguistic and cultural minority communities.

(2) It is further declared that the Canadian broadcasting system constitutes a single system and that the objectives of the broadcasting policy set out in subsection (1) can

best be achieved by providing for the regulation and supervision of the Canadian broadcasting system by a single independent public authority.

PART II
OBJECTS AND POWERS OF THE COMMISSION IN RELATION TO BROADCASTING

Objects

5. (1) Subject to this Act and the *Radiocommunication Act* and to any directions to the Commission issued by the Governor in Council under this Act, the Commission shall regulate and supervise all aspects of the Canadian broadcasting system with a view to implementing the broadcasting policy set out in subsection 3(1) and, in so doing, shall have regard to the regulatory policy set out in subsection (2).

(2) The Canadian broadcasting system should be regulated and supervised in a flexible manner that

a. is readily adaptable to the different characteristics of English and French language broadcasting and to the different conditions under which broadcasting undertakings that provide English or French language programming operate;
b. takes into account regional needs and concerns;
c. is readily adaptable to scientific and technological change;
d. facilitates the provision of broadcasting to Canadians;
e. facilitates the provision of Canadian programs to Canadians;
f. does not inhibit the development of information technologies and their application or the delivery of resultant services to Canadians; and
g. is sensitive to the administrative burden that, as a consequence of such regulation and supervision, may be imposed on persons carrying on broadcasting undertakings.

General Powers

10. (1) The Commission may, in furtherance of its objects, make regulations

a. respecting the proportion of time that shall be devoted to the broadcasting of Canadian programs;
b. prescribing what constitutes a Canadian program for the purposes of this Act;
c. respecting standards of programs and the allocation of broadcasting time for the purpose of giving effect to the broadcasting policy set out in subsection 3(1);
d. respecting the character of advertising and the amount of broadcasting time that may be devoted to advertising;

    e. respecting the proportion of time that may be devoted to the broadcasting of programs, including advertisements or announcements, of a partisan political character and the assignment of that time on an equitable basis to political parties and candidates;

    f. prescribing the conditions for the operation of programming undertakings as part of a network and for the broadcasting of network programs, and respecting the broadcasting times to be reserved for network programs by any such undertakings;

    g. respecting the carriage of any foreign or other programming services by distribution undertakings;

    h. for resolving, by way of mediation or otherwise, any disputes arising between programming undertakings and distribution undertakings concerning the carriage of programming originated by the programming undertakings;

    i. requiring licensees to submit to the Commission such information regarding their programs and financial affairs or otherwise relating to the conduct and management of their affairs as the regulations may specify;

    j. respecting the audit or examination of the records and books of account of licensees by the Commission or persons acting on behalf of the Commission; and

    k. respecting such other matters as it deems necessary for the furtherance of its objects.

(2) A regulation made under this section may be made applicable to all persons holding licences or to all persons holding licences of one or more classes.

❦ ❦ ❦

DISCUSSION

Broadcasting Act 1991, Section 3 (1) 5 (1&2), 10 (1&2)

1. Why does the *Broadcasting Act* define the essential character of Canadian broadcasting as a public service? Do you believe this principle is upheld in practice in radio and television broadcasting in Canada?

2. Using the Policy Analysis Framework on page 6 find a specific example of how Section 3(1) of the *Act* expresses each of the four broad policy rationales and the three concrete policy objectives listed in the framework.

3. What does Section 3(1) have to say about the role of the CBC? Look at the CBC's website (www.cbc.ca). Of the eight requirements for CBC programming specified in the *Act,* find current CBC programs that you think best achieve these goals.

4. What do you think the *Act* means by the phrase 'alternative television programming services'? Give examples of Canadian television channels that you think meet the criteria listed for these services.

5. The *Act* clearly describes the role of the CRTC ('the Commission'). What features of the Canadian broadcasting system does the *Act* say should be addressed through regulation by the CRTC?

Policy Source 4
Canada. Department of Canadian Heritage. (2005). *Sharing Canadian stories: Cultural diversity at home and in the world.* Retrieved from http://www.pch.gc.ca/pc-ch/publctn/ raconter-story/index-eng.cfm

Sharing Canadian Stories
Cultural Diversity at Home *and* in the World

INTRODUCTION

Through the Canadian Heritage portfolio, the Government of Canada plays a vital role in the preservation and promotion of Canada's heritage and culture. This portfolio includes both the Department of Canadian Heritage and a number of independent partner agencies and corporations with a specific mandate. Collectively, they provide support for the literary, visual and performing arts, for sports, broadcasting, film, new media, museums and archives, and more. In the most fundamental sense, the Canadian Heritage portfolio shares Canadian stories and diversity, both among Canadians and with others around the world.

Sharing Canadian Stories

Canada's cultural policies and programs are designed to encourage artistic excellence in all its diversity, to foster access for the largest audience possible, and to strengthen the administrative foundations and governance of the cultural sector. In addition, these policies and programs enable us to promote Canadian interests and values externally, while keeping Canada open to the best the world has to offer. As the world becomes more interconnected, our writers, performers, artists, athletes and scholars become our ambassadors. They are reflections of who we are and what we stand for as a country.

By 2017, visible minorities are expected to make up 20 percent of the Canadian population. (Source: Statistics Canada)

With nearly 10 million square kilometres of land, 10 provinces, three territories and six time zones, Canada is one of the largest countries on Earth. Most of the Canadian population lives within a thin strip along the southernmost border; the remainder lives in small towns and rural areas, some of which are remote from major population centres. Canada's two official languages are English and French; however, nearly 200 other languages are spoken in Canada on a daily basis, including

61 Native languages. In order of significance, Chinese, Italian, German and Spanish are the most widely spoken foreign languages in Canada.

The Canadian Heritage Portfolio

The **Department of Canadian Heritage** is responsible for policies and programs related to arts and heritage, broadcasting, cultural industries, new media, Canadian identity, multiculturalism, official languages and sport.

The **Canada Council for the Arts** encourages and promotes the study, enjoyment and production of artistic works through financial support to artists and art organizations in the performing, literary, visual, media and interdisciplinary arts.

The **Canada Science and Technology Museum Corporation,** which includes the **Canada Science and Technology Museum,** the **Canada Agriculture Museum** and the **Canada Aviation Museum,** collects and exhibits information that fosters scientific and technological literacy throughout Canada.

The **Canadian Broadcasting Corporation** provides national radio and television broadcasting services, predominantly Canadian in content and character, as well as multilayered Internet services that include special interactive platforms for children and youth.

The **Canadian Museum of Civilization Corporation,** which includes the **Canadian Museum of Civilization** and the **Canadian War Museum,** collects, maintains, and exhibits Canada's national military and human history collections, thereby promoting a greater understanding and appreciation of human achievement both within Canada and around the world.

The **Canadian Museum of Nature** collects, maintains and exhibits Canada's natural history collection, conducts research, and shares its expertise in the natural sciences both within Canada and around the world.

". . . Canada must now preserve its identity by having many identities."
NORTHROP FRYE, Canadian literary critic

The **Canadian Race Relations Foundation** works to combat racism and all forms of racial discrimination in Canada by promoting intercultural understanding.

The **Canadian Radio-television and Telecommunications Commission** regulates and supervises Canadian broadcasting and telecommunications industries according to their respective legislation.

Library and Archives Canada, which includes the **Portrait Gallery of Canada** program, is an innovative knowledge institution responsible for acquiring and preserving Canada's documentary heritage in all its forms, and for providing all Canadians with easy, one-stop access to the texts, photographs and other documents that reflect their cultural, social and political development.

The **National Arts Centre** develops and promotes the performing arts in the National Capital Region and elsewhere in the country, and assists the Canada Council for the Arts with development of the performing arts throughout Canada.

The **National Battlefields Commission** is responsible for administering the National Battlefields Park in Quebec City, which includes the Plains of Abraham and Des Braves Park.

The **National Capital Commission** fosters pride and unity by making the National Capital Region a meeting place for all Canadians, and by safeguarding and preserving the national treasures of the Capital, including the official residences.

Statistics Canada indicates that, by 2017, the Aboriginal population should continue to grow at an average rate of 1.8 percent per year, more than double the rate of 0.7 percent for the general population.

"This harsh and beautiful land has never ceased to accommodate what can further enhance its beauty. And the Canadian cultural mosaic, symbolizing unity in diversity, has a charm of its own."

WALI A. SHAHEEN, Canadian poet

The **National Film Board of Canada** produces and distributes films, videos and multimedia products that interpret Canada to Canadians and to the world. The NFB has received numerous awards, including 11 Oscars.

The **National Gallery of Canada,** which includes the **Canadian Museum of Contemporary Photography,** collects and exhibits outstanding works of visual art throughout Canada and internationally.

Status of Women Canada promotes gender equality and the full participation of women in the economic, social, cultural and political life of the country.

Telefilm Canada is devoted primarily to developing and promoting Canadian film, television and new media industries.

Each of these institutions maintains a Web site that provides more detailed information. Access to each of these Web sites is available from www.canadianheritage.gc.ca.

CANADIANS *AND* THE WORLD

Seeing Ourselves Through the Eyes of Others

The second half of the 20th century was marked by the introduction of television, satellite communications and the Internet. These technologies have changed our relationship to the world and the way in which we perceive the arts, culture, work and communications. International cultural and commercial exchanges have intensified and accelerated in recent years, so that the world has become a kind of "global village." Canada believes that even with our many differences, the citizens of this global village share a lot of common ground. Each country's unique heritage is enriched through its openness to that of other countries. In this context, respect for diversity is becoming a priority for more and more countries around the world, and Canada favours it within and beyond its own borders.

The Government of Canada has been actively pursuing the development of an international agreement that will recognize the unique character of cultural goods and services, and reaffirm the right of governments to enact policies in support of the diversity of cultural expression. In this regard, Canada is pleased that a draft Convention on the Protection and Promotion of the Diversity of Cultural Expression—negotiated multilaterally within UNESCO—meets these fundamental objectives.

> *Creation draws on the roots of cultural tradition, but flourishes in contact with other cultures. For this reason, heritage in all its forms must be preserved, enhanced, and handed on to future generations as a record of human experience and aspirations, so as to foster creativity in all its diversity and to inspire genuine dialogue among cultures.*
>
> (UNESCO Universal Declaration on Cultural Diversity, Article 7.)

This Convention will be an important tool, allowing each country to transmit its own stories and history to its citizens and the rest of the world.

As an officially bilingual country, Canada is also a very active member of both the Francophonie and the Commonwealth. In addition, Canada is a major player in the multilateral French-language channel TV5. This initiative for promoting cultural diversity provides an international showcase for the achievements of Canadian producers and artists, and offers the Canadian public an additional French-language channel where all parts of the French-speaking world are on view.

In the international arena, Canada has signed a large number of major international conventions, agreements and protocols in the areas of culture and sport. It also played a dynamic role in the development of the Universal Declaration on Cultural Diversity, which was adopted and proclaimed by UNESCO in November 2001.

Diversity, human rights and democracy are values at the very core of Canadian identity. We believe that the Canadian experience and the lessons we can learn from it provide added value to current discussions on cultural diversity.

This experience is shared at international forums where the international community focuses on the concepts of shared citizenship and social cohesion.

Canadians have long been convinced that support for the arts and culture is essential to the expression of a country's identity, and that arts and culture directly influence social development.

Canada's approach to diversity is based on the belief that the common good is best served when everyone is accepted and respected for who they are. This faith in the value of diversity recognizes that respect for social and cultural differences is necessary for promoting self-worth and identity. A society that treats everyone equally is one that encourages achievement, participation, harmony and a sense of belonging.

> *"If we do not now arrange to get to know one another better, to understand the rich variety of our differences and to rejoice in each other's triumphs . . . we will never have a country. Mutual understanding of this kind has always been best carried on through the creative arts and letters, whether 'live' or as the 'software' of modern communications. A country which does not read, hear or watch its own artists is bent on severing its own lifeline."*
>
> Mavor Moore, Canadian playwright, actor and arts administrator

All societies must nourish the roots of their heritage if they are to truly flourish. Mindful of this, Canada has worked hard to develop a comprehensive approach to preserving and managing its cultural resources. From the Arctic Ocean to the Great Lakes, from the Atlantic Ocean to the Pacific, Canadians can visit museums, archives, libraries, and re-enactments of living history, giving them a strong sense of how Canada has evolved. All these activities are a reflection of Canada's mosaic. It is this binding together of all our peoples in a rich tapestry that enables us to create a place for our cultural products on the world stage. Canada takes advantage of the opportunities presented by international expositions to showcase its cultural diversity to the rest of the world, such as during EXPO 2005 AICHI JAPAN, with the theme *Nature's Wisdom*.

By also promoting the values of fairness and ethics in sport, Canada was asked to play an active role in managing and funding the World Anti-Doping Agency, and Canada played a leading role in developing and negotiating the UNESCO Convention on Anti-Doping in Sport.

Canada is also a major promoter of the role that sport can play as an international development tool, and has supported international projects to encourage women, youth and persons with disabilities to get involved in sport. In recognition of our leadership in this area, Canada was one of three countries invited to join the International Working Group on Sport for Development and Peace, created to help countries include sport in their policies and programs. In 2010, Canada will host the XXI Olympic and Paralympic Winter Games in Vancouver, British Columbia.

DIVERSITY *OF* EXPRESSION IN CANADA

A Rose by Any Other Name

To encourage the creation of works that reflect Canada's cultural mosaic, Canadian Heritage has developed a number of strategic objectives. Chief among these is recognition of our cultural diversity.

Canada is officially bilingual. Government of Canada services are offered in both English and French across the country, and more than two million students are taking second-language courses—350,000 in immersion programs. In addition to Canada's two official languages and Aboriginal languages from Cree to Inuktitut, community centres and schools in many parts of the country offer courses in the languages of Canada's numerous cultural communities, including Arabic, Cantonese, German, Hebrew, Hindi, Ukrainian, Vietnamese and many others. Community centres and municipally funded continuing education programs support classes in traditional dance and music. The Canada Council for the Arts, provincial arts councils, and regional and municipal governments support artists from diverse cultural backgrounds and disciplines. Municipal, regional and national museums, archives and libraries showcase the cultural and scientific achievements of Canada's many peoples. Other Canadian institutions provide funding and support for artistic expression from diverse cultural traditions.

The Canadian Cable Television Association is a national organization representing 78 Canadian cable companies that provide a wide range of telecommunications, Internet, information and entertainment services. The cable industry currently provides television services to 7.6 million subscribers and high-speed Internet services to 2.3 million Canadians.

National Film Board (NFB) productions reflect the diversity of Canadian society. They often explore subjects related to immigration and the cultural mosaic. The NFB provides opportunities for ethnic communities in Canada to tell their stories. In 2003–2004, there were 147 original films and multimedia titles: 94 original NFB productions and 53 original co-productions. Of these, 79 were in English, 42 in French, and 26 in other languages. In addition, 25 percent of all productions were the work of artists from Aboriginal and ethnocultural communities. The NFB supports numerous festivals that screen films representing diverse cultures, such as the First Peoples Festival, the *Journées du cinéma africain et créole,* the Toronto Hispano Film Fest and the Toronto Reel Asian Film Festival. Established in 1939, the NFB remains major cultural institution. To date, it has received 4,724 awards in Canada and abroad, including 11 Oscars.

The wealth of Canadian diversity is also reflected in our broadcasting system. In addition to broadcasting across the country in English and French, CBC/Radio-Canada broadcasts programs in eight Aboriginal languages in Canada's North. A wide range of private, community, and educational broadcasters deliver radio and television programming in both official languages and a number of other languages. There is also a network that broadcasts Aboriginal programs exclusively. Many local stations also allocate a portion of their daily schedules to a mix of programming from nations around the world. For its part, Radio Canada International (RCI), one of the most respected shortwave services in the world, broadcasts programs in eight languages worldwide. The CBC Newsworld in English and the Réseau de l'information (RDI) in French broadcast news and current events programs across the country 24 hours a day, 7 days a week.

Organizations such as Telefilm Canada and the Canadian Television Fund (CTF) also ensure that funding is available for projects that tell a diverse range of stories. Both have a dubbing and captioning assistance fund to increase the exchange of cultures, ideas and stories between Canada's French-, English- and Aboriginal-language communities, and the CTF has funding set aside specifically for Aboriginal-language projects.

In turn, Canada's grassroots cultural vibrancy has led to an arts scene that embraces new forms of expression. This means that beyond the established audiences for Canada's renowned dance, theatre and opera companies and orchestras, you will also find many Canadian artists experimenting with innovative ways of bringing disparate cultural traditions together. Musicians combining the sounds of a Newfoundland jig with a Pakistani *qawwal,* for example, or an author using her traditional upbringing in China as a lens through which to view small-town life in Alberta. A visual artist interpreting his ancestral Aboriginal roots using multimedia computer technology, or a filmmaker charting the experience of Japanese immigrants in Canada through the eyes of her century-old ancestor. The excitement of Canadian culture today lies in fusion, based on freedom of expression, and an inherent acceptance of, and interest in, the cultural traditions of others.

> *"In the morning, I go to the Korean corner store to buy* Le Devoir *and* The Gazette. *Then I get my fresh challah at the European Kosher Bakery and say bonjour to my Greek neighbour. This may or may not be your Canada, but it's my neighbourhood. And my neighbourhood is my Canada."*
>
> MARIE-LOUISE GAY, Canadian author and illustrator

NURTURING EXCELLENCE

From Tiny Acorns

Encouraging the widespread acceptance of other cultural traditions involves recognizing and nurturing excellence. This nurturing process comprises two major activities: maintaining existing artistic and cultural excellence, and encouraging the talent of the future.

Significant support for Canada's cultural industries is set out in legislation and regulations. Since 1971, Canada has had content rules that ensure Canadian-produced television and radio programming is prominently represented on Canadian airwaves. Today, at least 60 percent of programming by traditional Canadian television stations must be Canadian. On radio, 35 percent of popular music selections must be Canadian on English-language stations, and on French-language stations, 65 percent of vocal music must be in French. The Canadian Radio-television and Telecommunications Commission administers these rules, and is responsible for giving particular impetus to Canada's music and television production industries.

Many of Canada's internationally known recording artists have benefited from broadcast regulations that ensure a place for them on Canadian commercial radio. They include such diverse talents as Susan Aglukark, Céline Dion, Shania Twain, Alanis Morissette, The Tragically Hip and Simple Plan, all of whom have succeeded in very different musical styles.

The same is true of Canadian television. Canada's cultural policies have led to the production of many popular programs and series, such as *DaVinci's Inquest, This Hour Has 22 Minutes, Annie et ses hommes, Corner Gas* and *Les Bougon*. The availability of excellent training opportunities has benefited Canadian talent for many years. Government of Canada support to centres such as the National Theatre School, the National Ballet School and the Banff Centre for the Arts ensures that Canadians do not have to leave their own country to receive professional training of the highest calibre. This training enables them to create new, original, and exciting works that speak to our identity as Canadians and to our role in the world.

Canada shares its vision with the world in various ways: by signing international agreements, by attracting foreign expertise and investment in its cultural industries, and by participating in a growing international network on cultural diversity. Canada also encourages its artists to form alliances with artists from other nations. The Government of Canada currently manages audio-visual co-production treaties with 53 countries. In 2004, 63 co-productions generated economic activity valued at more than $371 million, representing roughly 20 percent of all Canadian productions. Some of the largest co-productions in recent years include: *Les Invasions barbares (The Barbarian Invasions)*, a Canada/France co-production that won an Oscar for best foreign language film in 2004 and a César in France for best film; *Les Triplettes de Belleville (The Triplets of Belleville)*, a Canada/France co-production that was selected for the Cannes Film Festival and nominated for an Oscar in the best animated film category in 2004; and *Spider*, a Canada/UK co-production that was nominated for a Palme d'or at Cannes and awarded "Best Canadian Film" at the Toronto International Film Festival.

Canada also protects the rights of creators internationally. The *Copyright Act* protects the work of authors, playwrights, songwriters, performers, software designers and other creators. Canadian legislation reflects Canada's obligations under international copyright treaties, protecting the rights of foreign creators to the same extent as Canadian creators are protected under the laws of other countries when their works are used abroad. The principle of "national treatment" ensures that Canadians have access to the best the world has to offer, while opening up international markets to Canadian creators, our stories and our culture. The Act is currently under review to ensure that it reflects the latest in technology and remains at the forefront of international copyright measures.

> *"The societies which have succeeded best in winning and maintaining the most tolerable existences for their members have been those that have given very free scope to their poets, artists, philosophers, scholars, inventors . . . critics and innovators."*
>
> J. BARTLETT BREBNER, Canadian author and scholar

Policies that help encourage and support cultural industries often come under fire during negotiations with those trading partners seeking access to our market in cultural services. Paradoxically, while increased trade and globalization offer greater opportunities for exporting cultural products, they also challenge existing cultural policies. As part of globalization, increased trade promotes export of our cultural products. The government promotes cultural expression in a Canadian market that is among the most open in the world to foreign content. Canada plays a critical role in various multilateral, cultural and economic forums—including the G-8, La Francophonie, the Commonwealth, the Organization of American States, UNESCO and the International Network on Cultural Policy—in order to promote the importance of cultural diversity internationally.

PROMOTING CULTURAL EXPRESSION

Taking Our Show on the Road

Providing legislative and policy support is not enough. We must also look to the future, identifying the means by which new artistic voices can make themselves heard. To accomplish this, the Government of Canada has developed a number of organizations and programs designed to encourage outstanding artistic and cultural achievement. In May 2001, the Government of Canada announced the most significant long-term investment in arts and culture since the creation of the Canada Council for the Arts in 1957. This investment was renewed in 2005.

The Canada Council for the Arts remains the pre-eminent Canadian organization in support of the arts. Increased funding has enabled it to award even more grants to established Canadian creators in all fields of artistic endeavour. The Canada Council for the Arts also provides ongoing support to cultural treasures such as the Montreal Symphony Orchestra, the Stratford Shakespearean Festival, the Charlottetown Festival, the Royal Winnipeg Ballet, the Canadian Opera Company, and major travelling exhibitions of works by Canada's visual artists. Other Canada Council programs support individual artists in various disciplines, Aboriginal artists and arts organizations, as well as artists seeking new markets for their work at home and abroad.

The National Arts Centre shares a mandate with the Canada Council for the Arts to stimulate the performing arts in Canada. From the national and international tours of its resident orchestra to its role as one of the country's largest co-producers of dance and English and French theatre, the NAC is the country's national stage—a catalyst for Canada's artists and audiences.

When it comes to film, television and radio, Telefilm Canada, the National Film Board of Canada, the Canadian Television Fund and the Canadian Broadcasting Corporation have long-standing traditions of supporting and encouraging unique Canadian productions. As the pre-eminent public broadcaster in Canada, the Canadian Broadcasting Corporation has been the cornerstone of Canada's broadcasting system since 1936, providing an electronic stage for our performing artists, musicians and writers. Many productions broadcast on the CBC/Radio-Canada, such as the popular *Road to Avonlea* television series, have gone on to garner international acclaim. Financial assistance for film production is also available through a number of federal programs, including Telefilm Canada's Canada Feature Film Fund, the Canadian Film or Video Production Tax Credit Program, Canada Council for the Arts grants, and the Cultural Industries Development Fund. The Canadian Television Fund, a public/private partnership, is also an important supporter of the Canadian television and film industry.

Canada is a leader in new media, with government programs providing a springboard to success. The work of Daniel Langlois is a good example. Building on his background as a filmmaker with the National Film Board of Canada, he founded the Montreal-based Softimage. This company designed animation tools that were essential to such blockbuster feature films as *Jurassic Park* and *Star Wars: The Phantom Menace*. Daniel Langlois received a Scientific and Engineering Award from the Academy of Motion Picture Arts and Sciences in 1998. CBC/Radio-Canada also produces new media programs that have received many awards in Canada and abroad.

> *At present, more than 500,000 Canadians make their living in Canada's cultural industries, which inject more than $40 billion a year into the country's economy. In recent years Canada's cultural sector has grown faster than other key sectors such as agriculture and the automotive industry. (Source: Statistics Canada)*

The Canada Music Fund (CMF) aims to strengthen the entire Canadian music industry, from creators to audiences. It supports the production, distribution and marketing of Canadian music. The CMF's various funding programs support creators, artists, entrepreneurs, industry associations and joint initiatives. They also help preserve Canadian music for future generations.

In publishing, the Book Publishing Industry Development Program ensures the viability of the Canadian industry through its support to Canadian publishers. It provides the industry with tools to promote Canadian authors, to support projects that promote books in Canada, and to help Canadian publishers gain access to foreign markets and boost exports. The Canada Magazine Fund supports Canadian magazines that specialize in Canadian arts and literature, and projects designed to enhance the periodical industry. The Publications Assistance Program, together with the Canada Post Corporation, assures reduced postal rates for Canadian periodicals, such as community, ethnic and agricultural magazines and newspapers.

Trade Routes, the only trade development program established specifically to meet the international development needs of Canadian arts and culture entrepreneurs, helps arts and cultural businesses and not-for-profit organizations maximize international development opportunities. A financial support program and expert assistance for new and existing cultural exporters are offered from Trade Routes' head office, from the regional offices of International Trade Canada, and from key missions abroad. Other departments and programs support various international initiatives, ranging from cultural exchanges to exhibitions and international sporting events.

Canada also celebrates athletic excellence. Some of the most acclaimed athletes of our times, such as Alexandre Despatie, Beckie Scott and Chantal Petitclerc, are Canadian. Canadians participate in sport competitions at all levels, from local tournaments to major international games such as the Olympics, Paralympics, Special Olympics, the Games of La Francophonie, the Commonwealth Games and the Pan American Games, all of which have been hosted by Canada. The Department of Canadian Heritage actively promotes sporting excellence from the development of top coaches to the support of gifted athletes at the national and international levels. The 2010 Olympic and Paralympic Winter Games to be held in Vancouver and Whistler, British Columbia, provide a unique opportunity to promote sport and physical activity. Canadian Heritage encourages all Canadians to engage in sport. For example, the Sport Participation Development Program helps women, youth, children, Aboriginal people and persons with disabilities to participate in community sports programs.

> Some of the world's most popular sports were either invented or first played in Canada. Sports such as lacrosse and hockey are widely accepted as Canadian inventions; however, few people are aware that basketball was invented in 1891 by a Canadian professor, and that "American football" was invented as a combination of soccer and rugby by Canadian soldiers and university students in 1874. Even the modern game of baseball was actually first played in Canada in 1838.

To ensure the vitality of Canada's cultural future, government policies must assist young Canadians to develop their creative skills. Today's youth are already more global in focus than their parents, and it is vital to recognize the valuable role they already play in a world that is increasingly interconnected. Youth today have been exposed to new technologies and myriad peoples and cultures from an early age. They are the future of any comprehensive cultural strategy. The Government of Canada is committed to assisting youth through internships, cultural exchanges, training programs, sports initiatives, Aboriginal youth centres and other programs, many of which are already administered within the Canadian Heritage portfolio.

The results of Canada's cultural policies and programs speak for themselves. The $3-billion-a-year Canadian film and television industry includes innovative filmmakers such as Léa Pool, Denis Villeneuve, Denys Arcand, David Cronenberg, Patricia Rozema, Atom Egoyan, François Girard and Deepa Mehta. Canadians have created an estimated 60 percent of the software used within the American motion picture industry. And Canadian films such as La grande séduction, Being Julia, The Blue Butterfly, Atanarjuat: The Fast Runner and Les invasions barbares have gone on to worldwide acclaim.

"In Canada, a world-class performance is a world-class performance, regardless of whether it was achieved on foot, on a bicycle, in a kayak or in a wheelchair."
CHANTAL PETITCLERC, Olympic and Paralympic Champion

Musical artists Céline Dion, Diana Krall, Bryan Adams, Garou, Daniel Lavoie, Anne Murray, Oscar Peterson, Sarah McLachlan and Shania Twain have also achieved international stardom. Canadian authors Margaret Atwood, Daniel Poliquin, Yann Martel, Gaétan Soucy, Rohinton Mistry, Michael Ondaatje, Alice Munro and Evelyn Lau are read around the world. The works of visual artists such as Jean-Paul Riopelle, Alex Colville, Paul-Émile Borduas and Betty Goodwin are exhibited from Paris to Rio de Janeiro. Performing troupes Le Cirque du Soleil, the National Ballet of Canada, and the Canadian Opera Company and playwrights Michel Tremblay, Robert Lepage, Brad Fraser and Tomson Highway attract audiences from Australia to Alaska.

The Government of Canada, together with all the organizations that make up the Canadian Heritage family, supports this quest for excellence. By ensuring Canadian content in broadcast, digital and print media, by harnessing the power of the Internet and the Virtual Museum of Canada to showcase Canada's heritage, by supporting film, television and new media, and by awarding grants to individual artists and Canada's performing arts giants, organizations within the Canadian Heritage portfolio are helping Canadians of all cultural backgrounds to find their own voices, express themselves and flourish.

EMBRACING NEW TECHNOLOGY

Shaking Hands Online

In a nation as large and as diverse as Canada, the evolution of electronic media—radio, television and the Internet—has greatly advanced our ability to connect with one another and the world.

Since the first radio broadcast in 1906, broadcasting has come to play a critical role in our understanding of what it means to be Canadian. As early as 1936, Canada's public broadcaster was reaching into even the remotest corners of our country. Today, Canada's broadcasting system offers more than 600 private radio and television stations, a strong public broadcaster in CBC/Radio-Canada, educational channels, Aboriginal services, services for official-language minorities, multicultural and third-language channels, community services, and a wide range of foreign offerings. We have built a uniquely Canadian broadcast system that informs, enlightens and entertains Canadians of all ages, one that enriches our cultural, political, social and economic fabric and enhances our sense of national identity. As communications and broadcasting technology continue to evolve rapidly and to change the very notions of "content" and "choice," the Government of Canada remains committed to ensuring that Canadians have access to the best the world has to offer, while providing a space for uniquely Canadian voices, talent and ideas.

"During the mechanical ages we had extended our bodies in space. Today, after more than a century of electric technology, we have extended our central nervous system itself in a global embrace, abolishing both space and time as far as our planet is concerned."

MARSHALL MCLUHAN, Canadian professor, author and communications theorist

Canadians are also now among the world's forerunners in the use of the Internet. Indeed, more than two-thirds of Canadians report using the Internet every day, and over a quarter say they have more than one computer in their home. The Government of Canada is committed to cultivating a strong Canadian cultural presence in cyberspace. Through the Canadian Culture Online Strategy, the Canadian Heritage portfolio is actively stimulating the development and accessibility of quality Canadian digital content in both official languages. It is helping Canada's cultural industries, institutions, creators, and communities produce and showcase their creative works to Canadians and to the rest of the world. The Canada New Media Fund, for example, supports production of new cultural works, devoting one-third of its resources to French-language projects. As well, Canadian cultural collections and treasures are being digitized for online presentation with the help of programs such as the Canadian Memory Fund and the Partnership Fund. The New Media Research Networks Fund and Applied Research in Interactive Media further support Canadian innovation in new media.

The results of these efforts have been nothing short of astounding.

Canadian creators are benefiting from the proliferation of exciting new platforms for their works. Many are taking risks, pushing artistic and technological boundaries, and being recognized internationally for their achievements.

Launched in March 2001, the Virtual Museum of Canada (www.virtualmuseum.ca) is a one-of-a-kind portal featuring countless stories and treasures from 1,200 museums across Canada. It receives more than eight million visitors per year.

The Internet is also being used to bring Canadian history and culture to life in the form of exciting new learning products, virtual tours, information and entertainment products. Today, Canadian youth can discover the history of music, theatre and dance in Canada through the National Arts Centre's *ArtsAlive.ca*.T hey can learn about Canada's colourful history through Library and Archives Canada's Confederation for Kids Web site. Canadians of all ages can relive their shared history with Canadian radio and television over the past 70 years through the online CBC Archives. They can look in on Canadian museum sites, projects and exhibitions through the Virtual Museum of Canada portal. They can learn about the history of Aboriginal peoples in Canada through the Aboriginal Canada Portal. They can also gain a new appreciation for Canada's ethnic and cultural diversity through a broad range of new online sources, such as the Caribbean Tales Site and the Acadian Historical Village. Canadians can also discover more about culture and make their views known on this topic by visiting *Culture.ca*, which features more than 13,000 links to quality Web sites on Canadian culture.

In these and many other ways, the Canadian Heritage portfolio is helping to:

- promote greater understanding of Canada and its rich diversity;
- facilitate communication among the communities that make us so diverse;
- strengthen Canada as a learning society; and
- broaden and deepen the capacity of our cultural industries, institutions and creators.

As the pace of change and progress in the world marches on, Canadians can confidently rely on their nation's television, radio and Internet services to keep them connected to one another and the rest of the world.

A LONG TIME AGO *IN* THE FUTURE

Inuit storytellers from Canada's North traditionally began their tales with the words, "a long time ago in the future," implying that what has happened in the past can help us to understand the world to come.

The world over, people look to their histories for clues to their future. By listening to the voices of our nation's many peoples, by putting in place policies, programs and legislation that encourage artistic and cultural expression, and by working with all levels of government and the private sector, the Canadian Heritage portfolio ensures that Canadians have more opportunities to celebrate their rich histories, current achievements and promising futures.

> *"Science and technology are themselves neither good nor evil. They are the product of human curiosity—the mind's relentless urge to explore, to know, to change. And that is a quality we must always nourish."*
> DAVID SUZUKI, Canadian scientist and broadcaster

> *"If we do not tell ourselves funny or satirical or tragic or ironic stories about ourselves, if the teller of tales in the corner does not sing our songs, speak our sorrows, narrate our wars, then we will not exist as a nation."*
> MARY JANE MILLER, Canadian academic

In a world where communication is vital and information is the coin of the realm, our cultural touchstones are more important than ever. We must constantly remind ourselves where we come from and what we want to become. We can best do that by communicating our stories, by creating lasting monuments to who we are, and by reaching out to each other so that the mosaic we form presents a clear and cohesive image to the wider world. It is by being rooted in a sense of place, history, and cultural identity that we will thrive and prosper as a nation. And it is our artists and athletes, archivists and museologists, conservationists, creators, innovators and broadcasters who will lead the way.

DISCUSSION

Department of Canadian Heritage. *Sharing Canadian Stories: Cultural Diversity at Home and in the World.*

1. This report from the Department of Canadian Heritage lays out objectives of Canada's cultural policies and programs. Find three examples of specific media policy objectives mentioned in the report.
2. Of the 15 federal institutions that fall within the Department of Canadian Heritage portfolio, which ones do you think are most directly relevant to the creation and implementation of media policy, and why?
3. The report mentions the importance of international intergovernmental agreements as a policy tool. Which international convention is discussed and what is its purpose?
4. The report emphasizes the importance of supporting Canada's cultural diversity as a means of implementing the policy rationale of national unity. Find examples of two specific policies or programs that the report mentions with reference to cultural diversity. What actual outcomes of these policies or programs are given as evidence for the effective implementation of the Department of Canadian Heritage's policy goals?

Interest Groups and Stakeholders in the Policy Process

INTRODUCTION

In this chapter, we are examining the role of interest groups and the wide range of stakeholders in the formation of media policy. The chapter focusses on those non-governmental organizations (NGOs) and industry lobby groups that represent public and private interests in various domains of policy-making. As Hackett and Anderson argue, Canadian media policy contributes to the formation of a democratic public sphere. Throughout the history of Canadian broadcasting and media, a variety of national, provincial, and local interest groups have sought to influence the policy process and shape potential and actual policy outcomes. Broadly-based citizens' groups, like the Canadian Radio League in the 1930s, Friends of Canadian Broadcasting since 1985, and OpenMedia.ca today, have worked to support the public service aspects of media and develop the creation of Canadian media content. Specific industry lobby groups like the Canadian Association of Broadcasters, the Canadian Media Production Association, or Magazines Canada represent the private interests of cultural creators and entrepreneurs who depend on various government policies and programs for some aspects of their economic survival.

As Hackett and Anderson argue, a variety of NGOs in areas such as politics, professional associations, independent media, arts and culture, gender, religion, human rights, First Nations, and environmental activism also have a broad interest in media policy and media reform. The authors argue that these interest groups are active in movements for social change and depend on access to media for reaching the public with their messages. Thus, citizen advocacy is linked to calls for independent media and resistance to the increasing corporate concentration of media ownership in fewer and fewer hands. Hackett and Anderson have carried out a survey of Canadian social movement groups with the goal of determining how involved they are in media campaigns. The authors use aspects of social movement theory to ask why and under what conditions different interest groups might be involved in media policy. The authors' research questions focus on whether these interest groups have the resources to intervene in media policy and take collaborative action toward making Canadian media more accessible and democratic. The authors uncover common themes in how these groups would like to see the media change through better journalism, support for independent and community media or public service media, and protection for internet access and 'Net neutrality.' The article concludes by suggesting the frame of 'open media' as a way of bringing together a wide variety of types of media activism and public engagement in the media policy process.

Both of the primary policy sources presented here come from statements made by interest groups to the House of Commons Standing Committee on Canadian Heritage. Standing committees are permanent committees that sit while Parliament is in session and are made up of a combination of elected M.P.s from all the federal parties. Commons committees have the power to examine and report to the House on any subjects related to the mandate, operation, and administration of a specific government department. The Standing Committee on Canadian Heritage produced the 2003 Lincoln Report (part of which is reproduced in Chapter 2) among many other studies, reports, and hearings on aspects of federal broadcasting, media, and cultural policy. The Standing Committee makes reports and recommendations to Parliament with respect to such things as funding for the CBC, programs and policies to support the media industries in Canada, and economic and technological changes that affect media policy.

In Policy Source 5, you will read the presentation made by Ian Morrison, spokesperson for a citizens' group called Friends of Canadian Broadcasting. Mr. Morrison was addressing the Standing Committee on the question of the funding and mandate of the CBC. In an earlier session, the Committee heard from the President of the CBC who presented the CBC's five-year strategic plan for the national public broadcaster. The CBC President asked the Standing Committee to recommend that Parliament make a stable five-year commitment to CBC funding so that the plan could be implemented. In its presentation, Friends of Canadian Broadcasting argues that while there is strong public support for maintaining or increasing CBC funding, there is a gap between the mandate and role of the CBC as defined by the *Broadcasting Act* and what the CBC can deliver with its current lack of resources. As an independent citizen-funded group, Friends of Canadian Broadcasting are not affiliated directly with the CBC or any other broadcaster or with any particular political party. The group sees itself as a watchdog for protecting Canadian programming on radio, television, and through digital media.

The Canadian Media Producers Association (CMPA) is also making a presentation to the Standing Committee on Canadian Heritage in Policy Source 6. In this case, the Committee is examining recent ownership changes, mergers, and acquisitions in the Canadian film and television industry and the move toward new web-based and mobile viewing platforms. CMPA represents the independent companies who produce film and television in Canada. Most broadcasters and television networks do not create their own media content but purchase it from independent production companies. These production companies rely heavily on licences from the broadcasters to help finance their productions, but also to help them access public funding through the Canada Media Fund. In its presentation to the Standing Committee, CMPA (Canadian Media Production Association, 2010) points out how concentration of ownership in the Canadian television industry has made conditions more difficult for the production companies who supply the television programming. Two key issues highlighted in the presentation are the restricted nature of Canadian markets and rapid technological changes. CMPA suggests that the imbalance between the dominant economic power of the broadcasters and the financial needs of the producers leads to unfair and unreasonable licencing terms for television programs. Secondly, CMPA points out that more and more Canadians are shifting their viewing away from conventional cable and satellite services to internet platforms. The presentation argues that internet service providers should be contributing to the support of Canadian programming as cable and satellite distributors currently do. CMPA, on behalf of its members, makes a strong case to the Committee for addressing the negative impact of economic and technological changes on the companies, creators and workers who produce Canadian television content.

Critical Analysis

Hackett, R. A., & Anderson, S. (2011). Democratizing communication policy in Canada: A social movement perspective. *Canadian Journal of Communication, 36*(1), 161–168.

Research in Brief
Democratizing Communication Policy in Canada:
A Social Movement Perspective

Robert A. Hackett
Simon Fraser University
Steve Anderson
OpenMedia.ca

Partly due to citizens' coalitions like the Canadian Radio League in the 1930s, Canadian communications policy has long embodied elements of a democratic public sphere (see, for example, Raboy & Shtern, 2010). While quite concrete social interests helped to solidify such policies as public broadcasting, the common-carrier principle in telecommunications, and public consultation processes in policymaking, Canadian communications policies are also informed by broader democratic values, such as accountability of media institutions to publics and democratic policy goals; access to, and diversity of, citizen-relevant information; community-building, at both local and national levels; minority cultural and linguistic rights; domestic control over Canada's media system as a prerequisite for cultural sovereignty and democratic control over communication policy; and, yet more broadly, universal access to the key means of public communication as a basis for equality and participation in society, culture, and politics.

Never perfectly realized, these policies and values are under attack by neoliberal governments and ideologues. Communication policy has never fundamentally altered the commercial and corporate domination of Canadian media, which has arguably intensified in recent years. Ownership concentration continues apace: mergers and acquisitions since 1998 have aggregated over

Robert A. Hackett is professor of communication at Simon Fraser University. He has been active in media reform and policy advocacy organizations since 1984. Email: hackett@sfu.ca. **Steve Anderson** has an M.A. in Communication from Simon Fraser University and is co-founder and national co-ordinator of the national public interest advocacy group OpenMedia.ca. Email: steve@openmedia.ca.

Canadian Journal of Communication Vol 36 (2011) 161–168
©2011 Canadian Journal of Communication Corporation

half of all Canadian media revenues in the hands of three firms (Winseck, 2008), and the huge debts acquired during dot.com merger mania have contributed to a crisis of journalism. Regulatory and funding support for the CBC has been whittled down, its management and programming seemingly abandoning the philosophy of public broadcasting. Canadian ownership is being reconsidered by Stephen Harper's federal Conservative government and has been eroded by regulatory decisions allowing increasing American minority ownership of Canadian media companies (Moll & Shade, 2008). Community broadcasting, formally one of three pillars of the broadcasting system, struggles along with minimal resources. Once again, impending federal copyright legislation threatens to restrict users' rights of "fair dealing." Digital divides still characterize the Internet, and there is little public policy to offset access inequalities ultimately generated by unregulated capitalism, or to support Canadian new media content. Escalating violations of the principle of "Net neutrality" threaten to create an increasingly tiered Internet, in which fast-lane access is confined to content providers who can afford extra fees.

If neoliberalism succeeds in restructuring Canada's media, progressive social change will be more difficult across the board.

Fortunately, civil society has generated a growing movement for change. In the U.S., groups working for media justice have flourished in marginalized communities. Hundreds of local and national groups working on independent media, media education, and policy advocacy have been joined by Free Press, a national flagship for media reform with hundreds of thousands of supporters. Canadians have started to follow suit. The veteran Friends of Canadian Broadcasting has been joined by other groups lobbying on telecommunications and copyright issues. Media workers' unions have developed detailed policy proposals and launched collaborative policy-oriented campaigns. Activists and educators in Vancouver, Toronto, and elsewhere have organized an annual Media Democracy Day since 2001. In 2007, OpenMedia.ca (originally the Campaign for Democratic Media) was launched as a network of member organizations and individuals committed to expanding the public-interest voice in communications policy. Meanwhile, the World Association for Christian Communication (WACC), an ecumenical NGO concerned with communication rights for all, moved its global headquarters to Toronto.

In that context, and with key issues—Canada's digital strategy, Net neutrality, community TV—currently on the policy agenda, OpenMedia.ca and WACC, in collaboration with communications scholar Robert Hackett, decided to research the potential for building media reform in Anglo-Canada. Funding was supplied by the Necessary Knowledge for a Democratic Public Sphere program of the Social Science Research Council, with support from the Ford Foundation. An online survey of 57 NGOs in different stakeholder sectors (political, professional/service, independent media, arts/culture, gender, religion, human rights, labour, First Nations, environment, et cetera) was supplemented by 18 in-person interviews (as well as a workshop with 19 media producers and communication rights advocates in Toronto in May 2009).[1] Both online respondents and in-person interviewees were asked about the priorities, resources, strategies, challenges, partnerships, and achievements of each NGO, as well as use and perceptions of digital and news media. The objective was to identify opportunities and frames for successful media reform campaigns, projects, and partnerships.

Extrapolating from that research, this article considers the prospects for building a media reform movement in Canada. We draw selectively from social movement theory, particularly resource mobilization theory (RMT), to pose these questions:[2]

1. Do issues of media access, content, or policy constitute a *shared grievance* for Canadian NGOs? Do NGO perceptions of media indicate potential incentives to mobilize around communication issues? How do these issues relate to NGOs' overall goals and priorities?
2. Apart from incentives, do NGOs have *resources* that could be mobilized in media policy campaigns?
3. Do NGOs have a *shared diagnosis* of media problems, one that could help to form a coherent common platform or collaborative campaigns? What would be the most politically effective *frame*—a broad "symbolic container" to give shared meaning to collective action (Gamson & Wolfsfeld, 1993)?
4. To the extent that NGOs do have media-related grievances, diagnoses, and resources, are these translated into *collaborative action*? Does media activism constitute a *nexus* for progressive social movements, as argued by Hackett & Carroll (2006) and disputed by Napoli (2007)?
5. Beyond such short-term collaboration as may exist, is there consciousness of a *shared identity* as a movement for media reform?

MEDIA AS SHARED GRIEVANCE?

Among the 57 online respondents, the importance of media was widely acknowledged: 84.6% agreed that the quality and diversity of Canadian journalism affects their work. This view was often combined with discontent regarding coverage of their own NGO and issues: 62% expressed dissatisfaction, and only 26% expressed satisfaction. There was some sentiment (44%) that CBC was better than other media; only 8% identified CBC as worse. Independent media also received a vote of confidence: 88% said that such media had been helpful to their work, although a minority noted limitations to alternative media's resources, reach, and/or credibility.

Access to public communication is relevant to many of the priorities, achievements, and strategies of NGOs. The most frequently identified NGO priority for the near future was improving funding and sustainability, followed by advocating for changing government policy, improving benefits and representation of members' interests, improving circulation of NGOs' own media, strengthening the organization internally, improving the group's public visibility, and educating the public on pertinent issues.

Conversely, the major perceived challenges are lack of funding or other resources, various changes in the media and communications environment, lack of influence with government, lack of visibility or public awareness, and poor media representation. All of these challenges loomed larger than hostile groups.

The NGOs' dependence on mainstream media implies that they would benefit from democratic media reform. On the other hand, other factors militate against NGO investment of scarce resources in media reform. Some interviewees indicated that they had built positive relationships with at least some mainstream media, relationships they may be unwilling to jeopardize by overt advocacy of anti-corporate media reform. Several interviewees saw improved media relations practices by NGOs themselves as the best route to better coverage. Moreover, many NGOs have tried to reduce their dependency on mainstream media: the survey shows that NGOs put much more effort into their own websites, blogs, or published reports than into news releases or other ways to attract traditional media. Not surprisingly, then, respondents were nearly unanimous (88%) that the Internet is very important to their work. All respondents agreed that Internet access for Canadians and for their own work is at least moderately important. They valued the Internet for very tangible and instrumental reasons: research, public access, mobilization, outreach, education, advocacy, collaboration, community-building, and networking. Many of the respondents were emphatic. "It is our oxygen," said one.

RESOURCES?

Compared with some of their U.S. counterparts, the NGOs that responded are mainly modest in size, though there is a wide distribution. The median category of membership size was 500999. Seventeen of 57 NGOs had under 500 members; 14 are not membership-based. None had more than 100,000 signed-up members.

Median annual revenue was about $250,000. Thirteen had budgets of over $1 million, but fourteen had less than $100,000, including nine with under $25,000. We surmise that few organizations have surplus funds available for campaigns unrelated to their primary mandates, and some cannot afford paid staff at all. Lack of funding was the most frequently cited challenge facing the NGOs. Moreover, inequalities within the sector may well contribute to different organizational cultures and different levels of commitment to the existing field of state-recognized, politically legitimized advocacy.

That said, a cross-tabulation of organizational budget size with past and likely future participation in media/communication campaigns or coalitions revealed a striking contrast. Groups with budgets under $250,000 were much more likely to participate than their wealthier counterparts. Strategically, it would be important for a Canadian media reform coalition not to overlook the potential engagement of diverse small but dedicated organizations.

Asked to rate various sources of funding, respondents ranked the following as "very important": government grants/contracts (40.0%), individual membership (35.2%), individual donations (34.7%), foundations/philanthropy (30.6%), grants/contracts from business (18.8%) or from unions (6.4%), products/services provided by the NGO for a fee (18.0%), and membership dues from affiliated organizations (11.5%). Evidently, government funding helps to sustain NGOs in Canada, with potential influence on NGO agendas. The pursuit of government funding may be part of the reason for the current apparent conservatism of the environmental movement. But it also gives these NGOs a vested interest in intervening in government policy. On the other hand, 36% said government funding was "not important" at all, once again suggesting a bifurcation between elite/state-oriented and oppositional/independent or small marginal groups.

Many organizations have succeeded in building a base of support from individuals. Support from foundations is important, but probably less so than in U.S. Overall, the importance of external sources other than products/services marketed by the NGO itself implies a high degree of financial vulnerability and a good deal of effort absorbed by fundraising, contract-chasing, and/or membership servicing.

A SHARED DIAGNOSTIC FRAME?

Although the Harper government looms larger than mainstream media as a political opponent or problem for NGOs, they have at least modest incentives and resources for media policy campaigns. Do they share a perception of what policy solutions might improve the media?

On the abstract question of Canadian media's performance of their role in a democratic society, over half of respondents (55%) rated it as poor or very poor, though 45.1% rated media as average or better. Most of the 24 respondents who offered additional comments were critical, in ways resonating with the potential agenda for media reform. First, 13 respondents pointed to aspects of corporate control, media concentration, and/or state policy. Ten mentioned biased or inadequate coverage. Some respondents linked bias to corporate control, but others emphasized resource constraints (the third most common theme of critics), cultural power differentials, or journalists' own inadequacies.

These themes suggest somewhat divergent emphases for media reform: reduce market concentration; replace corporate ownership with public or community ownership; subsidize journalism; and/or change the cultural background and assumptions of journalists and their publics. These approaches are not necessarily mutually exclusive, however. Possibly by contrast with their American counterparts, Canadian NGOs do not appear to put much faith in market forces and greater competition as an antidote to concentrated corporate control.

A parallel range of views is evident among the 39 respondents who addressed specifically how they would like to see the media changed. Their (multiple) responses can be categorized into the following themes: structural changes in media (18 respondents), better journalism and content (17), regulatory and financial support for independent and community media (11) or for public-service media (9), improved media personnel (2), other regulatory measures (2), and miscellaneous (4).

Encouragingly, there is widespread support for using the instrumentality of the state to achieve democratic reform of media. Perhaps not surprisingly from a sample of institutionalized advocacy groups, many of them seeking to influence government policy, there is little evidence of hardcore libertarian or anarchist/autonomist sentiment. To be sure, there are issues that are not unanimous (such as relative support for mainstream journalism, public-service media, and community media) or that could even be divisive for media reform coalitions, such as copyright (free access versus revenues for creators).

There is no such ambiguity around the issue of fair access to the Internet, however. Respondents expressed a commitment to its democratic importance, one commenting that the Internet is "now a crucial medium for communication; effective citizenship depends on access." As noted above, however, NGOs' self-interest is also at stake. A full 98% agreed that Net throttling, the practice of prioritizing Internet traffic according to ability to pay, would negatively affect their work, especially outreach and finances. Net neutrality, the nondiscriminatory treatment of traffic, was described as essential, indeed "a life or death issue for us."

COLLABORATIVE ACTION?

The shortage of resources within individual NGOs reinforces the advisability of collaboration in mounting campaigns. Fortunately, the organizational culture in Canada seems favourable to coalitions. Asked how often their NGO engages in collaborative projects or campaigns with other organizations, only 13% of respondents said they "never" or "seldom" do so; 55.5% said they do so often or constantly.

Under what conditions might NGOs collaborate on campaigns related specifically to media issues? Our elementary data-analysis program enabled only limited bivariate analysis, but three correlations stand out. First, some NGO sectors are more likely than others to engage in media campaigns. One clue is provided by the sectoral response rate to our online survey. Of those invited to respond, peace and environmental groups were less likely to do so. With some notable exceptions (such as Adbusters magazine), groups in these sectors tend not to theorize the connection between dominant media and consumerism. Some NGOs in these sectors probably feel that they have won media access that they do not want to jeopardize through campaigns perceived as hostile to corporate media. A similarly low response rate from ethnic minorities may reflect a preference to work through their own media and communities.

By contrast, some of the "high" responders to the survey have a clear stake in communications policy: independent media, arts/culture, and arguably gender groups—in struggles for women's equality, in particular, media representations loom large. The welcome response from religious groups, perhaps encouraged by WACC's co-sponsorship of the project, suggests a media reform constituency often overlooked.

More direct evidence from the survey broadly corroborates the above ranking of sectoral participation. Civil and human rights groups, trade unions, media organizations, political advocates, and arts and culture groups were more likely than others to indicate past and likely future engagement with media policy campaigns.

A second variable influencing campaign/coalition participation is dissatisfaction with the mainstream media. Our sample was fairly evenly divided between participants and nonparticipants in media change campaigns. Respondents who had participated during the past five years were somewhat less satisfied with media coverage of their group and its issues or with Canadian media's democratic performance, compared with nonparticipants. There is a nearly linear relationship between dissatisfaction with media's democratic performance and the likelihood of future participation in media reform campaigns. A small group of respondents ranked Canadian media as quite good, but nevertheless indicated interest in future campaigns, perhaps to defend valued services such as the CBC.

A third factor possibly influencing participation is perceptions of the Internet. While it is only a small sample, those who rated Internet access as less than "very important" to their work or to Canadians generally also rated their likelihood of joining a media reform campaign lower than did other respondents.

Regardless of the factors that catalyze it, does media activism perform the role of articulating a shared grievance for progressive social movements and providing an arena for them to come together, as Hackett & Carroll (2006) speculated? Or do other organizations, such as trade unions or left-leaning political parties like the New Democratic Party, play that role in Canada?

Neither appears to be the case. Our respondents identified a total of 56 organizations as partners in the previous three years, but only three groups are mentioned more than once. The survey reveals no organizational hub for collaborative campaigns, although there may be passive partners, such as policy institutes, that consistently anchor campaigns with background advice or assistance.

CONCLUSION

The research summarized here is small in scale and thus must be considered exploratory. With that caveat, it does suggest that some of the building blocks identified by social movement theory are in place for media reform in Canada, such as shared dissatisfaction with the current state of Canadian media; a universal concern with and commitment to equitable and affordable Internet access; a tradition of engagement in collaborative campaigns; an expansive social movement and anti-neo-liberal orientation; a reasonable degree of awareness of media issues; previously untapped potential support among human rights, labour, and religious groups; and, arguably, an embryonic sense of media democratization as itself a social movement, especially among groups already in the independent media, culture, and arts fields.

Challenges remain, of course. Organizational resources are limited, even for NGOs' primary goals. Corporate media do not loom as "the" enemy for progressive groups in Canada to the same extent as in the U.S. NGO prescriptions for media change do not converge on a single issue or solution, though such diversity is also a resource for building different coalitions on different issues. And finding widely resonant frames for the seemingly abstract issues of media democracy is a longstanding challenge (Ó Siochrú, 2005).

From the viewpoint of movement-building strategy, several implications follow. First, it may be advisable to adopt different frames for different issues and constituencies. Second, NGOs are most likely to invest resources in issues that affect their organizational mandates and sustainability. Third, "positive" frames, such as support for community media or for reinvigorating Canadian journalism, may find broader (albeit likely less intense) support than would adversarial frames, such as opposition to corporate concentration. Fourth, the issue of Internet access and Net neutrality is likely to find wide support and to provide an entrée to ongoing collaboration for future campaigns. Finally, as we argue in the full report (Hackett & Anderson, 2010b) and elsewhere (Hackett & Anderson, 2010a), the frame of "open media" could appeal to younger activists, and it complements a focus on equitable access to digital media. At the very least, it should take its place alongside other current frames reflecting different emphases, such as media justice, free press, media democratization, and communication rights (Hackett & Carroll, 2006).

Endnotes

1. A list of potential respondents to the online survey was compiled partly through personal contacts established by OpenMedia.ca, but mainly (in the apparent absence of

an affordable and authoritative directory of Canadian organizations) through several online databases. For each organization, we sought to identify the individual responsible for media relations or policy development. Our list was intended to include NGOs in each of the following 16 categories: peace, environment, ethnic, gender, religion, labour/trade union, independent media, technology, arts and culture, civil and human rights, First Nations, professional/service, general political and advocacy, foundations, charity/education, and research "think tanks." (These categories can of course overlap. In analyzing the responses, respondents' self-identification with a sector, rather than our own initial categorization, was employed.)

2. The following groups (usually through their president, coordinator, executive director, or media relations officer) were interviewed between January and May 2009: the Rideau Institute; Douglas-Coldwell Foundation; Council of Canadians, Consumers Council of Canada; Friends of Canadian Broadcasting; Canadian Association of University Teachers; Alliance of Canadian Cinema, Television & Radio Artists; Canadian Conference of the Arts; Canadian Federation of Students; Columbia Institute; Check Your Head; The Tyee; W2 Community Media Arts Centre; Telecommunications Workers Union; The Maytree Foundation; NOW Magazine; Public Service Alliance of Canada; and Renewal.

3. We do not mean to imply that these questions are exhaustive; even within RMT, other questions are posed, such as the availability of political opportunities. Moreover, other traditions, such as new social movement theory, also offer valuable insights into media activism (see Carroll & Hackett (2006); Hackett & Carroll (2006)).

REFERENCES

Carroll, William K., & Hackett, Robert A. (2006). Democratic media activism through the lens of social movement theory. *Media, Culture & Society, 28*(1), 83–104.

Gamson, William A., & Wolfsfeld, Gadi. (1993). Movements and media as interacting systems. *The Annals of the American Academy of Political and Social Science, 528*(1), 114–125.

Hackett, Robert A., & Anderson, Steve. (2010a). Democratic media reform in Canada: Campaigns, coalitions aim to democratize media system. *The CCPA Monitor, 17*(3), 12–15.

Hackett, Robert A., & Anderson, Steve. (2010b). *Revitalizing a media reform movement in Canada*. Vancouver, BC: OpenMedia.ca. URL: http://openmedia.ca/revitalize [February 28, 2011].

Hackett, Robert A., & Carroll, William K. (2006). *Remaking media: The struggle to democratize public communication*. London, UK: Routledge.

Moll, Marita, & Shade, Leslie Regan (Eds.). (2008). *For sale to the highest bidder: Telecom policy in Canada*. Ottawa, ON: Canadian Centre for Policy Alternatives.

Napoli, Philip M. (2007). Public interest media activism and advocacy as a social movement: A review of the literature. *McGannon Center Working Paper Series, Paper 21*. URL: http://fordham.bepress.com/mcgannon_working_papers/21 [February 28, 2011].

Ó Siochrú, Seán. (2005). Finding a frame: Toward a transnational advocacy campaign to democratize communication. In R. A. Hackett & Y. Zhao (Eds.), *Democratizing global media: One world, many struggles* (pp. 289–311). Lanham, MD: Rowman & Littlefield.

Raboy, Marc, & Shtern, Jeremy. (2010). The horizontal view. In M. Raboy & J. Shtern, W. J. McIver, with L. J. Murray, S. Ó Siochrú, & L. R. Shade, *Media divides: Communication rights and the right to communicate in Canada* (pp. 63–90). Vancouver, BC: UBC Press.

Winseck, Dwayne. (2008). Media merger mania. *Canadian Dimension, 42*(1), 30–32.

DISCUSSION

Robert Hackett and Steve Anderson, 'Democratizing Communication Policy in Canada: A Social Movement Perspective.' *Canadian Journal of Communication.*

1. Hackett and Anderson argue that Canadian media policies meant to support democratic values, accountability, access, community building, national interests, and cultural sovereignty are being undermined by neo-liberal governments and ideologies. What features of neoliberal politics and economic changes do they suggest are negatively influencing the Canadian media environment?
2. Why do you think the authors chose to survey Canadian NGOs and interview group members about their actual and potential involvement in media activism and media policy? What type of groups were surveyed and why do they care about media policy?
3. The authors discover that these groups share a 'diagnostic frame' about what policy solutions might improve Canadian media. What three main things do social movement groups agree are wrong with the media and what solutions do they suggest to address these problems?
4. In their conclusions, the authors argue that the issues of Internet access and Net neutrality are likely to generate broad support for media policy activism. Visit the 'About Us' section of the OpenMedia.ca web site to learn more about this type of policy engagement. Do you agree or disagree with the OpenMedia principles on elements of access, choice, diversity, innovation, and openness in Canada's media system? Why or why not?

Primary Sources: Who Cares About Media Policy?
Policy Source 5
Friends of Canadian Broadcasting. (2011). *Presentation to the House of Commons Standing Committee on Canadian Heritage on the mandate and funding of the Canadian Broadcasting Corporation*. Ottawa: Friends of Canadian Broadcasting.

Presentation to the House of Commons Standing Committee on Canadian Heritage on the Mandate and Funding of the Canadian Broadcasting Corporation

Mar 21, 2011
Ian Morrison, Spokesperson

Mr. Chair and members of the Committee: thanks for inviting Friends of Canadian Broadcasting to appear today! FRIENDS is an independent watchdog for Canadian programming on radio, television and new media—supported by 150,000 Canadians. FRIENDS is not affiliated with any broadcaster or political party.

You are studying the mandate and funding of the CBC, a subject near to Canadians' hearts. Since the early 1990s, FRIENDS has periodically commissioned public opinion research on broadcasting issues. You can see all of them in the "Resources" section on friends.ca, our website. I want to take a moment to summarize a recent survey we commissioned from POLLARA on "Canadian attitudes and expectations towards public broadcasting":[1]

- 88% of Canadians believe that as Canada's economic ties with the U.S. increase, it is becoming more important to strengthen Canadian culture and identity. (page 26)
- 78% tune in to some form of CBC programming each week. (page 19)
- 81% believe that the CBC is one of the things that helps distinguish Canada from the U.S. (page 25)
- 74% would like to see CBC strengthened in their part of Canada. (page 25)

And finally, here is a question that might interest a group of parliamentarians: "Assume for a moment that your federal MP asked for your advice on an upcoming vote in the House of Commons on what to do about CBC funding. Which of the following three options would you advise him/her to vote for? Decrease funding? (9%), maintain funding at current levels? (31%), or increase funding (47%)." (Page 43)

There's a message here: CBC is popular with Canadians—of all political persuasions.

FRIENDS has appeared before this Committee on several occasions to underline our strong support for the CBC's mandate as expressed in Section 3 of the Broadcasting Act.

In our view, a key point is the large gap between Parliament's intentions and what CBC delivers daily to Canadians, in particular the mandate to "reflect Canada and its regions to national and regional audiences, *while serving the special needs of those regions*".[2]—and also the English Television Network's failure to "be predominantly and distinctively Canadian",[3] especially in prime-time.

As you know, this Committee has been a source of valuable and comprehensive information about public broadcasting, for example the graphic from the Lincoln Report[4] comparing public investment in public broadcasting in Western democracies as a share of the GDP:

These data show that CBC funding is near the basement—like the Ottawa Senators—with only Portugal, Poland, New Zealand and the United States investing less than Canada in public broadcasting.

So there's a disconnect between public sentiment and government investment, and this disconnect has become more severe in recent years. FRIENDS routinely tracks CBC's Parliamentary grant, factored for inflation, in order to identify changes in CBC's purchasing power. On friends.ca we have graphed these data over the past 21 years:[5]

Under each of the Mulroney, Chrétien, Martin and Harper governments, CBC has lost financial capacity. Canadians can hear and see the result of this gap every day. Regional programming is weaker and its reach is declining, more foreign content is televised in prime-time, and repetition of programs is increasing.

Ten years ago in prime-time, CBC's English Television Network broadcast 27 hours of Canadian programs and only one hour of foreign programs each week. Last year, seven hours of foreign programs appeared in prime-time—25% of CBC's prime-time schedule! And this in the face of a recommendation from your Committee that CBC television should be 100% Canadian in prime-time.

Each of you will probably have your own anecdotes on the results of under-funding. Earlier this year, New Brunswick residents learned that CBC proposed to end over-the-air television transmission in Moncton and Saint John next September, leading to a storm of protest at the CRTC. A few years ago, residents of the Comox valley lost their over-the-air CBC Television signal after an antenna fire, and it has not been replaced. CBC seems to be backing out of affiliate agreements in several communities, including Peterborough and Kingston. Examples abound of parts of the country that are denied CBC services, all because of a shortage of money.

FRIENDS thanks this Committee for its recent recommendation "that CBC/Radio-Canada's core funding be increased to an amount equivalent to at least $40 per capita."[6] This would be a good first step to addressing the funding gap—raising Canada's per-capita support for its national public broadcaster to half the OECD average.

Your recommendation is popular with Canadians. POLLARA found that:

- 54% of Canadians support this Committee's recommendation that CBC funding should increase to $40 per Canadian.
- 20% believe your $40 per Canadian recommendation is too low.

- And the balance, 26% of Canadians believe that your recommendation is too high. (page 33)

In our watchdog role, we keep close track of politicians' statements about broadcasting and cultural sovereignty. Our website is full of examples from years gone by—Liberal years—but today I want to focus on the current government.

Prime Minister Harper came up strongly on our radar when, as Opposition Leader in May 2004 he said: "I've suggested that government subsidies in support of CBC's services should be to those things that are not ... do not have commercial alternatives." He then added: "When you take a look at things like main-English language television and probably to a lesser degree Radio Two, you could there (sic) at putting those on a commercial basis."[7]

In seeming contradiction, a few months later Harper said: "we would seek to reduce the CBC's dependence on advertising revenue and its competition with the private sector for these valuable dollars, especially in non-sports programming."[8]

In office, the Prime Minister has gone silent on this file, at least in public. But troubling signs have emerged from Conservative Party fund raising letters where public broadcasting has been featured. For example in September 2008, on the eve of the general election, Doug Finley, writing as Campaign Director of the Conservative Party, sent donors a "2008 National Critical Issues Survey" and promised "I will personally share the overall results and any comments with the Prime Minister". Question 5 read: "The CBC costs taxpayers over $1.1 billion per year. Do you think this is a good use of taxpayer dollars (or) a bad use of taxpayer dollars"?[9]

This context might help you understand our concern when we read in the transcript of your November 23 meeting the following question from Mr. Del Mastro to a Corus executive: "Maybe it's time we get out of the broadcasting business and get into investing more money into content? ... Maybe I wasn't clear enough. The $1.1 billion, plus a whole bunch of other stuff that we're investing into the public broadcaster, should we look at reorganizing that in some fashion so we could put more money into content?"[10]

Getting out of the broadcasting business sounds a lot like killing CBC Radio, CBC Television, CBC NewsNet, cbc.ca and their French-language counterparts. And this disturbing comment was coming from the mouth of a Parliamentary Secretary who has a seat at the table beside the Minister of Canadian Heritage.

We also noted that twice in Question Period Minister Moore was invited to dissociate himself from Mr. Del Mastro's comments, and he failed to do so.

As you know, last month Immigration Minister Jason Kenney was quoted by Canadian Press as saying: "The CBC lies all the time".[11] Any one of these incidents could be written off as an isolated event. But taken together, it all adds up to a substantial concern: a government whose leadership may be out of sync with public opinion on Canadian public broadcasting.[12]

Eighty years ago, a Conservative Prime Minister introduced public broadcasting to Canada. I would like to conclude by quoting another prominent Conservative, the late Dalton Camp:

"Owning one national communications facility, such as the CBC, which owes nothing to Mitsubishi or General Dynamics or Krupp, is surely worth keeping. What we know about the CBC, in a world in which economics is power and so much power is out of our hands, is that the CBC would never willfully betray our national interest or sell off our Canadian heritage. And we are its only shareholders. When you hear people talk about reducing the role of the CBC, or selling off its assets, look closely at who's talking—it won't be a voice speaking for the people of Canada, but for shareholders of another kind of corporation."[13]

Endnotes

1. http://www.friends.ca/poll/8288
2. Section 3(1)(m)(ii) emphasis added.
3. Section 3(1)(m)9i)
4. These data are drawn from page 178 of the Lincoln Report, *Our Cultural Sovereignty,* published by the House of Commons Standing Committee on Canadian Heritage in 2003: http://www2.parl.gc.ca/HousePublications/Publication.aspx?DocId=1032284&Language=E&Mode= 1&Parl=37&Ses=2
5. http://www.friends.ca/fact-sheet/238
6. CBC/RadioCanada: Defining Distinctiveness in the Changing Media Landscape", 2008. Published by the House of Commons Standing Committee on Canadian Heritage. Page 139ff: http://www2.parl.gc.ca/HousePublications/Publication.aspx?DocId=3297009&Language=E&Mode= 1&Parl=39&Ses=2
7. May 19, 2004 http://www.friends.ca/News/Friends_News/archives/articles05190403
8. Speech to the Canadian Association of Broadcasters, November 29, 2004. http://www.friends.ca/news-item/6480
9. www.friends.ca/files/PDF/DougFinley.CPC-survey.pdf
10. http://www2.parl.gc.ca/HousePublications/Publication.aspx?DocId=4810757&Language=E&Mode=1&Parl=40&Ses=3
11. http://www.friends.ca/news-item/10022
12. Additional troubling comments are available here: http://www.friends.ca/fact-sheet/252
13. The Toronto Star, July 12, 1995, page A17.

DISCUSSION

Friends of Canadian Broadcasting. *Presentation to the House of Commons Standing Committee on Canadian Heritage on the Mandate and Funding of the Canadian Broadcasting Corporation.*

1. Friends of Canadian Broadcasting opens its presentation to the Standing Committee on Canadian Heritage by stating its role as a 'watchdog' group, independent from both broadcasters and political parties. Visit the 'About Us' section of the www.friends.ca website. How does the group support and organize its 'watchdog' activities in Canadian media policy-making?
2. The presentation provides results from research into Canadian attitudes and expectations towards public broadcasting showing strong public support for the CBC. Sum

up these findings in your own words. Do these results reflect your own attitudes toward the CBC? How would you have answered the survey questions?

3. The Friends of Canadian Broadcasting report illustrates the real dollar decline in government funding for the CBC and argues that this prevents the CBC from fulfilling the mandate of national public broadcasting as defined in the *Broadcasting Act*. Do you agree with this conclusion? What have been some of the results of long term cuts to the CBC?

4. The presentation ends with a quote from former Conservative strategist Dalton Camp arguing for the value of public broadcasting and the positive role of the CBC. Why do you think the presentation concludes with this example? Why does Friends of Canadian Broadcasting suggest that support for the CBC cuts across political parties and individual interests in Canada?

Policy Source 6

Canadian Media Production Association. (2010). *Remarks by the Canadian Media Production Association (CMPA) to House of Commons Standing Committee on Canadian Heritage: Study on the impacts of private television ownership changes and the move towards new viewing platforms.* Retrieved from http://www.cftpa.ca/government_relations/pdfs/CMPA_Remarks_to_Standing_Committee_re_Impact_of_Change_in_Television_Ownership.pdf

Remarks by the Canadian Media Production Association (CMPA) to House of Commons Standing Committee on Canadian Heritage

Study on The Impacts of Private Television Ownership Changes and the Move Towards New Viewing Platforms

November 23, 2010

NORM BOLEN

Good morning Mr. Chairman and Committee Members. I appreciate the opportunity to appear before you today. I will keep my remarks short so that we have more time for questions and answers.

But first, I offer my congratulations specifically to you, Mr. Chong, on your recent election as Chairman of this important Standing Committee. I look forward to working closely with you and the other Committee Members in the weeks and months ahead.

My name is Norm Bolen, and I am the President and CEO of the Canadian Media Production Association. With me today is Reynolds Mastin, Counsel for the CMPA.

We represent hundreds of independent companies across Canada. They produce and distribute English-language television programs, feature films, and interactive content. With a handful of exceptions, these are all small- and medium-sized businesses.

Our members produce content that is consumed by millions of viewers in Canada and abroad. That content is viewed on small, medium and large screens. Gone are the days when producers developed content for a single platform. Today, producers almost always develop content that will be exploited on multiple screens.

As most of you know, our organization was formerly the Canadian Film and Television Production Association. We rebranded a number of months ago to the Canadian Media Production Association. We did this specifically to better reflect the reality of today's independent production sector. And, in light of the multiplat-form universe that is already so prevalent in the lives of Canadians.

Our members have a significant impact on the Canadian economy. They generate most of the $5 billion in production that occurs in Canada each year. And, this activity sustains some 130,000 high-quality jobs.

While economic performance indicators are important, independent producers are about much more than just the money and the jobs. By the content they produce, inde-pendent producers reflect—I would even add celebrate—the broad diversity that exists across our vast country and the proud history that makes us so unique.

The fundamental role of producers has long been recognized and supported by successive governments.

This is why the *Broadcasting Act* recognizes the important role that independent producers play in the Canadian broadcasting system. Section 3 of the *Act* requires that "the programming provided by the Canadian broadcasting system should ... include a significant contribution from the Canadian independent production sector."

Independent producers are a key engine driving diversity, creativity and innovation.

I would like to think that our sector is well positioned to make a significant contri-bution to Canada's burgeoning digital economy. But lately, to be brutally honest with you, I'm beginning to wonder if this is at all true.

For independent producers to be well positioned to contribute meaningfully to Canada's economic and cultural future, certain things must change.... and, they must change quickly.

We therefore congratulate you for launching your study on the impacts of the changes in private television ownership and the move towards new viewing platforms.

Over the last decade, and certainly in the last few years, the massive consolidation and integration of the television sector has indeed had a significant impact on inde-pendent producers.

There is now a severe and unsustainable industry imbalance between independent producers and broadcasters. That imbalance is not only undermining content innova-tion and programming diversity, it is threatening the very existence of the independent production sector.

We remain hopeful, however, that the Government and all political parties continue to believe in the importance of the contribution made by independent producers.

The key question, as I see it, is really quite simple. Do we continue to believe it ben-eficial to all Canadians that a viable and healthy independent production sector not only exists but can flourish?

I, and many millions of Canadians, believe the answer to that question is an un-equivocal "YES."

So, I implore you to grasp the opportunity with this study to make concrete recom-mendations to address the imbalance that currently exists in the television sector be-tween independent producers and broadcasters.

Reynolds?

REYNOLDS MASTIN

So, you may be wondering what the problem is exactly between producers and broad-casters.

Simply put, there are only three large, integrated private broadcast corporate groups now in English Canada. As such, there are effectively few selling opportunities in the television market for our members.

And, more specifically, those three broadcast groups are now using—I would even say abusing—their dominant position in the market to secure unreasonable terms from independent producers. They are demanding more rights, including all digital rights, and often for very little additional fees, if any.

Broadcaster consolidation has virtually eliminated competition in the Canadian programming rights market, resulting in:

- Fewer incentives for broadcasters to experiment with multiplatform content production and distribution;
- Untenable and unsustainable rights deals for independent producers; and
- The virtual elimination of any return on investment for investors and funders, including the Canada Media Fund.

The equation is simple: where broadcasters control all of the rights, they will reap all of the benefits.

This leaves other key partners—independent producers, the Canada Media Fund, federal and provincial funding agencies, and independent production funds—with little or nothing to show for their investment in Canadian programming.

The situation for independent producers has gotten progressively worse over time.

Ten years ago, broadcasters were taking 3-year licence deals on programming.

Today, for very little additional compensation, they demand as many as 12 years. This virtually eliminates any possibility for a producer to sell in 2nd or 3rd markets.

Ten years ago, broadcasters negotiated for only one conventional station and maybe for 3 to 5 plays of the program over the 3-year licence term.

Today, with little additional compensation, they demand the rights for the same conventional station plus all their other owned and controlled broadcast platforms (e.g., specialty TV) . . . Plus, unlimited plays on all their platforms . . . Plus, Internet rights . . . Plus, all rights for all media . . . Plus, merchandizing rights . . . And, very often, foreign territories too.

Let's consider this last point for a second. A Canadian broadcaster whose sole raison d'être is the Canadian market is using its considerable clout to scoop up the rights for foreign territories. This is going way, way too far.

You may be asking yourselves why producers do not simply refuse these harsh business terms that are so damaging to their businesses.

There is a simple answer to that question. For most independent producers, turning down these terrible terms effectively means putting their businesses on hold, or even closing their doors permanently.

I would highlight that a broadcaster is also the only trigger to access a large majority of the financing available under the Canada Media Fund and one of the key triggers to access the Canadian Film or Video Production Tax Credit.

This puts broadcasters in a very strong bargaining position. Without a broadcast deal, our members have no access to most of the CMF and likely no access to the tax credit.

Without access to these crucial sources of funding, there would be far fewer Canadian content productions in under-represented genres. Thousands of key creative and technical craftspeople from coast to coast would lose their jobs.

Ultimately, Canada's diversity would be significantly lessened, and independent producers would fall considerably short of being able to effectively contribute to Canada's growing digital economy.

This is why we have been pushing so aggressively for the implementation of an equitable and enforceable Terms of Trade framework between independent producers and broadcasters.

This would provide a common-sense solution related to the ownership and exploitation of all rights, including digital rights, thereby maximizing the distribution of content across all platforms. This is a key Government policy objective that can be achieved at no cost to taxpayers and with minimal, if any, direct regulatory intervention.

Norm?

NORM BOLEN

Before we wrap up, I would like to make a short comment about the Canada Media Fund.

As you may know, the Department of Canadian Heritage's contribution to the Fund expires at the end of this fiscal year. This program is crucial for under-represented Canadian programming and the independent production sector. It is critical that it be renewed, long term.

As you may also know, we have been actively working with our colleagues in the creative sector in arguing before the courts that Internet Service Providers should be considered broadcast distributors under the *Broadcasting Act*.

Let me briefly explain why it is necessary to push so hard on this front.

Over time, Canadian audiences will increasingly migrate to platforms that are currently not regulated. As this trend accelerates, revenues earned within vertically integrated communications companies will shift from those generated by their traditional cable and satellite services to those derived from their Internet access services. Overall these companies could end up earning just as much—maybe even considerably more—from their customers' shift to broadband.

At the same time, they will end up contributing less and less to the Canada Media Fund, since their contributions are currently solely based on their cable and satellite revenues.

Data already show the CMF's revenue from BDUs flattening out.

This is not a positive trend for Canadian content, the independent production sector, or the thousands of jobs we sustain across Canada.

In closing I offer four specific recommendations that we ask you to incorporate into your study:

1. Recognize the imbalance that currently exists between independent producers and television broadcasters in the negotiation of rights, and the detrimental effect this has on diversity and innovation in the system;

2. Recommend that the Minister of Canadian Heritage issue a policy direction to the CRTC, pursuant to section 7 of the *Broadcasting Act,* requiring the Commission to ensure that broadcasters have taken all appropriate steps to reach an equitable arrangement with the independent production sector regarding the ownership and exploitation of program rights;

3. Support the renewal of the Department of Canadian Heritage's contribution to the Canada Media Fund on an ongoing basis. This will introduce much needed stability in the funding system. It will also allow all stakeholders to plan long-term and continue enhancing the effectiveness of the Fund;

4. Endorse the proposal that all distribution platforms, including those that are currently not regulated, be required to make a financial contribution to a Fund to support the creation of Canadian content.

With these key building blocks in place, I am confident that Canadian independent producers will be much better positioned to be able to contribute meaningfully to both our growing digital economy and our cultural future.

That concludes my presentation. I would be happy to answer any questions you may have.

Thank you.

DISCUSSION

Canadian Media Production Association. *Remarks to House of Commons Standing Committee on Canadian Heritage, Study on The Impacts of Private Television Ownership Changes.*

1. According to the CMPA report to the Standing Committee on Canadian Heritage, members of this interest group create content that is consumed by millions of viewers in Canada and abroad. Visit the 'Membership' section of the www.cmpa.ca website. Who are the members of CMPA and what services does the group offer to these companies?

2. The CMPA report mentions the role of independent production companies in fulfilling an important aspect of the *Broadcasting Act.* Why do you think the *Act* mentions independent media producers and which of the key policy objectives from the Policy Analysis Framework on page 6 do independent film and television companies help meet?

3. What are the different functions of independent producers and broadcasters in Canada's media industries? Why does the CMPA argue that there is a severe imbalance between broadcasters and producers, and how does the power of the broadcasters create negative conditions for CMPA members?

4. The CMPA presentation stresses how the move toward web platforms is changing the television industry. Why is the question of digital rights so pressing for independent media producers? Why does the CMPA think that internet service providers should help support Canadian television programming through contributions to the Canada Media Fund?

Public Interest, Public Service, and Public Ownership of Media

INTRODUCTION

As we have seen from our review of the history of media policy, the examination of policy instruments like legislation *(Broadcasting Act)*, and the survey of specific funding programs administered by the Department of Canadian Heritage, Canadian government interventions in media industries are based on underlying rationales of public good, national interest, and national unity. From this point on, we will be examining specific policy tools chosen and implemented by successive Canadian governments to support the creation of Canadian culture. In this chapter we look at one of the earliest policy tools: public ownership of media. This policy choice shaped the creation of CBC/Radio-Canada, Canada's national public broadcaster, and the National Film Board of Canada, a publicly owned documentary film producer. Governments also determine ways of defining what counts as 'national culture,' a question we will examine more closely in Chapter 6 when looking at the implementation of CRTC regulations, domestic content quotas, and spending requirements for television broadcasters. Media policy is also designed to protect Canadian ownership of media outlets, an issue we will examine in Chapter 7 with respect to efforts to protect Canadian magazines and periodicals. In Chapter 8 and 9 we consider the policy tool of direct expenditure, or public subsidies and grants, and their use in Canadian book publishing and music production. Chapter 10 examines the further implementation of subsidies in the television industry along with the tool of 'tax expenditure' or tax credits that help foster private investment in the film and television industries. These different policy choices complement the early government focus on public broadcasting and public ownership of media as a means of supporting national interest and national unity.

Public broadcasting in Canada dates back to 1932, with the creation of the Canadian Radio Broadcasting Commission (CRBC), the precursor to the CBC. The CRBC was designed to address the uneven access to radio signals across the country while supplying some Canadian programming. In an economic context where private investors did not have the resources to build a comprehensive national radio network, the state stepped in to address this instance of market failure (Armstrong, 2010, 28). Public broadcasting in Canada was developed as a response to the flow of American radio across the border. As the Massey Commission made clear, the public trust mandate for radio was meant to sustain the project of Canadian nation-building. Similarly, the National Film Board of Canada was created by the *National Film Act* of 1939. In the political context of the Second World War, the NFB first operated under British documentary filmmaker John Grierson as a national documentary film producer supporting the Canadian war effort with patriotic films (NFB, 2012). The NFB has created and distributed over 13,000 films in its seven decades. As Zoe Druick (2007, 9) has argued, documentary at the NFB was part of a much larger process of dialogue about citizenship, reflecting narratives of nationhood and "putting into practice the modernizing policies of industrial societies." Today the NFB has embarked on an ambitious project of streaming many of its films for free on the Internet in order to reach new national and global audiences with its vision of Canada and the world.

Public media like the CBC and NFB are funded by federal government, but they operate at arm's length from state control. In most Western democracies, public broadcasting is recognized for its independence from government, politics, and business interests. As indicated in the *Broadcasting Act,* radio and television licences are a public resource with social and cultural impact (like education) and should be allocated in the public interest. While the notion that broadcast frequencies are a 'scarce resource' has been challenged in the age of digital channel compression and on-line delivery, there are still many convincing arguments for public service broadcasting. Public broadcasters are often established to create specifically non-commercial, non-profit programming that provides a public service, and that private broadcasters do not produce. These include educational programs, in-depth news and current affairs, and arts and heritage programming. Grant and Wood (2004) sum up the main elements of mandates for public service broadcasting as it is practised in countries around the world. These elements include:

- Access to programming for all tastes, interests and needs—even those minority groups for whom content provision would not be profitable.
- Content for linguistic minorities, indigenous people, children and elderly, remote areas and poorer regions, and disabled or disadvantaged groups.
- Pluralistic content that reflects multiracial and multicultural societies, or political and religious differences.
- Non-commercial and high-quality programming that informs, educates, and entertains.
- Contributing to national and international understanding of people in their multiple social and economic environments.
- Treating audiences as citizens rather than only as consumers (Grant & Wood, 2004, 171)

Both the CBC, through radio, television, and Internet content, and the NFB, through documentary film production, embody many of these elements of 'public service' media. Policy objectives of creation of Canadian content and enhancing access to it are also clearly carried out by publicly-owned media.

The critical analysis for this chapter is a study conducted by Nordicity Group for the CBC. The consultants on this study undertook to address three key research questions: how funding for the CBC compared to funding for public broadcasters in other countries, whether the decline in funding for the CBC was matched with a general decline in funding for culture in Canada, and finally, which countries might be expected to most benefit from public broadcasting and how the potential benefit compares to actual levels of public funding. The study found that among 18 other countries, Canada had the third lowest level of public funding per capita for its public broadcaster. The study also found that while the real value of federal funding for CBC declined by 9 percent between 1996 and 2004, overall spending on other federal support to culture increased by 31 percent. Nordicity also conducted a 'benefits assessment' to test which countries, under what conditions, would seem to have the strongest need for a national public broadcaster. The indicators of 'potential benefit' included the country's need for promotion of common culture and values, the relative size of the domestic language market for media content, the proximity to another country with a similar language and larger economy, and the audience appeal of domestic programs. According to these criteria, out of all the countries surveyed, Canada stands to benefit most from the potential social and cultural outcomes of public broadcasting.

Policy Source 7 is a presentation by the president of the CBC to the Standing Committee on Canadian Heritage during the Committee's 2007 study of the role and mandate of the national public broadcaster. The presentation outlines the need for public broadcasting, considers the challenges facing CBC, overviews its services and provides information about the audience appeal of CBC programs. Making a strong case for support and funding for the CBC, the presentation argues that CBC has historically delivered on the policy objectives for public broadcasting by building a sense of belonging and national pride. The report details specific attributes of CBC programs and services that clearly distinguish it from private or commercial radio and television. Finally the CBC's presentation makes reference to the Nordicity study also included in this chapter to argue that while Canada's need for a public broadcaster is quite strong in comparison to most other countries, its per capita funding level is comparatively low. The presentation concludes with the offer of a 'new contract' for national public broadcasting that would support fundamental principles of a public/private system, programming independence, distinctiveness, and accessibility along with a strong government commitment to provide the necessary resources to support these objectives.

In Policy Source 8, the National Film Board states its positions and principles before the Standing Committee on Canadian Heritage, during the Committee's 2010 review of emerging and digital media. The NFB presentation sketches out the current context of digital and on-line media use in Canada, especially for the downloading and viewing of film and video. Highlighting the extent to which the Internet dissolves national borders and challenges conventional distribution of visual media content, the NFB report argues that new market models for the creation and distribution of film must be developed. These new models must meet the need of consumers and citizens to control their media choices and address people's desire to use media as a means of self-expression, not just passive observation. The report argues that Canada needs to carve out space for its own cultural products in this new environment, to tap into on-line advertising revenue, and find opportunities in emerging digital markets. The NFB has been at the forefront of the migration to digital platforms for Canadian documentary film production and distribution. It streams hundreds of films for free on its website and has launched highly successful iPhone and Android apps for mobile viewing of this content. This public media outlet has reached a younger national and international audience with these strategies and established a new relationship with Canadians.

Critical Analysis

Nordicity Group Ltd. (2006). *Analysis of government support for public broadcasting and other culture in Canada*. Ottawa: Prepared for Canadian Broadcasting Corporation/ La Société Radio-Canada.

Analysis of Government Support for Public Broadcasting and Other Culture in Canada

Nordicity Group Ltd.

1 INTRODUCTION

1.1 Background and Mandate

In late 2005, the Canadian Broadcasting Corporation (CBC) asked Nordicity Group Ltd. ("Nordicity") to analyse the financial resources provided by governments to public broadcasters in Western countries for a comparison to the CBC. This analysis produced results on a per-capita basis; as well, the results were adjusted based on the relative benefits of public broadcasting in each country. It was noted that while Canada appears to derive a significant benefit from public broadcasting, that public broadcasting in Canada receives substantially less support than it does in most other countries. Based on these results, CBC asked Nordicity to examine whether poor funding of Canadian public broadcasting was indicative of Canada's treatment of its cultural sector overall or whether this was peculiar to Canadian public broadcasting. Nordicity consequently examined federal government support provided to culture in Canada, including that provided to Canada's private broadcasters, using English-language television as an example.

We begin our analysis with an international comparison of levels of public funding for public broadcasters in 18 Western countries including Canada. This comparison of public funding levels is expressed on a per-capita basis. It demonstrates that Canada has one of the lowest levels of public funding for its public broadcaster.

We then refine this population-adjusted comparison to take into account the socio-political environment within each the 18 countries, and the potential benefit that a public broadcaster could bring to each country, in light of this socio-political environment. Certain Western countries, such as the United States (U.S.), may have less potential to derive large benefits from a strongly funded public broadcaster; and so, may require little public funding. In contrast, one could argue that a country such as Switzerland, which has four official languages and borders three large countries with similar languages, can derive greater benefit from a public broadcaster, and therefore should fund public broadcasting accordingly.

In order to assess the potential benefit of public broadcasting in Western countries, we constructed a potential-benefit index to demonstrate the extent to which the potential benefits derived from public broadcasting vary around the world. The index was based on a number of measures that gauge the socio-political environment and structure of the media sector within each country. Among the 18 Western countries in our analysis, Canada was seen as having the potential to derive the greatest benefits from public broadcasting, despite the fact that it has one of the lowest levels of government funding for public broadcasting, among the 18 countries.

As an additional comparison we examined the level of overall support provided to culture in Canada by the federal government. Thus, in the final section of the report, we review trends in the CBC's government appropriation over the last decade and compare it to other areas of federal government spending during the 1995/96-to-2004/05 period. This comparison demonstrates that while the federal government increased its overall program spending, as well as its spending on culture programs, its spending on the CBC actually remained below the 1995/96 level, on both a current- and constant-dollar basis.

1.2 What is Public Broadcasting?

In this report, we analyze the financial support provided by governments for public broadcasting—both in Canada and other Western countries. While the concept of public broadcasting may be fairly well understood, the formulation that it has taken has changed both through time and across geography. At the core, public broadcasting is a form of broadcast communications that serves the social, political and cultural needs of a community—typically defined by national (or regional) borders—without strong influence from either government or commercial interests.

The concept of public broadcasting originated out of the view held by many governments and citizenry at the introduction of broadcast communications in the 1920s and 1930s—a view that it was a public resource to which citizens should have universal access.

Today, with the increasing array of commercial broadcast outlets available to viewers and listeners in Western countries, the role of public broadcasting is to provide media content that is universal in content, universal in access, independent from political and commercial influence, and of high quality.[2]

While the current role of public broadcasting from a conceptual basis may be clearly stated, the actual role and mandate for public broadcasters in Western countries does vary. In the U.S., public broadcasters are an outlet for programming that commercial over-the-air broadcasters will not pursue. In contrast, in the United Kingdom and other European countries, the public broadcaster is considered a public service, akin to public education or public spaces. The public broadcaster is tasked with ensuring that all citizens have access to high-quality programming and the kind of discussion that is central to a well-functioning democracy.

One attribute that all public broadcasters around the world share is that they derive a significant portion of their income from a publicly imposed licence fee or public sources. In many countries, a television licence fee is set by a government body, and is collected either by the government, the broadcaster, or a third party. In other countries, the public funding comes in the form of some direct grant from the government. Our analysis focuses on the amount of public financing that supports public broadcasting and how the amount varies across borders and through time.

2 GOVERNMENT SUPPORT FOR PUBLIC BROADCASTING IN WESTERN COUNTRIES

The last several decades have seen a wave of de-regulation and privatization of media industries in the major Western developed economies. Even in the face of this trend, all Western countries maintain some type of public broadcasting. While this is the case, it is also true that government support for public broadcasting in Western countries varies tremendously from country to country. In this section we present a comparison of the relative levels of government financial support for public broadcasting in Western countries. We do this by way of a comparison of the per-capita levels of public subsidy received by public broadcasters in 18 Western countries, including Canada. We further enhance this international comparison by taking into account the potential benefits that public broadcasting can bring and how these potential benefits also vary across Western countries.

2.1 International Comparison of Government Support for Public Broadcasters

To construct the 18-country comparison, we totalled all amounts of public funding for the public broadcaster(s) in each country. We included all types of funding that were determined by some branch of the government, including licence fees levied on owners of television/radio receivers, government appropriations, and other forms of direct government aid or grants.

The per-capita comparison demonstrates that, among major Western countries, Canada has one of the lowest levels of population-adjusted funding for its public broadcaster. Among 18 Western countries, Canada had the third lowest level of public funding for its public broadcaster (see Figure 1). At $33 per inhabitant (all amounts in Canadian dollars, unless indicated otherwise), Canada's level of funding was only ahead of New Zealand ($20), and the U.S. ($5). We also note that Canada's funding was less than one-half of the $80 average across the 18 Western countries. Canada's level of funding was about one-fifth of the level of Switzerland—the leading country among those included in the comparison—where public funding totalled $154 per capita in 2004.

In preparing the comparison we took into account the fact that government financial support for public broadcasting can take various forms. In Canada, the CBC[3] receives direct government financial support in the form of an annual parliamentary appropriation. In 2004, this appropriation totalled $1,066 billion, or $33 per inhabitant.

The same can be said of Australia. In Australia, the two national public broadcasters, Australian Broadcasting Corporation (ABC) and Special Broadcasting Service (SBS) both receive government financial support in the form of parliamentary appropriations from the Commonwealth of Australia (the federal government). While ABC does not access advertising revenue, SBS does use advertising to supplement its government appropriation. New Zealand's TVNZ is another public broadcaster that receives its government financial support by way of an appropriation or grant. In the case of TVNZ, it

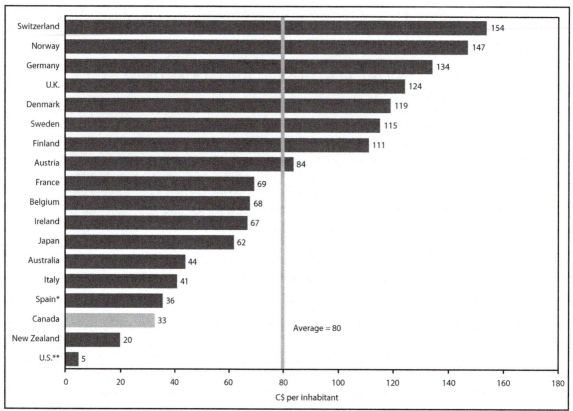

Sources: Public funding data obtained from various sources; see Appendix A for list of data sources. Exchange rates from Bank of Canada. Population data from CIA World Factbook.
* Figures for Spain include an estimate for the public broadcasters of the autonomous regions.
** Data for fiscal year 2003

FIGURE 1   Per capita public funding for public broadcasters, 2004

receives part of its government financial support in the form of direct appropriation, and part through grants from New Zealand On Air—a Crown entity established to support domestic programming in New Zealand.

In the U.S., government appropriation, at both the federal and state levels, is also the main method for supplying government monies to public broadcasters. The federal government provides an annual appropriation to the Corporation for Public Broadcasting (CPB), which in turn, makes financial contributions to public broadcasting through the Public Broadcasting Service (PBS), National Public Radio (NPR), Public Radio International (PRI) and local broadcast stations. The federal government also contributes to public broadcasting through additional grants for education programs delivered by public broadcasters, and certain technology initiatives (such as the transition to digital television). State and local governments also make significant contributions to public broadcasting both directly and indirectly through publicly funded state colleges and other public schools.

Instead of receiving some type of government appropriation, most European public broadcasters collect the bulk of their income by way of a television/radio licence fee levied on users of broadcast receivers. While the licence fee income does not directly come from a government or public body, per se, it is a creation of government regulation or legislation. In effect, the licence fee is imposed by the government. Instead of funding the public broadcaster out of general government revenues, the financial burden is spread across users—that is, households and businesses with broadcast receivers. So, while the method for collecting and remitting the funding for the public broadcaster is different from that in Canada, the substance is the same.

In preparing the comparison, we also took into account the structural differences in public broadcasting in Western countries. In Canada, there is a single national public broadcasting corporation, CBC/Radio Canada, which provides television and radio broadcasting services. In addition to the CBC/Radio Canada, Canada also has five provincial public broadcasters—TVOntario, TéléQuébec, Saskatchewan Communication Network, Knowledge Network (British Columbia) and Access Alberta. The provincial public broadcasters have a tradition of providing largely educational and informational programming; indeed, their broadcast licences from the CRTC require them to televise a certain amount of education programming as part of their schedules. Since our focus is on the CBC and federal government expenditures on Canadian public broadcasting, we have excluded Canada's provincial public broadcasters from the comparison. Had we included these five broadcasters in the analysis, then it would have added another $4 per inhabitant to the CBC's $33 per inhabitant. While this additional amount does increase the public funding picture for Canada's public broadcasters, and provides a more suitable basis for international comparison, it does not have a material impact on the conclusions of the analysis: it does not move Canada very much in ranking among the Western countries included in the comparison. Nevertheless, it is important to note this because in many of the comparison countries the public broadcaster has a wider mandate that often includes public-education objectives similar to Canada's public educational broadcasters.

From the per-capita comparison three distinct country groupings emerge. The first group includes the high-funding nations; those with per-capita funding levels in excess of $100 per inhabitant. The second group is comprised of the medium-funding nations. This group includes those countries with per-capita funding levels of between $60 per inhabitant and $100 per inhabitant. This range includes funding rates that are within plus or minus 20% of the 18-country average of $80 per-inhabitant. The third category includes the Western countries with per-capita funding rates of less than $60 per inhabitant. This third category includes the U.S.; however, with a funding level of $5 per inhabitant, the United States is arguably in a category of its own.

High-Funding Countries

The high-funding category is comprised of seven countries: Switzerland; the Scandinavian nations of Norway, Denmark, Sweden and Finland; Germany; and the U.K. All of the countries in this group appear to follow the European Anglo-Saxon model of public broadcasting. Two of the countries in this group—Germany and Switzerland—have public broadcasting systems which are highly fragmented; this aspect may add to the cost of maintaining the systems.

Under the European Anglo-Saxon model of public broadcasting, there is a strong tradition of ensuring that the public broadcaster remains independent from government and commercial interests.[4] To achieve this, the European governments in this group have put in place systems that give the public broadcasters sufficient funding so that they can easily maintain independence from both government and the influences of the market.[5]

The U.K. is the prime example of the European Anglo-Saxon model.[6] The British Broadcasting Corporation (BBC) has grown to become the world leader in public broadcasting. Over the last several decades, the U.K. government has provided the BBC with the mandate and resources to be an innovator in broadcasting and to build a global brand.

The Scandinavian governments have also followed the European Anglo-Saxon model.[7] Scandinavian governments and citizens have looked to their public broadcasters to make significant contributions to cultural and social development, and democracy within their countries. They have provided their public broadcasters within sufficient resources to fulfill this role, while at the same time maintaining their independence.

Germany's current public broadcasting system emerged following World War II. Germany's system also follows the European Anglo-Saxon model.[8] Another reason for the high levels of funding in Germany may be due to the highly fragmented structure of its public broadcasting system. Under German law, the states (Lander) are responsible for broadcasting. Instead of a single national public broadcaster, there are two national public broadcasting networks, ARD and ZDF, each comprised of several state-level public broadcasters. This regional fragmentation is further compounded by limits on advertising faced by ARD and ZDF.

In Switzerland, the fragmentation of the public broadcasting system is along linguistic lines. In order to serve each of its three major linguistic communities—French, German and Italian—Switzerland has to maintain three public broadcasters. While Switzerland's public broadcasters are under a single corporate umbrella, they produce full program schedules in all three languages. It is interesting to note that even with the highest level of per-capita public funding for public broadcasting, Switzerland's public broadcasters derive about 25% of their revenues from advertising. It appears that high levels of public funding are insufficient to cover the demands of operating in three languages, particularly when three large neighbours—France, Germany and Italy—offer programming in Switzerland's official languages.

Medium-Funding Countries

The medium-funding category is comprised of five countries: Austria, France, Belgium, Ireland, and Japan. While there is no apparent common thread among these countries, some characteristics do start to emerge which make them distinct from the high-funding countries. Except for Japan all the public broadcasters in this group of countries are permitted to access advertising revenue to supplement their public funding. While these countries may aspire to follow the European Anglo-Saxon model, they have either chosen to or been forced to expose their public broadcasters to some commercial influence.

Canada's national public broadcaster also accesses advertising revenue to supplement its public funding. So, in a way the Canadian government has exposed it to some degree of commercial influence. Despite having this characteristic, Canada's public-funding levels are well below the countries in this group.

Within this group of medium-funding countries, governments leverage commercial broadcasters through regulation as an additional means to meet public policy goals. In

TABLE 1   Public Broadcasting and Public Funding Mechanisms in Comparison Countries

COUNTRY	PUBLIC BROADCASTERS	FUNDING SYSTEMS
Australia	ABC (Australian Broadcasting Corporation) SBS (Special Broadcasting Service)	ABC and SBS receive an annual appropriation from the federal government.
Austria	Austrian Broadcasting Company (ORF) • 2 television channels • 4 radio channels	Licence fee
Belgium	VRT—Flemish-language public broadcaster RTBR—French-language public broadcaster	Public funding for RTBR is granted by the Belgium French Community and it covers 75% of the PBS budget. The amount granted by the French community is determined in the management contract stipulated every four years. The VRT mission is linked to the financial envelope granted to it by the Flemish government each year. This financial envelope is laid down in the coordinated media decrees. Further provisos are stipulated in the management contract.
Denmark	DR (Danish Broadcasting Corporation) • 2 television channels • 4 FM radio channels • 16 DAB radio channels	Public funding for DR is the form of a household licence radio/television fee. Parliament sets the licence fee for a four-year period. The proceeds of the licence fee are allocated to DR and TV2. The bulk of the licence fee proceeds go to DR.
Finland	YLE • 2 television channels • Radio services	The government determines the household licence fee. It is collected by the regulatory authority, FICORA.
France	France Télévisions • 3 public television channels • Radio France • Radio France Internationale • Réseau France Outre-mer	Public funding for France's public broadcaster is derived from a television licence fee set by Parliament.
Germany	ZDF ARD	Licence Fees
Ireland	RTE (Irish Public Television) • 2 television channels • 4 radio channels	RTE derives approximately 50% of its revenues from a television licence fee. The government sets the licence fee.
Italy	RAI • 3 television channels • 3 radio channels • International, educational, theme channels	Licence Fees
Japan	NHK	The Broadcast Law requires any person with equipment that can receive NHK broadcasts to pay an receiving-system fee.
New Zealand	TVNZ • 2 television channels	About 10% of TVNZ revenue is derived from contestable funding from New Zealand On Air and direct Charter Specific Government funding

Continued.

TABLE 1	Public Broadcasting and Public Funding Mechanisms in Comparison Countries—cont'd	
COUNTRY	**PUBLIC BROADCASTERS**	**FUNDING SYSTEMS**
Norway	NRK (Norwegian Broadcasting Corporation) ■ 2 television channels ■ 9 radio channels	Public funding for NRK is the form of a household licence radio/television fee. Parliament sets the licence fee.
Spain	RTVE (Radio Televisión Española) ■ operates national public television and radio channels as well as international and theme channels ■ Broadcasters serving the autonomous regions: Telemadrid, TV-3, Canal 33, Canal Sur, Canal 9, TVG, ETB-I, ETB-2.	Television licence fee
Sweden	SVT (Sveriges Television) ■ 2 television channels ■ SR (Sveriges Radio) ■ 4 radio channels ■ UR (Utbildningsradion, Swedish Educational Broadcasting Company)	Public funding for Sweden's three public broadcasters comes from a television licence fee. Parliament decides the size of the licence fee and the allocation among the three public broadcasters. Currently, Sveriges Television receives 58%, Sveriges Radio receives 37%, and UR receives 5%.
Switzerland	SF DRS—Schweizer Fernsehen DRS ■ 3 German-language television channels ■ TSR—Television Suisse Romande ■ 2 French-language television channels ■ TSI—Televisione svizzera di lingua italiana ■ 2 Italian-language channels ■ TvR—Televisiun Rumantscha ■ 1 Romansch-language channel ■ 4 language-based radio networks	Public funding for public broadcasters is derived from a radio/television licence fee.
United Kingdom	BBC S4C	BBC derives its public funding through television licence fees. BBC World Service's income is form a Grant-in-Aid from the Foreign and Commonwealth Office S4C receives annual grant from Department of Culture, Media and Sport
United States	PBS (Public Broadcasting Service) NPR (National Public Radio) PRI (Public Radio International)	PBS, NPR, PRI and other public broadcasters receive government funding through the Corporation for Public Broadcasting (CPB), other federal government grants, state and local governments, state colleges, and public schools.

particular, France has imposed domestic content regulations on commercial broadcasters. This type of approach allows the government to achieve some of its public broadcasting goals outside the public broadcaster, per se.

Once again, Canada has a similar environment; it too uses regulation to leverage commercial broadcasting to meet public policy goals. Nevertheless, its level of public funding for public broadcasting does not put it in this category of countries.

Low-Funding Countries

The low-funding category is comprised of six countries: Australia, Italy, Spain, Canada, New Zealand and the U.S. In several of the low-funding countries, governments have put more reliance on the market to meet the public's broadcast needs. From the introduction of radio broadcasting, the U.S. eschewed government influence in the broadcasting sector; lawmakers looked to commercial broadcasters to satisfy consumers' needs.[9] Though an innovator and leader in many respects, PBS is a modest component of the overall broadcasting system.

Over the last several decades, Canada, Australia and New Zealand have liberalized their broadcast sectors and introduced more privately owned domestic commercial broadcasting. Canada and Australia have also imposed content regulations on commercial broadcasters as a means to achieve some public broadcasting goals outside of the public broadcaster.

In Italy, the public broadcasters operate almost as if they are commercial broadcasters. The RAI channels broadcast the same type of programs as the private broadcasters, and they compete for advertising dollars. Spain is similar to Italy, although in Spain there are several regional public broadcasters representing the autonomous regions, which operate alongside the national public broadcasters. All of them raise income through a mixture of television/radio licence fees and advertising.

In some respects, Italy and Spain can be classified under the Latin model of public broadcasting.[10] Under this model, governments have traditionally underfinanced the public broadcaster, so that it would be financially dependent on the State, and therefore never have *real* independence from the government.[11]

The per-capita comparison, and the categorization of countries on the basis of it, places Canada among a group that either has had low regard for public-broadcaster's independence from the State, or would rather leverage commercial broadcasters to fulfill public policy goals. Either way, these approaches are unlikely to yield the type of innovative public broadcaster that is needed to properly serve Canada's small French-language market and compete with American programming in the English-language market.

2.2 The Potential Benefits of Public Broadcasting

In this section, we further develop the international comparison addressed in the previous section by exploring the potential benefits of public broadcasting. We postulate the potential benefits that a public broadcaster can provide to a country, and rate the 18 Western countries as to how valuable these benefits would be to that country. We then compare each country's rating in this benefits calculation to its per-capita level of public funding for public broadcasting. This comparison helps us identify which Western countries are possibly under-funding their public broadcasters, when the public broadcaster could be delivering substantial benefits in that country's particular socio-political circumstances.

2.2.1 Benefits of a Public Broadcaster

We begin with the assumption that all countries can benefit from public broadcasting—even the U.S.; that there is a role for public broadcasting in the social, political, and cultural life of a country. Our operating assumption is that that role encompasses more than providing infrastructure and services that are not provided by commercial broadcasters.

While the emergence and development of commercial broadcasting may shape the benefits of public broadcasting, they do not replace the public mandate of public broadcasting. Commercial broadcasters may fill many entertainment and other programming needs of a national community; they do not replace the broader role of public broadcasters. We also assume that in Western democracies, public broadcasters have moved away from being a government organ, a role that state-owned broadcasters assumed for some countries in past decades.

As we have described earlier, the role of a public broadcaster does vary somewhat by country, as there are different traditions and different expectations. For example, the following five roles were described by the BBC in its 2004 *Building Public Value* document prepared for its Charter review: (i) democracy, (ii) cultural, (iii) educational, (iv) society/community, and (v) global presence. In Canada, CBC has a relatively similar role in "democracy" (stimulate debate and offer a trusted news source), but does not have an explicit educational role (to some extent taken up by the provincial educational broadcasters), nor the resources to have more than a relatively small global presence role. CBC does have strong cultural and a societal/community roles, though the challenges and the expression of those roles would be different from the BBC.

In contrast in the U.S., PBS carries no responsibility to provide popular entertainment programming; rather, it bills itself as a "public non—profit media enterprise . . . that uses the power of non-commercial television, the Internet and other media to enrich the lives of all Americans through quality programs and education services that inform, inspire and delight."[12] While PBS serves nearly 90 million people per week (through on-air and on-line connection), it is specifically designed to appeal to audiences when they want to be informed and educated (through a range of educational programs) on a range of subjects. It is assumed that private networks and cable channels provide general interest, popular programming of all genres and for various niche audiences—and generate 95+ percent of TV viewing.

As technology drives changes in communications, and radio-listener and television-viewer habits, public broadcasters have adapted to different contexts. They have not adhered to a traditional definition of radio and television.

- In the U.K., the BBC is proposing to redefine itself in terms of the personal communications promise of digital media, i.e., not to be stuck in passive broadcasting. It is assumed that nations will expect their public broadcaster to remain relevant to citizens as the platforms evolve, partly to maintain community in a universe of increasing personalization.
- In the U.S., PBS has assumed a leadership role in digital media. It claims to be one of the most visited dot-org Web sites in the world and the home of comprehensive companion Web sites for more than 1,000 PBS television programs and specials. PBS member stations are digital television leaders, in interactive TV, high-definition programming, and multicast services.

2.2.2 A Framework for Assessing the Potential Benefits of a Public Broadcaster

The benefit of public broadcasting is heightened when the jurisdiction served by the public broadcaster displays certain challenges related to the structure of its media industry, and its social, political and cultural environment.

In this part of the analysis, our goal is to assess which Western countries can benefit most from public broadcasting. Such an assessment requires a broad review of the social, political and cultural environment, as well as the media-industry structure in each country. While this assessment is qualitative in many respects, we have developed a systematic approach. We have selected indicators that we believe are indicative of the relevant socio-political conditions and media-industry structure for each country. For each indicator we use a simple five-grade scale (high to low) for rating each country. As indicated earlier, this approach does not eliminate subjectivity, but it does force a discipline to the ranking of the countries.

There are two broad areas to our assessment: community/social cohesion, and culture and domestic programming. We address each of these below.

Promotion of Culture and a Shared Value System

It is posited that a homogeneous and highly inclusive society would benefit less from public broadcasting than societies with less cohesion where issues can be partly addressed through effective public broadcasting. Public broadcasting can benefit these countries by attempting to bridge some of the gaps through information, education, and by example.

It is difficult to determine which countries would benefit more from public broadcasting on this point, as threats to social cohesion can rise and fall. For example, while France is a very homogeneous country, it has a large Arab minority and less tradition in addressing the needs of minorities than other countries. Canada has a more pluralistic tradition and a more diverse population, but perhaps has a greater tolerance for minorities who may be more easily integrated in Canada. Canada may very well benefit from an effective public broadcaster that can contribute to ensuring social cohesion; however, some European countries may benefit even more urgently because of their difficulties in addressing issues raised by minorities in this way. One could argue that Western European countries benefit from public broadcasting because it can facilitate more effective integration of minorities in their societies—more so than Canada. However, Canada is composed of a far more diverse population that is growing rapidly in its diversity—so can also benefit greatly from a public broadcaster.

The development of community and social cohesion through communications requires an infrastructure to deliver messages. Broadcasting is an efficient medium for this activity; it reaches a large community simultaneously, but it does require a significant and sometime costly communication infrastructure. Commercial broadcasters with goals to maximize profit will often not commit to constructing an infrastructure which reaches the whole population; a public broadcaster is one avenue for overcoming these economic limitations.

Canada's relatively sparse population strung out along the U.S. border would seem to indicate that a public broadcaster with government financial backing would be very beneficial because it could shoulder the economic burden of the infrastructure requirements brought on by geography. This includes not only the physical infrastructure, but also the organizational infrastructure to deliver regional or local programming, in two official languages and sometimes more. A well-established communications infrastructure enables individual and mass communication, but public broadcasting provides the content and leadership in national discourse. We considered this category an important one in which to rate Canada versus other countries.

Accordingly, in developing our assessment of the relative benefit that a public broadcaster could bring in terms of community/social cohesion, we considered the following criterion, whose attributes reflect the geographic, social, cultural and political environment. It incorporates indicators related to population density and dispersion, the number of broadcasting languages, and cultural diversity and national unity.

- **Promotion of culture and common values**
  - A lower population density suggests an environment in which a public broadcaster would have to absorb the costs of building and maintaining an infrastructure offering universal coverage of the population. Even with satellite transmission now available, CBC has had to build an enormous terrestrial infrastructure, and operate in five time zones.
  - As noted earlier, countries with large ethnic populations, in theory, face more challenges to social cohesion than countries with more homogeneous populations. In practice, it is more complicated, since some countries have more problems arising from a small ethnic population than other countries more experienced in accommodating multiple cultures.

Creation and Availability of Cultural/Indigenous Programming
Another role or benefit of public broadcasting is that it can contribute, in part, to protecting and strengthening a country's culture, i.e., that which is expressed in radio and television formats (and other platforms). It could be argued that the benefit is greatest where foreign television broadcasters or foreign television programming attracts large audiences versus the audiences for domestic programming. By this criterion, English-language countries face enormous challenges in terms of a public broadcaster attracting audiences in competition with American programming exported the world over. Switzerland, Belgium, Ireland and Austria face similar challenges because they share languages with larger neighbours.

To measure the relative potential benefit, we reviewed Western countries in terms of the relative size of the domestic language market, proximity of a much larger country with strong programming, as well as the record of domestic broadcasters in terms of audience appeal for indigenous versus foreign programming. Accordingly, the criteria for assessing the relative potential benefit of public broadcasting for culture and domestic programming rationale are the following:

- **Relative size of the domestic language market**—In comparison to most manufacturing or service industries, the broadcasting industry is characterized by relatively high sunk and fixed costs of operation, and relatively low incremental costs. The high sunk costs arise largely from the unrecoverable investment that must be made to create broadcast programming. The high fixed costs arise largely from the broadcast infrastructure (e.g., production studios, transmission facilities) that must be acquired or constructed to reach the first viewer. The incremental cost of reaching the second and subsequent viewers is relatively low in comparison to other the costs involved in broadcasting. Because of these economics, broadcasting to a larger audience can be much more economical for a broadcaster; it can realize lower average costs by spreading the sunk and fixed costs over a larger audience base. Countries with relatively small populations may require more government intervention in broadcasting. The small broadcasting market may not attract enough private-sector investment into the production and broadcasting of domestic program content. Domestic viewers, thus, end up receiving relatively less domestic content. Countries with relatively low populations, then, can benefit from a public broadcaster that is not compelled to realize commercial returns on sunk and fixed investments.

- **Proximity to a large larger country with the same language**—It is contended that large and powerful border countries with significant media sectors generating television services in the same language pose a greater threat to indigenous culture. A strong public broadcaster can provide relatively more of benefit in such situations, by providing a continuous stream of television programming in multiple programming categories. A subset of this indicator would be countries whose populations are primarily English speaking. While not necessarily bordering the US as in the case of Canada, these countries are subject to the same dominant English language television programming emanating from the US.
- **Audience appeal of indigenous programming**—Any dominance by foreign programming can be determined through a review of audience tuning to domestic vs. international programming. The greater the tuning to foreign programming, the greater the potential benefit of a public broadcaster that can devote a large share (or all of) its airtime to exhibiting indigenous programming. Of course, the mere exhibition of indigenous programming does not in itself create a benefit, as the programming must be of sufficient quality and audience appeal to be competitive with the foreign programming.

2.2.3 Assessment of Environment for Public Broadcasting

We undertook basic research of some 18 countries to compare them to Canada along the following four criteria and associated indicators. For each indicator we were able to obtain specific data in order to establish the scale for a relative scoring for each country.

Based on these four criteria, we rated each country against six different indicators on a five-point scale. The details of the scoring systems and the data used to derive the scores are presented in Appendix B. In summary:

- A rating of **high** and a numerical score of **five** was assigned when the indicators pointed to an environment where a public broadcaster could potentially generate relatively high benefits to its citizens.
- A rating of **medium** and a numerical score of **three** was assigned when the indicators pointed to an environment where a public broadcaster could potentially generate a relatively moderate level of benefits.
- A rating of **low** and a numerical score of **one** was assigned when the indicators pointed to an environment where a public broadcaster could generate a relatively modest benefit.

Countries could also obtain scores of two or four.

We did not weight the indicators or the criteria in terms of level of importance, and recognize that not doing so is somewhat arbitrary. Nevertheless, this approach provides

TABLE 2   Potential-benefits Analysis Criteria and Indicators

CRITERIA	INDICATORS
1. Promotion of culture and common values	<ul><li>Population density</li><li>Number of broadcasting languages—number of official languages broadcast by the public broadcasting services (note: must be rough equivalency in broadcast, not just occasional minority programming broadcast)</li><li>Ethnic-diversity challenges (third-party risk ratings)</li></ul>
2. Relative size of domestic language market	<ul><li>Population of country or population of various official language groups within a single country</li></ul>
3. Proximity to a large larger country with the same language	<ul><li>Countries bordering countries of similar language with a much larger economy</li><li>Countries whose mother tongue is English (which are subject to greater pressure from American programming, even if not bordering on the U.S.)</li></ul>
4. Audience appeal of indigenous programming	<ul><li>The number of indigenous programs' among the top ten programs</li></ul>

TABLE 3   Scoring of Environment for Public Broadcasting Benefits

COUNTRY	AGGREGATE RATING (MAXIMUM POINTS OF 30)	COUNTRY	AGGREGATE RATING (MAXIMUM POINTS OF 30)
Canada	23	Finland	14
Switzerland	20	Sweden	14
New Zealand	20	Denmark	11
Australia	18	France	11
Belgium	18	U.K.	11
Ireland	18	Germany	9
Austria	17	Italy	9
Norway	15	U.S.	9
Spain	15	Japan	7

Source: Nordicity analysis

a systematic basis for gauging and comparing each country's environment, and thereby the relative benefit that public broadcasting could bring to the country.

In the table above, we report the aggregate score for each country across the four criteria and six indicators. A higher score indicates that the environment is such that a broadcaster could potentially deliver relatively large benefits. A lower score indicates that the environment is such that a public broadcaster is likely to deliver relatively lower benefits in comparison to other countries. The maximum possible score is 30.

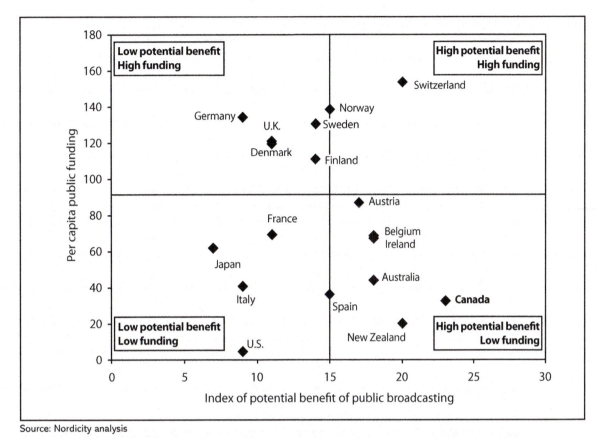

Source: Nordicity analysis

FIGURE 2   Comparison of potential benefit and funding of public broadcasting

The analysis shows that:

- Among the 18 countries included in the analysis, Canada stands to benefit the most from public broadcasting, according to this evaluation. It obtained a score of 23 out of a possible 30 points.
- Other countries that are positioned to realize relatively high benefits from public broadcasting include Switzerland, New Zealand, Australia, Belgium, Ireland, and Austria. They obtained scores of between 17 and 20.
- The next group of countries—with scores of between 11 and 15—are: Norway, Spain, Finland, Denmark, France, and the U.K.
- The final group with the lowest scores (seven to nine) are: Germany, Italy, U.S. and Japan.

Based on the aggregation of these qualitative ratings, we positioned each country along a potential-benefit axis in a two-by-two grid. This allowed us to graphically compare the potential benefits of a public broadcaster to the existing relative level of per-capita government funding provided to the public broadcaster. The resulting plot shows Canada with an environment that is likely to generate relative high potential benefits from public broadcasting. The plot also shows that, despite this high potential for benefits, Canada has one of the lowest levels of government financial support for public broadcasting.

3 THE FEDERAL GOVERNMENT'S ECONOMIC SUPPORT FOR CULTURE

In the previous section we compared the federal government's financial support for the CBC to levels of public financial support provided through public subsidy in other Western countries. In this section, we examine the Canadian federal government's overall economic support for culture in Canada. As part of this examination we consider both direct and indirect forms of economic support.

The federal government provides direct economic support for culture by way of grants and contributions, and other direct program expenditures related to Canada's culture and heritage. The Department of Canadian Heritage oversees the vast majority of these expenditures. They include funding and tax-based support provided to the CBC, Telefilm Canada, Canadian Television Fund, Canada Council for the Arts, museums and art galleries, movable cultural property, Library and Archives Canada, and other programs and agencies with mandates to preserve, promote and develop Canadian culture.

The federal government also provides indirect economic support to Canada's cultural sector through policies and regulations derived from various legislative authori-

TABLE 4 CBC/Radio Canada Annual Appropriations (current and constant 1995 dollars)		
FISCAL YEAR	**CBC/RADIO CANADA'S TOTAL GOVERNMENT APPROPRIATION, OPERATING, CAPITAL, AND WORKING CAPITAL**	
	CURRENT DOLLARS ($ MILLIONS)	**CONSTANT 1995 DOLLARS ($ MILLIONS)**
1995/96	1,171	1,171
1996/97	997	981
1997/98	806	772
1998/99	896	859
1999/00	879	828
2000/01	902	828
2001/02	983	880
2002/03	1,047	917
2003/04	1,066	908

Source: CBC Annual Reports; and Statistics Canada (CPI, Catalogue 62–001-XPB, table 4)
Notes:
1. Appropriations for 1995–96 include $106 million in funding for downsizing.
2. Beginning in 2003–04 appropriations include RCI; for the years 1991–92 through 2002–03 RCI was paid by contract and is therefore not included.

ties. Two measures in particular provide significant indirect economic benefit to Canada's private broadcasters. One of these measures is the CRTC's policy of simultaneous substitution; the other is section 19.1 of the *Income Tax Act*.

First, we review the different components of federal-government support for culture. We begin with CBC's annual parliamentary appropriation—its main source of income. We then use data from Statistics Canada to construct a time series of the federal government's other direct financial support for culture. We also derive estimates of the annual financial impact of the federal government's indirect economic support measures for television broadcasters. We address, separately, the indirect support garnered by private broadcasters and the CBC.

We conclude this section by comparing the trends in CBC's annual support (direct and indirect) to the trends in the federal government's overall spending, its other direct support for culture, and the financial impact of its indirect support for private broadcasters.

3.1 Components of Government Support for Culture

3.1.1 CBC's Parliamentary Appropriation

Each year, the CBC receives a financial appropriation from the federal government to finance its operations, capital improvements, and working-capital requirements. While the CBC does earn advertising and subscriber revenues from some of its broadcast services, the government appropriation represents its largest single source of income.

Between 1995/96 and 2003//04, the CBC experienced a significant swing in its annual government appropriation levels. In the 1995/96 fiscal year, the CBC's government appropriation totalled $1,171 million. Over the next two fiscal years, it dropped by 31% to $806 million in 1997/98.

Between 1997/98 and 2003/04, the CBC saw its government appropriation make some recovery; however by 2003/04, the total amount of the appropriation was still 9% below the 1995/96 level.

The drop in the appropriation is even larger when viewed in terms of constant dollars.

3.1.2 Other Federal Government Direct Expenditures on Culture and Heritage

In addition to the monies provided to the CBC, the federal government makes other direct expenditures on operations and programs related to culture. In order to assess the federal government's expenditures in this area, we examined Statistics Canada figures for federal government expenditures on culture. For the purposes of comparison with the CBC, we deducted the CBC's annual appropriation from the federal government's total culture expenditures to arrive at a time series for all other culture expenditures.

Between 1995/96 and 2003/04, the federal government's total expenditures on culture increased by 20%, from $2,920 million to $3,500 million. Because the CBC's annual appropriation comprises such a large share of the federal government's expenditures on culture, it is better to compare the CBC to all other culture expenditures. Between 1995/96 and 2003/04, the federal government's other expenditures on culture (excluding the CBC) increased by 39%, from $1,749 million to $2,433 million. Evidently,

TABLE 5 Federal Government Expenditures on Culture						
FISCAL YEAR	FEDERAL GOVERNMENT EXPENDITURES ON CULTURE		CBC GOVERNMENT APPROPRIATION		FEDERAL GOVERNMENT EXPENDITURES ON CULTURE (EXCLUDING CBC)	
	$ MILLIONS	% CHANGE	$ MILLIONS	% CHANGE	$ MILLIONS	% CHANGE
1995/96	2,920	—	1,171	—	1,749	—
1996/97	2,760	(5.5%)	997	(14.8%)	1,763	0.8%
1997/98	2,670	(3.3%)	806	(19.1%)	1,864	5.7%
1998/99	2,817	5.5%	896	11.2%	1,921	3.1%
1999/00	2,809	(0.3%)	879	(1.9%)	1,930	0.5%
2000/01	2,954	5.2%	902	2.6%	2,053	6.3%
2001/02	3,216	8.9%	983	9.0%	2,234	8.8%
2002/03	3,426	6.5%	1,047	6.5%	2,379	6.5%
2003/04	3,500	2.2%	1,066	1.9%	2,433	2.3%
Increase/(decrease) 1995/96 to 2003/04	580	19.9%	(105)	(9.1%)	684	39.1%

Source: Figures for federal government expenditures on culture are from Statistics Canada; figures for CBC government appropriation are from CBC.

after one strips out the effect of the CBC parliamentary appropriation, the data show that the federal government's culture expenditures rose, for the most part, consistently between 1995/96 and 2004/04. Federal government expenditures made through the CBC, however, dropped sharply during the mid-1990s before posting somewhat of a recovery.

REFERENCES AND DATA SOURCES

British Broadcasting Corporation. *Building public value: Renewing the BBC for a digital world*. June 2004. Available at http://www.bbc.co.uk.

Council of Europe. *Public service broadcasting*. Report to the Committee on Culture Science and Education. January 12, 2004. Available at: http://assembly.coe.int/Main.asp?link=/Documents/WorkingDocs/Doc04/EDOC10029.htm.

Donner, Arthur and Fred Lazar. *An Examination of the Financial Impacts of Canada's 1976 Amendment to Section 19.1 of the Income Tax Act (Bill C-58) on U.S. and Canadian Broadcasters*. Department of Communication. January 1979.

Donner, Arthur and Mel Kilman. *Television Advertising and the Income Tax Act: An Economic Analysis of Bill C-58*. Prepared for the Department of Communications, November 1983.

Donner, Arthur. *An Analysis of the Importance of U.S. Television Spillover, Bill C-58 and Simulcasting Policies for the Revenues of Canadian TV Broadcasters.* Taskforce on Broadcasting. February 1986 (mimeograph).

Donner, Arthur. *The Financial Impacts of Section 19.1 of the Income Tax Act (Bill C-58) and Simultaneous Substitution.* Her Majesty the Queen in Right of Canada as represented by the Minister of Communications. 1990.

Donner, Arthur and Fred Lazar. *Cable, Canadian Program Production and the Information Highway.* Discussion paper prepared for the CCTA. August 1994.

Donner, Arthur and Fred Lazar. *The Financial Effects of Simulcasting on Canadian TV Broadcasters.* June 1997.

Grant, Peter and Chris Wood. *Blockbusters and Trade Wars: Popular Culture in a Globalized World.* Toronto: Douglas & McIntyre, 2004.

Endnotes

1. In this section we have reverted to single-year denominations, e.g., 1996, to account for different year-ends for federal government financial statistics and broadcasting sector statistics. The former have a March 31 year-end; the latter have an August 31 year-end. The term 1996 refers to statistics form the government fiscal and broadcasting years ending in 1996.
2. Council of Europe, *Public service broadcasting,* Report to the Committee on Culture Science and Education, January 12, 2004, para. 12.
3. In addition to the CBC, Canada also has five provincial public broadcasters. We address these public broadcasters later in this section of the report.
4. Council of Europe, para. 31.
5. *Ibid.*
6. *Ibid.*
7. *Ibid,* para. 33.
8. Council of Europe, para 31.
9. Peter Grant and Chris Wood, *Blockbusters and Trade Wars: Popular Culture in a Globalized World,* Toronto: Douglas & McIntyre, 2004, p. 176.
10. Council of Europe, para. 32.
11. Council of Europe, para 32.
12. PBS Web site

DISCUSSION

Nordicity Group, *Analysis of Government Support for Public Broadcasting and Other Culture in Canada.*

1. Compare the funding levels per inhabitant for public broadcasting shown in the first table in the Nordicity study. From what you know about the countries with the highest amount of funding (Sweden), and the lowest amount (US), suggest some reasons for this wide range of government support for public ownership of media.
2. In your own words, sum up what you think are the most important attributes of public broadcasting in all the countries that have this type of media.

3. The Nordicity study creates a framework for conducting a 'benefits assessment' of public broadcasting. What two broad areas does the framework look at and what are the six specific indicators that it uses to rank each of the 18 countries that were compared?

4. According to this study, Canada is the country likely to benefit most from public broadcasting. How did Canada rank on the six indicators used? Do you think this is a fair and accurate assessment of how public broadcasting can promote social cohesion and develop and support domestic cultural content? If you were to revise this study what other criteria might you consider?

Primary Sources: Media in the Public Interest
Policy Source 7
Canadian Broadcasting Corporation. (2007). *Public broadcasting in Canada: Time for a new approach*. Submission to the Standing Committee on Canadian Heritage. Retrieved from http://www.cbc.radio-canada.ca/submissions/pdf/Mandate.pdf

Public Broadcasting in Canada: Time for a New Approach

Submission to the Standing Committee on Canadian Heritage

Presented by Mr. Robert Rabinovitch
President and CEO
March 22, 2007

"Neither commercial nor State-controlled, public broadcasting's only raison d'être is public service. It is the public's broadcasting organization; it speaks to everyone as a citizen. Public broadcasters encourage access to and participation in public life. They develop knowledge, broaden horizons and enable people to better understand themselves by better understanding the world and others.

Public broadcasting is defined as a meeting place where all citizens are welcome and considered equals. It is an information and education tool, accessible to all and meant for all, whatever their social or economic status. Its mandate is not restricted to information and cultural development—public broadcasting must also appeal to the imagination, and entertain. But it does so with a concern for quality that distinguishes it from commercial broadcasting."

—World Television and Radio Council, May 2001:
Public Broadcasting: Why? How?

Why Canada Needs a National Public Broadcaster

In the 1930s, US-based radio networks expanded quickly into Canada. The cultural influence of predominantly American programming became a source of apprehension for many. How could Canadians maintain an independent and distinct cultural identity if their cultural programming was American? Canadians chose public broadcasting, and the Government of Canada created CBC/Radio-Canada to ensure a Canadian space in the new broadcast age.

Today, Canadians face the same questions of culture and identity. Programming content from the world over is available to Canadians on countless platforms: a new world of choice is in their hands. At the same time, Canadians have become increasingly diverse, with diverse interests and values. The cultural challenge facing Canada is immense.

If Canada believes that it is important for its citizens to have universal access to distinctive content created by, for and about Canadians, then expectations of what public broadcasting is have to evolve. It is less about what Parliament can do for CBC/Radio-Canada than it is about what the public broadcaster, working with Parliament, can do for Canada and for the benefit of Canadians.

Indeed, some argue that the need for public broadcasting has diminished in this new digital age. Yet, significant questions and issues remain:

- How do we nurture a strong Canadian cultural identity in a sea of global content?
- How do we ensure that Canadians are not only exposed to the world and the reality of globalization, but that they also have access to a Canadian perspective on it?
- How do we sustain opportunities for national, regional and local expression?
- How do we promote social cohesion and shared values in an ever-more diverse society?
- How do we encourage engaged discussion and debate that advances common democratic principles?
- Given that storytelling, especially drama, is the single most pervasive catalyst of popular culture, how do we create a critical mass of drama that is first-rate and inimitably Canadian?

A CHANGING CULTURAL AND INDUSTRIAL CONTEXT

The role of public broadcasting in Western nations is generally to provide content that is universal in access; diverse in scope; independent from both political and commercial influence; and, distinctive in its offering and quality. It is to be a broadcaster that treats its audience as citizens to be served, not simply as consumers.

In Canada, the challenge of serving citizens is complicated by the fact that Canada has one of the most diverse populations in the world. It is an open and tolerant society that encourages the free flow of political and cultural ideas. And it inhabits the single most competitive broadcasting environment on the planet, bordering on the most powerful and successful exporter of popular culture the world has ever known. All these traits are sources of strength and potential only so long as we maintain the things that make us distinct.

Even more than in 1932, when R. B. Bennett's Government first articulated the need for a public broadcaster, CBC/Radio-Canada is interconnected with Canada's democratic, social and cultural needs. Public broadcasting offers a unique value proposition as an effective instrument of Canadian public policy in a mixed public and private broadcasting system.

Improving Democratic and Cultural Life in Canada

While there is a tendency to focus on technology and consumer choice in the digital era, there is also a need to explore the bigger questions, particularly underlying issues of democracy and culture.

How people experience democracy and culture has changed a great deal in the last decade. Public broadcasting helps to give form to people's experience of intangible concepts like informed citizenry; national identity; and the reflection of diversity in its many forms, be it geographic, ethnic, cultural, or communities of interest.

If culture matters, then broadcasting matters, since television is still the most pervasive cultural medium and radio still has the broadest reach. Moreover, with the rise of globalization and its inherent challenges, Canadians need a reliable, credible and trusted source of home-grown content that is free from commercial and political interest.

A national public broadcaster that is mandated to reflect the full spectrum of opinion and perspectives is a guarantor that various views are shared among Canadians, in turn helping them to form their self-, social and political identities.

Diversity, Fragmentation and Social Cohesion

The need to create coherence in a fragmenting world is a second daunting test for policymakers around the world. When broadcasters speak of fragmentation, it is usually about audiences, diminishing advertising revenues and the resulting strain on media business models. But, culturally speaking, the concern is weightier than that.

A deeper, more meaningful social, political and religious fragmentation has come to pass around the world. It is due in part to the cumulative effects of globalization, shifting immigration patterns, and global instability and insecurity. These changes are causing a profound transformation in the political and social fabric—no less in Canada than in other countries—which poses some important questions about the role of the media in general, and public broadcasting in particular. In this context, the public broadcaster can be seen as a vehicle for cultural identity and social cohesion.

It is not easy to offset fragmentation and embrace diversity at the same time. A public broadcaster is, however, uniquely positioned to do just that. A public broadcaster can create community-building spaces that serve as a buffer against fragmentation. These same spaces can also facilitate interaction and dialogue among different communities locally, regionally, nationally, and internationally.

Public broadcasting also ensures the availability of places where large numbers of Canadians can gather to share in important national moments. A healthy and relevant public broadcaster is able to foster a broad sense of belonging and national pride. It is one of the few means at our disposal to connect Canadians with each other, with this country and with the world.

Delivering on Public Policy Objectives and Priorities

Democracy and culture are important, and Canada must ensure that it has the means to deliver on its public policy goals in this area. Where the laws of the market alone will not achieve those goals, other mechanisms need to be found. In broadcasting, only a mixed system, whose success is based on striking the right balance between private and public media outlets, and having strong partnerships, can make the achievement of those goals feasible.

It is no secret that the broadcasting industry is in the midst of upheaval. Consolidation has created an industry dominated by a handful of well-funded private companies that offer a wide range of services, but a narrow spectrum of perspectives. Meanwhile, audiences are disintegrating. The visibility and usage of existing and new services lessens as a result, which dilutes the advertising value of broadcasting time. Revenues diminish as audience size shrinks, resulting in less money to fund programming. The existing threat to revenue streams for conventional broadcasters is a stark reality. The funding available for television production is no longer sufficient to sustain this most popular programming format.

As the environment in which we operate shifts and the business models upon which we depend become more and more unreliable, there is an escalating need to consider how best to bring the system back into balance. And strength of the Canadian system hinges on a robust national public broadcaster, since there are some things that private broadcasters either cannot or will not do, but that a public broadcaster can and will do.

For example, CBC/Radio-Canada provides:

- Content that is predominantly Canadian and distinctive;
- Programming that establishes and maintains connections in the North and other remote parts of the country;
- Commercial-free, safe, entertaining programming for kids;
- Original Current Affairs programming;
- A full-bodied Canadian perspective on international events;
- Comprehensive coverage of federal and provincial elections;
- Amateur sports programming;
- High-culture programming;
- Robust content created specifically for new immigrants to Canada;
- Nation-building dramatic and documentary programming;
- The ability to communicate to all Canadians in an emergency; and,
- A substantial amount of Canadian programming in prime time on television.

With respect to the attributes to which a public broadcaster's content should aspire, no single program or piece of content can be all things to all people on all platforms. But, individual programs and content should speak to one or more of the eight following descriptors, recognizing that few would realistically speak to all:

- Canadian: it should contribute to shared national consciousness and identity by serving cultural and societal needs, diversity of audience and perspective;
- Distinctive: it should stand out from what is provided by the private sector;
- Intelligent/Challenging: it should make audiences think and it should stimulate debate;
- Entertaining: it should aspire to be engaging, fascinating, even funny;
- Inspiring Trust: it should inspire confidence in the integrity of the source;
- Rassembleur (a place of shared experience): it should provide a focal point for large numbers of Canadians to share common experiences;
- Reflecting our Communities: it should reflect Canada and its regions and reflect the multicultural and multiracial nature of Canada; and,
- Innovative: it should present new ideas and invent exciting approaches.

Relative Value of Public Broadcasting

The question of why Canada needs a public broadcaster warrants an analysis of the relative value of public broadcasting in Canada compared to other Western nations. In late

2005, Nordicity Group Ltd. was commissioned by CBC/Radio-Canada to analyze the financial resources provided by governments to public broadcasters in Western countries, including Canada; and, to assess the relative value of public broadcasting in Canada vis-à-vis other Western nations.

This comparative analysis called for a broad, methodical review of the social, political and cultural environments, as well as the structures of the media industry in each country. It focused on four criteria: promotion of culture and common values; relative size of domestic language market; proximity to a larger country with the same language; and audience appeal of indigenous programming.

Among the 18 countries included in the analysis, Canada stands to benefit the most of all from public broadcasting. Canada's need is the greatest. At the same time, the per-capita comparison demonstrates that at just over $30, Canada had the third-lowest level of public funding for its national public broadcaster in 2004 among 18 major Western countries and was less than one half of the $80 average.

Value for Money of Public Broadcasting

Finally, the value for money invested in public broadcasting also figures prominently in any discussion of public broadcasting. Justifiably, no taxpayer would choose to invest in institutions, however important they might be, that do not spend their money responsibly. Public broadcasters around the world have recognized this fact in the face of financial constraints, an economically strained conventional business model, and mounting inflationary pressures. All have consequently taken strides to operate more efficiently—none more so than CBC/Radio-Canada.

For just over $30 each per year, Canadians enjoy a unique, distinctive and comprehensive offering from their public broadcaster. With 28 services offered on Radio, Television, the Internet, satellite radio, digital audio, as well as through its record and music distribution service and wireless WAP and SMS messaging services, CBC/Radio-Canada is available how, where and when Canadians want it.

Through this array of activities, CBC/Radio-Canada brings diverse regional and cultural perspectives into the daily lives of Canadians in English, French and eight Aboriginal languages, in nine languages on its international Radio service, RCI, and in eight languages on its Web-based Radio service, RCI viva, designed for recent and aspiring immigrants to Canada.

A NEW CONTRACT

So, if it is clear why Canadians need a public broadcaster, then the next step is to ensure that the public broadcaster provides the service Canadians need. For over a decade, CBC/Radio-Canada has tried to do this while hampered by: a lack of consensus on its role in a rapidly changing environment; a lack of stability in the resources required to fill that role; and, a lack of opportunity for Canadians to clearly state what they expect from their public broadcaster.

A new context, both cultural and industrial, calls for a new contract. We believe that the challenges of the future demand a new approach: a contract between the national public broadcaster and the citizens it serves. Other countries have followed a similar path. Following mandate reviews that involved widespread consultation, similar agreements have been put in place with public broadcasters in Ireland, Hong Kong and South Africa. And in Britain, the Government has just concluded a new Royal Charter, which spells out the expectations of the BBC and the resources it will receive, for the next ten years.

In Canada, a new contract would provide clear expectations of what Canadians could expect from their national public broadcaster in return for the public funding they provide.

There are many questions about the kind of public broadcaster Canadians need for the future, and this Committee's current review of the mandate of CBC/Radio-Canada is an important first step in finding the answers. We would suggest, however, that there are some fundamental principles which must be maintained in order to ensure its continued success. Most of these are common to public broadcasters around the world.

Principles

Mixed Public/Private System

Since the outset, the Canadian broadcasting system has recognized the unique strengths of both public and private components. Together they provide Canadians with a range of services they could not get without this partnership. The industry includes an extensive range of players—broadcasters, independent producers, distributors, etc.—each of which makes a central contribution to the system's success and vitality.

Programming Independence

Crucial to the very definition of a public broadcaster is its independence. History is full of examples of state broadcasters whose content is controlled by government—who serve government and not its citizens. Public broadcasting is a cornerstone of freedom of expression—a space where ideas are expressed freely, and where information and opinions circulate unencumbered. An arm's length relationship between the state and the public broadcaster is deeply rooted and is essential to the broadcaster's survival and its ability to serve its citizens.

Distinctiveness

Public broadcasting's content must offer a quality and character that sets it apart from other providers. Distinctiveness not only includes services, content, and both audiences and subjects neglected by others; it also means doing things differently. A broad definition of distinctiveness ensures that public broadcasting is inclusive and innovative, and that it sets high standards in content quality. CBC/Radio-Canada's programming should be overwhelmingly Canadian.

Accessibility and Ability to Serve All Canadians

If a public broadcaster is to serve its citizens, it must be able to reach them, where, when and how the audience chooses. It is no longer sufficient to be only a television and radio company. Canadians will choose their programming on television, radio, the Internet, on satellite radio, on mobile devices, as well as via new technologies just being developed. Public broadcasting is the content; the platform is only the means of ensuring that Canadians have access to it. These platforms not only ensure that content reaches new generations of Canadians, but that the diverse stories, perspectives and voices from Canada's regions and communities have a place where they can be seen and heard.

Resources to Meet Requirements

A fundamental principle that underpins any contract is that it sets out the explicit obligations of each party subject to it. In this case, CBC/Radio-Canada would be provided with resources and would, in turn, undertake to provide specific services. The noblest goals for public broadcasting mean nothing without the resources necessary to fulfill them. A broadcaster stretched too thinly serves no one well. We believe a new contract must build a consensus with Canadians, not only on the expectations for the public broadcaster, but also on sufficient resources to fulfill those expectations. In short, it must be a contract.

DISCUSSION

Canadian Broadcasting Corporation. (2007). *Public broadcasting in Canada: Time for a new approach. Submission to the Standing Committee on Canadian Heritage, 22 March 2007.*

1. What aspects of changing cultural and industrial contexts for public broadcasting are outlined in the CBC presentation to the Standing Committee on Canadian Heritage?
2. Why does the CBC presentation suggest that social fragmentation is increasing around the world? How can public broadcasting help offset these trends?
3. What specific features of CBC program content does the report list? Visit the CBC website at CBC.ca and the CTV television network site at CTV.ca and look at examples of news programs and drama or entertainment programming. How does CBC programming differ from that on CTV and what are its most distinctive attributes?
4. From your review of programming on the CBC, can you find concrete examples of how the public broadcaster provides a shared experience for Canadians and reflects Canadian communities?
5. What key principles does the CBC report propose as part of a 'new contract' for public broadcasting? Do you agree that in order to fulfill these principles the CBC should be assured of sufficient resources to support its services? By whom and how should these resources be determined?

Policy Source 8

National Film Board of Canada. (2010). *Emerging and digital media: Opportunities and challenges, presentation to the House of Commons Standing Committee on Canadian Heritage, 29 April 2010*. Retrieved from http://www.onf-nfb.gc.ca/medias/download/documents/pdf/publications/NFB-ONF_Presentation_10–04–29.pdf

Emerging and Digital Media: Opportunities and Challenges Standing Committee On Canadian Heritage By The National Film Board Of Canada

29 April 2010

Good morning, Mr. Chairman and members of the Committee.

I am very pleased to appear before you again on behalf of the National Film Board (NFB). My name is Tom Perlmutter and I am the Government Film Commissioner and Chair of the NFB. With me today are Claude Joli-Coeur, the Assistant Film Commissioner, and Deborah Drisdell, Director General of Accessibility and Digital Enterprises.

The NFB is a federal cultural agency, established in 1939, to produce and distribute original audiovisual works that are creatively innovative and contribute to Canadians' understanding of the issues facing our country and raise awareness of Canadian viewpoints around the world. Over a 70-year period the NFB has become Canada's best known cinematic brand. Last year on the occasion of our 70th anniversary we were fêted in China, Brazil, Japan, France, England, and Ireland among many other countries. In the past week alone I have received requests for partnerships from Malaysia, Korea, Singapore and Columbia. The value of the NFB brand for Canada is immeasurable.

Today, in a rich and diverse audio-visual world, the NFB remains distinct as a creative laboratory, a leader in exploring terrain that cannot be undertaken by the private sector, a voice for underrepresented Canadians, a prime means to assure the vitality of a francophone culture and, not least, one of Canada's leading pioneers in the digital realm. The latter is playing a crucial role in many of the international requests for partnership that I mentioned above.

The digital revolution is seismic. Today we are focusing on its impact on the cultural industries but it is important to bear in mind that the reach of this revolution is much broader. It touches everything: how we organize our lives personally, socially, economically, politically, and culturally. It is a revolution which, in its impact and its consequences, is as profound, if not more so, than the industrial revolution of the late 18th and 19th centuries.

Consider that worldwide over 1 billion users are now connected to the Internet—close to 20% of the planet. 20% of all human beings. Connected. Across borders. Across languages. Across cultures. And that number grows daily. The impact of mobile will be even more profound because of its ability to penetrate where landlines and electricity are not widely available. I traveled through some remote parts of Africa last summer and was astonished at the extent to which cell towers proliferated where there was little else in the way of infrastructure.

In Canada we are among the most avid users of digital technology. According to the Comscore 2009 report[1], the digital media universe in Canada has grown 11 percent over the past three years. On average there are more than 24.5 million Canadians online each month—among the world's highest Internet usage rates. In March of this year Ipsos reported that for the first time ever in their tracking research, the weekly Internet usage of online Canadians has moved ahead of the number of hours spent watching television. Crucially, Canadians are also the greatest consumers of video on line. Total videos streamed grew 123% in 2009 versus a year earlier—a monthly average of 263 videos per viewer.

Time spent watching online video surged even more dramatically with a 169% increase. By the end of 2009, the average unique viewer was spending 20.6 hours per month watching video. While YouTube accounted for the largest share at 30%, significant growth also occurred among long tail sites (such as our own NFB.ca), which held 55% share.

The impact has been very disruptive on Canadian cultural industries, which have been structured on the basis of a protected universe with high barriers to entry, enforceable regulations such as for content quotas, and clear ways to monetize content. All of that is increasingly subject to the corrosive effects of digital technology and the freedom it allows users to disregard national frontiers or established ways of delivering and consuming content—what we used to call the orderly marketplace with theatrical windows, pay windows, over the air broadcast windows, specialty channel windows and home video windows. It is a model that will soon have as much currency as the singing telegram—perhaps less.

And we are only in the early days of this revolution. Google is just over ten years old. YouTube celebrated its fifth anniversary last week. Twitter was launched in March 2006. Facebook extended beyond its original college circuit only four years ago. Now, one in two Canadians has a Facebook page. In four years.

The point is that the digital world is in constant transformation and we have no way of predicting what that world will look like in five years and who the new conquerors of the digital space will be. It may be players who don't exist . . . they could be Canadian—some of the extraordinary companies or creative talent, for example, represented by your next witness—a former colleague and friend. Given the range of talent and smarts here one of the questions we need to ask is why haven't any of the big players emerged from Canada? And what can we do to ameliorate the picture for the future.

Here is another reminder of the nature and rapidity of change. A few months ago the New York Times did a 10th anniversary piece on the Time-Warner/AOL merger. You may remember that it was the ten-day wonder of the then incipient brave new digital world, marrying old and new to create the media behemoth of the future. It crashed spectacularly. This is what Gerald Levin, architect of that merger, had to say about it:

"I used to think at the time it was a clash of cultures and a misreading of the dot-com bubble, but I now upon reflection believe that the transaction was undone by the Internet itself. I think it is something no one could have foreseen. What I call the rolling thunder of the Internet started actually to eat its own, which was AOL. AOL was the Google of its time. It was how you got to the Internet, but it was using some old media business ideas that were undone by the Internet itself, and that's why Google came along."

Ten years ago AOL seemed as invincible as Google does today. Things aren't set in stone—we can seize the day if we are ready to take risks and push boundaries.

We hear a lot about technology driving change. It is not technology in a vacuum. There are scores of examples of technologies that had the potential to create change and fell flat. Telidon was a pre-Internet Canadian innovation of the 80s. It went nowhere. The current wave of digital technology is so potent because it strikes at two core needs in audiences, in consumers, in citizens: the need to exert greater control over our lives and the irrepressible urge to express ourselves, to be players and not just observers.

This, I think, is one of the great engines of the ongoing growth and strength of social networks which today account for over 40% of Canadian Internet usage. Social networking now also includes significant cultural marketing and consumption. Another opportunity. For example, the whole of NFB's national screening room is embedded within Facebook allowing users to engage with our videos and continue with their social networking activities.

But as much as the consumers want to seize control, the purveyors of that technology want to seize it back. The recent controversy over Facebook and privacy is exactly about that issue: who owns, controls and has the right to exploit the information that I as an individual put on the 'net?

It is critical to note that the information that I or any Canadian upload is not on some neutral, transparent net. I insert it within a pre-existing framework. It may be Facebook or Twitter or Google's YouTube or Murdoch's MySpace. As Canadians we may log into Youtube.ca or Facebook.ca but the fundamental fact is that the information is always potentially controlled by others and often is.

We are unique in the world that our engagement as Canadians is almost overwhelmingly with non-Canadian—American—sites. There is no Canadian owned and operated company in the top ten web destinations. This is in contradiction to the case in UK, Australia, France, Italy and many other countries. One of our leading digital executives operating in the private sector notes that Canadians are "drawers of electricity and hewers of bandwidth". We are in danger of replicating the situation that currently exists in broadcast where great sums of money flow south to buy programming and Canadian content is the poor stepchild.

Let me be clear: none of this is leading to an argument for walled gardens or restricting choices for consumers. It is about looking level headedly and with clear eyes at the problem and finding the innovative solutions that will leverage Canadian creativity and output into the digital sphere.

Even as we recognize that change is on us I fear that many of the discussions I am hearing are still anchored within a terminology of a traditional media universe and thus by definition hampered by what Gerald Levin called "old media business ideas". The justification has been that television remains dominant in the marketplace in terms of viewers and revenue generation. There is a concession that we need to take account of digital media but only to the extent that we can deliver the old wine in the new bottles and collect on the wine and the bottle.

On the first issue, even as television holds steady or even may show some small increase in audiences, Internet use has grown even more, and most spectacularly in the under 18 category, our audiences of the future. On the second, it is true that television retains the lion share of dollars but we are seeing the shift of ad dollars into the online world. With no equivalent of broadcast's simultaneous substitution, 60% of online ad revenue goes south. Over the next few years the loss of this revenue will be a major hit on the ways in which we finance cultural production. On the third issue of what kind of content will dominate, sure, there is a lot of traditional media viewing on the net but there is no assurance that that will continue to be the dominant form in five or ten years.

Price Waterhouse Cooper in their most recent global media survey concedes that television remains dominant but adds that all the momentum is with online and mobile. Much of our industry's response to the shifting sands has been essentially to tuck our heads into those sands.

We are working on an assumption of incremental, manageable change. However, something different may be happening. Instead of incremental change we may be pushing to a tipping point when, bang!, everything becomes undone with enormous rapidity. I cannot say with certainty that this will be the case. But, whether it is a longer or shorter transition, we need to figure how to prepare for that eventuality. Yet our discourse tends to be how to protect the horse and buggy trade while the gas piston engines are being knocked up in the woodsheds.

What are some of the things that might push us to that tipping point? Let me point to a couple of examples. The centre of competitive gravity is shifting east. I returned from MIP, the world's largest television market, last week. The dominating presence of Asia—with large delegations from China, Korea and Singapore—was inescapable. Singapore, for example, is throwing incredible amount of resources into the media sector and into digital specifically. They offer a reach of 3 billion people within a 5-hour radius. There are 5,600 media companies there, 1,000 of them foreign including many the Asian headquarters for global brands such as Discovery and National Geographic. It is a test bed centre for digital innovation and stereoscopic production. They are phasing in optic fibre network to every home offering speeds of 1 gigabit per second. Singapore is out to conquer the world.

You may say that it is a different audience and a different kind of population, but consider this: last month Statscan released their Projections of Diversity of Canadian Population. Our country is in the process of transformation. Major urban centres will be composed of what we today call visible minorities: Toronto and Vancouver at 60%; Calgary and Ottawa 35%; Montreal, Edmonton and Winnipeg pushing towards 30%. It is not uniform and it is not across the country. But these urban centres tend to be the drivers of our cultural and media industries. Very little of that diversity is reflected in our traditional media. If I'm a Chinese Canadian, I may want to connect with the world in a different way because I want to see a world that reflects more of who I am. Digital provides me options that traditional does not.

Secondly, as we move to higher end digital infrastructure, change becomes qualitative. Connection speeds of 1 gigabit per second <u>alter</u> the universe. It is a tipping point. That's the kind of technological change that happened between Web 1.0 and Web 2.0

and that triggered the current wave of disruption. The changes to come are potentially more dramatic.

Coming from the point of view of content creation and given the NFB's drive to innovate I can tell you that we are on the threshold of something quite radical. This isn't simply about platforms. We are witnessing the birth of a new art form that will be immensely transformational . . . more powerful than the movement to television was in the 1950s. Incidentally, our intention at the NFB is to be at the forefront in these new forms of creation—not simply for Canada. For the world. I am happy to note, for example, that we are currently up for five Webby nominations. The Webbys are the Oscars of the digital world.

I think the example of the NFB and how we have embraced the digital challenge provides a sense that there are remarkable opportunities for Canadian culture. I will touch on this briefly but it is more developed in an annex which we have submitted with this presentation.

Since the launch of the NFB's national screening room at the beginning of last year we have had over 5 million views of NFB films. In October we launched our iPhone app which quickly became both a critical and popular success. iTunes called it one of the ten best apps of the year. In less than half a year we've had 700,000 views of films on the iPhone. We are ready to launch on the iPad when it comes to Canada. ONF.ca was the first platform in North America for viewing works in French by francophone creators.

These are engaged viewings; these are audiences making a decision to watch distinctive Canadian films, niche works, longtail works—serious documentaries and auteur animation. The industry norm for completed on line viewings is between 5 and 10%. On NFB.ca it is over 40%. Our youth audience has increased exponentially. Even more interesting is the level of engagement; our audiences are writing, blogging and sharing their experience.

We've made the films available for free by streaming. We will continue to do that. It is a public policy decision and, paradoxically, a sound commercial decision. We are reconnecting and reinvigorating our relationship with Canadians. But we are about to move into a second phase which will see us testing various models for generating revenues: deals with partners such as YouTube and other syndicated sites, online transactions, micropayments and a range of other possibilities. I have no doubt that as the models evolve solutions will be found.

In the interim, however, for Canada and the cultural industries there are a number of critical issues. It is clear we need to ramp up our infrastructure both in online and mobile. We need massive investment in training. Our own experience has shown that it is not simply possible to transfer linear production models to digital productions; it involves radically different ways of organizing budgeting, work processes and work flows and it requires additional and different technical skills—the artisanal basis that is fundamental to any art form based on technology. We need to look at copyright legislation and balancing the interests of creators of intellectual property and consumers and citizens. That latter distinction is important.

We need to understand what the barriers to investment are and why Canadian success stories often do not evolve into the global success of a Facebook or Twitter. Look at the example of Flickr, developed in Canada in 2004. A year later it was bought by Yahoo and all the content was migrated from Canadian servers to US ones. We need to look at how to ensure that the great wealth of existing content generated by the public and private sectors (often with public subsidies) can be digitized and made available to Canadians.

We shouldn't be taking a piecemeal approach to this. We need to do two things: devise a national digital strategy that is more long term in its thinking. Many jurisdictions have advanced in this area such as Britain (Digital Britain), France (France Numerique), New Zealand (Digital Strategy 2.0) and Australia (Digital Economy Future) to name a few. The process would bring together many diverse sectors: technological innovation, finance, cultural industries, communications industries, and so on.

As government film commissioner I have taken the initiative in this area calling for such a strategy well over a year ago. Since then I have assembled a broad based group of people from the private and public sectors to brainstorm ideas. I am heartened to hear that Minister Clement will soon be leading a consultative process for such a strategy and we look forward to enriching it with the work of our group.

But we also need a transitional strategy. How do we ensure that we can capitalize on our traditional media industries, not cannibalize their revenue base and build rapidly the new digital businesses of the future? What Minister Moore has done with CMF is a step in the right direction.

One final point: we talk about the digital revolution in terms of an economic strategy and global competitiveness. There is a larger story. As much as it is said that digital democratises media it is also a solvent dissolving social cohesiveness; it facilitates the formation of communities of interest as much as communities. The paradox of the virtual world is the isolation of connection. In moving forward we need to understand that there is something crucial at stake here—it has to do with nation building. If we park that at the door we do ourselves and our country an enormous disservice. Canadians have a yearning to connect beyond their individual interests—we saw that in the phenomenal outpouring of pride during the Vancouver Olympics. It tapped into a deeply felt need. If we recognize this then digital can also become a powerful tool to create social cohesiveness. This has to do with ensuring the public space in an online world.

One of the most interesting things for us has been the comments of audiences, across all age groups, about NFB.ca. For the first time, they had in one place, easily accessible and at their convenience a unique view of our country crossing time, geography and language and ethnic barriers. They came and saw something that we often forget—the immeasurable beauty and wonder of our country. Our audiences watched, understood, and took it to heart. And their hearts swelled with pride.

We know this because they haven't been shy about telling the world. Here are some comments young audiences—an 18–25 demographic—made on an online survey by Michael Adams, which we did not commission and about which we knew nothing until after the results were published:

"To me, the NFB is yet another one of the low-key yet crucially important bearers of Canadian identity."

—male, 19

"The NFB helps provide meaningful insight into the little aspects of Canadian culture, which are often forgotten."

—male, 19

"To conclude, I find that Johan Huizinga says it best when he states, "If we are to preserve culture we must continue to create it." That in a nutshell describes Canada's National Film Board, it is able to preserve our culture through film and yet help other artist aspire to create more representations of our Canadian identity."

—female, 25

Thank you.

ANNEX

The following document is a complement to the presentation by Government Film Commissioner and president of the NFB, and it provides a brief overview of the NFB's digital transformation.

The transition from analog to digital formats is one of the technological changes that is transforming the media environment in the present era. The network of ways in which we interconnect through digital media, including the Web and mobile platforms, will have enormous long-term consequences for Canada in the political, social, economical and cultural areas.

Two years into the NFB's five-year Strategic Plan, we are setting the standard among Canadian institutions for creative innovation in digital media. We experiment with new models, doing what the private sector cannot do because the risks are too great or business models have not yet sufficiently evolved. At the heart of our strategy is a reaffirmation of the NFB's core values: working with creators across all technologies, stimulating imaginative and socially engaged creation, and ensuring accessibility for all Canadians—while making maximum use of the possibilities of digital technology. Our audiovisual content is 100 percent Canadian—it reflects this country's diversity. It gives a powerful voice to Aboriginal creators and those from our diverse cultural and regional communities. It is available in French and in English, and crosses all our geographic boundaries.

NFB.ca has recently been named one of the "Top 50 Canadian Websites" by *Canada's Web 50*, a collection of Canadian creative designers, marketing managers and online media buyers, and "Best Online Video Portal" by the Canadian New Media Awards, Canada's only nationwide digital media awards show. Even more encouraging is how enthusiastically the NFB's growing audience has embraced our new digital products and services. To date, the online Screening Room at <NFB.ca> has generated over five million screenings worldwide, with more than 1,400 NFB productions currently available, and new titles being added weekly. Two days after its launch last October, the NFB iPhone application ranked as the third most downloaded application, ahead of Facebook and Skype. The total volume of iPhone application downloads has now reached 220,000 and of iPhone plays, more than 720,000 worldwide.

This month, the NFB received five nominations and four honourable mentions at the 14th Annual Webby Awards—a record number for the NFB in a single year. Leading the way with four nominations was the *Waterlife Interactive* website, nominated in three website categories—Society/Education, Society/Green, and Media/Movie and Film—as well as for Best Online Film and Video in the Documentary/Individual Episode category. Called the "Internet's highest honour" by the *New York Times,* the Webby is the leading international award honouring excellence on the Internet.[2]

DEVELOPMENTS IN EMERGING AND DIGITAL MEDIA AND THEIR IMPACT ON CANADIAN CULTURAL INDUSTRIES

The NFB's digital media strategy addresses three distinct market segments: consumers; the educational sector; and media content aggregators such as portals, broadcasters, and so on. Our primary goal is to provide value and accessibility to Canadians with an array of free and payable content. This involves maximizing the opportunities provided by the NFB's extraordinary archives and current catalogue while safeguarding, enriching and strengthening our film collection and name brand.

Here is a sample of some our most recent achievements:

- The NFB has undertaken a digital transformation involving all aspects of our organization, including our production and distribution services—a transformation that has been fully financed internally.
- Digital transformation of the NFB has required institutional renewal, including an organizational restructuring that flows from the new priorities contained in our strategic plan. By these means, we have been able to put significantly more dollars into making and delivering to Canadians the programming that is at the heart of our mandate.
- The NFB has totally revamped its website, which features our "screening room" with over 1400 NFB productions available free of charge online, via streaming technology, including recent HD and 3D productions. We have developed a special interest in mobile applications for portable devices such the iPhone, BlackBerry and Google Android.
- The NFB has arranged for the syndication of our digital content via distribution channels such as the NFB channel on YouTube.com, the YouTube screening room, an NFB-moderated channel on dailymotion.com, and a dedicated NFB channel on Rogers-on-demand and on Videotron's Illico—all of which involve some form of revenue-sharing.
- The NFB is the caretaker of one of the world's great audiovisual collections, dating back to the 1940s—13,000 titles, 500,000 still images and an extensive sound library—which constitutes an invaluable heritage for Canadians and for the rest of the world. The digitization and on-line distribution of this extensive collection is rapidly progressing. And just over two weeks ago, the NFB and Radio-Canada announced their intention to join forces to showcase over 2,000 hours of new stock footage online at <NFB.ca/images>, our web destination for stock footage professionals.
- We launched *Waterlife Interactive*, a web project inspired by the documentary *Waterlife* by Kevin McMahon. This co-production between Primitive Entertainment and the NFB, is the story of the last great supply of fresh drinking water on earth. It is a creative and educational portrait of a pressing social issue that directly affects over 350 million people. *Waterlife Interactive* builds on the film's stunning visuals and soundtrack to create an immersive experience that allows users to explore the beauty of water and the danger in taking it for granted. It was one of two winners of the City of Karlsruhe Prize at the BaKaFORUM 2010 TV and Media Forum in Karlsruhe, Germany. The prize honours the best educational, societal or science multimedia project.

- We launched *GDP -Measuring the human side of the Canadian economic crisis/* ***PIB—L'indice humain de la crise économique canadienne,*** the country's first bilingual web documentary, a pan-Canadian project that bears witness to the far-reaching effects of the economic crisis in our lives and communities. Under the direction of documentary filmmaker Hélène Choquette, over 250 documentary shorts and photo-essays, each about four minutes in length, create a mosaic showing how Canadians are experiencing the crisis.
- ***100 mots pour la folie*** by Fayad Ghassan is the first interactive music video and the first such work on the NFB's interactive platform. This innovative project uses the words of each visitor to the site as a navigation interface to let them create a unique video clip based on Malajube's music with visuals from the NFB's archives spanning over 70 years of production.
- We are devoted to the training and mentoring of emerging and established Canadian filmmakers. Equally essential is the commitment to support our employees with more training and opportunities to better adapt to the new realities of the digital environment. We have worked with l'Institut national de l'image de du son (INIS) to deliver a digital training program: a series of training and knowledge-sharing workshops with NFB and other industry experts.
- To better reach official language minority communities in remote and under-served areas, we have launched the first e-cinema network in five francophone communities in Acadia. This pilot project provides a rich collection of otherwise unavailable digitized documentaries, animation and features, on the big screen, in French.

Where are All These Developments Coming From?

Digital technology allows for the exact reproduction, widespread interconnectivity, instantaneous transport, mobility, accessibility, and the broad multi-purposing of cultural content on a scale never before imagined. As a result, an array of overlapping and interrelated new digital markets has arisen that are complementing, competing with, and transforming traditional media such as broadcasting and telecommunications. These online markets are characterized by a mix of free and premium content, more and more frequent micropayments, streaming technology, and downloading by rental or sale.

The NFB's general strategy for the gradual monetizing of initially free services is to, first, build a strong and compelling free offering that offers greater accessibility to the NFB's collection, builds audiences and creates a solid customer base. In a second phase, we will move to a tiered approach that, while continuing to improve accessibility and increase the volume of content available, also offers premium content and services, such as new releases, for a price. In this stage, we will experiment with subscription models, video-on-demand (VOD), downloading by loan or sale, and links with online stores for DVD purchase.

WHAT FEDERAL INSTITUTIONS COULD DO TO ASSIST

Canadian cultural institutions must embrace the digital transition and accept continuous change and upheaval as part of their daily lives. To achieve this objective, the NFB favours the creation of a national digital strategy by the Government of Canada to ensure that the various components of new media are part of a coordinated national approach. In its *Review of broadcasting in new media* last June, the CRTC pointed out that several countries have already recognized the value and the importance of a national digital strategy and have developed plans that respond to the perceived challenges and take advantage of the expected opportunities presented by the digital age. In the Commission's words, "given the breadth and magnitude of the issues and their importance to Canada's future, the Commission fully endorses the call by the NFB for the Government of Canada to develop a national digital strategy."[3] According to the Minister's remarks before this Committee on April 13, we understand that a national digital strategy is now on its way.[4]

The NFB is in favour of a comprehensive study of the measures that could increase the resources available for investment in digital media. Investment incentives should also encourage greater promotion and visibility of Canadian content, to ensure that Canadians have access to high-value Canadian content on new platforms.

The NFB intends to extend the work it has done in the last few years to develop low-cost, highly effective programs that fill the void between film and training schools and a graduate's first professional production experience. With First Person Digital, Engagetoi, Newscreen and Calling Card, we have pioneered an integration of master classes and full professional production to assist the next generation of digital artists and artisans. This has been done in partnership with a range of institutions, including provincial government agencies, broadcasters and independent production companies. For example, the First Person Digital production program for women informs and inspires creators by engaging in discussion with some of the most extraordinary individuals working in new media today. First Person Digital offers the support and tools necessary for six teams to create a new media experience with the NFB, Studio XX and other partners. Projects will premiere on CBC, be webcast by the NFB and the CBC, and be considered for NFB festival and non theatrical distribution.

Homegrown institutions like the NFB have become breeding grounds for creativity and innovation, allowing not only emerging creators but also seasoned artists the opportunity to experiment and create what they could not do in the private sector. Films such as Couleur Z by Phillipe Baylaucq and *Glimpses/Impressions* by Jean François Pouliot explore innovative cinematic experiences, using digital media to experiment with new ways of reflecting and engaging the reality of our country.

The financing and nurturing of initiatives for professional development in emerging and digital media ought to be increased. Canadian cultural institutions must foster the development of the fullest possible range of Canadian innovation and content within the fast changing digital environment.

CONCLUSION

Canadian government policy should ensure the availability of a wide array of Canadian cultural content of all kinds alongside the high-quality internationally-available alternatives. The NFB is an essential policy instrument in achieving this objective in the new digital environment. We have committed ourselves to taking the creative, technological and financial risks that the private sector cannot.

Since its inception, the NFB has served Canadians by producing and distributing programming designed to reflect Canadian realities and to engage Canadians in issues of importance. The NFB is a creative laboratory, where we can test the future today. Without the burden of a traditional broadcasting infrastructure, the NFB can push further and deeper into areas that are risky, even for public broadcasters. We can and will increasingly be focusing on delivering unique content on digital platforms. In fact, we've been taking the lead in this area for some time.

The NFB is at its best when it serves as a laboratory, when its creators can research and develop the new forms of the future, as was the case with direct cinema in the fifties or with the big screen technology IMAX. We are creating and distributing works that are unique, original and trailblazing—that have their natural home in the digital universe—projects such as *Waterlife* or PIB-GDP.

The possibilities for new platforms, new approaches and new ideas remain wide open. Canadians have proven they can compete with the best in this arena. We need to provide the support that will make Canada a world centre for digital innovation that will then help drive the creation of Canadian content.

Endnotes

1. The ComScore 2009 Digital Year in Review, A Recap of the Year in Canadian Digital Marketing
2. Winners will be announced on May 4th, 2010.
3. Broadcasting Regulatory Policy CRTC 2009–329, 4 June 2009, para. 78.
4. During his appearance at the Standing Committee on April 13, Heritage Minister James Moore said the Minister of Industry, Tony Clement, will launch a digital strategy in the next month or two.

DISCUSSION

National Film Board of Canada, *Emerging and Digital Media: Opportunities and Challenges, Presentation to the House of Commons Standing Committee on Canadian Heritage.*

1. The NFB presentation to the Standing Committee on Canadian Heritage argues that Canadians are active consumers of on-line film and video, but that on-line viewing allows viewers to ignore national borders and conventional film and television distribution systems. In your experience, is this true? If so what do you think are the potential positive and negative outcomes for Canadian film and television creation?
2. This report suggests that from the point of view of content creation, digital production and delivery infrastructure has put the NFB at the 'birth of a new art form.' Visit www.nfb.ca/interactive to experience some of the Film Board's interactive documentaries. Do you agree that these digital works present a new opportunity for the creation of Canadian culture? Why can publicly-owned media take creative, technological, and financial risks that the private sector media cannot?

3. The NFB report calls for a national digital strategy. Do you agree that this is an important area for developing media policy? If so what types of policy rationales and objectives should inform a digital strategy and what types of specific outcomes could such a strategy trigger in Canada's media industries?

4. According to this report, what are the NFB's core values? How has it adapted these values to film production in the digital and on-line environment?

Regulating Shelf Space for Canadian Content

INTRODUCTION

Governments everywhere have defined various attributes of 'national culture,' which they strive to maintain and enhance through policies for media and culture. John Foote, in the selection in Chapter 1, suggests that clear definitions of Canadian culture are developed so governments can create policy tools to protect 'shelf space' for Canadian content. As Grant and Wood have argued, the nationality of culture can be defined in different ways. National culture can be determined based upon the citizenship of the individuals who contribute to the creation of cultural content, the physical location and financing of media production, or through a more subjective assessment of the aesthetic and formal attributes of the content itself (Grant & Wood 2004, 151). For example, 'Canadian content' for media such as music, radio, television, and film can be defined according to who made the content, where it was actually produced, or what type of imagery and stories are used. CRTC television regulations assign points to each Canadian who plays a creative role in content production, in order to determine whether or not broadcasters have met CanCon quotas. Department of Canadian Heritage funding programs like the Canada Media Fund or the Canada Book Fund, on the other hand, determine eligibility for grants based on a combination of citizenship criteria for the creators and a qualitative assessment of the 'Canadianess' of the television programs or books being created. Thus we see that media policy has different ways of determining what should count as 'Canadian' in determining how to regulate or subsidize the creation of national culture through media content.

Once governments determine how national culture is to be defined, they have a number of policy tools to choose from for enabling its creation and ensuring that citizens have access to it. One key tool is the implementation of exhibition requirements, or content quotas, in radio, television, and film. Quotas for locally or nationally produced media content exist in many other countries besides Canada and are a key component of media regulation in countries around the world. In Canada, domestic content quotas were first introduced at the same time as private television stations in 1961 (Grant & Wood 2004, 199). Since that time, the CRTC has been developing content quotas that require radio and television stations to devote at least part of their schedule to Canadian television productions or Canadian popular music. According to Grant and Wood (2004, 198), there are four other types of quotas that can also be applied to media industries:

1. Quotas for language programming: CRTC rules specify that French radio stations must play 65% French language music.
2. Quotas for genre of programming: CRTC licence requirements indicate the amount of local news required by television stations.
3. Quotas for programming directed to certain audiences: CRTC specifies minimum amounts of children's programming on TVO and CBC.
4. Quotas for independently produced programs: CRTC expects that television programming should be acquired from production companies not owned or controlled by the networks.

In this chapter we are closely examining CRTC regulations for Canadian-produced content. Recall from Chapter 3 that the CRTC is tasked with implementing the objectives of the *Broadcasting Act* and takes its mandate for promoting Canadian content production directly from the *Act*. As a public policy choice, regulation is often perceived as a negative imposition on private industry—a way of forcing businesses to do things that may curtail their profits, but that are deemed to be central to the public good. In the critical analysis for this chapter, Robert Babe compares the concept of 'regulation' to that of 'incentives' in the realm of media policy and argues that they are not as dissimilar as one might first expect. Writing in 1985, leading up to the last round of revisions to the *Broadcasting Act,* Babe points out that broadcasting and media industries do not exist in a realm of pure competition, nor do they operate within a completely 'free market' upon which government controls are then enforced. Existing laws and policies already protect broadcasters and media companies through the allocation of licences, giving media outlets guaranteed access to viewers and listeners in a certain area or region. Therefore, Babe argues, Canadian content obligations that come with licences should actually be viewed by broadcasters as incentives to keep those licences and maintain the profits that flow directly from them. Babe also points out that the idea of 'deregulation' of media industries is misleading. Since governments already enforce property laws and guarantee the smooth operation of business on a day to day basis, it is more accurate to speak of 're-regulation' when existing rights, responsibilities, and obligations amongst parties are altered. If Canadian content obligations for broadcasters were lessened or removed, the rights of Canadian creative artists and audiences to produce and consume Canadian culture would be diminished, while the rights of broadcasters to increase profits would increase. With these economic facts in mind, Babe's recommendations for reforming media policy include a more competitive process of television licence renewals tied to positive performance on the screening of Canadian content and an increased requirement for financial contributions from the cable companies to support Canadian programming.

In Policy Source 9, the CRTC lays out its most recent policy for commercial radio in Canada, including expectations for playing Canadian content and contributing to the development of Canadian music. The statement begins with a review of the policy objectives for Canadian privately-owned radio mandated by the *Broadcasting Act*. As is common with CRTC policy documents, this one was produced after a series of written submissions and oral presentations at public hearings. The document makes reference to participants in the hearings, and addresses points raised in written submissions, to arrive at the Commission's current policy position. The Commercial Radio Policy surveys technological changes in the creation and distribution of music brought about by the Internet and considers the impact of these changes upon the profits and ad revenues available to private radio stations. As overall levels of radio tuning fall among youth and young adult audiences, the CRTC cautions that radio stations will have to consider new delivery modes on new media platforms.

Despite these changes, commercial radio remains in reasonable financial health and so the CRTC lays out expectations that broadcasters will continue to contribute to the economic support of Canadian musical talent. Using the MAPL formula (Music, Artist, Production, Lyrics), this policy source clearly lays out the criteria by which Canadian Category 2 music (popular music) is defined for the purposes of meeting the 35 percent quota for Canadian music on commercial radio. The policy also prescribes a 65 percent quota for French-language music on French stations (although this French language music does not have to be Canadian to meet the quota). After considering the pros and cons of increasing the quota for Canadian music on radio, the CRTC states its intention to leave the 35 percent level unaltered. Finally, the document introduces the new term 'Canadian content development' and describes the objective of having privately-owned commercial stations contribute to the support, promotion, training, and development of Canadian musical talent. This financial support for existing and emerging Canadian musicians will have the desired outcome of increasing the supply of quality Canadian music in a variety of genres. The policy statement describes some of the various agencies to which radio broadcasters must contribute, including RadioStarmaker, FACTOR (see Chapter 9), and MusicAction and other non-profit music industry associations (MIAs).

Policy Source 10 is the most recent CRTC policy for private television stations. The document reviews the state of private television in light of both increased concentration of ownership in the industry and the decline in ad revenue that occurred after the 2008 recession. Like commercial radio policy, commercial television policy is also rooted in the requirements of the *Broadcasting Act* that private networks contribute to the creation of Canadian programming. The policy recognizes that technological changes are affecting television and introduces changes to allow large ownership groups like Rogers, Shaw, and Bell to better support and deliver Canadian content through all of their networks and specialty channels, and across multiple platforms. Under this policy, large ownership groups will be subject to new spending requirements for Canadian programs. Expenditure requirements are designed to ensure the creation of high quality Canadian content, alongside quotas to protect the overall quantity of Canadian content. Specialty channels have always had Canadian program spending requirements, set at different levels according to the type of content carried. In 1999 however, expenditure rules were eliminated for conventional television channels and this resulted in a rapid decline in the amount and quality of Canadian television drama being produced. The 2010 reintroduction of the Canadian Program Expenditure (CPE) is set at 30 percent of each ownership group's gross revenue with the objective of increasing the overall quality of Canadian content on television.

The new television policy also revises 'exhibition requirements,' or content quotas, for television. It keeps the requirement that 50 percent of all evening (6:00 P.M. to midnight) programming be Canadian, but lowers the minimum average over the whole broadcast year from 60 percent to 55 percent. The policy updates the idea that there should be a separate screening quota for under-represented and costly 'priority programming' categories like drama, documentary, variety, and regional content. The term 'priority programs' is replaced with the concept of 'programs of national interest' and now includes drama, documentary, and specific Canadian award shows. The quota of eight hours per week of priority programs during peak time is replaced with an expenditure requirement for programs of national interest set at 5 percent of each ownership group's gross revenue. Finally, the television policy recognizes that conventional over-the-air (OTA) networks no longer have guaranteed access to local ad revenue in the new 'on-demand' on-line media environment. Because of these market shifts and technological changes, the policy allows the OTA networks to negotiate a fee from cable and satellite distribution undertakings that formerly carried these networks without any form of compensation. Each of these different forms of industry regulation—content quotas, expenditure requirements, and licencing—are developed around the overall policy objectives of ensuring the creation of, and access to, Canadian cultural content in our media.

Critical Analysis

Babe, R. (1985). Regulation and incentives, two sides of any policy. In C. Hoskins and
S. McFadyen (Eds.), *Canadian broadcasting, the challenge of change*. Edmonton:
University of Alberta and ACCESS.

Regulation and Incentives:
Two Sides of Any Policy

Robert E. Babe
Department of Communication
University of Ottawa

While recognizing that the Task Force on Broadcasting has both a very practical mandate and quite severe time constraints, nonetheless, some abstract discussion is vital—to avoid possible confusion at a time when important structural changes to our broadcasting system are being contemplated. In particular, a comparison of the two terms or policy approaches central to this session, namely incentives and regulation, is called for.

It is my main point that these two terms or policy approaches are not nearly so dissimilar or dichotomous as they are frequently made out to be, that generally the choice of which term to use is merely that, a choice, depending not so much on the policy measure itself as upon the vantage point (or self interest) of the particular commentator or spokesman. If, on balance, one expects to make more money from a policy initiative, there will be a natural tendency to call this change an *incentive,* connoting positive feelings of freedom, expansion and growth. On the other hand, if a policy measure on balance is expected to reduce one's profit or revenues, there will be an inclination to call it a *regulation,* with the accompanying negative connotations of restriction, direction and control.

So much of our thinking and evaluation depend on word choice.

Therefore, I propose to delve more deeply into these two concepts to detect their complex relationship.

The two terms, regulation and incentives, are actually quite closely related, even to the point of being mutually interdependent, indeed being inextricably bound together as the two necessary sides of every policy, rule or law.

Briefly stated, an incentive to one person or group will be a regulation or restriction to another, and vice versa; furthermore, a regulation *is* an incentive, and vice versa, for each person or group, if and when the privilege awarded is circumscribed. Few privileges, rights or benefits are unlimited or uncircumscribed. To note one authority on the subject of property, for example,

To permit anyone to do absolutely anything he likes with his property in creating noise, smells or danger of fire, could be to make property in

167

general valueless. To be really effective, therefore, the right of property must be supported by restrictions or positive duties on the part of owners, enforced by the state, as much as by the right to exclude, that is the essence of property.[1]

To illustrate the close interrelation between incentives and regulation, between "freedom and control", consider first the economist's model of pure competition, said by many to depict an ideal of economic freedom inasmuch as the incentive system is seen to be in full operation.

While from one perspective the model of pure competition may exemplify economic freedom (no special licences are required to enter a field, no special or explicit regulations or standards are imposed by fiat, and so forth), nonetheless, the model of pure competition is also the ultimate in economic control: price is imposed on each firm by the abstract forces of supply and demand; no firm can expand or contract levels of output; technology is given by the state of the art; even the consumer is looked upon as being merely a conditional automation responding mechanically, in Skinnerian fashion, to the pushes and pulls of his/her utility function. Incentives here mean necessities, spontaneity is abolished; pure competition is a model of total control and unfreedom.

Let us look at a second, more immediate example, namely Canadian content quotas, in order again to explore the intimate relationship between incentives and regulation, between freedom and control. Most of us are accustomed to calling content quotas regulations, not incentives, since they are commonly viewed as restricting the programming options of Canadian broadcasters; we see them as being contrary to broadcasters' financial interests. But this point of view depends very much upon what one's initial premises are. If it is assumed that a broadcaster already has a licence and that this license in and of itself entails no programming requirements or obligations, then of course Canadian content quotas, superimposed on the licensee, restrict his freedom and hence could be termed "regulations".

On the other hand, if the licence is not absolute and if restrictions on it are enforced (as through revocation or non renewal in the absence of compliance), then restrictions or regulations can be viewed also as being incentives. Broadcasters obviously have incentives to apply for and to hold licences; if obligations such as content quotas are not segregated from the licence, then broadcasters have incentives to comply with these quotas, meaning they have incentives to undertake Canadian content.[2]

Far from an arbitrary imposition, content quotas can be seen as being central to the awarding of the privilege of broadcasting, similar in nature to technical specifications pertaining to power, frequency, directionality, and so forth. These boundaries or definitions, both technical and programming, taken together, constitute the boundaries circumscribing the privilege of broadcasting.

Looking at the question again from another level it can be seen that any restriction or obligation for one group entrails an expansion for another. Again using the example of Canadian content quotas, even if these quotas are declared to limit broadcasters' freedom as compared to hypothetical state of unencumbered licence tenure, nonetheless this very restriction enhances the freedoms of others by creating incentives in other sectors—for example, for writers, actors, producers, musicians and audiences wishing to view Canadian programming. Incentives are created for these groups since broadcasters are obliged by their licences to offer some Canadian programming and to employ some Canadians. Without these obligations, or others substituting for them, there would be little opportunity, or incentive, for these other groups to ply their trade in the private sector.

The discussion now leads naturally to the meaning of "deregulation", a currently fashionable but misleading term. It is far more accurate to speak of *reregulation* than of *deregulation*. This is because *all* economic activity takes place only within the framework of law.[3] Law explicitly and implicitly apportions rights among contending interests; it is never neutral. It is never the case of the government being absent either from our economic system or from *any* market transaction. Government or law defends ownership of property against theft, for example; it enforces contracts, permits unionization, prohibits price fixing, allows incorporation, treats the corporation as an artificial person, allows limited liability and on and on.[4] Without law to back up economic transactions, it would certainly be survival of the strongest; ownership would be based on immediacy of possession and on capacity to defend possessions by force. When we use the term "deregulation", then, we are never speaking of the government getting out of an area of economic activity; we are merely speaking of government reapportioning rights and obligations amongst contending interests. Returning again to the example of Canadian content, if the CRTC were to abolish all such quotas I am sure that many broadcasters would applaud this action as "deregulation". But in fact what would have taken place is the withdrawal of rights and benefits from some groups (namely creative artists, technicians and audiences), and apportionment of increased rights and benefits to other groups (principally broadcasters). But in so doing the government certainly has not withdrawn. It still enforces and apportions privileges: the broadcaster still sells advertising time; imports (and perhaps even exports) programs; it can sell its transmitter, and so on. *All* of the broadcasters' rights are supported by the underlying legal system, and in no sense has the government withdrawn.

Having put to rest the ideologically-motivated distinction between incentives and regulation, and having exposed "deregulation" as merely the reapportionment of rights and duties, it remains to offer comment on future strategies. Here I can be brief because elsewhere I have set forth my proposals in some detail. At the outset it must be emphasized that Canadian television broadcasting is a subsystem of the larger North American system. This means that changes in laws, policies, regulations, incentives intended to apply to and affect Canadian broadcasting must be studied within the context of the North American system as a whole.

When this is done certain conclusions are apparent.

Canadian broadcasting, a subsystem less than ten percent the size of the full North American system, has immense outside pressures put upon it, while conversely its influence on the North American system is minimal. This implies that our policies, whether termed incentives or regulations, will be ineffective, even invisible, unless focused, concentrated and dramatic. It is no longer a question of playing around with the Income Tax Act to increase per capita advertising expenditures on television from 40 percent to 49 percent of the U.S. level, as with Bill C-58; nor is it a question of making marginal adjustments to Canadian quotas and to licence conditions.

With respect to private television broadcasters, the most dramatic and productive change can come, I suggest, from a vigorous, competitive licence renewal and licence transfer process, as I have described in a previous document.[5] Licence conditions, content quotas, promises of performance, and general responsibility in broadcasting should become inextricably tied to the licence to broadcast. Broadcasters should have *incentives* to participate in the objectives set for broadcasting in this country by facing the real possibility of losing their licences if they do not.

With respect to cable television, the most dramatic and productive change can come, I believe, through the infusion of new funds to public broadcasting and to independent producers based on cable copyright liability, as I have described elsewhere.[6] Cable copyright payments of one hundred million dollars a year (or about 20 percent of cable revenues) do not seem too large when it is realized that cable now appropriates without compensation programming rediffused from off-air sources. Added to the budgets of CBC and independent producers, these funds would be significant.

Finally, the most effective and dramatic step has already been taken, indeed was taken in 1932, namely the creation of a public broadcasting corporation with a focused, cultural mandate. All data and statistics point to the CBC as *the* success story in Canadian broadcasting. Therefore, we should be contemplating means of strengthening and expanding the role of the CBC: in particular, additional channels and new sources of funding, as from cable copyright payment. Also we should be encouraging the development of provincial, indeed municipal broadcasting.

Market-based incentives and constraints stemming from the North American context are fundamentally hostile to indigenous Canadian productions targeted to domestic audiences.

This was realized in 1929 when Sir John Aird reported; it is likewise true today. While not wishing to minimize regulatory and incentive approaches that can be applied to the private sector, I would be most remiss to not reaffirm the centrality of public broadcasting in this country.

To close, I wish to cite an important insight contained in the 1965 Fowler Committee Report on Broadcasting:

> There is no point in asking where a national broadcasting system is going. It will go only where it is pushed by conscious and articulate public policy, or where it drifts if there is no policy. The State is inescapably involved in the creation of a broadcasting system, and should accept responsibility for the powerful agency it has created, so as to ensure that broadcasting serves the people with distinction; for the ultimate test of a society may well be the quality of the artistic and intellectual life it creates and supports.[7]

Endnotes

1. Morris Cohen, "Property and Sovereignty" in C. B. Macpherson (ed.) *Property: Mainstream and Critical Positions,* (Toronto: University of Toronto Press, 1978), p. 167.
2. This is, of course, the heart of the policy problem. As Herschel Hardin and I have both argued, the CRTC has allowed obligations of broadcasters to become segregated from their licenses through automatic license renewals and the absence of licence revocations, irrespective of their compliance with these obligations; it is in this way that content quotas and other obligations have come to be viewed as a self-contained package of regulations, rather than as essential components of or boundaries to the privilege of broadcasting. See Herschel Hardin *Closed Circuits: The Sellout of Canadian Television* (Vancouver: Douglas & McIntyre, 1985); and Robert E.

Babe *Canadian Television Broadcasting Structure, Performance and Regulation* (Ottawa: Supply and Services, 1979).

3. I have addressed this point in greater detail in Chapter 2, "Copyright as Property" in Robert E. Babe and Conrad Winn *Broadcasting Policy and Copyright Law: An Analysis of a Cable Rediffusion Right,* (Ottawa: Department of Communications, 1984), pp. 16–37.

   Two other references must be noted: Warren J. Samuels, "Interrelations Between Legal and Economic Processes", *Journal of Law and Economics* LIV (October 1971); and Walter Lippmann, *The Public Philosophy,* (New York: Mentor, 1955).

4. John P. Davis, *Corporations: A Study of the Origin and Development of Great Business Combinations and of Their Relation to the Authority of the State,* (New York: Capricorn Books, 1961), first published in 1905 by G. P. Putnam's Sons, New York.

5. Robert E. Babe and Philip Slayton, *Competitive Procedures for Broadcasting—Renewal and Transfers.* (Ottawa: Department of Communications, 1980).

6. Robert E. Babe and Conrad Winn, *Broadcasting Policy and Copyright Law: An Analysis of a Cable Rediffusion Right.*

7. Committee on Broadcasting *Report,* (Ottawa: Queen's Printer, 1965), p. 5.

DISCUSSION

Robert Babe, 'Regulation or Incentives' from *Canadian Broadcasting, the Challenge of Change.*

1. Babe suggests that our word choice between 'regulation' and 'incentive' reflects the point of view or position that we might hold on media policy. In your own words, explain what he means when he says that regulations could be seen as incentives for broadcasters to get and keep a licence.

2. Babe argues that even if we see regulations as restrictions on broadcasters, they enhance the freedom of other groups in the media industries. What groups is he referring to and how do these groups benefit directly from Canadian content rules?

3. Do you agree that a more competitive licencing process would increase broadcasters' commitment to supporting Canadian content? What would be some of the advantages and drawbacks of having media companies compete for their licence renewals every seven years?

Commercial Radio Policy 2006

In this public notice, the Commission sets out its revised policy for commercial radio. Areas addressed include airplay and financial support for Canadian music and French-language vocal music, cultural diversity, local management agreements and local sales agreements, local programming and infomercials. The Commission considers that the measures announced in this policy, particularly its new approach to Canadian content development, will allow the commercial radio sector to contribute more effectively to the achievement of the goals set out in the Broadcasting Act, *while enabling it to operate effectively in an increasingly competitive environment for the delivery of audio programming.*

This public notice is one of three issued following the Commission's review of its policy for commercial radio announced in Review of the commercial radio policy, Broadcasting Notice of Public Hearing CRTC 2006–1, 31 January 2006, *and that was the subject of a public hearing in the National Capital Region that began on 15 May 2006. The other two public notices are* Revised policy concerning the issuance of calls for radio applications and a new process for applications to serve small markets, Broadcasting Public Notice CRTC 2006–159, 15 December 2006, *and,* Digital Radio Policy, Broadcasting Public Notice CRTC 2006–160, 15 December 2006.

Dissenting opinions by Commissioners Cram and Langford are attached.

INTRODUCTION

1. In *Review of the Commercial Radio Policy,* Broadcasting Notice of Public Hearing CRTC 2006–1, 13 January 2006 (the Notice), the Commission announced that it would hold a public hearing commencing on 15 May 2006 to review its commercial radio policies and invited comments on the matters set out in the Notice.
2. The Notice set out the following overall objectives for the review:
   To develop policies that assist in creating conditions for:

   - A strong, well-financed commercial radio sector in both official languages capable of contributing to the fulfillment of the policy objectives set out in the *Broadcasting Act* (the Act).

- A commercial radio sector that makes effective contributions to Canadian artists through airplay of Canadian music, French-language vocal music, and contributions to Canadian talent development (CTD) that are commensurate with the financial health of the sector.
- A commercial radio sector that provides listeners with a greater diversity of musical genres, and airplay for a greater variety of Canadian artists in both official languages.
- A commercial radio sector that reflects the multicultural and multiracial nature of Canadian society and the special place of Aboriginal peoples within society.
- A commercial radio sector that provides listeners with an appropriate amount of regularly-scheduled, locally produced news and information.
- A commercial radio sector capable of making the transition to digital transmission, and of exploiting new and emerging distribution platforms in a manner that furthers the objectives of the Act.

3. The Commission received 194 written comments in response to the Notice, and 48 parties made oral presentations at the hearing, which took place between 15 May and 18 May 2006. Participating parties included private individuals, unions and guilds, commercial radio broadcasters, including the Canadian Association of Broadcasters (CAB), not-for-profit radio broadcasters and various representatives from the Canadian music industry.

4. In general, commercial radio broadcasters stressed that, since the Commission's last review of radio in 1998 (the 1998 Review), which resulted in *Commercial Radio Policy 1998*, Public Notice CRTC 1998–41, 30 April 1998 (the 1998 Commercial Radio Policy), there has been a proliferation of alternative technologies for the distribution of music to consumers. In their view, it is likely that these devices will continue to proliferate and become more sophisticated and attractive in the next few years. While there is little evidence so far of an impact on broadcasters' revenues, commercial radio broadcasters submitted that a significant effect on listeners' habits is inevitable, and the financial performance of commercial radio stations may well decline as a result. Commercial radio broadcasters also presented their views on the Commission's current radio policies and discussed possible changes in some areas.

5. Other parties cited the generally positive financial results that commercial radio broadcasters have enjoyed since 1998 and argued that the commercial radio industry was in a good position to strengthen its contributions to the achievement of the objectives set out in the Act, particularly with respect to the airplay of Canadian and French-language music, the exposure of emerging artists, and monetary assistance for CTD. The parties also raised a number of other issues, which are addressed throughout this public notice.

6. During the public hearing, the Commission asked seventeen parties to file additional information by 29 May 2006. All participants were afforded the opportunity to file final comments on any topic covered by the review by 12 June 2006.

THE RADIO BROADCASTING ENVIRONMENT

The Evolving Marketplace for the Delivery of Audio Programming

7. The delivery and consumption of audio programming has changed dramatically since the 1998 Review. The marketplace within which commercial radio stations compete is evolving with the advent of new regulated and unregulated technologies. Such new audio technologies include MP3 players, iPods and other personal media devices, Internet music services and radio streaming, including streaming over wireless broadband, podcasting, peer-to-peer file sharing and downloading, cell phone radio, and satellite radio. New technological innovations are constantly being introduced into this marketplace. However, despite this competitively challenging economic environment and a decline in overall tuning to conventional radio since 1999, the Canadian commercial radio industry remains healthy from a financial perspective, as discussed below.

Tuning to Conventional Radio

8. Overall weekly listening levels to conventional radio decreased by roughly one hour and twenty-five minutes from 1999 to 2005 to 19.1 average weekly hours tuned per capita. The decrease is most notable in the teen demographic (12–17) and for adults aged from 18 to 34.

9. Emerging technologies and more media choices will continue to erode in-house and at-work listening. Higher cell phone, MP3 and satellite radio penetration will increasingly challenge in-car listening. As a result, audiences to conventional radio are expected to decline over the next several years.

AIRPLAY AND FINANCIAL SUPPORT FOR CANADIAN MUSIC, INCLUDING FRENCH-LANGUAGE VOCAL MUSIC

32. The Canadian broadcasting system has an important role to play in showcasing the work and contributing to the development and promotion of Canadian artists. Section 3(1)(d)(ii) of the Act provides that the Canadian broadcasting system should "encourage the development of Canadian expression by ... displaying Canadian talent in entertainment programming ..." Section 3(1)(e) of the Act provides that "each element of the Canadian broadcasting system shall contribute in an appropriate manner to the creation and presentation of Canadian programming." Section 3(1)(f) provides that "each broadcasting undertaking shall make maximum use, and in no case less than predominant use, of Canadian creative and other resources in the creation and presentation of programming unless the nature of the service provided by the undertaking, such as specialized content or format or the use of languages other than French and English, renders that use impracticable, in which case the undertaking shall make the greatest practicable use of those resources."

33. The commercial radio sector contributes to the fulfilment of the objectives set out above in two ways. The first is through the airplay of Canadian music, including French-language vocal music, which provides a showcase for the work of Canadian artists. The second is through financial contributions to CTD that are commensurate with the financial health of the sector. These development initiatives help ensure the availability and promotion of high quality Canadian music, and other creative material, for broadcast.

Current Approach

Airplay

Canadian Music

34. Section 2.2 of the *Radio Regulations, 1986* (the Radio Regulations) sets out the minimum levels of Canadian musical selections required of radio stations holding commercial licences. The Radio Regulations require that at least 35% of the popular (category 2) musical selections and at least 10% of the special interest (category 3) musical selections aired during each broadcast week be Canadian selections.

35. To ensure that Canadian selections are not relegated to times when relatively small audiences are tuned to radio, such as on weekday evenings and on weekends, the Radio Regulations also require that at least 35% of the category 2 musical selections broadcast between 6:00 a.m. and 6:00 p.m., Monday through Friday during any broadcast week, be Canadian selections.

36. The Radio Regulations provide that a musical selection must generally meet at least two of the criteria set out below in order to qualify as a Canadian selection. This is commonly referred to as the MAPL system.

37. M (music)—the music is composed entirely by a Canadian.
   A (artist)—the music is, or the lyrics are, performed principally by a Canadian.
   P (production)—the musical selection consists of a live performance that is recorded wholly in Canada, or performed wholly in Canada and broadcast live in Canada.
   L (Lyrics)—the lyrics are entirely written by a Canadian.
   - The musical selection was performed live or recorded after 1 September 1991, and a Canadian who has collaborated with a non-Canadian receives at least half of the credit as a composer and lyricist.

French-language Vocal Music

38. To ensure that French-language radio stations holding commercial licences serve the needs and interests of their audiences, section 2.2 of the Radio Regulations requires that at least 65% of the category 2 vocal musical selections aired by French-language stations during each broadcast week be in the French language. To ensure that French-language vocal selections are not consigned to periods with relatively small audiences, the Radio Regulations also require that at least 55% of the category 2 vocal musical selections aired by French-language stations each week between 6 a.m. and 6 p.m., Monday through Friday during any broadcast week be French-language selections.

❋ ❋ ❋

Commission's Analysis and Determinations

81. In this section, the Commission sets out its revised approach to airplay for Canadian music, including French-language vocal music, and to development initiatives. In order to reflect a new emphasis on development initiatives that lead to the creation of audio content for broadcast using Canadian resources, the Commission considers that it is appropriate to replace the expression "Canadian talent development" (CTD) with "Canadian content development" (CCD). The Commission's approach involves a number of changes to the requirements related to airplay, and focuses primarily on CCD. The Commission considers that well-targeted CCD initiatives allocated to the support, promotion, training and development of Canadian musical and spoken-word talent will increase the supply of and demand for high-quality Canadian music in a variety of genres as well as enlarge the supply of spoken word material for broadcast.

Airplay

Category 2 Selections

82. The Commission has taken note of the suggestions made, mainly by representatives of the music industry, that there are supplies of Canadian music in most genres that would permit increases in the required minimum levels of Canadian category 2 musical selections. It also notes, however, the arguments made by the commercial radio industry that demand by listeners for more Canadian music has not been demonstrated, and that listeners, especially youth, are turning more and more to unregulated sources of music.

83. The minimum levels of Canadian category 2 selections were increased, by regulation, from 30% to 35% in 1999 as a result of the 1998 Review. This has led to a substantial increase in the total amount of Canadian music available to radio listeners. Many stations, especially French-language stations, have exceeded the minimum levels. However, Commission studies have not indicated that there has been a meaningful increase in the airplay of selections by new and emerging Canadian artists by English-language stations.

84. A number of statistics were cited with respect to the sale of Canadian recordings. Evidence provided by CIRPA, and according to *The Canadian Music Industry 2005 Economic Profile* issued by the Department of Canadian Heritage, indicates that Canadian artists' share of the top 2,000 album sales tracked by Soundscan increased upward between 16% and 25% between 1998 and 2005. The CAB cited data from Statistics Canada indicating that Canadian recordings comprised 17% of total sales of recordings in 1998 and 16% of total sales of recordings in 2000 and 2003. The Commission is of the view that these sales figures do not indicate a level of demand that would support a further increase in the required levels of Canadian category 2 selections at this time.

85. The Commission is also not convinced that a further increase in the required levels of Canadian category 2 music is the best way to foster the airplay of music by

emerging Canadian artists, and is concerned that an increase could lead to more repetition of the musical selections by Canadian artists that are already established. Further, it does not consider that an increase to the required level of Canadian category 2 music is appropriate at a time when the radio industry must respond to the challenge of competing with new, largely unregulated sources for the delivery of audio programming.

86. **Accordingly, the Commission will retain the existing requirements respecting the levels of category 2 Canadian selections set out in the Radio Regulations.**

French-language Vocal Music

87. With respect to French-language vocal music, the Commission notes comments by representatives of the music industry that increases in the required minimum levels would be achievable. It also notes, however, the comments by French-language broadcasters that MVF levels are too high, leading to high levels of repetition for the most popular selections and artists.

88. The Commission notes suggestions for bonus systems related to MVF, whereby selections by emerging Canadian French-language artists would receive additional weight in meeting the required MVF levels. However, the Commission is concerned that implementation of a bonus system, such as that suggested by the CAB where a selection by an emerging Canadian French-language artist would receive a 150% credit toward meeting MVF requirements, would lead to a decrease in the total number of MVF selections that are played. It further notes that, since the more stringent MVF requirements were established in 1999, Commission studies indicate that there has been an increase in the airplay of selections by emerging Canadian artists on French-language stations. The Commission is satisfied that the current MVF requirements are having a positive effect and does not consider that they should be amended at this time. As is the case with category 2 music, the Commission is concerned about raising the required MVF levels at a time when the radio industry must respond to the challenges of competing with new, largely unregulated technologies for the delivery of audio programming.

89. **In light of the above, the Commission will retain the existing requirements respecting the levels of French-language vocal musical selections in category 2 for commercial broadcasters set out in the Radio Regulations.**

🍁 🍁 🍁

Canadian Content Development

97. In light of the growth in revenue and profitability that the radio industry has experienced since the 1998 Review, and given that an increased demand for Canadian music has not been demonstrated as discussed earlier, the Commission considers that additional emphasis should be placed on the development and promotion of Canadian talent through financial contributions by broadcasters to the development of audio content for broadcast. Such initiatives will not only help to develop and advance the careers of emerging Canadian artists but

will increase the supply of high-quality Canadian music in a variety of genres and the demand for Canadian music by listeners. They will also enlarge the supply of spoken word material for broadcast. Further, the initiatives can also be tailored in a flexible manner that is representative of the programming and revenues of particular stations. Stations make CCD commitments at the time of licence renewals, when applications for new licences are considered, and as tangible benefits at the time of the transfer of ownership and control of radio undertakings.

98. In order to make the most effective use of these financial contributions, the Commission considers that such contributions should be used to fund initiatives that lead to the creation and promotion of audio content for broadcast using Canadian resources. This is achieved by the support, promotion, training and development of Canadian musical and spoken word talent, including journalists. In light of this approach, initiatives not targeted to the development of Canadian audio content, such as visual arts exhibitions, theatre and dance will no longer qualify for contributions by radio broadcasters.

99. CCD initiatives by broadcasters are important at the local, regional and national levels. In reflecting the circumstances of their local communities, local initiatives by broadcasters can provide an important first step in the discovery and showcasing of new artists. Not-for-profit MIAs, operating in most regions, foster new and emerging talent. They do valuable work with those very early in their careers, providing various forms of support, information, communication, education, as well as business and market development services. These also support artists as they develop their professional careers.

100. At the national level, FACTOR and MUSICACTION are the most important vehicles for the development of a variety of Canadian artists, including new and emerging artists. In operation since the mid-1980s, FACTOR and MUSICACTION are well-known and established organizations that have implemented a variety of programs that have resulted in the emergence of many well-known Canadian artists.

101. Programs such as those supporting new recordings, touring and showcasing are especially valuable for artists who do not qualify for funding from the Radio Starmaker Fund or Fonds Radiostar. The Collective Initiative grants program, supported, in part, by funding from the Department of Canadian Heritage, underwrites initiatives by music organizations, including the MIAs, that sustain the development of such artists, including emerging songwriters.

102. The Commission notes that the Department of Canadian Heritage has initiated a program providing financial assistance to certain Canadian recording firms. These firms, as participants in this program, are no longer eligible for funding from FACTOR or MUSICACTION. More funding from FACTOR or MUSICACTION will therefore likely be available for programs that support emerging Canadian artists.

103. The Commission notes comments by parties concerning the necessity for accountability and transparency with regard to CCD. In this regard, the Commission commends FACTOR and MUSICACTION for the very detailed accounting of their activities in their latest annual reports.

104. The Radio Starmaker Fund and Fonds RadioStar were created following the 1998 Review. These funds provide support for the marketing and promotion of established artists, contributing to their national and international success. The Radio

Starmaker Fund and Fonds RadioStar are the largest recipients of financial support from radio broadcasters, and the Commission commends them for adjusting their eligibility criteria for certain less-established categories of music. The Commission encourages these funds to provide similar flexibility to other types of music for niche audiences, thereby further recognizing the diversity of Canadian musical talent.

DISCUSSION

CRTC, *Commercial Radio Policy 2006.*

1. The CRTC *Commercial Radio Policy* begins by setting out specific objectives for developing policy in the private radio sector. List three of these objectives and explain which of the key policy objectives from the Policy Analysis Framework on page 6 they most directly relate to.
2. This document lists some of the stakeholders in commercial radio policy who participated in the policy review process. Which groups are mentioned and which ones represent predominantly public or private interests?
3. The *Commercial Radio Policy* quotes sections of the *Broadcasting Act* that pertain to radio. In what two important ways does commercial radio contribute to the fulfillment of the *Act?*
4. What four criteria does the policy use to determine whether music on commercial radio qualifies as a 'Canadian selection'? Are these criteria related to the citizenship of the creator, the location of music production, or the aesthetic content of the music?
5. Currently, at least 35 percent of the music played on commercial radio stations between 6:00 A.M. and 6:00 P.M. must be Canadian. What reasons does the policy statement give for not raising this level to 40 percent as suggested by some stakeholders? Do you agree or disagree with these reasons?
6. What is the objective of Canadian Content Development as laid out in the *Commercial Radio Policy?* How will this part of the policy be implemented?

Policy Source 10

Canadian Radio-Television and Telecommunications Commission. (2010a). *Broadcasting Regulatory Policy CRTC 2010–167, A group-based approach to the licensing of private television services.*

A Group-based Approach to the Licensing of Private Television Services

In this regulatory policy, the Commission sets out its determinations on issues relating to a group-based approach to the licensing of large English-language private television ownership groups. The key areas addressed are the following:

- *Canadian programming expenditures;*
- *Canadian content requirements;*
- *programs of national interest;*
- *maintaining local programming;*
- *expenditures on non-Canadian programming;*
- *Canadian independent production;*
- *regional production;*
- *continuing application of social policies;*
- *ownership issues;*
- *administrative renewals; and*
- *appropriate length of licence term.*

The Commission also addresses the following issues relating to revenue support for English- and French-language conventional television broadcasters:

- *review of the Local Programming Improvement Fund; and*
- *proposed regime for value for signal and the question of the Commission's jurisdiction to be referred to the Federal Court of Appeal for expedited hearing and determination.*

Further, the Commission notes its determinations, set out in broadcasting regulatory policies to be issued shortly, relating to advertising on the video-on-demand platform and to the sale of commercial advertising in the local availabilities of non-Canadian specialty services. It also states its intention to conduct a review of its policies concerning direct-to-home (DTH) services prior to the next licence renewal proceedings for the two DTH undertakings currently in operation (Shaw Direct and Bell TV).

Finally, the Commission addresses various issues relating to the digital television (DTV) transition for English- and French-language conventional television broadcasters, including its revised list of mandatory markets, the date set for the DTV transition, and the operation of analog transmitters in and outside the mandatory markets. A dissenting opinion by Commissioner Suzanne Lamarre is attached.

INTRODUCTION—LEGISLATIVE CONTEXT

1. Section 3(1)(s) of the *Broadcasting Act* (the Act) states that:
   (s) private networks and programming undertakings should, to an extent consistent with the financial and other resources available to them,

   i. contribute significantly to the creation and presentation of Canadian programming, and
   ii. be responsive to the evolving demands of the public [. . .]

2. Further, section 3(1)(t) of the Act states that distribution undertakings:

   i. should give priority to the carriage of Canadian programming services and, in particular, to the carriage of local Canadian stations,
   ii. should provide efficient delivery of programming at affordable rates, using the most effective technologies available at reasonable cost [. . .]

3. In order to give effect to these and other objectives set out by Parliament in the Act, the Commission has developed and modified its policies and regulations in light of the broadcasting environment of the time.

4. For over fifty years, individual television broadcasting undertakings, in return for regulatory supports and protections, have been obligated to meet requirements for the exhibition of a diversity of Canadian programming. To ensure sufficient quality of that programming, expenditure requirements have been imposed where required.

5. This model has served Canadians and all of the other stakeholders in the Canadian broadcasting system well. Its application through the introduction of new services and new platforms has provided Canadian viewers with a world leading diversity of both Canadian and foreign content. This has been accomplished in the face of significant geographic, economic and linguistic challenges.

6. The advent of digital technologies for the distribution of broadcasting and for the broader exchange of all digital information has fundamentally changed the basis for existing approaches to television broadcasting regulation. The ownership structure of Canadian television has also changed with a relatively few large ownership groups now controlling the majority of services, audience share and revenues.

7. The Canadian broadcasting system will succeed or fail to the degree that Canadian creative talent, producers, broadcasters and distributors provide a quality Canadian television experience for the viewer. At the heart of this experience is the ability of the system to continually create attractive new Canadian programs.

8. There is significant opportunity to deliver programming from both within and outside the regulated broadcasting system. The Commission recognizes that models for distributing Canadian content to Canadians increasingly include non-linear platforms, such as video-on-demand (VOD) and the Internet. Canadians' expectations

for the delivery of content have evolved considerably since the Act came into force in 1991. The desire to view content at any time on any platform is changing Canadians' viewing habits. Yet the Act clearly enjoins private networks and programming undertakings to be responsive to the public's evolving demands. Therefore, attractive Canadian content available at anytime and on any platform represents a goal towards which the Canadian broadcasting system should strive in order to remain not only responsive to the public's demands, but also relevant and competitive in the new digital era.

9. It is, in part, with a view to meeting the challenges of this new on-demand world that the Commission undertook the current revision of its regulatory policy with respect to television programming services. In its view, a shift in regulatory focus from program exhibition to program creation will help to ensure the continued presence of Canadian programming options for Canadians, however the broadcasting system may evolve.

10. Indeed, the process launched with Broadcasting Notice of Consultation 2009–411[1] sought to develop a new approach to the creation and distribution of Canadian programming in a new broadcasting landscape.

11. One of key features of the Canadian broadcasting system has been its openness to foreign television services. Broadcasting distribution undertakings (BDUs) have benefited from being able to offer subscribers diverse packages of Canadian and foreign services, and consumers have benefited from a significant degree of choice. On the other hand, the widespread availability of foreign services has fragmented the audience and revenues available to Canadian broadcasters.

12. The framework described in the new regulatory policy set out in this document recognizes both the increasing fragmentation of viewing audiences and the reality of corporate consolidation in the marketplace. Its intention is to remove unnecessary barriers to the continued viability of private broadcasters and to ensure that broadcasters are able to obtain, through market-based negotiations, fair value for the distribution of the programming they broadcast.

13. The Commission continues to recognize the importance of regulation to meet the objectives of the Act where the market cannot do so, but considers that, in a broadcasting environment characterized by ever increasing choice, the application of regulation must be directed towards the creation of quality Canadian content. This framework is an important and timely step in preparing the Canadian broadcasting system for its digital future.

🍁 🍁 🍁

PART 1—ISSUES RELATING TO A GROUP-BASED APPROACH TO THE LICENSING OF LARGE ENGLISH-LANGUAGE PRIVATE TELEVISION OWNERSHIP GROUPS

22. The Commission regulates television programming services on an individual basis. Currently, where expenditure requirements have been imposed, they apply to a single service in relation to the financial situation of that service and without regard to the overall financial situation of the other television services controlled by a single ownership group.

23. The television programming services controlled by the largest ownership groups in broadcasting now account for the large majority of viewing to all Canadian television,[2] although this viewing is fragmented among multiple individual programming undertakings. These large, private broadcasting groups, by launching or acquiring multiple specialty services, have embraced the opportunity to offer a greater choice of programming to audiences.

24. As conventional television profitability is challenged by a downturn in advertising revenues and the fragmentation of those revenues, specialty services have demonstrated continued financial strength on the basis of their dual advertising/subscription revenue streams. This has contributed to the overall profitability of the large groups and their ongoing ability to contribute to the creation of high-quality Canadian programming.

25. In Broadcasting Notice of Consultation 2009–411, the Commission noted that the present proceeding would examine how to structure and conduct group-based conventional and specialty television licence renewals. The Commission sought to establish a comprehensive framework that would take into account systemic changes in the broadcasting industry, including those relating to the horizontal and vertical integration that has taken place.

26. Through group-based licence renewals, the Commission's objective is to provide private broadcasting groups with greater flexibility in the allocation of resources amongst their various television platforms. These groups require the flexibility to respond quickly to changes in viewer behaviour. Such an approach will allow the Commission to consider factors including, but not limited to, the total audience reached by a broadcasting group, the totality of its revenues and the totality of its programming commitments and obligations.

27. The greater flexibility that will result from a group-based approach should have a positive impact on the viability of the Canadian television industry. Further, it will permit the Commission to ensure continued support for the creation of Canadian programming, particularly in categories that continue to be under-represented in the Canadian broadcasting system, such as scripted drama and documentaries.

28. In the following sections, the Commission sets out its determinations on group-based requirements relating to the following issues:

   - Canadian programming expenditures (CPE);
   - Canadian content requirements;
   - programs of national interest;
   - maintaining local programming;
   - expenditures on non-Canadian programming;
   - Canadian independent production;
   - regional production;
   - annual reporting;
   - continuing application of social policies;
   - ownership issues;
   - administrative renewals;
   - appropriate length of licence term; and
   - application of the group framework—detailed determinations.

A Flexible Canadian Programming Expenditure Requirement

Commission's Analysis and Determinations

41. The Commission must supervise and regulate the broadcasting system in order to fulfil the policy objectives of the Act. These include encouraging the development of Canadian expression; being readily adaptable to scientific and technological change; and ensuring that each element of the Canadian broadcasting system contributes in an appropriate manner to the creation and presentation of Canadian programming.

42. The Commission considers that these objectives, particularly the adaptability of the broadcasting system to change, are best met through a regulatory approach that recognizes the significant challenges to conventional television broadcasting and the stronger role that both regulated and unregulated, on-demand platforms are playing in providing Canadians with the television programming they need and want.

43. The Commission notes that there has been a significant shift in Canadians' viewing habits since the publication of the 1999 Television Policy.[5] The subsequent widespread introduction of digital cable has rapidly brought Canadians a wide variety of programming choices, from both Canadian and non-Canadian sources. The availability of new services on conventional and specialty television platforms has been significantly augmented by content available from alternative, unregulated platforms.

44. The exclusivity of broadcasters' programming has eroded as a result of increased choice and increasing cost of foreign programming. This has resulted in a diminishing of the profits realized from the exhibition of popular foreign programming. The profitability of this programming has, in the past, provided conventional television broadcasters with the resources to spend on less profitable Canadian programming, such as programs of local reflection, local news, and especially high-quality scripted Canadian environment.

45. In the short and medium terms, because of their continued ability to attract mass audiences, conventional television broadcasters play a particularly important role in fulfilling the objectives of the Act. However, in the longer term, as audiences continue to move to other platforms, this role may become less important. As a step in adapting the broadcasting system to the digital age, the Commission considers it appropriate to pursue a new approach regarding the regarding the requirements for the exhibition and creation of high-quality Canadian programming.

46. First, in order to ensure that the designated groups continue to contribute to the creation of Canadian programming, the Commission will establish a minimum, aggregate level of spending on Canadian programs for each designated group.

47. Second, in order to permit the designated groups to adapt quickly to a changing environment, the Commission will provide them with the greatest possible flexibility so that they may allocate that spending among their various licensed undertakings. Since these ownership groups are not licensees of the Commission, this policy will be implemented through the imposition of conditions of licence on the relevant individual licensees controlled by the groups, as set out in detail below.

48. All qualifying specialty services controlled by a designated group will continue individual CPE requirements imposed by condition of licence (as is the current practice for Category 1 and analog specialty services). In addition, the Commission will impose, by condition of licence, a CPE requirement on the conventional tele-

vision services controlled by the designated groups. These CPE requirements will be expressed as a percentage of the previous year's revenues.

49. The Commission has also determined that Category B specialty services controlled a designated group and with more than one million subscribers will be subject to a CPE requirement. This requirement will be determined at the licence renewal of these services, using as a base the actual spending by the services over the previous three years.

50. It is the Commission's preliminary view that the base spending level for each designated group, as an aggregate, should be a minimum of 30% of the group's gross revenues. The Commission considers that this is an appropriate level given the record of the groups' actual spending on Canadian programming in the years 2007, 2008 and 2009, and given the Commission's intention not to impose, at this time, additional obligations on the groups beyond their recent historical expenditures.

51. In order to establish the appropriate CPE for the conventional television services controlled by a designated group, the Commission will calculate the dollar amount of the CPE obligations for qualifying[6] Category A and Category B specialty services. This amount will be subtracted from the dollar amount of the group's 30% CPE obligation. The difference will be the dollar amount of the CPE obligation for the conventional television services controlled by the group.

52. The difference established in the above paragraph, calculated as a percentage of the average of the previous three years' gross revenues for the conventional television services, will constitute the CPE for the designated group's conventional television services and will be imposed as a condition of licence on those services.

53. In order to permit the groups to adapt quickly to changing circumstances, qualifying specialty licensees within a designated group will have the flexibility to attribute 100% of their required CPE to any other qualifying specialty service, or to conventional television services, within the same designated group. Each licensee will be required to report annually the attributed amounts and each of the service(s) to which they were allocated.

54. Designated groups will also have flexibility to attribute a portion of the required CPE for the conventional television services controlled by that group. However, as the Commission attaches particular importance to CPE spending for conventional television services, this flexibility will be limited. Only a maximum of 25% of the required CPE for conventional television services may be attributed to any other qualifying specialty services within the same designated group. Each licensee will be required to report annually the attributed amounts and each of the service(s) to which they were allocated.

🍁 🍁 🍁

Canadian Content Requirements

Positions of Parties

61. Currently, conventional television broadcasters are required to devote, by regulation, a minimum average of 60% of the broadcast year and not less than 50% of the evening broadcast period (6:00 p.m. to midnight) to the broadcast of Canadian

programs. Further, Canadian content exhibition requirements for specialty services vary according to the nature of the programming provided. In Broadcasting Notice of Consultation 2009–411, the Commission sought comment on a conceptual model whereby each ownership group would be required to devote, across all of its services, not less than 55% of the programming broadcast over the broadcast year to Canadian programming and, on each specific service, not less than 35% of the programming broadcast over the broadcast year to such programming.

62. Although broadcasters were generally supportive of the conceptual model, many indicated that it would be inappropriate to establish a single Canadian content requirement at the group level. Most of the broadcasters stated that exhibition requirements should be tailored for specific types of services in order to reflect the particular character of each service. As well, many broadcasters supported the exclusion of an evening exhibition requirement.

63. Various parties representing the creative sector strongly discouraged the Commission from lowering the overall Canadian content level to 55%, while other parties indicated that the amount could be lowered if the Commission combined the exhibition requirement with an expenditure requirement. In addition, most parties from the creative sector argued for the maintenance of the evening Canadian content requirement on conventional television stations.

Commission's Analysis and Determinations

64. With respect to conventional television, the Commission recognizes the importance of providing maximum regulatory flexibility while ensuring the availability of Canadian programming during times when most Canadians are watching television. Accordingly, the Commission is of the view that, for conventional television stations, it would be appropriate to amend the *Television Broadcasting Regulations, 1987* so that a licensee is required to devote not less than 55% of the broadcast year while maintaining the current requirement of devoting not less than 50% of the evening broadcast period (6:00 p.m. to midnight) to the broadcast of Canadian programs.

65. As for the Canadian content requirements for specialty services, the Commission concurs with the position of most parties that exhibition requirements should be tailored to reflect the character of each service. Accordingly, the Commission will continue to impose Canadian content exhibition requirements for specialty services on an individual basis.

Programs of National Interest

Positions of Parties

66. Priority programs, as currently defined, are Canadian programs in the categories of drama, long-form documentary, music/variety, entertainment magazines and regionally-produced programs other than news and sports.

67. In Public Notice 1999–97, the Commission required the largest conventional multi-station ownership groups to broadcast, over the broadcast year, on average,

at least eight hours per broadcast week of priority Canadian programs during peak time, which was defined as the period from 7:00 p.m. to 11:00 p.m.

68. In Broadcasting Notice of Consultation 2009–411, the Commission sought comment on how the current exhibition requirements for Canadian content and priority programs could be simplified, streamlined or amalgamated. Further, the Commission sought comment on the measures that might be required in a group-based framework to ensure appropriate exhibition of programs of national interest, such as dramas and documentaries.

69. There was general consensus among parties representing broadcasters and the creative sector that the concept of priority programming needed to be updated. Broadcasters, for the most part, proposed an expansion of the definition of priority programming to include additional categories, and proposed greater flexibility in how such programming could be exhibited. Conversely, producers and creators proposed a narrowing of the definition of priority programming to the difficult-to-finance categories of scripted drama and long-form documentaries, and children's programming.

Commission's Analysis and Determinations

70. The Commission recognizes that broadcasters require increased flexibility to program their various services in order to maximize audiences and revenues. However, such flexibility must be balanced with continuing support for the creation of programs that clearly serve the national interest. To achieve these two objectives, the Commission has deemed it appropriate to eliminate the current exhibition requirement for priority programming and replace it with an expenditure requirement that will apply to categories of programs that the Commission considers to be of national interest and that, in its view, require continued regulatory support.

Defining Programs of National Interest

71. The Commission considers that there is a continuing need for regulatory support for key genres of Canadian programming. The Commission notes that over 40% of all viewing to English-language television in Canada is to drama programs;[8] drama is thus the genre of programming that Canadians choose to watch more than all others. Drama programs and documentary programs are expensive and difficult to produce, yet are central vehicles for communicating Canadian stories and values. In addition, the Commission considers that programs that celebrate Canadian creative talent in English Canada, such as The Geminis, The Junos, The Giller Prize, The National Aboriginal Achievement Awards, The East Coast Music Awards, and The Aboriginal Peoples Choice Music Awards, promote Canadian culture and are also of national interest.

72. The Commission has therefore determined that the new designation of programs of national interest will consist of programs from program categories 7 Drama and comedy and 2(b) Long-form documentary,[9] as well as specific Canadian award shows that celebrate Canadian creative talent, such as those noted above.

73. The Commission notes that programs directed to children are not considered to be a separate program category. Such programs may be categorized in a variety

of program genres. Therefore, programs directed to children that are in categories 7 and 2(*b*) will also be considered programs of national interest.

Canadian Programming Expenditure Requirements for Programs of National Interest

74. In order to ensure that programs of national interest are created and available on whatever platform Canadians choose to consume their media, the Commission will impose on each designated group, at the next licence renewals of their services, an expenditure requirement specific to the creation and acquisition of programs of national interest. Licensees will have the flexibility to attribute 100% of their required spending on programs of national interest to any qualifying specialty service or conventional television services within the same designated group so long as the aggregate group CPE is met.

75. The Commission does not, at this time, collect separate expenditure information for category 2(*b*) programs. Consequently, it is not possible to evaluate licensees' past expenditures in this category. Analyzing past expenditures for drama (category 7) only, the Commission has determined that group expenditures of at least 5% of gross revenues over the licence term is appropriate. The large groups will be required to file, as part of their renewal applications, their historical spending on long-form documentaries and award show programming. Based upon its analysis of these past expenditures, the Commission will establish, at licence renewal, a base level spending requirement for programs of national interest and determine whether any increases over the licence term may be necessary.

76. The Commission's view is that this approach, with its emphasis on the creation of programming, will best ensure that Canadian stories are told and made available to viewers in Canada and abroad, whatever the platform.

77. The Commission notes that, in order to ensure transparency and accountability, the manner by which the licensees report programming-related expenditures in their annual returns will require modification. Specifically, licensees will be required to report programming expenditures related to long-form documentaries (category 2(*b*)) and award programs as separate line items in their annual returns. This reporting modification will apply to all conventional, specialty and pay television programming undertakings.

❋ ❋ ❋

Endnotes

1. Amendments to certain paragraphs of that notice of consultation were provided in Broadcasting Notice of Consultation 2009–411–3.
2. See CRTC Communications Monitoring Report 2009.
3. Conventional television services have not had a requirement for a minimum level of Canadian expenditures since the issuance of Public Notice 1999–97.
4. See Public Notice 1999–97.
5. See *Navigating Convergence: Charting Canadian Communications Change and Regulatory Implications,* available on the Commission's website under "Broadcasting Reports and Publications."

6. See section 4 of the appendix to this regulatory policy.
8. See CRTC Communications Monitoring Report 2009.
9. These program categories are set out in Public Notice 1999–205 and in Item 6 of Schedule I to the *Television Broadcasting Regulations, 1987*.

DISCUSSION

CRTC, *A Group-Based Approach to the Licensing of Private Television Services 2010.*

1. The policy for private television suggests that Canadian broadcasting will succeed or fail to the degree that it is able to provide a quality Canadian television experience for the viewer. In your opinion, what does a 'quality Canadian television experience' include, what features of this policy do you think support it, and what things do you think are missing?
2. In this policy, the CRTC hopes to ensure the economic stability of the industry while focussing on the creation of quality Canadian content and it allows large ownership groups to be flexible in meeting requirements across multiple platforms. To what extent are economic profits and creation of Canadian content potentially competing goals? Do you think this policy successfully strikes a balance between them? Why or why not?
3. In your own words explain the main elements of the 2010 Canadian Programming Expenditure requirement and describe how the CRTC plans to implement it for large ownership groups in the television industry.
4. The quota for the average amount of Canadian content screened over the broadcast year was lowered from 60 percent to 55 percent. Using Babe's contrast between regulation and incentive, explain which stakeholders were likely to be for or against this reduction and why.
5. What specific types of programs are included in the category 'programs of national interest'? Why does the CRTC suggest that private television networks should devote some of their profits to creating this type of content?

Protecting Media Industries and Ownership Restrictions

Chapter

7

INTRODUCTION

In this chapter, we will look at how governments have used various policy tools to protect Canadian ownership of Canada's media industries. National ownership is not the same as public ownership or public broadcasting. In this case governments are using media policies to protect private and commercial media companies from take-over by foreign interests. Many countries require that radio and television services be owned by their own citizens. The US, for example, restricts ownership of television networks, but not film studios, to US citizens. This legal requirement led to Australian Rupert Murdoch's decision to become a US citizen in 1985 so that he could expand his ownership of the 20th Century Fox film studios into the realm of television by buying TV stations for his new Fox Network (Grant & Wood, 2004, 247). In Canada, foreign ownership and control of radio and television is restricted by the CRTC. The Commission requires that no less that 80 percent of voting shares of companies with broadcast licences be held by Canadians. The CRTC carefully monitors Canadian media ownership so that even parent companies or holding companies with interests in radio or television licences must have a majority (66 and two-thirds percent) voting share ownership in Canadian hands (Armstrong, 2010, 206). In an era of expanding concentration of media ownership and rapid changes in majority control of media companies, determining the actual locus of financial control in large corporations can be complicated and is sometimes disputed by companies subject to unfavourable CRTC rulings.

Outside of broadcasting, under the *Investment Canada Act,* Heritage Canada monitors the sale and

191

acquisition of other media and cultural industries to be sure they are in keeping with Canada's cultural policies. This *Act* has led to review of foreign acquisitions in the book publishing and film and video production industries. Foreign ownership is not directly restricted in the magazine or newspaper industry, but here other policy tools make take-overs or acquisitions unappealing to non-Canadians. Successive Canadian governments have recognized not only the value of protecting Canadian ownership of media indus-tries, but also in protecting Canadian advertising revenue for Canadian media compa-nies. This form of protection occurs in two main areas, through income tax deductions for advertising in Canadian media and through the CRTC's 'simultaneous substitution' rules. Provisions of the *Income Tax Act* stipulate that in order to count advertising costs as a business tax deduction in Canada, those ads must be placed in majority Canadian-owned newspapers, television, or radio stations, or in Canadian-content magazines. While Canadian companies might believe that they can reach more Canadian readers with advertisements in American mass circulation magazines or on US television and ra-dio stations with cross-border reach, Section 19 of the *Income Tax Act* makes it eco-nomically prohibitive to advertise in anything other than Canadian-owned media. This has the outcome of preserving advertising revenue for Canadian media outlets. In the area of cable television, a related policy protects Canadian ad revenue for the Canadian-owned networks. If a cable company carries a US network like NBC and a Canadian network like CTV, the programming is often identical since CTV purchases the rights to broadcast major US series in Canada and these programs are usually scheduled at ex-actly the same time on both networks. The CRTC's 'simultaneous substitution' rule means that cable viewers watching the NBC channel actually see the CTV ads inserted during the program breaks. This rule is designed to ensure that Canadian ads reach the largest possible viewership and to protect a steady supply of ad revenue from local sources for Canadian television networks.

In the 1990s, some of these national ownership rules and protectionist policies came under scrutiny in the international context of free trade agreements. This was particu-larly the case in the magazine industry. Historically, Canadian governments developed several policies to support and protect Canadian magazines. The oldest policy tool in this area is the application of a subsidy to postal rates for magazines. As indicated in Pol-icy Source 12 below, the objective of the postal subsidy was to lower prices for Canadian magazines and make them uniform across the country, ensuring fair access for Canadian readers to Canadian publications. In 1961, the O'Leary Royal Commission on Publica-tions discovered that most of Canada's magazines were foreign-owned. In response to this finding, the *Income Tax Act* was amended in 1965 to disallow tax deductions for ad-vertising directed at Canadian markets that were placed in foreign-owned magazines (Dubinsky, 1996, 43). The same year, the government also created Tariff Code 9958, which prohibited the entry of 'split-run' magazines into Canada at customs. A split-run magazine includes editorial content already produced in the US, where the American ads are removed and replaced with ads targeted at Canadians and then distributed in the Canadian market. Split-runs require no new editorial content, so American magazines are able to sell ad space in Canada at a highly discounted price (Szeman, 2000, 214). Be-cause up to 60 percent of a magazine's revenue comes from ad sales, split-runs were si-phoning off a substantial proportion of possible income for Canadian magazines, while driving down the prices for ad space. By the late 1980s, the customs tariff was no longer effective because US magazine publishers began simply transmitting magazine content electronically to printing plants in Canada where the Canadian ads were inserted. Even with protections under the *Income Tax Act,* these technological changes meant that Canadian magazines were still struggling against foreign competition. In 1993, the introduction of a split-run edition of *Sports Illustrated Canada* triggered the creation of a federal Task Force on the Magazine Industry. On the recommendations of this body, the federal government in 1995 added a further excise tax of 80 percent on the ad revenue of split-run titles.

In a move that significantly altered the history of Canada's magazine policy, the US directly challenged the excise tax and other protectionist policy tools before the World Trade Organization (WTO). In its complaint, the US argued that Tariff Code 9958, the application of the excise tax, and Canada's postal subsidies, all violated the General Agreement on Tariffs and Trade (GATT) to which Canada is a signatory. After a hearing and appeal process during 1996–97, the WTO panel found that Canada's various policy measures in support of its magazine industry were indeed in contravention of GATT (WTO, 2012). The dispute then led to an overhaul of magazine policy in a formal agreement with the US. The final result was the elimination of the tariff code and the excise tax, and the creation of the *Foreign Publishers Advertising Services Act* (FPASA) in 1999. As described in Policy Source 11, FPASA allows US-owned magazines to publish in Canada with Canadian advertising under two controlled situations. First, US titles published in Canada with less than 50 percent Canadian-originated content may have up to 18 percent of their advertising targeted at the Canadian market without penalty (amounts greater than 18 percent are subject to fines under the *Act*). Secondly, US companies may own and publish magazines in Canada with Canadian ads, but those magazines must have 80 percent Canadian-authored content to qualify for full tax deductions on advertising costs under the *Income Tax Act.* Foreign-owned titles with between 50 and 80 percent Canadian content may carry ads targeted at the Canadian market, but those ads only qualify for half of the tax deduction on advertising costs.

The Canada-US Agreement on magazines did not directly affect the postal subsidies, and at the same time in 1999 the federal government also established the Canada Magazine Fund (now Canada Periodical Fund). The Magazine Fund provided direct subsidies for content creation and business development to support magazines facing the impact of increased US access to advertising revenues in the Canadian market. More than 10 years after the FPASA was passed, however, the dire impact of US presence in the Canadian magazine industry has not materialized. Canadian magazines still face competition from US titles imported directly into Canada, especially on newsstands where foreign titles dominate. However, over 70 percent of magazines bought by subscription in Canada are Canadian titles, and the total market share for Canadian magazines is over 40 percent (Canadian Heritage, 2008b, 12). Today, the Canadian federal government still actively supports the magazine industry through the Canada Periodical Fund. Created in 2010, this new subsidy program incorporated the former Magazine Fund and the Publications Assistance Program. Canada Post and Canadian Heritage phased out postal subsidies for magazine and newspaper subscriptions in 2010, but recipients of Periodical Fund 'Aid to Publishers' (ATP) support can use this money for both content and distribution. Currently the Canada Periodical Fund devotes $75.5 million annually toward direct support for magazine publishers and innovation in the magazine industry. Canadian-owned magazines are eligible for up to $1.5 million in support each year, but the funds are tied directly to the size of each magazine's or non-daily newspaper's readership (Canadian Heritage,

2009b). The Periodical Fund is targeted toward support for small and medium sized titles and some of the larger ones, such as *Maclean's* or *Chatelaine* are capped at $1.5 million. Book publishing is also supported by direct subsidy and we will take up the question of subsidies in more detail in the next chapter.

In conclusion, we can consider some of the arguments for and against protecting national ownership of the media industries in Canada. In support of policy tools that protect domestic media industries from foreign ownership, we can see that domestically-owned companies are more likely to identify and develop local content and local talent. Canadian companies are also more likely to reinvest profits into local media development, thus keeping industry revenues in Canada. This is especially true in industries with high production costs, such as film and television. As Grant and Wood (2004, 241) argue, "When the copyright and cash flow from one domestic winner wind up in foreign hands, so does the green light for future projects. Those foreign investors may simply take the money and run—or invest it in a project in some other country." It can also be argued that nationally-owned media may have more respect for domestic content quotas and regulations, although this argument is less convincing since foreign-owned companies in any sector are obliged to respect the laws and regulations of the country within which they operate.

Some of the limitations of national ownership policies in the media industries can also be seen in the Canadian case. In small domestic markets like Canada's, licencing and ownership rules act as barriers to entry and reduce competition, leading to a greater concentration of ownership among a few powerful companies. This has been the case across all of Canada's media sectors, where concentration and cross-media ownership have been accelerating rapidly over the past decade. As Imre Szeman suggests, sometimes arguments in support of protecting national culture disguise the economic and political interests at stake in maintaining the profitability of media industries. In his 2000 analysis of the impact of the Canada-US Agreement on Magazines and the implementation of FPASA, Szeman suggests that the larger mass-market Canadian magazines like *Maclean's* or *Flare* are already globalized cultural commodities whose 'protection' as a form of national culture is somewhat dubious: ". . . the weekly new magazine format already suggests a framing and approach to news events that is similar to other, foreign (American) magazines. Most contemporary media forms already embody cultural values and ideologies—those of capitalist modernity often, though incorrectly, associated with America in particular—and thus the defence of the magazine industry on cultural grounds is problematic to say the least" (Szeman, 2000, 221).

National ownership policies have protected Canada's media industries from outside competition and ensured their profitability in our small market. However, allowing for foreign ownership might bring more capital into Canadian industry to finance technological innovation, thereby also increasing competition and freedom of choice for consumers. At present, the arguments in favour of protecting national ownership in media industries continue to hold considerable weight with the federal government, but as the pressures of digitalization, globalization, and international trade increase, this political position could change.

Policy Source 11 gives a clear overview of the Canada-US Agreement on Magazines and the FPASA. The Canadian Heritage backgrounder explains how foreign magazine publishers may gradually increase the number of Canadian advertisements in their periodicals, up to a maximum of 18 percent after 2002. The report also explains the transfer of authority for foreign investment reviews in Canadian cultural industries to the Department of Canadian Heritage and describes the conditions under which foreign publishers may publish Canadian content magazines. As the information makes clear, tax deductions for advertisements in magazines will no longer be based on Canadian ownership of the periodical, but on its level of Canadian-authored content. The new requirements of the FPASA led to subsequent amendments to the *Income Tax Act* in 2000 in order to implement these changes.

Policy Source 12 provides a snapshot of policy tools and their outcomes in the book and periodical industries in Canada. The report describes the role of the Cultural Affairs sector of Canadian Heritage in implementing legislation and regulations that support national ownership in these industries, while fostering creation of and access to Canadian books and magazines. Presenting economic statistics that reveal the varying degrees of profitability in these industries, the report also highlights the rapid technological and market changes occurring in both book and periodical publishing. The report focuses on government support for the creation of content through subsidy programs for books and magazines, while enhanced access to this content is fostered through various programs that support industry infrastructure, development of new technologies and promotion. In each case, the report highlights 'success stories,' giving detailed examples of actual outcomes of media policies drawn from specific companies, magazine content, and book titles.

Backgrounder, Canada—U.S. Agreement on Magazines, Foreign Publishers Advertising Services Act

Accessed original source October 13, 2011
http://www.pch.gc.ca/eng/1289312410707/1289312410708

BACKGROUNDER

Updated June 5, 2000
CANADA—U.S. AGREEMENT ON MAGAZINES

Foreign Publishers Advertising Services Act

- The Foreign Publishers Advertising Services Act (FPASA) received royal assent on June 17, 1999. It came into force on July 1, 1999.
- The prohibition on foreign publishers selling advertising services aimed primarily at the Canadian market was amended to allow two controlled forms of access to the Canadian advertising services market:
  - an exemption that allows foreign publishers to invest in Canada, create new businesses and produce a majority of Canadian content if they want to have greater access to advertising revenues.
  - a de minimis exemption of up to 18% of the advertising in any foreign periodical. This exemption will be phased in over three years from the date of enactment of FPASA (12% as of July 1, 1999, 15% as of January 1, 2001, and 18% as of July 1, 2002).

INVESTMENT

- A foreign publisher will not be able to sell more than 18% of advertising aimed at Canada unless it invests and creates new businesses, hires Canadians, and produces magazines containing majority Canadian content.
- New investments that result in ownership and control by a foreign investor will be reviewed under the *Investment Canada Act* for net benefit to Canada, using policy guidelines that will be made public. These guidelines

will ensure that, in addition to any economic benefits, new businesses will have to generate majority Canadian content in their magazines. Accordingly, authority for the review and approval of investments related to all cultural industries, including periodicals, was transferred to the Minister of Canadian Heritage from the Minister of Industry on May 26, 1999.

- Acquisitions of Canadian publishers will continue to be not permitted.

CANADIAN CONTENT

- For the purposes of investment review, and for determining eligibility for tax deductibility, Canadian content is content that is created for the Canadian market or that has been authored by a Canadian.
- Editorial content is everything that is not advertising pages, such as stories, illustrations, graphics and photographs. Canadian means a citizen or permanent resident of Canada. Original means it does not also appear in other foreign editions of a magazine.
- There will not be any subjective assessment of themes or subject matter to determine what is Canadian content. Stories, illustrations and photographs created by Canadians will count, regardless of subject, even if they appear in foreign editions. Content created by non-Canadians will count only if it was created for the Canadian edition and is not reproduced in other editions.

TAX DEDUCTIBILITY

- The proposed amendments to section 19 of the *Income Tax Act* become effective June 1, 2000. A deduction will be available for advertisements placed in periodicals—regardless of whether the ownership of the periodical is domestic or foreign.
- A full tax deductibility is available for advertising placed in periodicals for an advertisement directed at the Canadian market if the original editorial content in the issue is 80% or more of the total non-advertising content in the issue.
- A 50% tax deductibility is available for advertising placed in periodicals for an advertisement directed at the Canadian market if the original editorial content in the issue is less than 80% of the total non-advertising content in the issue.
- The proposed changes to section 19 apply only to periodicals. There are no fundamental changes on the availability of the tax deductibility for newspapers. The tax deductibility remains available for advertising placed in newspapers with a minimum of 75% Canadian ownership.

OTHER ISSUES

- The federal government will provide a package of assistance to the Canadian magazine publishing industry, details of which will be announced by the Minister of Canadian Heritage, following consultations on its design with the industry.

% OF EDITORIAL CONTENT THAT IS CANADIAN	ADS THAT CAN BE SOLD BY THE PUBLISHER THAT ARE AIMED AT THE CANADIAN MARKET	TAX DEDUCTION TO THE ADVERTISER OF THE ADS
less than 50%	up to 18%	50% of deduction
between 50 and 79%*	up to 100%	50% of deduction
more than 80%	up to 100%	100% of deduction

*Foreign publishers who make an investment in periodical publishing which has been approved under guidelines set out in the *Investment Canada Act* will have unrestricted access to the Canadian advertising services market.

- The agreement does not affect the Publications Assistance Program, operated by agreement between Canadian Heritage and Canada Post, that supports the mailing costs of paid circulation Canadian magazines and small community newspapers.
- Nothing in the agreement directly affects newspapers or electronic magazines, just as was the case with FPASA.

DISCUSSION

Department of Canadian Heritage, *Backgrounder, Canada-US Agreement on Magazines, Foreign Publishers Advertising Services Act.*

1. According to this report, circulation of Canadian magazines is declining while advertising is shifting from print to on-line sources. How would you describe the potential impact of on-line magazines in the periodical industry and what types of policy initiatives might help publishers respond to these technological changes?
2. The report describes the *Income Tax Act* as an 'incentive for advertisers to do business with magazines that have high levels of Canadian content.' How do tax deductions work as an incentive to attract revenue for Canadian magazines and why would this particular policy tool be popular with both magazine publishers and the government?
3. The report discusses the 'success stories' and actual outcomes of policies for the book and magazine industries in Canada. What kind of economic and cultural outcomes are mentioned and how important do you think these are to Canadians?
4. According to the report, over 5,000 new Canadian books were published by government subsidized publishers in 2009. Can you think of any Canadian books that you have read or heard about recently? Do you think that these Canadian titles would be published without some form of government subsidy? Why or why not?

Policy Source 12

Canada. Department of Canadian Heritage. (2008a). *'Perspective: Publishing' Intersections: Updates from the cultural landscape. Cultural Affairs Sector 2008–2009 Annual Report.* Retrieved from http://www.pch.gc.ca/pc-ch/org/sectr/ac-ca/pblctns/anl-rpt/2008-2009/ra-ar-eng.pdf

Perspective: Publishing in Intersection: Updates from the Cultural Landscape

Read

While digital technologies reshape the art and business of publishing, the written word continues to hold powerful appeal for Canadians—spinning stories, delivering news and keeping communities connected.

PERSPECTIVE: PUBLISHING

Canadians continue to show a love for reading. A 2008 Decima survey found the average Canadian bought some 14 books over the previous 12 months and read about 17 titles for leisure. Despite the challenging economic environment, Canada's total book sales improved in 2008–2009, growing by 4.4 percent[48] in Quebec and 6.2 percent[49] in the English-language market.

Unlike news—where free online sources are garnering ever-larger audiences—readers have yet to embrace digital book formats in large numbers. A mere eight percent of Canadians reported having read one or more digital books within the period covered by the Decima survey. The remaining respondents cited a preference for printed books (40 percent), a lack of time (8 percent), and a lack of interest (8 percent) among their primary reasons for not reading digital books.[50] That said, several applications were launched that allow readers to access e-book content on their existing handheld devices, and Amazon's Kindle e-book reader hit the Canadian market late in 2009. Major Canadian retailers expanded their online bookselling in 2009 to include dedicated e-book ventures.

Likely related to the growth in e-media, print circulation of Canada's 100-some paid daily newspapers fell by eight percent in 2008.[51] Paid circulation for Canadian magazines also fell by about five percent in the last six months of 2008 compared to the same period in 2007.[52] Advertisers followed their readers to the Web: online advertising accounted for 11 percent of the estimated $14.6 billion total for periodicals, a 29 percent increase over 2007.[53] Newspapers and magazines were affected financially by this shift and, by the fall of 2008, more than 200 magazine and 1,000 newspaper layoffs had been announced.[54] By the middle of 2009, magazine closures were on their way to significantly outnumbering launches.[55]

Publishers have recognized the evolution toward online content and have extended their presence to the Web and mobile devices. Many newspapers produced digital editions and Web-only content and encouraged their writers to start blogs. In January 2009, Rogers Publishing created mobile editions of two of its magazines, *Maclean's* and *Canadian Business*, for download by Web-enabled phones.[56] In February 2009, Hearst, which publishes several prominent American magazines and newspapers, announced it was developing a "wireless e-reader with a large-format screen suited to the reading and advertising requirement of newspapers and magazines." The device is designed to "approximate the reading experience of print periodicals" while providing space for advertising content.[57]

Community newspapers remained a stronghold for the print format in periodicals, retaining their readers and revenues likely because of their "monopoly on truly local content."[58]

The Role of the Cultural Affairs Sector

The Sector's primary goals in supporting book and periodicals publishers are to foster the creation and distribution of Canadian works that reflect the country's diversity of Canadian experiences and perspectives, and to help ensure the sustainability of the industry over the long term. The Sector's efforts are carried out within a broader government context that includes bodies such as the Canada Council for the Arts and the following tools:

- The *Foreign Publishers Advertising Services Act*, which strengthens the financial viability of Canadian magazine publishers by helping them compete on more favourable terms with lower-cost foreign companies for ad sales.
- The *Income Tax Act*, which stimulates production by providing incentives for advertisers to do business with magazines that have high levels of Canadian content—important given that advertising generates the most revenue for the majority of magazines.
- The *Investment Canada Act*, which ensures that foreign investment in books and magazines benefits Canada, including the production of Canadian editorial content.
- The Book Importation Regulations of the *Copyright Act*, which protect the exclusive distribution agreements signed by Canadian publishers and distributors.
- The National Translation Program for Book Publishing, introduced in 2009 as part of the Roadmap for Canada's Linguistic Duality, will provide $5 million over four years to help publishers in Canada translate Canadian-authored books from one official language to the other.

Reaching a world of readers
Canada is home to more than 21,000 full-time writers and countless other
part-time wordsmiths producing all manner of fiction, creative non-fiction,
personal journalism and essays.[59] Works by many of these writers are on
bookshelves all over the world, with Canadian authors receiving nearly every

Highlights: 2008–2009

- The appetite for Canadian books continues to grow at home and around the world. In 2008–2009, Sector-supported publishers sold **$350 million** worth of books in Canada and **$103 million** in other countries—a six percent increase over the past five years, after adjustment for inflation.
- Canadian-owned book publishers supported by the Sector published nearly **2,000** English-language authors and **2,000** French-language authors, including Margaret Atwood (*The Door*), Rawi Hage (*De Niro's Game*), Elizabeth Hay (*Late Nights on Air*), David Suzuki (*David Suzuki*), Dave Bidini (*Around the World in 57½ Gigs*), Marie-Claire Blais (*Noces ê midi au-dessus de l'abîme*), Marie-Louise Gay (*Les malheurs de princesse Pistache*), Aude (*Chrysalide*), Lise Tremblay (*La Soeur de Judith*) and Michel J. LÄvesque (*Arielle Queen*). The Sector also supported the work of nearly **1,000** first-time writers.
- Among the books published were **400** translations—noteworthy among them being official language translations of *The Perfect Circle* (Pascal Quiviger translated by Sheila Fischman), *A Good Death* (Gil Courtemanche translated by Wayne Grady), *Divisadero* (Michael Ondaatje translated by Michel Lederer), *Les rescapés du Styx* (Jane Urquhart translated by Anne Rabinovitch).
- Canadian subscribers received more than **183 million** copies of Canadian magazines and non-daily newspapers with the help of the Publications Assistance Program. These included *The Carillon*, a non-daily newspaper based in Manitoba; *Down Home*, a news and leisure magazine from Newfoundland; and *Rénovation Bricolage*, a Quebec-based home renovation magazine.
- While the profit margin of the Canadian magazine industry as a whole increased by **8.7** percent between 2005 and 2007,[60] magazine publishers funded through the Support for Editorial Content component of the Canada Magazine Fund saw their profit margins increase by **22** percent.

major international literary award—among others the Man Booker Prize, the Prix Goncourt, *the Orange Prize for Fiction, the* Prix Femina *and the International IMPAC Dublin Literary Award.*

"The Book Publishing Industry Development Program (BPIDP) enjoys industry-wide recognition for its relevance, a point clearly re-articulated by ANEL members during their recent annual general meeting."
    GILLES HERMAN, Association nationale des éditeurs de livres (ANEL), Montréal, Quebec

YEAR IN REVIEW: CREATE

Part 1: Books

The Cultural Affairs Sector continued to support a broad range of book industry activities across the country in 2009. Through the Book Publishing Industry Development Program (BPIDP),* the Sector helped ensure a diverse range of Canadian-authored

---

* Effective April 1, 2010, BPIDP was renamed the Canada Book Fund.

Aid to Publishers Recipients by Region				
	NUMBER OF PUBLISHERS	NEW CANADIAN-AUTHORED TITLES PUBLISHED	NEW TITLES PER PUBLISHER (AVERAGE)	AID TO PUBLISHERS CONTRIBUTION
BC	26	423	16	$2,204,154
Prairies & North	26	345	13	$2,329,926
Ontario	65	1,278	20	$7,056,060
Quebec	105	3,138	30	$14,233,244
Atlantic	13	142	11	$718,521
Total	235	5,326	23	$26,541,905

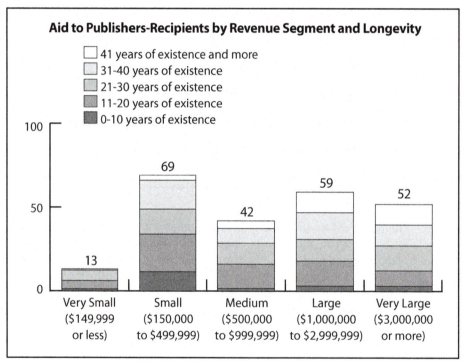

FIGURE 1

books were available in Canada and other countries. In 2008–2009, the largest component of BPIDP, Aid to Publishers, provided more than $26 million to publishers from coast to coast to coast. That funding reached 235 Canadian-owned publishers in all 10 provinces and more than 75 towns and cities—firms that directly employ, in total, more than 3,000 Canadians and that published 5,395 Canadian-authored titles.

The BPIDP continued to support both established publishers and relative newcomers, fostering a stable environment for book publishing in Canada. In 2009 Wilson & Lafleur became the fifth active BPIDP recipient to celebrate a century in publishing.

This diversity of firms—small and large, emerging and mature—is important to ensuring the overall sustainability of the country's book publishing sector. As the table below indicates, BPIDP recipients include companies with revenues under $150,000 and fewer than 10 years' experience up to those exceeding $3 million in sales and more than four decades in business.

"Magazine Canada's Professional Development Program is a great program, especially under the current economic circumstances and the best way of keeping up the standard of Canadian magazines. We would never be able to afford such high-level consultations otherwise."

ANDERS NEUMULLER, Swedish Press, Vancouver, British Columbia

Success story: *Les Éditions du Boréal*
Marie-Claire Blais, one of Canada's most popular and renowned authors, won her fourth Governor General's award for fiction in 2008. Her novel, Naissance de Rebecca à l'ère des tourments, *was published by* Les Éditions du Boréal, *which is supported by the Sector.*

Part 2: Periodicals

The Cultural Affairs Sector administers the Canada Magazine Fund* to develop and maintain Canadian content levels in magazines and to build industry capacity by supporting small magazine publishers' business development efforts, industry development projects, and arts and literary magazines. The Sector also works at the policy level to address market forces and inequalities that affect Canadian magazines and newspapers.

In 2008–2009, through the Canada Magazine Fund, the Sector provided $13.7 million to 277 Canadian magazines and supported 75 projects to develop Canadian content, improve efficiency and sustainability, and enhance marketing and professional development. This was divided among four components: Support for Editorial Content (SEC), Support for Arts and Literary Magazines (SALM), Support for Industry Development (SID), and Support for Business Development for Magazine Publishers (SBDMP).

Success story: *Consumer Magazines Get the Nod*
The Sector sponsored eight prizes at the 32nd annual National Magazine Awards, which recognized excellence in Canadian consumer magazines produced in 2008. Several Sector supported magazines took home major awards: Toronto Life, *which won most awards overall, and* The Walrus, *which received the most gold awards.*

Recipients of Canada Magazine Fund's SEC component reported higher profit margins than the industry as a whole for two of the last three years for which data are available. In the two most recent years on record (2005 and 2007), SEC recipients increased their margins by 22.2 percent while the industry's overall profits went up by just 8.7 percent.[61]

---

* Effective April 1, 2010, the Canada Magazine Fund and the Publications Assistance Program were replaced by the Canada Periodical Fund.

Total Canada Magazine Fund Funding by Component						
	2006–2007		2007–2008		2008–2009	
COMPONENT	RECIPIENTS	FUNDING	RECIPIENTS	FUNDING	RECIPIENTS	FUNDING
SEC	197	$9,938,884	201	$9,645,709	196	$9,468,964
SALM	60	$1,000,000	57	$1,000,000	56	$1,000,000
SID	28*	$2,263,686	31*	$1,998,634	25*	$1,802,714
SBDMP	82*	$2,299,538	58*	$1,876,734	50*	$1,384,880
Total	367	$15,502,108	347	$14,521,077	327	$13,656,558

*For SID and SBDMP, "recipients" refers to the number of individual projects.

The Canada Magazine Fund also contributed to the creation of a diverse range of Canadian-authored content as publishers supported by the Support for Editorial Component in 2008–2009 produced approximately 113,000 pages of Canadian content in 196 titles.

Success story: *Quebec Awards Recognize Science Writing*
Since 1962, Québec-Science *has informed readers about the latest developments in science and technology. The magazine, which received support during the year for developing editorial content, won top prize in the reporting category at the Concours des Grands Prix 2008 des Magazines du Québec—the province s highest awards for magazine excellence.*

YEAR IN REVIEW: ACCESS

Part 1: Books

The Sector helps Canada's book publishing industry strengthen its infrastructure, enhance its use of technology, and market Canadian authors both in Canada and around the world to ensure Canadian works are accessible to the broadest possible audiences.

The Collective Initiatives, Supply Chain Initiative and International Marketing Assistance components of the BPIDP are the Cultural Affairs Sector's key instruments in ensuring access to Canadian books. Together, these provided nearly $10 million of additional support for collective and individual projects in professional development, publishing internships, business planning and export market development.

Success story: *The Porcupine's Quill*
In 2008, Tim and Elke Inkster were named to the Order of Canada for "their distinctive contributions to publishing in Canada and for their promotion of new authors, as co-founders of the Porcupine's Quill, a small press known for the award-winning beauty and quality of its books." Their influential publishing

house, established in 1974 and supported by the Sector, has helped launch the careers of authors such as Jane Urquhart, Elizabeth Hay and Russell Smith.

Providing Full-spectrum Support

The Sector's work touches all aspects of the book publishing industry, from management and production to distribution and marketing. On the supply chain side, in 2008–2009, Cultural Affairs Sector funding enabled the *Association nationale des éditeurs de livres* to develop a new system for digitally warehousing and distributing French-language e-books published by Canadian-owned publishers. This innovation reduces costs for participating publishers while allowing retailers and other interested parties to access a large collection of French-language content within a single repository.

Embracing Technology

Since 2000, BPIDP has helped develop the next generation of Canadian publishing professionals by providing funding for internship opportunities at Canadian-owned publishing companies. In 2008–2009, as publishers continued to adapt to the evolving digital environment, BPIDP increased its support for internships focused on emerging technologies. These involved Web marketing, digital content design and digital rights management, and accounted for nearly two-thirds of the 42 internships funded by BPIDP during the year.

> **Success story: *Brick Books***
> *In 2008–2009, Randall Maggs' Night Work: The Sawchuk Poems proved a triumph for Sector-supported publisher Brick Books. From a launch at the Hockey Hall of Fame in Toronto to author interviews with major radio, television and print media—rare occurrences for a book of poetry—Brick Books ran an innovative, multifaceted marketing campaign to connect the book to its readership. By artfully intertwining two of Canada's favourite pastimes—hockey and reading—Night Work struck a chord and became the third best-selling Canadian poetry book of 2008 behind works by literary titans Leonard Cohen and Margaret Atwood.*

Fostering Diversity

The Sector supports a number of initiatives to ensure that Canada's cultural and linguistic diversity are reflected in its books. In 2008–2009 it funded *Un monde à lire*, a special project of Communication-Jeunesse, an organization that makes cultural products more accessible to children. *Un monde à lire* is a thematic list of Québécois and French-Canadian children's books for recent immigrants aged 5 to 11. Its aim is to help these young people learn French. The list organizes 143 titles according to eight themes including friends, school, holidays and traditions, and the French language. A special index card was developed for each book to give information on the author and publisher.

In 2009, the Sector continued its support of the First Nation Communities Read program, a campaign that helps Ontario's First Nation public librarians build interest in Aboriginal literature and in the province's First Nation public libraries. The 2009 Friends of Ontario's First Nation Public Libraries Honour Program recognized BPIDP for its ongoing support to the Southern Ontario Library Service, which administers the program.

Part 2: Periodicals

Through its policies and funding programs, the Sector enables periodicals and non-daily newspapers to develop Canadian content, reach out to diverse audiences and adapt to changing technologies in the marketplace.

The Publications Assistance Program (PAP)* is a key tool for ensuring access to content, subsidizing postal delivery of magazines and non-daily newspapers and helping ensure that Canadian readers have access to a diversity of Canadian periodicals. In 2008–2009, the program subsidized the postal costs of 1,130 recipients.

---

* Effective April 1, 2010, the Publications Assistance Program and Canada Magazine Fund were replaced by the Canada Periodical Fund.

Reaching Diverse Communities with Postal Subsidies	
COMMUNITY	NUMBER OF COPIES 2008–2009
General	177,141,165
Official language minority	2,014,594
Aboriginal	256,792
Ethnocultural	4,272,665
Total	183,685,216

Total PAP Funding, 2006–2007 to 2008–2009						
	2006–2007		2007–2008		2008–2009	
	RECIPIENTS	FUNDING	RECIPIENTS	FUNDING	RECIPIENTS	FUNDING
Consumer magazines	603	$44,438,431	597	$41,628,271	584	$42,811,238
Non-daily newspapers	479	$15,719,226	474	$15,724,317	460	$14,845,677
Trade magazines	479	$1,414,562	82	$1,628,019	86	$1,623,837
Total	1,161	$61,572,219	1,153	$58,980,607	1,130	$59,280,753

The trend in funding from the PAP over the past three years reflects a mature industry under pressure from online competitors and a slowing economy. There have been slight declines in total publications and the total amount of funding over this period. The drop in the number of publications could indicate closures outpacing launches or that some titles have shifted from print to online distribution. The amount of PAP funding from year to year is based on three main factors: postal rates, the weight of the publications, and the total number of copies sent in the mail. The decline in total funding over the three years is in spite of annual postal rate increases from Canada Post, indicating that magazines and newspapers are either thinner, mailed less frequently, or both. These changes could be indications of declines in advertising and circulation revenues.

Endnotes

48. Observatoire de la culture et des communications du Québec.
49. BookNet Canada Sales Data.
50. Decima Research, *2008 Canadian Books Readership Study.* Prepared for PCH. May 2008.
51. Canadian Newspaper Association, "Daily Newspaper Paid Circulation Data." http://www.cna-acj.ca/en/aboutnewspapers/circulation, accessed on September 15, 2009.
52. Audit Bureau of Circulations, FAS-FAX Report – December 31, 2008: Chicago: Audit Bureau of Circulations, 2009. Also noted in ABC news bulletin, March 2009. http://www.accessabc.com/newsbulletin/askabc_0309.htm
53. Interactive Advertising Bureau of Canada, *2008 Actual + 2009 Estimated Canadian Online Advertising Revenue Survey,* 2008, http://www.iabcanada.com/reports/IABCanada_2008Act2009Budg_CdnOnlineAdRev_FINAL.pdf, accessed on September 10, 2009.
54. Compilation prepared by the Department of Canadian Heritage.
55. Masthead Online, "Mid-year tally: Closures outnumber launches by almost three-to-one", July 7, 2009, http://www.mastheadonline.com/news/2009/20090706711.shtml, accessed on September 18, 2009.
56. Mobile Marketer, "Canada's largest magazine publisher uses push for mobile", August 18, 2008, http://www.mobilemarketer.com/cms/news/media/1548.print, accessed on September 10, 2009.
57. Fortune, "Hearst to launch a wireless e-reader", February 27, 2009. http://money.cnn.com/2009/02/27/technology/copeland_hearst.fortune/index.htm
58. The Future of Publishing, "The Future of Newspapers", September 24, 2008, http://www.thefutureofpublishing.com/industries/newspapers.html, accessed on September 10, 2009.
59. Hill Strategies, *A Statistical Profile of Artists in Canada,* 2004.
60. Statistics Canada, Survey of Periodical Publishers 2007, Catalogue no.87F0005X, June 2009.
61. Ibid.

DISCUSSION

Department of Canadian Heritage, *'Perspective: Publishing' in Intersections: Updates from the Cultural Landscape.*

1. In your own words describe the two 'controlled forms of access' that foreign magazines have to advertising revenue in the Canadian market under the *Foreign Publishers Advertising Services Act.* How was the *Income Tax Act* amended to account for these changes to Canada's magazine policy?
2. The Canada-US Agreement on Magazines allows foreign magazines to sell up to 18 percent of their advertising space to Canadian advertisers. This implies that Canadian magazines could miss out on these amounts of ad revenue. Why might even this small amount of Canadian advertising allowed in foreign magazines negatively affect Canadian magazines' profits?
3. The FPSA allows foreign companies to invest in magazine publishing in Canada so long as they create a majority of Canadian-authored content. For the most part, no American or foreign publishers have launched Canadian-content magazines since the legislation was passed. What reasons can you think of for this lack of foreign interest and investment in the Canadian market?
4. According to this agreement on magazines, Canadian content is defined as: 'Stories, illustrations, and photographs created by Canadians.' How does this definition compare to the MAPL definition of a 'Canadian selection' used by the CRTC in the Commercial Radio Policy discussed in Chapter 6? What are some of the advantages and disadvantages of defining content solely in relation to the citizenship of its creators?

Using Direct Subsidies to Address Market Failure

Chapter 8

INTRODUCTION

While national ownership policies work in various ways to prohibit foreign ownership of media industries and to attract and protect advertising revenue and market share for Canada's commercial media, these policy tools may not fully overcome the conditions of market failure. Canada's small domestic market cannot generate enough revenue to sustain adequate profits from either ad revenue or individual consumption of media products. Our open cultural economy and shared border with one of the world's largest producers of entertainment and popular culture makes it very difficult for Canadian media to compete and survive. The Canada-US magazine dispute highlights the complexity of this situation. The combined use of national ownership strategies, tax incentives, and direct subsidy through the Canada Periodical Fund attempts to strike a balance between domestic media policy goals and international trade regimes. The book publishing industry faces many of the same forms of foreign competition in getting Canadian books out to Canadian readers, however this industry relies completely on consumer sales and so tax incentive policies for advertisers are not relevant. Canadian authors and book publishers rely heavily on forms of direct subsidy, either through Canada Council for the Arts grants to writers or Canadian Heritage subsidies to publishers who publish Canadian books.

Canada's book industry was, in its early days, dominated by foreign publishers—British, French, and later American. Canadian-owned publishers emerged in the early twentieth century, but these were primarily 'agency publishers' who imported and distributed foreign titles in Canada. In the post-World War II era, American 'branch plant' publishers were established in Canada and in English Canada they bought up many of the British companies. Their role was to import and distribute US titles in Canada while also creating 'derivative' titles, especially for text books that, like split run magazines, were primarily foreign content with some Canadian facts or references inserted for the Canadian market (Lorimer, 1991). There were very few Canadian publishers supporting Canadian authors and the variety and international success of Canadian non-fiction, literature, and poetry that we see today simply did not exist.

In the late 1960s and 70s, the baby-boom generation, inspired by a growing national and global consciousness in Canada, began to create and seek out Canadian writers on Canadian themes and subjects. As Roland Lorimer describes this era:

> . . . the baby boomers came hard upon the blockage to the publication of Canadian creative writing and discussion of Canadian issues that the branch plant and agency system represented. Their response was to take control of the printing presses themselves. For approximately $5,000 they became publishers of their colleagues and themselves. As they persuaded bookstores to accept their titles, and as the political and intellectual elite became aware of these titles and the quality of the content and writing they contained, only one conclusion could be reached. Far from being vanity publishers, this new wave of publishers was bringing forward issues, ideas and writing that had been silenced by the agency system and that deserved a hearing in Canadian society if not the world (Lorimer 1991, 6).

While these culturally and politically aware publishers developed Canadian authors and helped them reach Canadian readers, they quickly came up against economic realities. Although their goal was to displace some of the foreign books in the Canadian market with new Canadian writing, they were competing for readers with larger foreign-owned publishers who set the price for the majority of books. This competition proved to be too great for many small Canadian-owned presses and they began to go into debt. Further, in 1970 three of the oldest Canadian-owned publishers were threatened with foreign take-over (Boggs, 2010, 26). This led to the call for government intervention to support the project of Canadian publishing for Canadian books.

The primary policy instrument for Canadian writing and publishing is the use of direct subsidies, first introduced in the 1970s. In 1972, the Canada Council launched a 'block grant' program for new Canadian publishers, along with direct grants to Canadian authors. Larger grants to publishers were also introduced by the Secretary of State in 1979. This program was the predecessor to the Book Publishing Industry Development Program (BPIDP) administered first by the former Department of Communication and then by the Department of Canadian Heritage when it was created in 1995. Today, the Canada Book Fund provides $39.5 million support for eligible Canadian-owned publishers. It includes both sales-based annual funding and project funding for industry activities such as export development, marketing, professional development and technological adaptation (Canadian Heritage, 2010b, 5). In order to be eligible for Canada Book Fund support, publishers must be at least 75 percent Canadian-owned, have Canadian headquarters, at least 75 percent Canadian employees and may not be unincorporated divisions ('imprints') of a larger organization. In addition, eligible publishers must meet minimum levels of publication and sales of Canadian-authored titles (Canadian Heritage, 2012). The Canada Council continues to support culturally significant Canadian literature through its $19 million Publishing Support program, but also has a variety of grants for Canadian creative writers and literary arts.

A second key policy tool for books and publishing is regulation of foreign ownership of Canadian publishers. As in radio, television, and periodical publishing the government does concern itself with ownership of publishing houses in Canada, but has not historically prevented foreign-owned companies or subsidiaries of multinational companies from operating in Canada. Instead, beginning in 1985 with the Baie Comeau policy, the government tried to limit the creation of new foreign publishers and the indirect or direct sale of Canadian-owned publishers to foreign interests (Lorimer, 1991). In 1992, the 'Revised Foreign Investment Policy in Book Publishing and Distribution' was developed in conjunction with review of foreign investment in the cultural industries under the *Investment Canada Act*. This revised version of the Baie Comeau policy "sets out preferred areas for undertakings from foreign investors . . . and advises potential investors of the Government's objective of generally favouring Canadian control of book businesses. Since, in the majority of cases, foreign investors choose not to invest in the Canadian book sector because of the policy, the use of the *Act* as a tool to provide for investments that are of net benefit to Canada typically only occurs in the review of indirect acquisitions" (Canadian Heritage, 2010b, 9). In order to prove a 'net benefit' to Canada, foreign purchasers in publishing are required to meet such criteria as using Canadian suppliers for the Canadian business, marketing Canadian books, maintaining or increasing Canadian employment and the autonomy of Canadian management, and increasing or maintaining the level of Canadian content, among other things (Canadian Heritage, 2010b). French-language publishers and booksellers in Quebec further benefit from a 1979 provincial government policy, Bill 51, that creates a system of regulated distribution and pricing and accredited book stores from which all major institutional purchases, including schools, colleges, and universities, must be made. This has had the effect of creating a strong and stable publishing and retail environment for books in Quebec.

Today, the Canadian publishing industry in both English and French is predominantly Canadian-owned and relatively successful as a result of these policy tools. However as Jeff Boggs (2010, 37) points out, a small number of foreign-controlled publishers still dominate the industry in terms of revenue and productivity. At the same time, while smaller Canadian presses with predominantly Canadian titles are marginally profitable, the report in Policy Source 14 clearly indicates that these profits would disappear without the support of BPIDP and its successor, the Canada Book Fund. Publishers of Canadian books are heavily reliant on government subsidy and this economic reality is very unlikely to change as the impact of on-line book purchasing and e-book sales is increasingly felt in Canada.

Policy Source 13 describes the evolution of the Canada Council's support for the arts, including grants for Canadian writers and Canadian book publishing. It outlines the wide variety of programs and funds for the creation of culture and the arts in Canada and touches on changes in Canadian society that influence the government's support for cultural production. The Council's programs adapted to the changing roles of women, cultural minorities, and Aboriginal people. The time-line also describes the Canada Council's growing emphasis on the professionalization of the arts through services to arts organizations and arts education. In the current era, the Council is one among many public and private sources for funding the arts. Federal funding for the arts, through the Canada Council, has stabilized and in some cases increased. This reflects a corresponding change in the number, size, and scope of cultural and arts activities in Canadian society. Today, the Council distributes over $150 million in direct subsidies to artists and arts organizations in Canada.

Policy Source 14 is a part of a detailed evaluation of the BPIDP in the year before it became the Canada Book Fund. The evaluation describes the key challenges facing Canadian publishers, including concentration in the book retail sector, competition from multinational 'branch plants,' and the cost of using new technologies and of entering export markets. The evaluation of BPIDP relied on surveys and interviews with publishers and other stakeholders in the industry. For the most part, the Aid to Publishers (ATP) program was highly valued by its recipients. The International Marketing Assistance (IMA) and Supply Chain Initiatives (SCI) are also evaluated positively as addressing specific issues and changes in Canadian publishing. The report assesses the relevance of the program components in meeting federal media policy objectives such as the goal that Canadians have access to Canadian voices and Canadian stories. BPIDP addresses the policy rationales of national unity, Canadian identity, and internal social linkages through its support of linguistic duality, cultural diversity, and regional expression in the publishing sector. As well, direct subsidies to publishing play a key role in economic growth in the cultural industries, while the evaluation shows that programs like BPIDP, and now the Canada Book Fund, clearly contribute to the viability and diversity of the Canadian-owned book industry.

Primary Sources: Grants for Writers, Books, and Publishing.
Policy Source 13
Canada Council for the Arts. 2007. The evolution of the Canada Council's support of the arts. (August 31), http://www.canadacouncil.ca/aboutus/Background/
xp128565418182821011.htm.

The Evolution of the Canada Council's Support of the Arts

The Canada Council was created by an Act of Parliament in 1957 with a very broad mandate—"to foster and promote the study and enjoyment of, and the production of works in, the arts." Originally funded by the revenues from an endowment fund, it began receiving annual appropriations from Parliament in the late 1960s. Today, Parliament provides the majority of the Council's resources.

The *Canada Council for the Arts Act* did not specify what kind of organization the Council should be or how it should carry out its mandate. Among the most crucial decisions the Council made in its early years was that it would focus on professional artists and arts organizations and operate primarily as a granting organization.

Over the years the Council has significantly evolved as it adapted to new ways in which art was being created, produced and disseminated and to changes in Canadian society.

- In the **Council's early years,** it frequently discussed whether its priority should be to lift standards of excellence by responding to the best in the arts or distribute its resources more broadly and democratically ("to raise" or "to spread," as the Council put it). In the early years, the Council generally preferred the former option. It devoted much of its energy and most of its resources to developing a professional arts infrastructure in both official languages, principally in urban areas.

- The **late 1960s and early 1970s** marked the arrival of the first generation of artists and arts managers trained and developed in Canada. It was a period of social change and ferment, with citizens calling for more democratic public institutions and one federal minister responsible for culture (Gérald Pelletier) announcing a policy of "democratization and decentralization". The Canada Council began to be much more active in bringing the arts to people. It improved access to its programs for new artists, expanded the disciplines it funded, and launched special initiatives to address underserved regions. Examples included the creation of the Touring Office, the Explorations program, the Block Grant program for book publishers, and the Art Bank in the 1970s. Special measures were taken to address the under-representation of Council funding in the Atlantic provinces and to reach out to artists in the North. The early 1970s also saw the end of peer assessment committees made up exclusively of men.

- From the **mid-1970s to the mid-1980s,** the Council recognized Canadian work as an important priority. It began supporting a new stream of creator-based organizations and encouraged repertoire-based arts organizations to present new Canadian works. It also put a special focus on grants to individual artists. These changes responded to the emergence of new arts organizations, some of them led by young people initially funded through federal youth-work grants, and the emergence of new creative voices, including those of women and francophone artists outside Quebec. In addition to incentives for new Canadian work, the Council provided support to artist-run centres, alternative theatres, contemporary dance companies, arts magazines, new music groups and small classical music ensembles. It also made grants available to a substantially larger number of organizations and, in the early 1980s, set up the Media Arts Section. Over this decade, arts funding by the provinces expanded significantly.

- During the **1970s and 1980s,** recognizing that as a national agency it had sources of information and insight that could help strengthen the arts community, the Council began expanding its support by providing services and tools (such as workshops, showcases and professional development opportunities) to artists and arts organizations. It put a new emphasis on disseminating research and information on the arts.

- In the **1990s,** in response to calls for action from the culturally diverse and Aboriginal arts communities, the Council acknowledged that its programs, committees and staff did not reflect the face of modern Canada. With the advice of committees for both racial equity and Aboriginal arts, it made an active commitment to Aboriginal and culturally diverse arts practices and to equity as a corporate goal. The Equity Office and the Aboriginal Arts Secretariat were established and their respective advisory committees constituted. In this decade, the Council also established the Inter-Arts Office as a means of responding to shifting disciplinary boundaries and new artistic practices. The Council began giving operating grants on a multi-year basis, and it greatly expanded its prizes and awards for artists. Across the country during this period, some municipalities were becoming much more active in arts funding.

- Internal changes in the **1990s** included an increased communications capacity and a greater emphasis on reaching the arts community, the public, government, members of Parliament and the media in multiple ways, including the Council's website.

- In the **mid-1990s,** during a period of federal program review, the Council experienced dramatic internal changes. To cope with financial cutbacks, it reduced its staff by 50% and eliminated or consolidated a number of programs. The Council's goal with these measures was to prevent reductions in its grants budget.

- In the **current decade (since 2000)** the Council has received a series of new funds from the federal government. To encourage greater stability among arts organizations, it has emphasized capacity building and long-term organizational health. With its most recent increase from government, the additional $20 million in 2006–07 and $30 million in 2007–08 announced in the May 2006 federal budget, it provided additional support to arts organizations receiving operating grants, including significant funding for large institutions. In response to the new ways in which artists are working, the Council has also introduced several changes that make its programs more flexible, increased its support for project grants, and made its Artists in Community Collaboration program permanent. It also developed projects that bring artists together with other sectors of society such as science.

- In the **current decade,** responding to the continuous growth in the number of artists, a high rate of applications, and the advent of new technologies, the Council has introduced an online process for grant applications. It has filled a gap in its planning processes by adopting three-year corporate plans, and it is paying greater attention to evaluation and accountability issues. Acknowledging that the funding landscape has shifted dramatically and that it is no longer the only or even the largest public funder in many regions of Canada, the Council has fostered the creation of a collaborative network of provincial and territorial arts funders. It has also increased its work in arts promotion, in recognition of the need to engage the public more deeply in the arts. Finally, in this decade the Council has expressed a desire to assume a more proactive leadership role in the arts, by contributing to an improved federal framework for arts support and sharing its national knowledge of the arts more broadly with others.

The growth of the Canadian arts community since the Council was created in 1957 has been so extraordinary that comparisons are almost impossible. But two differences stand out above all others:

- The sheer difference in **quantity and scope of professional artists and arts organizations in Canada:** In 1957, the Council funded 29 arts organizations, most of them repertoire companies in the performing arts, and two individual artists. Today it funds over 2000 organizations and 2000 artists annually in a wide variety of disciplines and arts practices, and more than 900 of the organizations receive operating support. Nearly 16,000 applications are received each year and some 6000 grants awarded. In 2005–06, the Canada Council awarded more than $120.5 million in grants:
  - close to $102.3 million through 4,068 grants to organizations; and
  - close to $18.3 million through 2,122 grants to individuals.
  While final data is not yet available, this amount will increase in 2006–07 as a result of the $50 million in new money provided to the Council in the federal budget of May 2, 2006. These funds were over two years: $20 million in 2006–07 and $30 million in 2007–08.
- The **diversity and maturity** of the arts community: In its early years the Council helped to foster and develop the professional arts infrastructure of Canada. Today the arts community, while still lacking adequate financial resources, is mature and well-developed, diverse in its practices and forms of expression, and recognized for its quality across the country and internationally.

Further information is available from the website of the CCFA: www.canadacouncil.ca
August 2007

DISCUSSION

Canada Council for the Arts, *The Evolution of the Canada Council's Support of the Arts.*

1. The Canada Council for the Arts emerged from the recommendations of the Massey Commission. How does the description of the Council's 'early years' correspond with what you know about the era of the Massey Commission and its emphasis on the role of high culture in Canada?
2. How does this brief time-line describe the expanding role of the Canada Council in the 1970s and 80s? Do you think the Council's focus on Canadian work in this era can be related to the rise of Canadian-owned publishers and the emergence of new Canadian writing and if so, how?
3. Visit the Canada Council's website at www.canadacouncil.ca and explore the 'Writing and Publishing' section. Describe two of the specific Council funding programs from this section in your own words. What specific policy rationales and objectives from the Policy Analysis Framework on page 6 are met by these programs for writers and publishers?
4. The final entry in the evolution of the Canada Council's support for the arts describes the diversity and maturity of the arts community in Canada today. Read the description for 'Emerging Publisher Support' on the Canada Council website and explain how you think this program might help add to the diversity of publishing in Canada.

Policy Source 14
Canada. Department of Canadian Heritage. (2008c). *Summative evaluation of the book publishing industry development program*. Retrieved from http://www.pch.gc.ca/pgm/em-cr/evaltn/2008/2008-11/bpidp-eng.pdf

Summative Evaluation of the Book Publishing Industry Development Industry Program

3. KEY FINDINGS

The following sections present the findings of the summative evaluation by main evaluation issue.

3.1 Program Relevance

The evaluation concluded that the program remains relevant in light of the multiple and persistent challenges Canadian-owned book publishers encounter. The program remains consistent with Departmental and federal government priorities and policies for the cultural industry.

3.1.1 Key Challenges Faced by Canadian-owned Book Publishers

The challenges that Canadian-owned publishers face are enduring. Numerous analyses since the Ontario Royal Commission on Book Publishing (1973) have emphasized structural economic constraints on publishers who originate books for Canada's relatively small English-and French-language markets. Similarly, the report of the Standing Committee on Canadian Heritage (2000) noted that "increased consolidation among retailers and foreign publishers and the lack of access to capital make it difficult for Canadian firms to compete in the changing environment".

Publishers surveyed for the evaluation confirmed that these structural factors constitute their most important challenges today. Other realities, such as competition from multinational firms, the cost of entering the export market, and the cost of adapting new technologies, are also important challenges for Canadian-owned publishers. Changes in institutional markets (e.g. educational and library markets) and succession planning represent further significant challenges with which publishers must contend. Exhibit 1 provides an overview of the key challenges English and French language Canadian-owned publishers surveyed in the context of this evaluation face.

When comparing English- and French-language book publishers (Exhibit 1), retail concentration is reportedly the most important issue for English-language

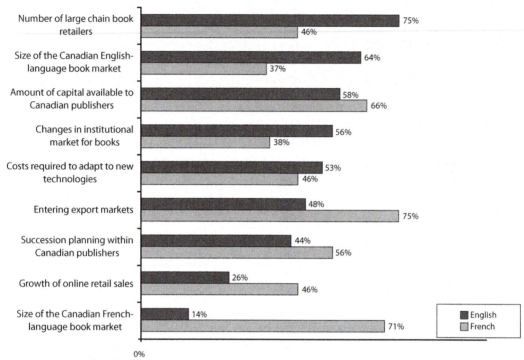

Source: Survey of Publishers (English *n* =80; French *n* = 68)

EXHIBIT 1   Key challenges for English and French language Canadian-owned Publishers (large challenge)

publishers (75%), with the size of the Canadian English-language book market being the second most important challenge (64%). The third most important challenge for English-language publishers is accessing capital (58%). For French-language publishers, entering the export market is the single most important issue (75%), followed by the size of the Canadian French-language market (71%), and accessing capital (66%).

The fragmentation of the French-language market was also mentioned by several key informants in interviews.[12] These results are consistent with those obtained in both key informant interviews and focus groups. (See Table 1 and 2 in Appendix 4 for a breakdown of survey results.)

Challenge: Concentration in the Retail Market

In the English-Canadian market, where in 1985 there were three national bookstore chains, there is now only one, Chapters/Indigo. In the smaller Quebec market, two chains, Archambault and Renaud-Bray, hold between them a market share comparable to that of Chapters/Indigo outside of Quebec (44%). A 2007 PCH study[13] on the Canadian book retail market estimated the market share in retail bookselling throughout Canada (excluding sales of educational texts) as shown in Exhibit 2.

The impact of retail concentration on book publishing is double-edged. On one hand, the expansion of chain and non-traditional sectors can be seen as an opportunity for publishers, because those retailers have enlarged the national retail space for books

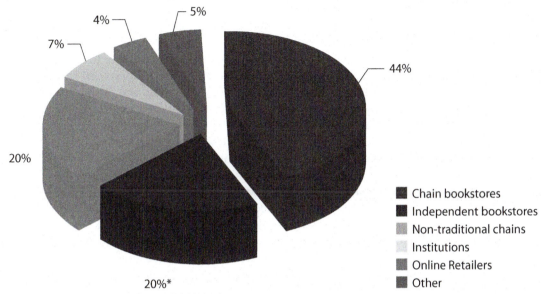

Source: The Book Retail Sector in Canada, PCH (2007)

*20%–Independent bookstores includes two major Quebec retailers (Renaud Bray and Archambault) that hold 44% market share in that province.

EXHIBIT 2   Canadian Market Share-by Book Retail Channel

and have attracted new customers for books. On the other hand, as the study notes, deep discounts offered by chains, discount stores and online retailers such as Amazon, and other in-store promotions by the big-box retailers, have contributed to a decline in number of independent booksellers over the past decade. The independents often represent key accounts for smaller publishers, particularly publishers of specialized literary, regional or children's books, accounting for 27% of sales for publishing firms with revenues of $449,999 or less, compared to 15% for firms with revenues of $3 million or more[14].

The PCH study notes that warehouse clubs such as Costco typically stock a relatively narrow range of books (500–600 titles) and move high volumes of books at a discounted list price, estimated at 30%. They also can return high volumes of unsold copies[15], with the overall effect of concentrating a large number of sales among a small number of bestselling titles. In addition to aggressive price discounting, the study describes how other industry practices, such as handling of returns, co-op promotions, whereby publishers pay booksellers to promote specific titles, price conventions for different types of trade titles, and list prices of comparable imported titles, particularly from the US and France, affect customers' expectations and leave little flexibility to publishers on pricing. In addition, the steady strength of the Canadian dollar against the American dollar since 2006 created parity between the currencies toward the end of 2007. One result was a public controversy over book prices, featuring strong public pressure to reduce cover prices on American books imported into Canada. As American cover prices came down, pressure increased on their Canadian competition to be priced accordingly, further diminishing profit margins on Canadian-authored titles.[16]

Challenge: Competition from Multinationals

In addition to direct competition from imported books, competition from large, foreign-controlled multinational publishers with subsidiaries in Canada is an important challenge for Canadian-owned publishers. These firms located here primarily to sell their parent companies' products. Subsidiary publishers benefit from economies of scale from the parent company both in terms of production and marketing. They can also market and distribute their own books more aggressively through infrastructures built on high volume sales of imported titles. Their presence in Canada also limits opportunities for Canadian-owned publishers to generate revenues by acting as distributors of imported books. Competition from existing multinational subsidiaries remains more challenging than ever, particularly as a result of international mergers creating ever-larger foreign conglomerates, such as Random House and Hachette.

Many multinationals have also become active in publishing Canadian-authored books, both in the educational and trade sectors. This confronts Canadian firms with powerful direct competition for rights to Canadian writers. Foreign-owned subsidiary publishers have access to substantially greater financial resources, allowing them to compete successfully for new books by the Canadian authors who command the highest sales and royalty advances.

Cumulatively, these challenges contribute to the lower profit margins of many Canadian-owned publishers. As illustrated in Exhibit 3, for the three years covered by the evaluation plus 2003–04[17], the median reported profit margins of BPIDP recipients as a percentage of total revenues for those publishers receiving funding ranged from 3% to was just under 5% (4.8%) across the four years. The very small firms (less than $150K in revenue) had median profit margins that moved considerably from year to year (between a low of—1.0% to a high of 11.7%). Overall, the other sizes of firms ex-

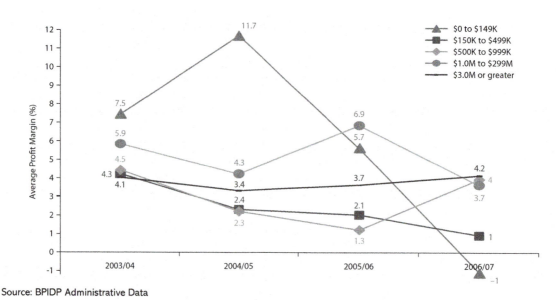

Source: BPIDP Administrative Data

EXHIBIT 3   Median Profit Margin as Percentage of Total Revenues by Size of Firm

perienced less volatility with median profit margins ranging within one to four percentage points across the four years. Larger Canadian-owned book publishers (>$1M) have the healthiest cost to sales ratios. Smaller publishers (revenues under $999K) tended to experience more fluctuation and larger declines in profit margin when compared with large publishers. Despite government support, about 25% of BPIDP-funded publishers reported losing money in at least two of the last four years, including approximately one half of BPIDP-funded Official Language Minority publishers.

Between 2003 and 2007, the proportion of aggregated annual revenues from government sources (all grants and contributions) when compared with total revenues for BPIDP recipients was relatively consistent across the four years at between 8% and 9%. When examined by firm size, this proportion varied considerably. For the larger firms, the proportion of aggregated revenues from government sources ranged between 5.0% and 6.0%. In contrast, the smallest firms with revenue less that $150K had proportions ranging from 40% to 53% across the same period.[18]

Similarly, when aggregated revenues from BPIDP funding were compared with total revenues, the proportions overall remained relatively consistent across the time period of 2003–2007 at between 4% and 5%. As would be expected, the proportion of aggregated revenue attributable to BPIDP funding was higher among the smaller firms (between 11% and 16% for smallest firms with less than $150K of revenues, compared with 3–4% among firms with $3.0M or greater in revenues).

When considering sources of government funding, for the larger firms, BPIDP funding overall makes up a larger proportion of the revenues from government sources (overall about 60–68% for firms with revenues $3.0M or greater). This is compared with the smaller firms that see BPIDP overall represent 22–32% of their revenues from government sources.

Despite these differences, when compared against the median profit margins reported above, the aggregate proportions of funding from BPIDP when compared with total revenues suggest that, in the absence of BPIDP funding, the profit margin of BPIDP-funded publishers would be negative for many firms in each size category, all other things being equal. In the absence of BPIDP, many recipients believe they would have to adjust their content production or could cease to be viable and go out of business.

Given the relatively low profit margins of many Canadian-owned publishers, it is not surprising that lending institutions are reluctant to lend money to publishers. As a result, public sources of funding are essential for publishers not to be driven solely by return-on-investment considerations in their editorial choices. The investments by BPIDP and likely other government sources allow them to produce content that may be less profitable but culturally more significant. BPIDP simultaneously encourages publishers' entrepreneurial behaviour though the ATP and EMAP funding formulas, which are based on sales of eligible Canadian-authored titles.

Other important sources of government support for Canadian-owned publishers include the Canada Council for the Arts (CCA), which is a significant source of funding for small literary publishers; the Société de développement des entreprises culturelles (SODEC) in Quebec; and the Ontario Media Development Corporation (OMDC). Publishers can also access funding from provincial arts councils and other provincially based funding sources. Three provinces offer tax credits to book publishers. Ontario provides refundable tax credits on a percentage of eligible pre-press, printing and marketing expenditures on Canadian-authored books; the credit is administered by the OMDC, which also funds other book industry projects. A key point is that these provincial credits are refundable regardless of whether the publisher has taxable profits. Ontario publishers interviewed or who participated in focus groups for the evaluation consider the tax credit an important component of their government support. Comparable tax credits are provided to book publishers in British Columbia and Quebec. In Quebec the credit is administered by the SODEC, which offers a program comparable to the OMDC.

In addition, the Quebec government has longstanding legislation (Loi 51) to support Quebec publishers by requiring the province's libraries and educational institutions to buy their books from accredited bookstores stocking minimum levels of books from Quebec publishers. While not a funding program, it is a helpful policy ensuring that many books produced by Quebec publishers will find a buyer.

Challenge: Cost of Adapting to New Technologies and Entering the Export Market
With some variations, publishers reported that the costs of adapting to new technologies and entering the export market posed a challenge for them. At the same time, participants in the interviews and focus groups indicated that while both these areas presented challenges, they also represent opportunities for Canadian-owned publishers, such as accessing nontraditional market channels (e.g. selling via the web).

3.1.2 Continued Validity of the Program's Rationale

The challenges identified during the evaluation by publishers contribute to the industry's challenges in producing a wide range of Canadian-authored books that reach readers in Canada and abroad. The evaluation confirmed that during the period of the evaluation, the BPIDP components were relevant in assisting the industry to address these challenges and contribute to program objectives. The various program components were viewed as relevant in assisting Canadian-owned publishers overcome identified challenges in order to be able to meet program outcomes; i.e., produce books that reflect Canadian culture and values for readers domestically and abroad.

For instance, when queried, a large majority (88%) of publishers who responded to the survey indicated that overall, BPIDP was relevant to a large or very large extent in assisting them in meeting various challenges they encounter. A similar rate of endorsement (89%) was found for the Aid to Publishers component. ATP was highly rated in focus groups, interviews and on the survey because it was viewed as allowing the most flexibility for recipients to use the funding to meet their business needs. According to the survey of publishers, the majority of recipients of IMA (76%) and SCI (57%) also indicated that these two specific BPIDP components are relevant to a large or very large extent in addressing the challenges they encounter in the industry (see Exhibit 4).

For the Collective Initiatives component, most of the funding is distributed among industry organizations for specific projects. The vast majority of these organizations (72%) reported on the survey that they viewed the CI component as relevant to a large or very large extent in addressing industry challenges. A small number of publishers participate in specific initiatives under the Collective Initiatives component (e.g. internships, business planning). Of these, slightly less than one-half (43%) indicated that CI is relevant to a large/very large extent in addressing their specific challenges.

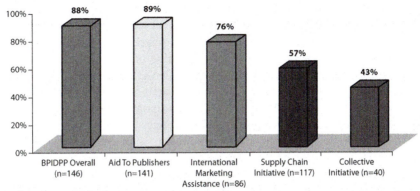

Source: Survey of Publishers

EXHIBIT 4   Relevance of Program Overall and by Components Based on Participation in Respective Program Components

3.1.3 Management Responsiveness

Studies such as *The Book Retail Sector in Canada* (2007), a study on succession planning for book publishers (2005), the *Reading and Buying Books for Pleasure 2005 National Survey,* and a study on the *Book Distribution System in Quebec for New Releases* (2005–06)[19] are examples of BPIDP management's efforts to research key areas of concern to the Canadian book publishing industry. Interviews confirmed that publishers found these studies useful. Publishers also indicated that the confidential performance reports that the program provides each publisher, which compare publishers with others in the same category, were also useful tools.

Both [Department of Canadian Heritage] PCH and the [Association for the Export of Canadian Books] AECB hold consultations with publishing industry stakeholders two to three times per year to hear concerns, exchange ideas and discuss issues of common interest. The program has been evaluated and audited periodically, with BPIDP management addressing many of the recommendations from the last evaluation (2004). This was another positive sign that the program is aiming to stay relevant over time. There is also a widely held perception among publishers, industry associations and academics that the AECB and the IMA component are relevant in terms of the support they offer to publishers in making more Canadian-authored books available to readers abroad. Several stakeholders noted this was in large part due to publishers' presence on the AECB board, which allows them direct input into programming.

3.1.4 Alignment with Federal Government Priorities & Policies for the Cultural Industries

The evaluation found that BPIDP is aligned with government priorities in several ways. First, the Government of Canada has long maintained programs and policies to support the production, distribution and promotion of Canadian books, magazines and newspapers that reflect Canadian culture. This support is premised on the belief that Canadians must have access to Canadian voices and Canadian stories.[20] The Contribution Terms and Conditions of BPIDP indicate that the program contributes to these overall objectives, as the principal objective of BPIDP is to "ensure access to a diverse range of Canadian-authored books in Canada and abroad." In working towards this objective, BPIDP contributes to the departmental strategic outcome as articulated in the Program Activity Architecture: "Canadians express and share their diverse cultural experiences with each other and the world."

In addition, the program offers support for the production of Aboriginal and Official Language Minority books and development of new authors from these communities across Canada. Hence it reflects the country's linguistic duality and promotes cultural diversity and cultural expression from all regions of Canada, an enduring priority of the Canadian government.

In addition, according to the Department of Canadian Heritage, in looking to the future, the cultural sector must continue to adapt so as to benefit fully from a changing global economy. For the Government of Canada, this means searching for innovative ways to support publishers so they can take advantage of opportunities available both at home and abroad.[21] Helping publishers harness the potential of new technologies is an example of the program supporting Canadian participation in the global economy, through its cultural industries. And, while not a program goal, indirectly the program also contributes to "helping Canadian businesses compete globally",a government priority, by helping Canadian publishers market their books in over one hundred countries.

The Program also contributes to Canada being "at the leading edge in science, business, the arts and sport".[22] One example of this is the recent development of "state of the art" bibliographic standards through the Supply Chain Initiative.[23] In addition, the Program has helped developed writers who have gone on to win prestigious international awards.

It can also be argued that by supporting Canadian book publishing, BPIDP contributes to the vitality of the cultural industries, which are considered internationally to be one of the cornerstones of the future economy because they foster creative communities.[24] The proponents of this thesis, developed by a US professor of economics in 2002,[25] argue that creativity, imagination, experimentation and appreciation of difference fuel economic growth in cities, and that what attracts creative people to these cities are a clean environment, a tolerant society, high levels of education and skills, and a rich and accessible arts environment. Supporting the Canadian book publishing industry is consistent with this vision and would support the Canadian government's view that "talented, skilled, creative people are the most critical element of a successful national economy over the long term".[26]

3.2 Program Success

The ultimate outcome of BPIDP is "increased access to a diverse range of Canadian-authored books in Canada and abroad". It is logical to assume that to achieve this ultimate outcome, it is important to foster a strong and diverse population of Canadian-owned publishers across all regions (immediate outcome) that in turn produce a diverse range of Canadian-authored books (intermediate outcome).

3.2.1 A Strong, Diverse Population of Canadian-Owned Book Publishers

The evaluation found that BPIDP contributed to the viability and diversity of the Canadian-owned book industry across Canada.

BPIDP's financial support to the Canadian-owned book industry has helped ensure its stability and the viability of Canadian-owned publishers during the period under review. Since 2003, BPIDP has contributed to the viability of approximately 220 publishers, which in turns enables them to develop new authors and diverse Canadian cultural content. These include regional publishers, Official Language Minority publishers (16 publishers) and Aboriginal publishers (two publishers[27]). English- and French-Canadian publishers constitute a highly diverse community in terms of editorial specialization, company size and regional location. For example, the BPIDP 2005–06 annual report indicated that the 220 qualifying BPIDP publishers were based in over 80 different Canadian communities. In addition to large concentrations of publishers in Quebec and Ontario, 23 are from British Columbia, 14 from Alberta, four from Saskatchewan, eight from Manitoba, and 10 from the Atlantic region, including linguistic minority community publishers. BPIDP's administrative data shows that the number of ATP recipients grew from 185 to 226 between 1993 and 2006–07.

> *"BPIDP has helped support the creation of publishing houses in many communities across Canada. Ten years ago there were very few publishers outside Montreal, Toronto and Vancouver. Now there are publishers in about 85 communities across Canada"*
>
> Key informant interviewee

For the years covered by the evaluation, the number of eligible publishers has remained relatively constant, fluctuating from 217 to 226, depending on the year. This has occurred during a period where there has not been an increase in funding since 2001. Taking inflation into account, this lack of increase translates into a decrease in funding for publishers, according to the analysis of BPIDP administrative data.

As illustrated in Exhibit 5, the majority of publishers surveyed in the context of the evaluation confirmed that BPIDP had a considerable positive impact on their firms' overall sales, profits and number of titles published. This allows Canadian-owned publishers to develop diverse Canadian cultural content for readers domestically and abroad, which is the program's ultimate goal.

While it is clear that BPIDP has contributed to the health of the Canadian-owned book publishing industry, the industry nonetheless remains in a fragile state. This vulnerability is more apparent for smaller firms, as demonstrated in section 3.1.

3.2.2 Increase in the Diversity and Range of Books and Authors

By supporting a wide range of publishers, BPIDP contributed to an increase in the diversity of titles and authors across the country, with smaller publishers contributing significantly to the development of new authors.

It can be assumed that the presence and diversity of publishers across Canada provides the basis for generating a substantial and diverse production of Canadian-authored titles. BPIDP supported the publication of over 6,000 new titles annually, ranging from 6,270 in 2003/04 to 6,738 in 2006/07—an overall increase of approximately 7% for all categories, as Table 3 indicates.[28] The average number of new titles per publisher rose slightly from 28.4 to 29.8 during the same period.

The BPIDP 2005/06 annual report indicated that, in terms of types of books being published by Canadian-owned publishers, based on BookNet's sales tracking in 50 categories, ATP-funded publishers were present in all categories.[29] According to the data, their sales were more evenly spread across subject groupings than the sales of other publishers operating in Canada, whose sales were concentrated in adult fiction and juvenile fiction.

Another indicator of diversity is the number of first-time authors that were published by BPIDP funded publishers. According to the administrative data provided for 2006–07, there were 988 first-time authors published by BPIDP funded publishers[30]. The median number of first-time authors published was 3, with very similar medians occurring across the various size categories of publishers (range of 2 to 6). Considering the total numbers of authors published by each firm, the smaller and medium-sized firms have considerably higher proportions of first-time authors. Many of the regional publishers are within the smaller size categories. Hence, it can be inferred that BPIDP

TABLE 3   Total Number of Eligible New Titles by Commercial Category

YEAR	EDUCATIONAL TOTAL	SCHOLARLY TOTAL	TRADE TOTAL	ALL CATEGORIES TOTAL
2003–04	1,302	414	3,588	5,304
2004–05	1,189	460	3,340	4,989
2005–06	1,273	476	3,316	5,065
2006–07	1,614	507	3,661	5,782

Source: BPIDP Administrative Data

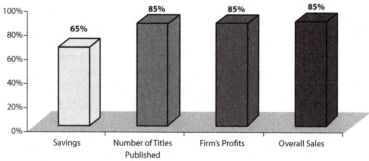

Source: Survey of Publishers

EXHIBIT 5   Percentage of Publishers Reporting Some or Considerable Positive Impact from BPIDP on Savings, Number of Titles Published, and Profits/Sales

has been contributing to the diversity and range of books in Canada, particularly through its support of small and medium-sized publishers.

3.2.3 Enhanced Professional Skills and Industry Knowledge

BPIDP contributed to enhancing the professional skills and industry knowledge of Canadian-owned book publishers. The reported impact varied among English- and French-language publishers but was more important for smaller publishers.

The evaluation found that BPIDP contributed to enhancing the professional skills of the majority of recipients, as well as their knowledge of the industry, which are considered necessary elements to remain competitive in the industry to meet program goals. The finding is based largely on stakeholders' view and publishers' own assessment gathered through the survey and key informant interviews, as it was not possible to quantify these types of results. As illustrated in Exhibit 6, the majority of BPIDP recipients (60% or more) surveyed reported that the support received from the program assisted them in achieving these results. Key informant interviewees reported many improved professional skills, such as improved production skills, management and marketing skills, website management, and improved computerization skills. And, while not a primary program objective, a majority of publishers reported the Program contributed to an increase in their capacity to use market intelligence as cited by 63% of survey respondents and key informant interviewees.

All BPIDP components and activities contributed to these results. However, the data indicates that an important contributing factor to these results has been improvements to the supply chain, discussed in section 3.2.6., a program outcome associated more with CI than SCI. This is likely due, in part, to the fact that a much larger portion of respondent publishers had benefited directly from SCI support rather than from CI support[31], which helps to support knowledge and skill development through funding for collective professional development projects undertaken by representative associations in various sectors of the book industry. Participation in book fairs and trade shows (with the support of CI and IMA) was another source of learning and skills acquisition for publishers, particularly attendance at international book fairs, and can be considered another unintended program outcome. For example, 53% of publishers who attended international book fairs indicated that this activity has considerable impact on

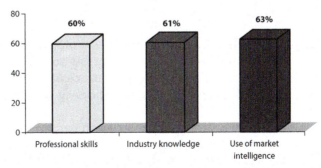

EXHIBIT 6   Percentage of Publishers Reporting Some or Considerable Positive Impact of BPIDP on Professional skills, Industry Knowledge

their professional skills and industry knowledge, compared to 33% for domestic book fairs. The Frankfurt Book Fair, the primary venue for selling and buying foreign rights, was singled out as the most important international book publishing fair.

> *"The AECB has a lot of experience with exporting. When you arrive at international book fairs, it's great to have someone knowledgeable about exporting to talk to."*
>
> Focus group participant, Montreal (original quote in French)

Approximately one-quarter of BPIDP recipients (32% of firms with revenues less than $1M versus 11% of firms with revenues over $1M[32]) received funding to hire an intern. The file review provided several examples of successful projects, as well as benefits for recipient organizations. Most of the information available in the files related to project outputs, as publishers had to report soon after the conclusion of their project. Nevertheless, in the files reviewed, all those who hired interns reported benefits for the firm. These varied across publishers and included being able to provide services in a more efficient and timely basis; contribution of the intern to the conclusion of several rights agreements; and increased industry knowledge. A few publishers reported the amount of paper work and reporting required from BPIDP, as a challenge resulting from hiring an intern.

A few book publishers indicated that they had employed the intern after the internship ended and being able to train that new employee was viewed as a benefit; other benefits cited included increasing marketing efforts or developing export markets. The main challenge of offering an internship was the lack of capital to offer a competitive salary for the intern after the internship was over. A few respondents noted that they were not able to retain the intern at the end of the training period for that reason; not having sufficient time to devote to the intern, or lacking sufficient physical space for the intern.

As for the few firms that received BPIDP funding for strategic business planning purposes (5% overall), some reported a significant impact for the firm. Reported benefits included: implementing a successful succession strategy by attracting new shareholders and private equity; developing a clearer marketing strategy and changes in the approach to grow the business successfully; or, introducing improvements in human resources management, budgets and other administrative functions.

3.2.4 A More Effective and Efficient Canadian Book Supply Chain

BPIDP support for the adoption of new technologies has significantly helped publishing firms in several areas, such as capacity to produce and transfer electronic bibliographic data, to digitize business processes, and to market via the Web, which in turn contributed to increased efficiency and savings for Canadian-owned publishers.

The book publishing academics interviewed concurred that there are two areas that can help Canadian book publishers achieve higher profit margins. One is increasing revenues through exports; the other is achieving savings through the supply chain.

With the support of BPIDP, both the French- and English-language book industries have taken advantage of new digital technologies to create efficiencies in the supply chain for books, connecting publishers and distributors to retailers and book-buyers. The results from interventions undertaken through the Supply Chain Initiative can be more directly attributed to BPIDP due to the targeted nature of the funding. Efficiency gains include a better understanding of the marketplace and enhanced abilities to make corporate decisions and implement management practices.

Through BookNet Canada (BNC) and the Société de gestion de la banque de titres de langue française (BTLF), the industry has committed itself to generating high-quality bibliographic data as the foundation for efficient digital ordering systems. Both agencies, which are funded through the BPIDP Supply Chain Initiative, have developed bibliographic data standards for book publishers and bibliographic certification criteria. By these means, publishers can achieve standardized levels of digital bibliographic capability and are certified by BookNet or the BTLF for their participation in online book ordering using an electronic data interchange (EDI) system, which is done according to widely used specifications known as ONIX[33].

Endnotes

12. Where appropriate, for qualitative analysis, the evaluation reports on the frequency of a particular response using the following quantitative adjectives to indicate the relative weight of the responses for each respondent group, as follows: "All/almost All"—90% or more of respondents; "Large Majority"—at least 75% but less than 90% of respondents; "Majority/most"—at least 50% but less than 75% of respondents; "Several"—at least 25% but less than 50% of respondents; and "A few"—at least two respondents but less than 25% of respondents.

13. Department of Canadian Heritage (PCH), *The Book Retail Sector in Canada*, 2007.

14. Source: BPIDP administrative data.

15. While the return of unsold copies is a common practice in the industry and in fact one of the challenges publishers face in terms of the supply chain, the volume of books that large retailers can order and return to publishers exacerbates the problem.

16. *Globe & Mail*, Jan. 9, 2008.

17. As noted elsewhere, while the evaluation covers three years, from 2004–05 to 2006–07, data from 2003–04 were included where appropriate, as information for that year could not be included in the 2004 evaluation.

18. All Gs&Cs include BPIDP funding.

19. While the first two studies were commissioned directly by BPIDP management, the latter was undertaken through Collective Initiative funding.

20. PCH, Cultural Affairs Policies, Books: http://www.pch.gc.ca/progs/ac-ca/pol/livre-book/index_e.cfm

21. PCH, Cultural Policies, Books: http://www.pch.gc.ca/progs/ac-ca/pol/livre-book/index_e.cfm

22. Government of Canada, 2007 Budget, http://www.budget.gc.ca/2007/pdf/briefe.pdf

23. Government of Canada, Speech from the Throne, April 4, 2206: http://pm.gc.ca/eng/media.asp?id=1087

24. http://www.washingtonmonthly.com/features/2001/0205.florida.html

25. 'Creative Cities': the role of the Melbourne 2030 strategy in enhancing Melbourne's competitive advantage as one of the world's most creative and liveable cities,

Speech to the Australian Fabian Society, 2 February 2004, http://www.fabian.org.
au/files/050202Creative_cities.pdf

26. Department of Finance, Mobilizing Science and Technology to Canada's Advan-
    tage, Executive Summary, http://www.ic.gc.ca/cmb/welcomeic.nsf/
    532340a8523f33718525649d006b119d/c682d92ba63a5e1e
    852572de00503b8e!OpenDocument

27. Overall, there about 20 organizations across Canada that publish Aboriginal con-
    tent but only three or four are "official" publishers. Given the environment in which
    Aboriginal publishers operate (e.g. small and isolated communities, characterized
    by lower education levels, various languages, and cultures in which the oral tradi-
    tions are still very alive) and, despite the fact that the Program has lower thresholds
    and proportionally higher support (through the ATP funding formula and CI intern-
    ships) for Aboriginal publishers, it is challenging for Aboriginal publishers to meet
    thresholds required to be eligible for ATP. Like other very small publishers, they rely
    more heavily on the Canada Council for the Arts for support.

28. These figures also include foreign-authored titles (though only a very small num-
    ber—those eligible by virtue of having been translated or adapted by a Canadian).

29. PCH, *The Book Report 2005–06*, p 17–18: http://www.pch.gc.ca/progs/ac-ca/
    progs/padie-bpidp/reports/bookreport/0506/05-06_e.pdf

30. "First-time" author means an author who has never been published before by any
    book publisher.

31. SCI publisher respondents n=106 vs. CI publisher respondents n=37. *Source: Sur-
    vey of Publishers*

32. The difference can be attributed, in large part, to BPIDP instituting a rule during the
    period covered by the evaluation limiting internship support to publishers with rev-
    enues under $1M.

33. Many book sales are driven by large retail chains and online retailers and distribu-
    tors that require that publishers provide them with title information in formats ac-
    cording to ONIX specifications. ONIX is both a data dictionary of the elements
    which go to make up a product record and a standard means by which product
    data can be transmitted electronically by publishers to data aggregators, whole-
    salers, booksellers and anyone else involved in the sale of their publications. ONIX
    was originally devised to simplify the provision of product information to online
    retailers.

DISCUSSION

Department of Canadian Heritage, *Summative Evaluation of the Book Publishing Industry Development Program*.

1. The evaluation of the BPIDP program outlines three key challenges facing the Canadian book publishing industry. Briefly summarize each of these in your own words
   and explain how direct subsidies like BPIDP (now the Canada Book Fund) help publishers overcome each of these challenges.

2. The largest component of BPIDP was the Aid to Publishers component. How satisfied with the program were publishers who received this support and why do they like it?
3. The evaluation found that BPIDP contributed to diversity within the book publishing industry and to the increased diversity of books and authors. What evidence is presented to support this assessment? Do you agree with this positive evaluation of direct subsidies for publishing in Canada? Why or why not?
4. Visit the Department of Canadian Heritage at www.pch.gc.ca and search on the Canada Book Fund. Find the list of recipients for 'Publishing Support' and choose one of the recipients for further research on the web. What types of books and specific titles does this publisher publish? How well do you think this publisher is meeting the objective of creating access to Canadian books?

Supporting Canadian Content through Public-Private Funding

INTRODUCTION

In the last two chapters of this book, we will examine the complex combination of direct expenditures, tax expenditures and compulsory contributions to subsidy programs that work together to support the creation of Canadian content in the media industries. As we have already learned in Chapter 6, governments can establish quotas for both television and radio content as a means of supporting the production of national culture. The CRTC imposes a Canadian programming quota on private television networks and a Canadian music quota on commercial radio. The quotas act as a 'stick' with which broadcasters are firmly encouraged to seek out Canadian content. While quotas effectively act as a way of increasing the **demand** for Canadian content, they cannot in themselves ensure an adequate **supply** of appropriate high quality TV shows or musical selections. For this, governments turn to the policy instrument of subsidies—in the form of direct expenditure such as grants and loans to content producers, or in the form of tax expenditure to generate private investment in Canadian content by providing tax deductions or refundable tax credits on some of the production costs. We have seen a form of tax expenditure at work in the magazine and newspaper industries, but these tax deductions under the *Income Tax Act* go to advertisers in print media, not to the actual producers of Canadian content. In the next chapter, we will look at a federal program of refundable tax credits that go to investors in Canadian film and television production.

In both of these final chapters we will consider another way of triggering investment in the creation of Canadian content, through mandatory contributions made by commercial media outlets to subsidy programs that are designed to support the creation of Canadian music and television programs. Radio broadcasters are required to make an annual contribution to the Foundation to Assist Canadian Talent on Recordings (FACTOR), or to its French equivalent MUSICACTION, while cable and satellite distributors must contribute to the Canada Media Fund. The Department of Canadian Heritage also contributes significant amounts to each of these funds, making them both examples of public-private partnerships for production subsidies in Canada's media industries. This particular type of policy tool evolved during the 1980s and 90s, as stakeholders in the media industries and government agencies experimented with ways of developing the supply of Canadian media content while building creative clusters in the music, television, and film industries. Media policy during this period was an often contradictory blend of both cultural and industrial goals, targeted at the creation of distinctively Canadian media products while also establishing viable and profitable private-sector media industries that could survive in an increasingly globalized economy.

This chapter focuses on the sound recording industry and its participants: musicians, record labels, music publishers, radio broadcasters, and Canadian music fans. It is important to distinguish between the creation of quotas for commercial radio and their actual outcomes in the music industry. As previously suggested, the Canadian commercial radio quotas are a tool for generating demand that has multiple and sometimes conflicting influences on the production of Canadian music. While the CRTC defines and implements the 35 percent radio quota, it has a much less direct role in influencing the actual creation of music in Canada. However, as explained in Chapter 6, the CRTC complements the quotas with explicit expenditure requirements for radio broadcasters. The 2006 Commercial Radio Policy clarifies the objectives of 'Canadian content development' (CCD) and requires that privately-owned commercial stations help finance promotion, training and development of Canadian musical talent. The 2006 policy lays out specific amounts for this contribution based on revenues of each individual radio station:

The total amount of each station's basic annual CCD contribution will be determined as follows:

- Stations with total revenues in the previous broadcast year of less than $625,000 will make a fixed contribution of $500.
- Stations with total revenues in the previous broadcast year between $625,000 and $1,250,000 will make a fixed contribution of $1,000.
- Stations with total revenues exceeding $1,250,000 in the previous broadcast year will contribute $1,000 plus 0.5% of the portion of the previous year's total revenues that exceeds $1,250,000. (CRTC, 2006)

The Commercial Radio Policy further specifies that in order to ensure continuity of funding, no less than 60 percent of the basic annual CCD contribution must go directly to FACTOR or MUSICACTION, while the remaining amount may be directed to any eligible CCD initiative. FACTOR and MUSICACTION also receive public funds from the Canada Music Fund. The agencies use these combined funds for direct grants and loans to Canadian musicians, record labels, and other non-profit associations in the music industry, as described in Policy Source 16.

As Robert Wright (2004) argues in the critical analysis that follows, the combination of radio quotas and public-private subsidies has both positive and negative outcomes for the Canadian music industry. Wright is quite critical of the music quotas for commercial radio. Although he recognizes that quotas have had an undeniable impact on increasing the quantity of Canadian music available for airplay, he is uncertain about the audience demand for and quality of the music that is supplied. In his historical overview of Can-Con rules for radio, Wright points to a disturbing trend of quotas being filled with generic Canadian popular music that meets the MAPL criteria, but does not always generate Canadian sales. At the same time, he suggests, Canadian musicians who truly want to succeed in the business attempt to escape the Canadian content 'ghetto' by getting deals with multinational record labels and moving into the US and other foreign markets. As Wright indicates, the Canadian-owned independent labels who do all the initial work of developing and promoting local musicians are then likely to lose these artists to the larger multinationals. The author points to the inherent contradiction between using quotas to create opportunity for Canadian musicians in a domestic industry that, like book publishing, is dominated by multinational 'branch plants.' In order to succeed in this context, musicians need to produce a 'global product' that may not be distinctively Canadian in anything other than the citizenship of the artists. For this reason, the quotas and the subsidies provided by private radio and the federal government through FACTOR have not, in Wright's view, succeeded in building a viable domestic recording industry.

Policy Source 15 describes the creation of the Canada Music Fund in 2001, based on the former Sound Recording Development Program. The Music Fund was renewed by the Conservative government in 2009, with an annual investment of $27.6 million over five years, but the Canadian Musical Diversity Program and the Support to Sector Associations were cut at this time (Canadian Heritage, 2009b). Today, the Music Fund supports five distinct components: Creators' Assistance Component (to be eliminated in 2013), New Musical Works Component, Collective Initiatives Component, Music Entrepreneur Component and Canadian Music Memories Component. These components are actually administered by different stakeholders in the music industry, including FACTOR and MUSICACTION. The Music Fund remains the core of support for music subsidies in Canada. As 'The FACTOR Story' in Policy Source 16 indicates, government funding accounts for 64 percent of FACTOR's combined funding.

In Policy Source 16, Larry Leblanc clearly shows how Canadian musicians themselves rely extensively on FACTOR support, especially in the early part of their careers. FACTOR funds can be used to make demo recordings, to go on tour, to create a music video, for promotion and marketing, and for actual album production. FACTOR also supports small and emerging independent record labels in Canada. These companies can apply to FACTOR for funds to help cover costs of business development and business travel. Larger, more established Canadian independent record labels can also apply directly to Canadian Heritage for funding under the Music Entrepreneur program. Leblanc traces the history of FACTOR from its early days as a joint initiative between key stakeholders in the music industry: radio station owners, the Canadian Independent Record Production Association (CIRPA) and the Canadian Music Publishers Association (CMPA). His history is full of evidence of actual outcomes of policy intervention, since he mentions many of the hundreds of Canadian artists and record labels who have benefited from public-private subsidies administered by FACTOR since 1982.

Critical Analysis

Wright, R. A. (2004). Gimme Shelter: Cultural Protectionism and the Canadian Recording Industry (Chapter 3). In *Virtual sovereignty: nationalism, culture and the Canadian question* (79–98). Toronto: Canadian Scholars' Press.

Gimme Shelter

Cultural Protectionism and The Canadian Recording Industry

"[S]tay away from the Canadian music business. It's full of politics and bureaucracy. It's trouble. Don't sign to a Canadian company. Don't sign to a Canadian publisher. Go south of the border. You'll get a better deal."

Bryan Adams (1992)[1]

"For all I know, Canadian content may become the last bastion for Canadian culture on radio after all the stations get bought up by American media groups and are programmed out of Dallas or somewhere . . . ."

Bryan Adams (2000)[2]

"Tears Are Not Enough," Canada's contribution to the 1986 campaign for Ethiopian famine relief, was notable not only for its saccharine sentimentality but also for demonstrating rather starkly that "Canadian-content" regulations had largely failed to deliver the musical "uniqueness" imagined by its pioneers. There was something unnerving about the pairing of ground-breaking veterans like Joni Mitchell, Neil Young and Geddy Lee with the lightweight "hair bands" of the era—Platinum Blonde, Honeymoon Suite and Corey Hart, for example.[3] The depth and the breadth of the talent of the generation that had risen to international prominence just prior to the introduction of Cancon was in particularly sharp relief, even if this was not immediately obvious to some of the participants. As Geoff Pevere and Greig Dymond have observed, during the "Tears Are Not Enough" recording session Young suffered the "ultimate indignity" of "being told he was singing off-key by blow-dried yuppie-pup producer David Foster." To this affront Young offered his now famous reply: "That's my sound, man."[4]

In 1992, having been denied Cancon status for his hit "(Everything I Do) I Do It For You," Bryan Adams angrily stated what many Canadian music fans had long since come to believe: Canadian content breeds mediocrity. Adams advised Canada's aspiring artists to pursue their careers "south of the border"; and as Canadians had done as a matter of course since the 1930s, many did. In the 1990s, some of Canada's most innovative musicians and producers—Daniel Lanois, the post-Band Robbie Robertson and the re-born Alanis Morissette, most notably—achieved massive critical and commercial success largely without reference to Cancon.[5] Yet at the end of the decade, by which time even beloved Canadian artists like Céline Dion had ceased to satisfy the criteria for Canadian content, the CRTC "arbitrarily" raised the Cancon quota for commercial radio from 30 per cent to 35.[6] The argument is now frequently heard that the success of "great" Canadian artists like the Tragically Hip, the Barenaked Ladies and Sarah McLachlan demonstrate that the original logic of Cancon was sound, at least in the sense that it gives Canadian acts a leg up in the domestic market at the start of careers that may become runaway successes. Yet the doubts expressed by Gordon Lightfoot and others in the 1960s and 1970s remain: if Canadian music is truly "world class," why are Canadian-content quotas necessary at all?

This chapter has two related objectives. Firstly, I would like to undertake a brief review of Canadian policy initiatives in the areas of music broadcasting and sound recording as they took formative shape in the 1970s and became entrenched in the 1980s. In particular, I shall focus on the legacy of discord that such initiatives—most notably those having to do with Cancon—seem to have left as a more or less perennial feature of these industries. Secondly, and more importantly, I would like to explore the question of what Canadian musicians, labels and music consumers might reasonably have expected from such a strategy of "official" cultural protectionism. I argue that the principal objective of Canadian-content legislation and of state involvement in the recording sector in Canada—the development of a strong indigenous recording industry—was a reasonable one given the structure of the music business internationally, but that it was undermined by the very policies which were implemented to bring it about.

CANADIAN CONTENT

Concern for the survival of "Canadian culture," particularly in relation to American mass culture, has been a central feature of national life in Canada since Confederation (1867) at least. As noted in Chapter One, various forms of cultural protectionism—ranging from tariffs against imported cultural goods to the patronage and later the subsidization of the arts—were a mainstay of Canadian public policy throughout much of the twentieth century. In contrast with the "high" arts and even with the broadcasting, magazine and book-publishing industries, however, all of which were thought to be directly threatened by increasing American competition, sound recording remained of little concern to cultural nationalists and hence to the state. The Canadian cultural élite in the era of the Massey Commission, for example, thought the music business both commercially marginal and culturally insignificant; indeed, "American" popular music was one of the very homogenizing cultural forces from which the Commission itself believed Canadian culture needed defending.[7] (This élitist bias seems somewhat puzzling in retrospect, given that cultural nationalists and the Canadian state had made an extremely high priority of public broadcasting in the 1920s and of regulating private radio broadcasting in the national interest the following decade.) The question of ownership and control of the recording industry in Canada did not become a matter of public discussion until the Centennial era, when a nationalist outcry on the part of journalists and industry pioneers like Walt Grealis compelled federal policy-makers to direct their attention towards it.[8] As noted in Chapter Two, this nationalist upsurge coincided with the coming-of-age of the baby boom generation and with it, the musical and lyrical "maturation" of rock-and-roll and its myriad blues, pop, folk and "protest music" hybrids.

The music business in Canada has been dominated throughout most of its history by a handful of foreign (multinational) "major labels," companies which have themselves been integrated, vertically and horizontally, into global entertainment empires. The Canadian role in this transnational record industry—one that is typical of all "small market" countries in the industrialized West[9]—has been to serve as a market for mostly non-Canadian recordings of non-Canadian musical performances. In part as a result of Canada's historically high tariff on imported recordings, all of the multinational "majors" had established subsidiary operations in Canada by 1920, where they came to dominate the domestic market (and where they continue to account for approximately 85 per cent of industry revenues).[10] These "branch plants" have been concentrated in Toronto, with a limited number of adjunct offices in other Canadian cities, where they have mainly been in the business of pressing records, tapes and CDs for domestic consumption, using foreign (usually American or British) master tapes. The Canadian subsidiaries operate with limited autonomy, signing and promoting some local talent, but this is a relatively recent development and one that is itself arguably a byproduct of Cancon regulations. The subsidiaries' sometimes distant relationship with their parent companies has, in fact, proven to be something of a mixed blessing for Canadian recording artists. For the most part, Canadian artists from Hank Snow in the 1930s to Neil Young in the 1960s recognized that they had little choice but to leave Canada if they hoped to have a musical career that included a record contract.

As noted in the last chapter, the project of mobilizing Canadian policy-makers in support of an indigenous recording industry was shaped in the late 1960s by a growing public taste for music about Canada—most notably for the music of Gordon Lightfoot—and, indeed, by a growing unease about the fact that Canadian recording artists had had to exile themselves to pursue their craft. Private radio broadcasters were singled out as having collaborated in the colonization of the Canadian recording industry, on the grounds that they had refused to sacrifice audience share (and hence advertising revenues) in order to promote Canadian artists. Responding to this growing public concern, the Trudeau Liberals implemented "Canadian-content" rules for commercial radio broadcasters under the terms of the Broadcasting Act, to be administered by the newly designated Canadian Radio-Television and Telecommunications Commission (CRTC). Starting in January 1971, AM radio stations in Canada were required to play a minimum of 30 per cent Cancon as a condition of the renewal of their broadcasting licenses. Musical selections considered Canadian content under the new legislation were those which met two of the following four criteria: (a) the instrumentation or lyrics were principally performed by a Canadian; (b) the music was performed by a Canadian; (c) the lyrics were written by a Canadian; (d) the live performance was wholly recorded in Canada. After Bryan Adams' 1992 hit "(Everything I Do) I Do It For You" failed to qualify as Canadian content, setting in motion an extraordinarily acrimonious public debate about state regulation of popular music in Canada, the rules were loosened so as to award Cancon status to "special cases" like Adams'. Henceforth, "in addition to meeting the criterion for either artists or production, a Canadian who has collaborated with a non-Canadian receives at least half of the credit for both music and lyrics" and is therefore considered Cancon.[11]

It was not until the early 1980s that the Canadian government arranged for the provision of direct subsidies to the sound-recording industry, several years after it had initiated financial support for the book-publishing and film industries. The institutional structure through which this support was channelled took the form of an ostensibly "private-sector" agency, the Foundation to Assist Canadian Talent on Record. FACTOR was created in 1982 by several Canadian-owned private broadcasting corporations, the Canadian Independent Record Producers Association (CIRPA) and the Canadian Music Publishers Association (CMPA). It was designed to "stimulate the growth and development of the independent sector of the Canadian recording industry" by making grants and interest-free loans available to Canadian acts on a competitive basis for the production of demos and video clips and for the organization of international tours.[12] Publicly, broadcasters expressed their desire to support the Canadian recording industry in selfless, often nationalist terms, while simultaneously reasoning that if they failed to cooperate they might run the risk of having too little Canadian "product" for their playlists. Under the terms of the Liberals' Cancon legislation, however, private broadcasters were required not only to play Canadian music but to actively promote Canadian talent off-air (although the CRTC never specified the proportion of profit each station was expected to spend on this promotion). To be sure, membership in FACTOR has not gone unnoticed by the CRTC in its consideration of broadcast license renewal applications.

With FACTOR in place but woefully underfunded—its first annual budget was $200,000, too little to capitalize the production of more than two record albums—the federal government announced the creation in 1986 of a Sound Recording Development Program (SRDP) which would pump $25 million into the Canadian recording industry over five years. The SRDP included three major components—production support ($18 million), promotion, touring and marketing support ($4.5 million), and business development ($2.5 million). FACTOR and its French-language counterpart, *Musicaction,* which was founded in 1985, received $2.2 million annually from SRDP funds. This amount, along with an increased commitment from the private sector, brought FACTOR's annual operating budget to roughly $4 million in 1990. The rationale for government involvement in the FACTOR program, as expressed in *Vital Links,* an influential booklet published by the Department of Communications in 1987, was that the "recent serious decline in the number of Canadian-content recordings—especially the precipitous 45 per cent drop in French-language production since 1978—had created problems for Canada's radio broadcasters, who were finding if difficult to obtain an adequate supply of new releases."[13] Partisan support for the indigenous recording industry continued to make good nationalist fodder, even fifteen years after the introduction of Canadian-content rules. At the press conference announcing the creation of the SRDP, held at a Montreal disco, Tory Communications Minister Marcel Massé was quoted as saying that "the sorry state of Canada's recording industry is due to the viselike control exercised by multinational companies over the distribution of records in Canada."[14] In November 1991, at the end of SRDP's first five years of operation, the federal government announced that it would become a permanent program, with an annual budget of $5 million. In 1999–2000 the SRDP's annual budget was $9.45 million; in 2002, FACTOR's annual budget stood at $11 million, of which $8.1 million was provided by the Department of Heritage.[15]

THE TROUBLE WITH NORMAL

From their inception, Canadian-content quotas, and to a lesser extent FACTOR, were contentious within the recording and broadcasting sectors, as well as among policy-makers and outside observers. Within the industries themselves, support for Cancon tended to co-alesce around the Canadian Independent Record Producers Association (CIRPA), while op-position emanated most noticeably from the Canadian Association of Broadcasters (CAB).

CIRPA was founded in 1975 as a voluntary association for Canada's independent record industry, assuming the crucial role of watchdog and lobbyist. CIRPA's position on Canadian content was unequivocal: it saw the very survival of the Canadian recording industry as hinging on radio exposure for Canadian acts. Thus, the Association lobbied in the late 1970s and the 1980s not only for increased Canadian-content requirements for FM radio—which, it argued, would represent simply a return to the "status quo ante of 1971, when AM was the band of choice"—but for a much more strenuous monitor-ing policy that would prevent broadcasters from playing their requisite Canadian con-tent in non-peak periods.[16] CIRPA's position was supported in these years by the influ-ential Canadian record industry trade paper *The Record* and explicitly by many of the country's most influential rock music critics, most notably Chris Dafoe of the *Toronto Star*. Notable for its relative silence in the debate over Cancon was the Canadian Recording Industry Association (CRIA), which represented the major label subsidiaries in Canada and for which, therefore, the country of origin of recorded "product" was of far less importance than its overall sales in the Canadian market.

The position of the CAB, the association that has represented private broadcasters in Canada since 1926, was explicitly opposed to that of CIRPA. Given that the CAB has always spoken exclusively for the interests of private-sector capital, it is not easy to dis-til its specific objections to Cancon from the Association's generalized resentment of reg-ulation of its industry. The broad outlines of its case are, however, clear. A CAB survey of FM-radio programmers conducted in 1990 revealed that very few broadcasters believed there was "enough Canadian music to sustain a higher quota." Radio entrepreneur Bill Gilliland—which the sponsorship of "concerned music industryites"—articulated in *The Record* what was undoubtedly a widely held view of the Canadian record industry among broadcasters:

> Throughout the '60s and '70s and '80s, radio programmers across Canada busted their buns devising creative and effective ways to present the nation's music artists to listeners. Beginning in the mid-'80s, music video programmers added their very, very substantial support to the record industry by imagina-tively presenting the nation's music artists to viewers. Radio and video support continues in the '90s. Why, then, aren't the made-in-Canada recording artists as successful as many critics think they should be? Is the market for domestic recording artists grossly overestimated?[17]

Clearly implicit in Gilliland's observations was the suggestion that some radio program-mers in Canada had reservations, not only about the quantity of Canadian musical recordings, but about their quality as well.

At the level of policy analysis, traditionally the domain of economists and academic observers, the debate over Canadian content as it evolved in the 1980s tended to cen-tre on the more generalized question of its value (utility) for Canadians and for "Cana-dian culture." Unlike the debate between independent recording companies and radio interests, this was a debate about first principles. For Paul Audley, one of several inde-pendent policy analysts whose writing echoed the official governmental line about Cancon, any discussion of the subject had to begin with the premise that "Canadians who are involved in the creation and performance of music ought to have a fair chance to have their music recorded and played on radio stations in Canada."[18] This position was restated in November 1990 by CRTC policy analyst John Feihl, who urged Canadians to "change [their] perspective" on the Cancon issue by asking not whether 30 per cent Cancon is too much, but whether 70 per cent non-Canadian content is too little.[19]

The widespread consensus in favour of Canadian-content regulations, outside of certain narrowly partisan circles, was evident in the low number of policy analysts who criticized the assumptions upon which it rested. I am aware of only one scholarly work from this period, William Watson's *National Pastimes: The Economics of Canadian Leisure* (1988), that came out squarely in favour of dismantling Canadian-content policy as it then existed, and the evidence suggests that because this work was published by the neo-conservative Fraser Institute, it was largely ignored within policy-making circles. Watson's methodology was simple, perhaps deceptively so: as an economist, he wanted to ask whether Canadians were getting their money's worth, quite literally, from Canadian-content regulations. Most of the leisure goods consumed within Canada, he observed, were not subsidized, while most of those that were eligible for designation as Canadian-content received some form of subsidy. Watson asked whether a performer or a recording may be said to have provided benefits to the people who had paid for it via their taxes, but who had not seen or heard it because it was of too little value to them to do so. With regard to sound recordings, Watson argued that, at most, the state ought to be subsidizing activities that teach Canadians about each other, and that the pertinent criterion for Cancon eligibility should therefore be the "Canadianness" of a recording's subject matter rather than of its production. He asked: "Should the state really have a position on where the generic rock music Canadians listen to is produced?" The answer: "[S]ound-alike recordings by such people as Corey Hart, Bryan Adams and Luba, [which are] destined for the US market have no claim to public support."[20]

Regardless of one's ideological proximity to Watson, his insistence that Canadian consumers be brought into the Cancon debate represented a challenge that had been simmering since the 1960s—one which would later burst upon the broadcasting and recording industries during the Adams controversy. Taken alongside data published by the Canadian Association of Broadcasters which revealed that domestic radio audience share decreased in direct proportion to the amount of Canadian content broadcast, there was a certain force to the argument that so-called ordinary Canadians were casting their votes on Canadian content with their ears, that is, with their radio tuners and record-buying dollars.

If *laissez faire* critics of Cancon like William Watson and the CAB had been alone in advancing the argument that the consumption of recorded music ought to be driven by "market forces," the suggestion that Canadians vote with their ears might be easily dismissed. The truth of the matter is that even ardent Cancon supporters acknowledged in the 1980s that the main preoccupation of the Canadian music industry—and therefore of the CRTC and FACTOR—was not that of protecting or enhancing Canadian culture so much as it was that of finding and developing international markets. And herein lay the rub: the path to success in New York and Stockholm and Tokyo lay in developing the generic sounds of the increasingly globalized corporate "playlist," which actually meant *reducing* the "Canadianness" of Canadian recorded product.

WILL IT PLAY IN BOISE?

Canadian-content requirements, as originally envisaged by the CRTC, were driven by two main goals: the development of a Canadian recording industry and the nurture and support of Canadian musical talent. However compatible these objectives might have seemed as matters of policy, in practice they have proven to be at odds. Because of the dominant position of the major multinational labels both domestically and internationally, Canadian recording artists have always recognized that their greatest success was likely to come in the form of an international record contract. This is as true for post-Cancon artists as it was for the pioneers of the 1930s: the top-selling Canadian acts have always been those that produce records for major foreign record companies. In 1984, a celebrated but by no means exceptional year, the top-selling Canadian rock acts—Bryan Adams, Helix, Platinum Blonde, Corey Hart and Honeymoon Suite—were all signed to major multinational record deals and actually broke first in the United States.[21] Today the same general rule applies. In 1991, Shania Twain was "discovered" at a Huntsville, Ontario, resort but signed her first record deal with Mercury Nashville. In a slight variation on the same theme, Alanis Morissette abandoned the Canadian music scene altogether in 1993 after two albums with MCA Canada, obliterating her dance-pop past and signing with Madonna's Maverick Records label.

What is more, the success—and arguably even the survival—of independent Canadian record companies has been tempered since the 1970s by their ability to expand into markets beyond Canada. The reason for this, simply stated, is that the Canadian market for records is too small in all but a handful of cases to recover the costs of production: an album has to go Gold (50,000 copies in Canada) before the costs of bringing a new act onstream—including recording, marketing, touring and videos—are likely to be recovered. Thus, the most successful Canadian independent labels (those unaffiliated with transnational firms) have been: those which distribute foreign product in Canada—as in the case of Attic Records; those which have managed to crack international markets with Canadian product—notably Nettwerk and True North; or, most ironically of all, those which have managed to break non-Canadian performers in international markets—Stony Plain, for example.[22]

Thus, to be a successful Canadian recording artist or Canadian record company is, paradoxically, to have broken into international markets. Consequently, the most successful Canadian musicians and record companies are those that fit most readily into the larger world of Anglo-American popular music. This has long been the rule of thumb for musicians and record executives in Canada; in the 1980s it also became the guiding principle of Ottawa's policy on the subsidization of the recording industry. As *Vital Links* puts it, "In most cases, export sales are . . . essential if Canadian-owned companies are to turn a profit on a recording project. Efforts must be made, therefore, to tour the artist internationally and to license Canadian products to recording and music-publishing companies in other countries."[23] To this end, it was decided in October 1990 that FACTOR funding for Canadian recording projects would be "earmarked for fewer artists in order to deliver product better suited for the international market," with the result that "individual labels would of necessity be eligible for fewer projects."[24] CIRPA followed suit in 1990, presenting a report to the Ontario Ministry of Culture and Communications requesting $5 million annually for, among other things, "assistance in expanding foreign markets."[25]

Since the objectives of the CRTC included strengthening the recording industry in Canada and supporting Canadian acts, the success of Canadian-content legislation was gauged in part in terms of its success in carrying Canadian musicians and Canadian product into foreign markets. When so judged, as virtually everyone in the broadcasting and recording industries agreed, Cancon was found wanting. As one Canadian record executive stated bluntly in 1980: "So much garbage was being recorded just to help fill the airways that a lot of third-rate stuff was called a hit. What was worse came when you took a good record that was a Canadian hit to the States. They wouldn't listen. To them, a Canadian hit meant second-rate."[26]

It was not only performers signed to independent Canadian labels who suffered this fate. On the contrary, as Toronto singer/songwriter Andrew Cash noted in 1986, the multinationals had even grown suspicious of the judgements of their Canadian branch offices: "Most Canadian record companies are US-owned subsidiaries and many of the local acts they've signed ... haven't been picked up in the US. What's the point in pinning your hopes on a big contract and allowing yourself to be moulded and processed if you end up getting dropped after one or two records, just because the US parent company wasn't interested ... ?"[27] Rather than stimulating exposure for Canadian product in non-Canadian markets, Cancon contributed to the perception in this period that this product was inferior. As veteran Canadian rock critic Peter Goddard suggested in 1980: "Ironically, the legislated Canadian-content regulations ... undermined [the] international impact [of Canadian acts]. Soon enough, artists who had the clout ... signed with either British or American companies; hits outside Canada were the name of the game."[28] Fellow critic Craig MacInnis called this "the sure-it's-a-gold-record-in-Canada-but-will-it-play-in-Boise syndrome."[29]

The central paradox of cultural protectionism in the recording industry—and this applied to both Cancon legislation and direct subsidization of sound recordings—was thus that the criterion by which Canadian acts qualified for support was their appeal in international markets. "Distinctive" Canadian recordings did not necessarily qualify since they were unlikely to make the tight playlists of commercial radio and were unlikely to sell well internationally. Thus, to echo William Watson, the argument can be made that Canadian-content legislation and government subsidization of the recording industry, rather than preserving whatever was distinctive about Canadian culture or teaching Canadians about each other, were effectively homogenizing Canadian musical culture along lines dictated by the multinational Anglo-American recording industry. As Goddard put it, "No one at the centres of pop power in New York or Los Angeles gives a gilt-edged hoot about regional sound or style unless it can move 50,000 units a day."[30]

Nowhere was this paradox more strikingly evident than in the designation of Canadian-content recordings for radio airplay. As they had since 1971, non-Canadian acts covering domestic copyrights qualified as Cancon. Notable examples of this phenomenon in the 1980s included the Neville Brothers' cover of Leonard Cohen's "Bird On A Wire" and Aerosmith's "The Other Side," which was produced by Canadian Bruce Fairbairn (and recorded in Vancouver). As Laura Bartlett, Promotion Vice-President of Virgin Canada, noted in July 1990: "A situation such as Aerosmith is completely absurd. If I phone my Los Angeles office and tell them that Colin James (lacking in sufficient Cancon points) is not Canadian content but Aerosmith is, they'll think I lost my mind."[31] Moreover, a Canadian artist living in Canada (and paying taxes here) who had gone to the United States and recorded an American song—as was the case, for example, of material from Colin James, k. d. lang, Lori Yates and others in the 1980s—failed to qualify for Cancon certification. Since it was axiomatic that private broadcasters would play only the minimum level of Canadian content to meet their quota obligations, Canadians' failure to meet Cancon regulations had the effect of actually shutting them out of their home market. The situation got so bad that BMG Canada adopted a policy of re-recording non-Cancon tracks by Canadian artists in Canada so as to meet the terms of Canadian-content eligibility. Michelle Wright and Jeff Healey were two artists distributed by BMG who re-recorded tracks in Canada using Canadian personnel. As CBS national-promotion director Shan Kelly stated bluntly in 1990: "[O]verall, I believe that Cancon ghettoizes Canadian music."[32]

CONCLUSION

The question of whether there is anything worth preserving in Canadian musical culture seems to me to be less salient than the more pragmatic question of what, in the last analysis, Canadians might reasonably have expected from a policy of cultural protectionism. Since for the most part Canadian-content legislation and direct subsidization of the record industry neither produced a competitive recording industry nor significantly affected musicians' aspirations, it seems fair to ask whether the nationalist vision that informed such policies—to produce made-in-Canada stars who achieved international success while remaining on a Canadian label—were ever viable. I would argue not only that these twin objectives were untenable but that, in truth, the pragmatic business of accommodating to the dominant agenda of the multinational music industry has always worked against such a vision.

Cancon regulations and the subsidization of the recording industry could never have produced a competitive Canadian recording industry because at a practical level these mechanisms evolved into means of improving Canadian musicians' chances in a global industry dominated by the multinationals. Cultural protectionism may have allowed—or forced—Canadians to hear more music by Canadian artists on the radio, and it may well have stimulated a taste for this recorded product nationally. However, by definition no interventionist policy was ever likely to enable Canadian record companies to compete with the multinationals internationally. On the contrary, there is strong evidence to suggest that official protectionism has limited the ability of indigenous companies and artists to compete outside Canada, while stigmatizing them to some extent within.

My argument is not that these protectionist policies were poorly conceived or even that they have failed in practice, but rather that they were inadequate when measured against the nationalist agenda out of which they arose in the 1970s and against which they were measured in the first two decades of mandatory Canadian-content quotas. Cancon legislation failed for the most part to serve as a launching pad from which Canadian performers could attain international stardom, and this failure was inevitable. The most Canadians might have asked of it is that it help local artists to a portion of the domestic market. The worst we might have feared is that it would ghettoize such acts and so reduce their chances of international success. Geoff Pevere and Greig Dymond expressed this ambivalence brilliantly in *Mondo Canuck*: "Sure, there was a fair amount of dreck (Terry Jacks, Paul Anka's midlife crisis), but the first half of the seventies was a great time to be an impressionable young radio addict: CanCon made it easy to believe that, as far as pop music was concerned, Canucks took care of business every bit as fiercely as anybody else in the world."[33]

Similarly, the most that Canadians might have asked from programs like FACTOR and the SRDP is that these programs foster independent record production in Canada. The key term here is not *Canada,* however, but *independent,* for it is the nature of independent labels—whether in Canada or elsewhere—to play an adjunct role in a world dominated by the majors. Independent labels have always borne the lion's share of responsibility for seeking out and nurturing new talent, knowing full well that, once discovered, this talent (or the label itself) is likely to be appropriated by a major. There are, in fact, few clearer examples of the monopolistic logic of global capitalism. As Jackie Luffman of Statistics Canada noted bluntly in 1999, "Canadian-controlled recording companies are holding their own in the marketplace but the marketplace is anything but stable. There have been several mergers involving companies which were already among the largest, and thus the industry is becoming even more concentrated and the big companies are becoming even bigger."[34] Official cultural protectionism could never have been expected to dramatically increase the Canadian indies' share of the international market, but what it has done over the years—and this point should be underscored—is to broaden dramatically the volume and range of Canadian recorded product available to Canadian consumers. If all that such institutions as FACTOR ever accomplish is keeping Canadian indies afloat—as a source of Canadian music for Canadian consumers, but also as a source of a new talent for world markets—they will have succeeded admirably.

As for Canadian artists, most appear to be ambivalent still. Bryan Adams' mixed views of Canadian-content regulations and the domestic recording industry—captured in the epigraph above—suggest strongly that the long shadow cast in Canada by the US recording and broadcasting industries continues to be the mixed blessing it was in the heyday of Cancon. The "American media groups" Adams felt free to disparage in 2000, at the twilight of his career as a pop star, were, of course, precisely those that had made him rich and famous in the 1980s. If there is an act that appears to demonstrate the triumph of the original logic of Canadian content, it is the Tragically Hip—homegrown heroes and nationalist standard-bearers for literally millions of Canadian music fans. Yet even here there is more than a little ambiguity. As journalist Joshua Ostroff has suggested, the Hip's elevation to "Canadian rock icon" is attributable at least in part to the awkward truth that, despite the band's many salvos at the American market, "[t]heir fans treat the band's lack of success in the U.S. as a badge of honor."[35] In any case, the Kingston quintet may well prove to be the exception that proves the historic rule, ending up as the first and only band to achieve true "superstardom" in Canada but nowhere else. Far more typical of "Canadian" musical success stories in the globalized world of twenty-first century pop are those squarely in the triumph-through-exile tradition—campus favourites the Barenaked Ladies, alt-rocker Alanis Morissette and chart-topping country-pop diva Shania Twain. One-time Quebec child-star (and French-language chanteuse) Céline Dion has travelled even further down the road of global superstardom, announcing recently that she has become a permanent fixture at Caesar's Palace in Las Vegas, where her nightly show is sponsored by Chrysler.[36]

Meanwhile, in the spring of 2003, Canadian broadcasters were facing the prospect of yet another increase in the CRTC's Cancon quota for commercial radio, from 35 per cent to 40 per cent. This upward revision was not entirely unexpected. During the regulator's 1998 review of "radio policy," certain "industry players" had argued that "a

40% Canadian-content level should be attainable across the board within five years." Once again, broadcasters and record labels girded for battle, resurrecting all of the old arguments. Rael Merson, president of Rogers Broadcasting, was quoted as saying that "there is not enough product in many genres to justify a playlist that is 40% Canadian" and, hence, that "a 40% Canadian-content rule would 'dilute' Canadian radio stations, causing them to lose listeners to U.S. stations whose signals come across the border."[37] Whether this argument will carry sway at the next round of CRTC hearings is doubtful, since Canadian FM stations have recorded average revenue growth of 31.4% since 1998, apparently reversing the inverse relationship between Canadian content and profitability. A sign of the times is that Standard Broadcasting Corporation, which owns 51 radio outlets nationwide, now "volunteers" a 40 per cent Cancon minimum when it goes before the CRTC for a new license—most recently in its successful launch of an urban music station in Calgary. But some things never change. Said one unnamed "radio executive" who resents the idea that Cancon quotas should be raised yet again: "You can only play so much Gordon Lightfoot."[38]

Endnotes

1. Bryan Adams, cited in Geoff Pevere and Greig Dymond, *Mondo Canuck: A Canadian Pop Culture Odyssey* (Toronto: Prentice Hall, 1996), p. 2.
2. Bryan Adams, cited in Stephen Cooke, "Adams Makes the Best of It," *The Halifax Herald* (4 January 2000).
3. See Michael Barclay, Ian A. D. Jack and Jason Schneider, *Have Not Been the Same: The CanRock Renaissance, 1985–1995* (Toronto: ECW Press, 2001).
4. Pevere and Dymond, *Mondo Canuck*, p. 171.
5. The subtext of Paul Cantin's biography of Alanis Morissette is that the artist was utterly dismissed in Canada in the period between her dance-pop career and her re-birth as the confessional rocker who penned *Jagged Little Pill*. This indifference was, arguably, a function of Cancon, though Cantin does not press the point. See *Alanis Morissette: You Oughta Know* (Toronto: Stoddart, 1997).
6. Céline Dion's album *Let's Talk about Love* did not qualify as Canadian under CRTC rules. See Canadian Association of Broadcasters, "CRTC's Arbitrary Decision to Hike Canadian Content Hurts Listeners and Broadcasters Alike" (Press Release 30 April 1998).
7. See Paul Litt, *The Muses, the Masses and the Massey Commission* (Toronto: University of Toronto Press, 1992).
8. Walt Grealis was publisher of the music-industry trade magazine *RPM* which, in the early and late 1960s, was a leading nationalist voice calling for government protection of the domestic recording industry.
9. This pattern is described in Roger Wallis and Krister Malm, *Big Sounds from Small People: The Music Industry in Small Countries* (New York: Pendragon, 1984).
10. Jackie Luffman, "Variations on a Theme: The Changing Music Scene," *Quarterly Bulletin from the Culture Statistics Program* (Statistics Canada) 11:4 (Winter 1999), p. 2.
11. "Canadian Content" (Toronto: CIRPA, 2000).
12. FACTOR [The Foundation to Assist Canadian Talent on Record], untitled pamphlet (no date).

13. *Vital Links: Canadian Cultural Industries* (Ottawa: Government of Canada, Department of Communications, 1987), p. 54.
14. "Ottawa To Help Record Industry Change Its Tune," *Globe and Mail* (10 May 1986).
15. *Evaluation of the Sound Recording Development Program* (Department of Canadian Heritage, Corporate Review Branch, April 2000).
16. "Executive Directors' Report," *CIRPA Newsletter* (August 1990), p. 1. See also David Farrell, "FM Regs Help Promote Fool's Gold," *The Record* (6 August 1990).
17. Bill Gilliland, cited in "Gilliland Proposes 30% Music Content for Daily Newspapers and Consumer Magazines," *The Record* (13 August 1990).
18. Paul Audley, *Canada's Cultural Industries: Broadcasting, Publishing, Records and Film* (Toronto: Lorimer, 1983), p. 139.
19. John Feihl, "The Impact of the Canadian Content Regulations on the Canadian Recording Industry," *Association of Canadian Studies Newsletter* 12:3 (Fall, 1990), p. 32.
20. William Watson, *National Pastimes: The Economics of Canadian Leisure* (Vancouver: The Fraser Institute, 1988), p. 112.
21. Greg Quill, "Record Industry Needs New Deal," *Toronto Star* (1 December 1984).
22. See Liam Lacey, "Little Labels Can Make a Big Mark," *Globe and Mail* (4 April 1986).
23. *Vital Links,* p. 53.
24. Jeff Bateman, "FACTOR Vetting Quality over Quantity," *The Record* (8 October 1990).
25. "CIRPA Study Recommends Ontario Support Program," *The Record* (15 October 1990).
26. Cited in Peter Goddard, "Pop Record Makers Ignore Borders," *Toronto Star* (15 November 1980).
27. Andrew Cash, cited in Greg Quill, "What Do Most Indies Want?" *Toronto Star* (21 February 1986).
28. Goddard, "Pop Record Makers Ignore Borders."
29. Craig MacInnis, "High Price of Selling Rock," *Toronto Star* (29 December 1987).
30. Ibid.
31. Laura Bartlett, cited in "Cancon Reg Has Industry Seeing Red," *The Record* (23 July 1990).
32. Shan Kelly, cited in "Canadian Artists Resort to Re-Recording Songs," *The Record* (23 July 1990).
33. Pevere and Dymond, *Mondo Canuck,* p. 168.
34. Luffman, "Variations on a Theme," pp. 5–6.
35. Joshua Ostroff, "A Hip Homecoming," *Ottawa Sun* (4 July 1998).
36. "Chrysler Sponsors Céline Dion in Las Vegas," (Chrysler Corporation news release) 16 January 2003. In the 1990s Twain, Morissette and Dion together sold 155 million albums worldwide, 95 per cent of which were outside Canada. See Luffman, "Variations on a Theme," p. 1.
37. Rael Merson, cited in Barbara Shecter, "Radio Fears Canadian Content Boost," *Financial Post* (4 April 2003).
38. Cited in ibid.

DISCUSSION

Robert Wright, 'Gimme Shelter: Cultural Protectionism and the Canadian Recording Industry' from *Virtual Sovereignty: Nationalism, Culture, and the Canadian Question*.

1. Why does Wright argue that Canadian content quotas risk creating mediocre and generic music and have left a 'legacy of discord' in the music industry?
2. Do you think radio quotas are necessary to help new Canadian artists to get a start in the music industry, or would other policy tools work better in the digital era? If so, what might these tools include?
3. Wright describes the impact of vertical integration in the Canadian music industry with the domination of foreign record labels. When and why did the federal government first introduce direct subsidies for the music industry?
4. Wright refers to the activities of several different stakeholders in the music industry. Who were these key groups and what type of public or private interests did they represent?
5. Since 1990, Canada's larger independent recording labels have focussed on expanding export markets for their artists. What does Wright say about this situation and why does he see it as creating a fundamental contradiction for policy in the music industry?

Primary Sources: Public-Private Support for the Music Industry
Policy Source 15
Canada. Department of Canadian Heritage. (2001). *From Creators to Audience: New Policy Directions for Canadian Sound Recording,* June 2001.

From Creators to Audience: New Policy Directions for Canadian Sound Recording June 2001

FOREWORD

The Government of Canada is pleased to launch the Canadian Sound Recording Policy. This policy signals an important evolution from project-based support to a comprehensive policy framework that invests in the Canadian sound recording sector at every level-from creators to audience.

Extensive consultations with the public and industry groups have helped shape the Canadian Sound Recording Policy. Our experience and success with the Sound Recording Development Program (SRDP), as well as studies of the sound recording sector, and an independent evaluation of the SRDP, also provided important direction. Three main objectives emerged from this process:

- To enhance Canadians' access to a diverse range of Canadian music choices through existing and emerging media;
- To increase the opportunities available for Canadian music artists and cultural entrepreneurs to make a significant and lasting contribution to Canadian cultural expression; and
- To ensure that Canadian music artists and entrepreneurs have the skills, know-how and tools to succeed in a global and digital environment.

The Canadian Sound Recording Policy addresses each of these objectives to ensure that Canadians and the world have access to a diverse selection of Canadian music on their radios, television sets, in stores, at public venues and on the Internet.

The policy establishes the Canada Music Fund, a series of eight programs in support of policy objectives. As well, it creates the Canada Music Council comprised of a diverse cross-section of music industry representatives to advise the Minister and the Department on the implementation of initiatives to support songwriting, composing, new musical works, specialized music, market development initiatives, sound recording entrepreneurship, and to give access to and preserve Canadian musical collections.

Ultimately, the Canadian Sound Recording Policy will measurably contribute to the success of Canada's sound recording sector. And, in building on the success of the SRDP, the policy will adopt a more holistic approach to developing this sector.

MUSIC COUNTS

Canada's sound recording industry encompasses a range of Canadian music artists and entrepreneurs who are responsible for creating, producing and promoting the vast majority of Canadian music-songwriters, composers, performers, studios, producers, engineers, record companies, artist managers, music publishers, manufacturers, distributors, publicists, retail outlets, and concert promoters. The industry generates thousands of jobs, many of them held by young Canadians.

Canadian music embodies the creativity and spirit of Canadians. It helps define who we are, and reflects the richness of Canada's linguistic and cultural diversity.

Canadian music artists are among our best known cultural ambassadors abroad. Nelly Furtado, Natalie McMaster, La Bottine Souriante, Nickelback, The Barenaked Ladies, Diana Krall, Céline Dion, Bruce Cockburn, The Tragically Hip, and many others enrich the lives of Canadians and help to shape how we are perceived in the world. So too do the thousands of Canadian musicians and entrepreneurs, from classical to country, who bring Canadian music to festivals and events around the world.

Canadian music is part of our everyday lives. This is especially true for young Canadians. We hear it on the radio on our way to work or school. We buy it in stores and access it on the Internet. We experience it live at concerts, in clubs and restaurants, at festivals and at parties. Canadian music sets the mood for television programs, commercials, and movies. We hear it in virtually every Canadian neighbourhood as today's youth gather in garages to practice.

Yet the Canadian music industry is undergoing fundamental changes. Faced with the challenges of a global digital economy, Canadian sound recording must transform itself to keep pace with our changing world, and to remain relevant and competitive.

The Government of Canada can contribute to a smooth transition for this industry in this period of flux. Ensuring that Canadians continue to have access to diverse Canadian music choices means developing the right policy framework and tools for meeting today's global and digital challenges.

PUBLIC POLICY AND THE CANADIAN SOUND RECORDING INDUSTRY

The Government of Canada has played a vital role in creating a supportive policy and program environment and in fostering partnerships with creators and entrepreneurs, with the goal of building a domestic sound recording industry.

The *Broadcasting Act* affirms the Government of Canada's commitment to a broadcasting system that encourages the development of Canadian expression and reflects Canada's cultural and linguistic reality.

Canadian Radio-television and Telecommunications Commission (CRTC) policies aimed at supporting the sound recording sector include Canadian content and French-language airtime requirements, contributions towards Canadian talent development, and requirements to offer tangible benefits to the music industry for certain ownership transactions.

The Canadian Broadcasting Corporation and the Société Radio-Canada provide important avenues through which youth, local and regional talent and culturally-specific music genres are disseminated across Canada.

Other federal government legislation also plays an important role. Canada's Copyright Act provides the legal framework for creators, publishers, performers and producers to control the use of their work and to be remunerated for it. The Investment Canada Act requires that investments in the cultural sector be reviewed for compatibility with Canadian cultural policies.

The Sound Recording Development Program (SRDP), introduced in 1986, helped increase the quantity and quality of Canadian sound recordings. Its principal function was to provide project assistance for the production, marketing and distribution of Canadian sound recordings.

The Canada Council for the Arts works with artists and arts organizations to create non-mainstream popular music, world music, classical traditions, Aboriginal music and various jazz and concert music genres. The Council also supports professional development, festivals, tours, concert rehearsals and productions, festival programming, orchestras and choirs.

The National Library of Canada ensures that Canadians have access to their music heritage by acquiring and preserving Canadian sound recordings for future generations. The National Library is also using the Internet and other technologies to make Canadian music recordings more broadly available.

THE CHANGING SOUNDSCAPE

While efforts at the federal and provincial levels have laid the foundation for a Canadian sound recording industry where Canadian creators are celebrated at home and abroad, the industry sector is facing major challenges brought on by the global and digital economy.

Globalization is taking down barriers, eroding borders and making way for a world of opportunities for Canadian artists and recording companies. It is also opening the door to even greater competition for the mostly smaller and undercapitalized Canadian firms.

The digital environment poses great challenges. The music industry was the first in the cultural sector to face the complex realities of the Internet when it became a new medium for accessing recorded music. The concerns surrounding Internet-based music services continue to challenge the industry worldwide.

It is critical that Canada's sound recording entrepreneurs be equipped to deal with these issues and make a smooth transition to the digital economy. An important part of this transition involves adjusting to the new ways in which audiences access their music. Music entrepreneurs must reach out to audiences through the Internet as well as market their artists through traditional routes such as retail stores, radio, television, and print media. They must embrace the Internet and other technologies as marketing and sales tools. Maximizing their market position will mean finding creative ways to reposition themselves, develop partnerships, bring their artists to audiences and remain competitive.

The Canadian-owned and -controlled sound recording industry is the main source of innovation, talent development and musical diversity in Canada. The Government of Canada is committed to ensuring that the industry develops the tools to succeed in this challenging environment and that Canadians continue to have access to a diverse range of quality Canadian sound recordings.

The Canadian Sound Recording Policy addresses the many challenges of the global and digital environment and aims to build a strong future for the Canadian music industry. It adopts a holistic approach, from creators to audience, to create the conditions for success. The policy will ensure that Canadian music artists continue to succeed at home and abroad and that new talent continues to emerge. It will also help promote viable Canadian music firms and make Canadian choices more widely available in the new borderless world.

CANADIAN VOICES, CANADIAN CHOICES

For generations, Canadians in every corner of the country have found their voice in music. Canadian artists have written and recorded music that has shaped the Canadian experience, created a sense of common citizenship and provided a source of pride. The Canadian Sound Recording Policy aims to ensure that the successes of the music industry are sustained in the 21st century.

The Canadian Sound Recording Policy sets out three clear objectives to guide the design and implementation of the Government of Canada's new and more comprehensive public policy approach to supporting the sound recording industry:

- To enhance Canadians' access to a diverse range of Canadian music choices through existing and emerging media;
- To increase the opportunities available for Canadian music artists and entrepreneurs to make a significant and lasting contribution to Canadian cultural expression; and
- To ensure that Canadian music artists and entrepreneurs have the skills and means to succeed in a global and digital environment.

THE CANADA MUSIC FUND

The principal means for achieving the goals of the Canadian Sound Recording Policy is the Canada Music Fund. This new fund absorbs the Sound Recording Development Program. It also introduces a new and integrated range of both innovative and proven programs designed to deliver on the policy's vision of supporting diversity, capacity, and excellence in the sound recording industry, at every level, from creators to audience. It will operate with advice from the Canada Music Council representing a broad cross-section of the sound recording industry.

The Government of Canada will work closely with program delivery partners in the music industry and the wider cultural sector to ensure the effective administration of the new programs. Important partnerships with FACTOR, Musicaction and the Canada Council for the Arts will continue and new ones will be forged with the Society of Composers, Authors and Music Publishers of Canada (SOCAN Foundation), Telefilm Canada, the AV Preservation Trust of Canada and the National Library of Canada.

The Canada Music Fund comprises the following initiatives:

- Creators' Assistance Program
- Canadian Musical Diversity Program
- New Musical Works Program
- Music Entrepreneur Program
- Support to Sector Associations Program
- Collective Initiatives Program
- Canadian Music Memories Program
- Policy Monitoring Program

CREATORS' ASSISTANCE PROGRAM

The Creators' Assistance Program will help artists create high-quality Canadian musical works, and give Canadian talent the tools to fully develop their creative and business skills. Songwriters and composers tend to work in isolation, with few opportunities to share their expertise and develop their talent in a collaborative environment. They also lack public profile, even though countless Canadians may enjoy their music. This initiative aims to support community building and skills development, and to increase awareness of their works.

CANADIAN MUSICAL DIVERSITY PROGRAM

The Canadian Musical Diversity Program will offer resources to produce and distribute specialized music recordings reflective of the diversity of Canadian voices. Specialized music is a musical production that places creativity, self-expression and/or experimentation above the current demands and format expectations of the mainstream music industry.

NEW MUSICAL WORKS PROGRAM

The New Musical Works Program invests in the Canadian sound recording stars of the future by providing assistance to entrepreneurs, creators, and artists. New resources will help develop their talent and expertise. This critical source of Canadian creativity and expression requires support and opportunities to grow. The program will provide project-based support to help develop and renew the sound recording industry.

MUSIC ENTREPRENEUR PROGRAM

The Music Entrepreneur Program (MEP) will ensure that Canadian music entrepreneurs build a strong, sustainable industry that continues to contribute to the Canadian musical experience.

The MEP will provide company-based funding to allow Canada's music entrepreneurs to make the transition to the digital economy, effectively develop Canadian talent, and ultimately become self-sufficient. This program will invest in eligible established industry professionals with viable multi-year business plans, giving them critical assistance to consolidate and develop their human, financial, and technological resource base.

The end result will be to empower entrepreneurs with solid business skills.

SUPPORT TO SECTOR ASSOCIATIONS PROGRAM

Continued support to sound recording sector associations will also encourage capacity building and effective representation. The Government of Canada is committed to working in partnership with the industry to ensure that Canada's voices of experience continue to contribute to shaping public policies for the sound recording sector.

COLLECTIVE INITIATIVES PROGRAM

Initiatives that bring together Canadian creators, entrepreneurs, and the media can offer significant and enduring returns for the sound recording sector. Conferences and awards shows, physical and online showcases, as well as market development initiatives offer the industry important opportunities to share best practices, inspire young artists and entrepreneurs, and build a star system. The Collective Initiatives Program will help provide the funding required to ensure that Canadian creators and entrepreneurs have opportunities to gain greater profile and showcase their excellence and creativity.

CANADIAN MUSIC MEMORIES PROGRAM

Long after the sounds have faded, Canadian music remains part of our cultural fabric, woven into our lives and our memories. A wealth of Canadian music has been captured on recordings and preserved at the National Library of Canada; however, much of the collection is deteriorating and the costs of preservation are high. The Canadian Music Memories Program will ensure that significant works are preserved, giving Canadians of today and tomorrow access to their musical heritage. It will also fund private sector initiatives to collect, consolidate and make available collections of Canadian music for the public.

POLICY MONITORING PROGRAM

To provide the maximum operational efficiency of the fund, this program will draw on a wide range of resources to establish an ongoing and timely monitoring of all programs. In doing so, the Department will ensure that the programs will meet policy objectives, change with the times, and address future challenges to come.

SAFEGUARDING OUR INVESTMENT

The Canada Music Fund has been designed to ensure increased transparency, representation and accountability. Agreements between the Department of Canadian Heritage and executing agencies will ensure that concerned parties are committed to successfully carrying out the Canadian Sound Recording Policy's vision. They will also commit the Fund's administrators and federal program managers to efficiently and effectively delivering the Fund's programs, measuring its performance, and regularly reporting its results.

MEASURES OF SUCCESS

The Canadian Sound Recording Policy will secure a cultural return on the Government of Canada's investment:

- Canadians will enjoy better access to high-quality Canadian music content through existing and emerging media;
- Canadian talent will have access to greater career development opportunities;
- New and established Canadian artists will be marketed more creatively and effectively in Canada and around the world;
- Canadian sound recording entrepreneurs meet the challenges of the transition to new technologies; and
- Canadian sound recording firms and Canadian artists will enjoy more fruitful long-term collaborations.

Achieving success will require a commitment on the part of all players. The Government of Canada will measure the policy's success through a variety of tools:

- Cultural indicators such as the number of new artist releases and the diversity of releases by genres;
- Audience and consumption indicators such as sales numbers, radio airplay, Internet traffic, festival and concert attendance, and royalties to creators; and
- Performance measures for Canadian labels, including revenues, profitability, and capitalization.

Ultimately, success rests in part in the hands of our youth-the music fans and talent base of today and tomorrow. Nearly half of Canada's young people write or play music. They are also Internet savvy. Capturing and retaining this important audience and talent base will be critical if Canada's sound recording sector is to meet the challenges brought on by today's rapid pace of change. The Canadian Sound Recording Policy sets the stage for achieving this ambitious goal. The rest is in the hands of the talented Canadians who create, market, distribute and preserve our musical memories.

DISCUSSION

Canada Music Fund, From Creators to Audience New Policy Directions for Canadian Sound Recording.

1. What are the three main objectives outlined in this policy statement for the Canadian music industry?
2. The statement outlines several different policy tools used for the Canadian sound recording industry. What are these tools and what role do they play in helping reach the goal of building a domestic recording industry?
3. What features of the 'changing soundscape' does the policy statement point to? How has the environment for recorded music further changed since the policy was announced in 2001? Do you think the policy objectives and tools discussed are still relevant and effective today?
4. Visit the Department of Canadian Heritage web site at www.pch.gc.ca and locate current information on the Canada Music Fund. What components of the Fund have been eliminated since 2001? What impact do you think these cuts to the amount of subsidies will have on production of music in Canada?

Policy Source 16
LeBlanc, L., & FACTOR. (2007). *The FACTOR Story: Fostering Emerging Artists and Musical Diversity.* Toronto: Foundation to Assist Canadian Talent on Recordings.

The Factor Story

HIGHLIGHTS

From April 1, 1982 to March 31, 2007 FACTOR has:

- processed 43,203 requests for funding totaling $398,117,290
- approved 16,184 projects for funding with offers totaling $124,609,233

On average 37.46% of all applications received an offer of funding.

On average 31.22% of funds requested were offered.

FACTOR supported sound recordings have sold over 31.6 million copies worldwide, generating retail sales in excess of $705,000,000.

From inception to March 31, 2007

FACTOR has received $135,966,529 in funding. It breaksdown as follows:

FACTOR received $86,986,457 in funding from the Department of Canadian Heritage FACTOR received $37,828,948 from private radio broadcasters

Loan repayments have totaled $7,239,440

Interest earned has totaled $3,911,684

On average FACTOR has spent 12.46% per annum on administration. During the early years administration costs were a much higher percentage of the budget. Over the past 5 years it has been approximately 10% of total revenue.

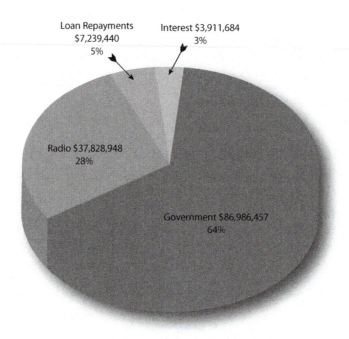

FACTOR: FOSTERING GRASSROOTS MUSICAL DIVERSITY

Written by Larry Leblanc

There is practically nothing drearier than being a developing musical act touring. The physical wear and tear on members is immeasurable. It's a nether world of loading up rented vans, staying in low-budget rooms, and fighting to be heard by audiences.

Artists traveling Canada know where they have been. Summer-time, it's driving across deserted prairie roads so hot the asphalt and tar have melted. Winter-time, it's snow storms in Atlantic Canada; snow drifts in northern Ontario and Quebec; and bears blocking the road in the Rockies. It's driving through the prairies at 25 km. per hour because the roads are so icy you aren't supposed to travel.

"Then, if you are an up-and-coming band, a good opening slot is about exposure," says guitarist **Josh Ramsay** of Vancouver-based **Marianas Trench.** "It's a series $100 shows. Between gas and food for four guys, $100 is like petty cash. Sell some merch, and you might get your own bed that night. We would not have had the same debut album ("Fix Me") if we didn't have tour support from FACTOR early on."

"The Trews may not have seen the inside of a tour bus if it wasn't for the support of FACTOR," adds the band's guitarist **John-Angus MacDonald.**

That Canada is a leading global source of commercial pop and rock music is underscored by the global popularity of Celine Dion, Avril Lavigne, Nelly Furtado, Shania Twain, **Nickelback,** Bryan Adams, **Alanis Morissette,** Diana Krall, **k. d. lang, Barenaked Ladies, Billy Talent,** Simple Plan, Finger Eleven, Deborah Cox, Glenn Lewis, and Three Days Grace—the bulk signed by multinational companies.

International markets have also clearly embraced—on varying levels—such musically diverse acts as **Arcade Fire, Broken Social Scene, Leslie Feist, Patrick Watson, Bruce Cockburn, Ron Sexsmith, Blue Rodeo, New Pornographers, Bedouin Soundclash, Metric, the Dears, Hot Hot Heat, Kid Koala, Buck 65, Sum 41, the Duhks, Tegan & Sara, Alexisonfire, Stars, the Trews,** Silverstein, and **Tokyo Police Club**—the majority being with Canadian-based independent labels.

As well, Canada has produced a significant number of folk/roots, jazz, urban, blues and classical performers that enjoy notable careers home and abroad.

This includes folk and roots-based **Loreena McKennitt, Sarah Harmer, Kathleen Edwards,** Paul Reddick, Jesse Cook, **the Bills, Blackie & the Rodeo Kings, Jorane, James Keelaghan, Alana Levandoski,** and **Fred Eaglesmith; George Canyon, the Roadhammers, Michelle Wright, the Wilkinsons,** and **Shane Yellowbird** in country; urban-based **K-os, Saukrates, Choclair, Jacksoul, Ivana Santilli,** and **Massari;** jazz acts like **Holly Cole, Jane Bunnett, Molly Johnson,** Denzel Sinclaire, and Dave Restivo; as well as the **Tafelmusik Baroque Orchestra,** Measha Brueggergosman, and **Angele Dubeau** in classical.

"The success of Canadian music in recent years has definitely been a factor in HMV Canada's continuing ability to expand into new markets." From HMV Canada's website.

PIVOTAL ROLE OF INDEPENDENTS WITH FACTOR SUPPORT

Four foreign-owned multinationals—EMI Music, Universal Music, Sony BMG Music, and Warner Music—dominate Canada's music market, and collectively account for 90% of revenue. They have significant advantages, of course, over Canadian-owned independent labels. This includes having sales and working capital from their parent company lines; their own national distribution systems; and access to distribution networks worldwide.

In recent years, as the multinationals in Canada cut back on direct signings, the Canadian independent label and artist sector, benefiting from the growth in popularity of MySpace, Last FM, and YouTube, has become the primary marketing window for emerging Canadian acts.

This pivotal role of independents is underscored by the fact that the majority of Canadian jazz, country, blues and classical music is issued by independent sources.

Another case in point also is that a coterie of entrepreneurial Canadian indies has developed such significant emerging acts as **Joel Plaskett Emergency, Belly, Jenn Grant, K'naan, Nathan, Champion, Dave Gunning, the Golden Dogs, Justin Nozuka, Malajube,** Emile-Claire-Barlow, **Final Fantasy, Cadence Weapon, the Deadly Snakes, Julie Doiron, Miracle Fortress, Joel Kroeker,** and Little Miss Higgins.

"I continue to be struck by the supportive nature of the community in Canada," wrote British DJ/historian Bob Harris in Maverick magazine (Oct. 2006 issue). "My strong impression is that the mix of financial support offered by FACTOR and other funding bodies, alongside Canadian government acknowledgement and the shared experiences of road and hardship, bond the people who are trying to make a living in this huge, sparsely populated country. They know that they are not going to sell a million copies of their records in Canada alone, so there is more small-label infrastructure, more awareness of the concept of building a following one fan at a time."

"FACTOR has really brought a profile onto Canada," agrees singer/songwriter **Kevin Drew** of **Broken Social Scene.** "Its support has enabled us to evolve, and tour overseas as a nine or ten piece band."

"FACTOR support is pivotal to my career every second of the day," says country star **George Canyon.** "Everybody makes the assumption that when you get a major record deal, it's all buttercups and roses. But the music business is a business, and everything costs money."

A private non-profit organization providing assistance toward the growth and development of the Canadian independent recording industry, the Foundation Assisting Canadian Talent On Recordings (originally called The Foundation to Assist Canadian Talent on Records) is the bedrock of Canada's music industry. It has played a pivotal role in Canada's emergence as a global music player.

"We would not be here if it wasn't for FACTOR," flatly states Nettwerk Productions president Ric Arboit. "We would not have been able to do a second or a third **Sarah McLachlan** album without FACTOR."

"Without FACTOR, I wouldn't be here," Bumstead Productions owner Larry Wanagas admits. "It's that simple."

"FACTOR support is crucial to our label," adds Jonathan Simkin, president of 604 Records in Vancouver. "It enables us to compete internationally."

FACTOR SUPPORT TRICKLES DOWN

In its 25 years, FACTOR has administered over $112 million in funding to assist in the development of the Canadian artists, and the independent music industry. In 2006–2007, it provided in excess of $14 million to support the sector.

"FACTOR's help for my first album ("Something Goin' On Here" in 2003) made a big, big difference," recalls British Columbia country star **Aaron Pritchett.** "For recording the album; for touring and having merchandising; and getting distribution of the album. If you compete with everybody on radio, it's tough. (As a Canadian country artist) you are up against Faith Hill, and Tim McGraw and all of these major country artists that record in Nashville with big budgets."

Jazz saxophonist/flautist **Jane Bunnett,** adds, "The key moment in my career, for sure, was my first record 'In Dew Time' in 1988. The fact we were able to do an international record with FACTOR's help was pivotal. We wanted to make the best record we could. FACTOR support allowed us to do that."

With a staff of 14, FACTOR administers contributions from sponsoring radio broadcasters as well as two components of the Department of Canadian Heritage's Canada Music Fund programs. Monies are allocated according to programs overseen by a 11-member board of directors with representation from music and broadcast industries.

FACTOR awards loans to Canadian-owned labels, and Canadian artists to aid in the production and marketing costs of recordings and/or DVDs for commercial release. It offers grants to defray production costs related to music videos. It supplies funds for domestic and international business development, and supports music industry tours and showcases. It also offers funding to three programs developed for emerging recording artists: the Independent Recording Loan, the Professional Demo Award, and the Professional Publishers and Songwriters Demo Award.

As Canada's music business evolved internationally, and with more opportunities available through more platforms than ever before, the significance and impact of FACTOR funding have also increased. While the major beneficiaries of its programs have been record companies and individual artists, branches of the Canadian music industry that now greatly benefit from its funding include managers, publishers, recording studios, video makers, and music industry associations.

"There's a trickle down effect," points out Wanagas. "A label applying to FACTOR for a recording will spend money working with studios, producers, engineers, graphic designers, photographers, wardrobe artists, make-up artists, and publicists. If the label applies for marketing support, they spend money on publicists, video directors, editors, and so on."

Blue Rodeo front man **Jim Cuddy** lauds FACTOR's support of musical diversity, and the grassroots sector, "You want the representatives of your culture to be more than just the pop hit," he says. "Although they are a great story, they don't tell the whole story of what's going on in Canada. FACTOR has been an enormous boost in telling Canada's musical story."

RADIO AND THE MUSIC INDUSTRY JOIN TOGETHER

Following the introduction of the Canadian Radio-television and Telecommunications Commission's 30% Canadian content radio regulations on AM in 1971, and on FM in 1975, many Canadian private broadcasters were, in principle, supportive of the need to help Canadian talent, and the need to build a solid record industry infrastructure. But it wasn't until the '80s, they offered to play a leadership role.

FACTOR was founded in 1982 as a result of discussions between the radio and music industries. It was founded by the Canadian Independent Record Production Assn. (CIRPA), the Canadian Music Publishers Assn. (CMPA), and by three major Canadian broadcasting compa nies—CHUM Limited, Moffat Communications Limited, and Rogers Radio Broadcasting Limited.

1982 was co-incidentally the year an unprecedented number of Canadian pop artists jumped onto U.S. radio charts and radio play lists. "BEAVER TAKES A BITE OUT OF UNCLE SAM" read a headline in the Toronto Star (April 10, 1982). Seventeen acts made it onto Billboard's Top 200 album chart in the year, including Rush, Loverboy, Saga, Aldo Nova, April Wine, Chilliwack, Triumph, Eddie Schwartz, and Bob and Doug McKenzie.

These successes, followed the next year by Prism, Red Rider, Aldo Nova, and Bryan Adams, as well as the solid domestic successes of such Canadian country acts as Carroll Baker, the Family Brown, and Terry Carisse, however, obscured the fact that competition from the United States, both in terms of superstar product and the dominance of the multinationals, dwarfed Canada's homegrown music industry.

The vast majority of Canadian recordings were then being produced by independent labels operating on shoestring budgets having almost no funds for promotion, sales campaigns and the other functions that enable hits.

While the CRTC's CanCon quota had served an important role in establishing opportunities of exposure for Canadian artists previously, private broadcasters then felt that there were now insufficient new Canadian releases to satisfy their CRTC broadcasting requirements. Due to individual CRTC licensing commitments, these broadcasters were also required to invest in Canadian talent, which included stations supporting local musical events and funding "homegrown" albums of emerging talent.

"We were concerned with the quantity and quality of product available," recalls Chuck McCoy, then a programmer at Moffat Communications. "There were concerns that the things we were doing with our money weren't effectively bringing forward more commercial product for our stations to play."

"We kept throwing things against the wall hoping they would stick," recalls Duff Roman, then director of industry affairs, CHUM Ltd. "But there weren't enough records (for airplay). FACTOR was a survival initiative (for broadcasters)."

Widely credited with the idea of launching FACTOR is Attic Records co-founder Tom Williams who first broached the idea of a funding foundation with the three co-founding broadcasters. There were also pivotal meetings in the same period between Roman, and Department of Communications policy advisor John Watts; and between J. Robert Wood, program dir. of CHUM Radio, and True North president Bernie Finkelstein.

Williams told broadcasters it'd be to their benefit to help improve the quality of Canadian recordings by providing production loans and grants.

Recalls Williams "CHUM had just given $30,000 to a big band festival. At the same time, Bob Wood was complaining there weren't enough Canadian records for CHUM to live up to its CanCon commitment. I tied those two things together. I told him, 'If you have to spend this money anyway, why don't you do something to help Canadian recordings?' Then I met with (vice-president) Jim Sward at Rogers, and with McCoy and Jim McLaughlin (vice-president Moffat Radio) and got their commitments."

"Tom argued the money broadcasters were spending on Canadian talent was not being used to the betterment of artists' careers," recalls McCoy. "He had the idea that the broadcasters donate money through a board, represented by broadcasters and record company people, and we would fund records. We thought it was a good idea. We had a few meetings with our friends at Rogers and CHUM. That's how FACTOR was born."

Funds would initially be provided by broadcasters as part of their Promise of Performance (POP) licensing commitment to develop Canadian talent as required by CRTC. "Broadcasters," recalls Roman, "looked at what commitments under our POPs we could bundle up and make available for funding. It came to a pot of $200,000."

Next came a meeting with executives at CIRPA—representing the interests of the English-speaking independent music sector in Canada—and the CMPA at CHUM's boardroom in Toronto.

This led to FACTOR's founding with a board of seven directors drawn from the radio and music industries. The organization was co-named by Roman—coming up with FACT— and CIRPA's executive director Earl Rosen who suggested adding "OR" for "on records."

"Already, it was a collaborative effort," jokes Roman.

FACTOR was initially administered by CIRPA, and Rosen was its president from 1982–1986.

FACTOR's sole mandate was to help produce Canadian recordings suitable for radio airplay and retail sales. It started with a single program—lending money through a jury process for production of recordings. "We wanted records for airplay; the music industry wanted to sell records," explains Roman.

"We didn't accept the broadcasters' argument that there wasn't enough good Canadian music," recalls Rosen. "We said if there was more money for labels to invest in production then Canadian recordings would sound more like the international productions."

Adds Rosen, "CIRPA wanted to support all genres of music, and broadcasters agreed to let selection juries recommend projects. Among the first applications approved, there were quite a few that were noncommercial."

FACTOR's requirement that independent labels or individual artists must own their own masters was an important precedent for the future. Few labels or acts working with multinationals then owned their masters. This requirement would give labels and artists significant clout over the years to negotiate better deals for themselves with multinationals or to better operate as production companies.

Soon afterwards, numerous private broadcasters transferred at least part of their local talent budgets to FACTOR. Says Roman, "We enticed other broadcasters saying, 'Nobody needs another homegrown album. Join us and be part of FACTOR.' "

At first, however, there was sizable wariness within Canada's music industry over the role of FACTOR. "People were skeptical," admits Roman. "We did gather credibility because we had some very good people involved from the music industry. And like them, we broadcasters checked our guns at the door."

By 1983, with an investment of $530,000 and over 70 recordings, the fund was being hailed as a true sign of industry-wide cooperation and accomplishment.

In Oct. 1983, newsletter "The CHUM Report" made note of Canadian private broadcasters' new responsibility: "If you are not a radio program manager or music director, your foremost concern as a broadcaster is likely not with the rise and fall in output of the Canadian recording industry. But it should be. The connection between the number of new Canadian content albums and singles released every week and success in reaching ratings and sales objectives is far more directly related than many realize . . . For radio teams to build audiences and increase revenues, the players we put on the field must be competitive with those of our opponents."

In 1985, private radio broadcasters and French-language sound-recording firms formed MusicAction to create a similar production fund to FACTOR, primarily for French-language recordings and videos.

FACTOR EXPANDS WITH CTL AND GOVERNMENT FUNDING

The same year, in order to increase its production fund, and support a wider variety of musical genres, FACTOR merged with the Canadian Talent Library Trust to form the shortly-lived FACTOR/CTL.

CTL was a non-profit trust, operated by Standard Broadcasting that had produced 268 popular and light classical albums since 1962, including those by **Hagood Hardy, Peter Appleyard, John Arpin, Keath Barrie, the Boss Brass,** and the **Laurie Bower Singers.** CTL had first distributed its recordings only to subscribing broadcast stations, but it began leasing its masters for commercial release in 1966.

CTL provided FACTOR with further funding of $300,000 annually. "It helped us a great deal," recalls Roman. "Then the feds came the next year, and we started talking real dole."

A significant benefit to FACTOR's future from the merger was attaining Heather Ostertag, then an administrative assistant at CTL. "My impression when I met Heather was she was a work in progress," recalls Roman. "A real work horse."

1985 was the year that Canadian artists had another rush on the domestic marketplace and American hearts again. Bryan Adams, Corey Hart, **Rush,** Loverboy, **Triumph** and Gino Vannelli each had a strong year. Domestically, there were also the successes of new Canadian acts such as Platinum Blonde, **Gowan, Parachute Club, Luba, Helix, Honeymoon Suite, Headpins, the Payolas** and **Jane Siberry.**

Meanwhile, however, there were growing concerns that Canada's independent sector needed to be more aggressive in providing financial backing for its artists' international efforts.

While multinationals have affiliates in most foreign markets, most Canadian independent labels must license their catalogs or specific product abroad either through a single worldwide deal with a multinational or on a territory-by-territory basis with a multinational or independent distributor.

For Canadian independents, securing a meaningful U.S. release had long served as a gateway to international success. Yet, despite an impressive international showing by Canadian artists in the 80s, there were still considerable obstacles in securing releases of Canadian masters in the U.S.

Generally, Canadian-based independents attempted to build an impressive sales success at home before trying to secure a "meaningful" release from as many of the international labels or distributors as possible, including a coveted U.S. release. But the wall was high. You could count without difficulty the numbers who'd made it over.

"When I got **k. d. lang** signed to Sire Records in 1985, she was one of the few Canadians signed directly to an American company," recalls Wanagas. "Nobody in Canada even had international releases with the major American companies controlling rights. How things have since changed."

Music video stabilized the record business after its late 1970s/early 1980s slump. Previously, it would have taken years of press coverage, in-store posters, concerts and albums for an act to reach that level of audiences. Music videos, besides selling records, could also fuse an artist's name with easily grasped personas.

However, the downside of video was that it substantially drove up the cost of releasing albums. While videos could be produced then for under $10,000, industry standards dictated minimal production costs of $1520,000 with maximum Canadian costs ranging from $75,000-$100,000.

FACTOR's role grew significantly in 1986 when, after consultations with the various segments of the recording and broadcasting industries, the Department of Communications (DOC), began the Sound Recording Development Program (SRDP).

Under SRDP, the DOC committed itself to invest $25 million over a five year period. The DOC chose FACTOR to administer 60% of the Fund for English & other-language companies, while MusicAction would administer the remainder for the French and other-language projects.

The SRDP program offered assistance to Canadian-owned companies for the production of Canadian audio and video music, and radio programs; and to support marketing, international touring, and business development. It was the government's first comprehensive program directed at strengthening the infrastructure of the Canadian-owned record industry.

SRDP was intended to create the most favorable conditions for Canadian-owned companies—one which would act as a stimulant to private-sector funding. The program's intent was to increase the number of quality productions by providing financial support from demo to master stage, as well as support for videos, touring, and radio syndication.

The influx of federal funding ensured FACTOR's effectiveness and enabled it to expand into other areas. In 1988, for example, FACTOR launched two new programs: Direct Board Approval Loans, intended to assist Canadian-owned active labels; and Professional Publisher and Songwriters Demo Awards to assist Canadian songwriters and publishers to produce quality demos.

However, with the public funding, FACTOR had to break away from being under CIRPA's administration due to its role as a lobby body. Rosen stepped down as executive director. A brief stint in the position by former WEA Music of Canada A&R head Gary Muth led to Roman and Ann Graham, director of Rogers Radio stepping in for a year. This was followed by another one-year stint by Mel Shaw, past president of CIRPA, and founding president of Canadian Academy of Recording Arts & Sciences (CARAS).

Shaw recalls that Roman, who was also president of FACTOR for its first six years, was "Not only a driving force, he was a logistical force at FACTOR." Shaw adds, "Duff knew what the broadcasters wanted to accomplish, and he fully understood the focus of the record industry. The programs were carefully thought out."

While SRDP funding allowed FACTOR to do so much more because there was so much more money available, it also led to the organization coming under blistering music industry attack, particularly in the regions which cited favouritism. There was criticism that many of FACTOR's loans, grant applications and approvals were rock music, and that the majority of approvals were from Ontario.

"Everybody had a different take on what FACTOR should be," recalls Roman. "The six early years were tough. I had everybody coming to me saying they could do it better."

"Everybody then was going, "Gimme, gimme, gimme," recalls Ostertag.

At the invitation of the Alberta Recording Industries Assn., Shaw returned to his hometown of Calgary to drum-beat FACTOR. He was overwhelmed by the reception. Performers Tom Kelly and Gene MacLellan encountered a similar reception when they went to Atlantic Canada for FACTOR a few months later.

After Shaw left, Roman and Graham began seeking a new head administrator, It eventually dawned on them that Ostertag, by now the director of operations, was the obvious choice.

"Heather is the classic case of an administrator who did much of the work, knew more than her bosses, and got none of the credit," recalls Vancouver songwriter Jim Vallance, then a FACTOR board member. "Duff and Ann realized the best candidate was already in the room, and Heather got the job. It's a bit of a Cinderella story."

"It took us awhile to learn that Heather was really backing up some of the people who passed through here," agrees Roman.

FACTOR SUPPORT IMPACTS BOTH DOMESTICALLY AND INTERNATIONALLY

As FACTOR evolved, a supportive Canadian media for Canadian artists evolved in the '80s. This included regular coverage from local daily newspapers and local TV stations and from such music-based national publications as Music Express, Canadian Musician and Canadian Country Music News. Regular national video coverage of Canadian acts was being provided by MuchMusic, MusiquePlus, and the YTV show "YTV Rocks." The recording industry was then serviced by two trade publications, The Record and RPM Weekly.

Still, despite inroads into markets outside Canada that seemed inconceivable a decade earlier, popularity in Canada often did not hold much weight elsewhere, particularly the United States. Although they enjoyed strong domestic success, recordings by such notable Canadian acts as **Honeymoon Suite,** Platinum Blonde, **Parachute Club,** Dalbello, **Frozen Ghost, Zappacosta, Headpins,** Payolas and **Rough Trade** disappeared into the backwater of regional American markets.

For those Canadian independent labels or acts seeking distribution outlets outside Canada, the obstacles were significant because they lagged behind the multinationals due to lack of finances and contacts.

Meanwhile, the escalating production costs of making records and videos, plus the marketing costs associated with co-op retail advertising and in-store positioning, was placing financial stress on many Canadian indies. Independent labels and artists needed the supplemental support that SRDP provided to meet the challenges of the marketplace.

Ideally, FACTOR financial funding was deemed a loan which Canadian-owned independent companies could use to record and support Canadian artists and eventually recoup on. However, FACTOR often represented a high-risk bank of last resort. Some labels knew they wouldn't be making money from what were essentially developmental projects which would take several albums before substantial revenue would be realized. Though the companies put up half the finances for recording and marketing support, FACTOR support was more appealing than putting up the full 100% of financing.

Nettwerk's Arboit, recalling the impact of early FACTOR funding on Nettwerk says, "We were three guys with day jobs who pulled nothing out of the company. FACTOR gave us $12,500 to start the Grapes of Wrath's 'Treehouse' album. That was like winning the lottery. Not only did we get that but we could get $25,000 to tour. Being young and resourceful, we made $25,000 go a long way."

Jim Cuddy recalls the benefits of FACTOR funding in building an international profile for Blue Rodeo. "We've been able to go to Australia, Europe, the U.K, and the United States, largely because of FACTOR. Those tours are large undertakings for a band our size. But you want to represent the kind of band you are when you tour. We opened for Edie Brickell in Europe in 1989. That put us at the Montreux Jazz Festival, and in front of a lot of international Warner affiliates."

By 1990, FACTOR had 12 sponsoring broadcasters and its budget for the fiscal year beginning April 1, 1990 was just over $3,000,000 covering funding for 7 programs.

SRDP was being recognized as a most useful government strategy because the program was effective in producing completed works which attracted significant public attention.

In a speech at the Music Canada Conference in Toronto on March 17, 1990, then federal Communications Minister Marcel Masse acknowledged the increasing demand in the industry for funding, saying, "The number of companies now qualifying for SRDP funding is growing at such a rate—over one hundred per cent growth—that the program is swamped by more applications than it can possibly fund."

INDIES AS LEADING A&R PLAYERS

(SRDP) was made permanent in 1991, the program, now known as the Canada Music Fund Council (CMFC), allocated $5 million annually to the development of the sound recording industry in Canada; 60% to the English-language industry, represented by FACTOR, and 40% to the French-language industry, represented by MusicAction.

By this time, FACTOR had provided recording assistance to more than 1,100 artists in all styles and supported more than 50 tours and the production of some 200 music videos.

The base of Canadian labels—almost doubled in 1984–85 to 1995–96 (+81%) according to the Apr. 2000 report "Evaluation of the Sound Recording Development Program—Final Report." The core of major companies under Canadian control with a revenue of $1 million represented 15%. It grew significantly from 9 companies in 1984–85 to 23 in 1995–96.

At the same time, the growth of foreign markets made artist development in Canada more globally oriented. Labels increasingly began to look to develop artists who could leap international boundaries.

Alannah Myles, Celine Dion, **the Cowboy Junkies, the Tragically Hip,** Jane Child, **Rita MacNeil,** the Jeff Healey Band, **Colin James,** Kon Kan, **Skinny Puppy,** Mary Margaret O'Hara, and **Jane Siberry** made significant international gains in the early '90s.

Still, some of Canada's biggest domestic successes of the period, including the Northern Pikes, Tom Cochrane, **Men Without Hats, Maestro Fresh-Wes, Gowan,** Luba, **Blue Rodeo, Barney Bentall & the Legendary Hearts** and **Sass Jordan** experienced practically no international profile.

But this began to change.

In 1992 **Sarah, McLachlan, Crash Test Dummies, the Holly Cole Trio, Loreena McKennitt, the Grapes of Wrath,** and **54:40** broke through internationally while enjoying success in Canada.

By the early '90s, FACTOR support became even more relevant as a vibrant, grassroots alternative scene developed with a high number of alternative-styled bands enjoying sizeable success releasing their own independent recordings, leading to intense A&R scrutiny from multinationals.

Initially leading the way were **Barenaked Ladies, Sloan, Moxy Furious, the Waltons, Doughboys, I Mother Earth, Ashley MacIsaac, King Cobb Steelie, Lowest of the Low, Change Of Heart,** and **Eric's Trip.**

While support from MuchMusic and alternative and college radio was vital in boosting the careers of these acts, it was also the enthusiastic support of such major retail chains as Sam the Record Man, and HMV Canada.

At HMV's Yonge Street flagship store, for example, the independent section ran from 600–1,000 titles, and was front racked near the high-traffic ground floor entrance. HMV promoted independent product by utilizing a chart, in-store displays, and in-store listening posts.

Noticing that Canada's independent sector had become a potent A&R source, multinationals in Canada began to eagerly seek out such talent via tie-ins with independent labels and artists via pressing and distribution agreements, co-ventures, or licensing deals.

Meanwhile, Canadian country music was attaining more credibility. A star system had been established by the likes of Ian Tyson, **George Fox, Michelle Wright, Prairie Oyster, Gary Fjellgaard, Patricia Conroy, the Good Brothers, Lisa Brokop,** and the **Johner Brothers.**

As well, Canada's urban acts, including **Dream Warriors, Michie Mee** & LA Luv, Kon Kan, **Maestro Fresh-Wes,** and Main Source, were spreading the word internationally that Canadians could make great dance music.

1995 provided one of Canada's most productive years, as McLachlan, McKennit, Siberry, and Crash Test Dummies set the pace internationally.

At home, the most popular Canadian independent artist was Toronto-based singer/songwriter Hayden. His album "Everything I Long For" topped indie charts in the country for months. Other leading independents releases were registered by Pluto, Treble Charger, Glueleg, Len, Eric's Trip and Monoxides.

The following year, releases by Celine Dion, **Alanis Morissette** and Shania Twain dominated the global music marketplace. Canada finally was being widely recognized as a leading repertoire source.

Wanagas noticed significant differences to Canada's music industry when he returned in 1999, after 8 years in the United States. "I became aware very quickly how things had changed," he says. "When I left Canada in 1991, it was very difficult to have a full time job in the music business in this country unless you were employed by a major record company, a major publisher, SOCAN or CIRPA. "When I came back, I could see you could make a living in the music business in Canada. That there was an infrastructure. I could see it the minute I got here. A lot of the change had to do with FACTOR."

FACTOR'S CONNECTION COAST TO COAST TO COAST

In its efforts to ensure that there was a national presence having a voice in who received funding, FACTOR started working with the provincial music industry associations (where they existed). The associations represented FACTOR to their local industry and helped with the dissemination of information about the various programs. As well, they shared the responsibility with FACTOR of conducting juries. The associations assigned a staff member to act as a Regional Evaluation Co-Ordinator (REC). In 1991, it started out with the associations doing it on a volunteer basis. As the relationship developed and the associations became comfortable with representing FACTOR and holding juries, more and more time was dedicated to program development and in 1995 the National Advisory Board was created.

At the bi-annual meetings the associations bring forward any feedback (both negative and positive) they had received. This ensures that FACTOR continues to remain responsive to the needs of the industry coast to coast to coast.

"I am very proud of our National Advisory Board and the relationships FACTOR has developed with the provincial and territorial music industry associations throughout Canada. One could say they are a cornerstone in the success FACTOR supported projects have had" states Ostertag.

FACTOR CHALLENGES

In 2001, the Canadian government renewed its commitment to the recording industry by developing the Canadian Sound Recording Policy under the Canada Music Fund (CMF), which includes those support programs FACTOR administers.

However, CMF was rolled into a new three-year overall cultural program, Tomorrow Starts Today. This led to CMF—including those programs administered by FACTOR—being switched to "temporary" status, and being subject to annual federal cabinet approval.

This "temporary" status, and perceived threat to FACTOR's future, spurred an independent committee of 20 Canadian music industry figures to launch the "Save Canadian Music" campaign in 2003.

There have since been concerns that FACTOR was being sidelined to a lessened industry role by the Music Entrepreneur Component (MEC) program launched by Canadian Heritage in Sept. 2005. Initial funding for the program began to flow April 1, 2006.

MEC—with an annual $10 million budget funds 19 established Canadian-owned labels. Nine of these—including Justin Time, Aquarius, Analekta, Tox, all in Montreal; Marquis, and True North in Toronto, and Nettwerk in Vancouver—previously drew funding from various FACTOR programs.

"The launch of MEC shows a measured result of what we did for over two decades," points out Ostertag proudly. "We grew companies. We still have plenty of labels at FACTOR, and will continue to have success stories."

However, due in part to evolving new communication technologies, there has been a dramatic shift in the recording industry in recent years. Downloading of music via the Internet and widespread CD-R copying, coupled with competition from such leisure products as DVD video, and computer games, has adversely affected recorded music sales worldwide.

FACTOR realized that the Canadian-owned label and artist sector needed additional supplemental support to enhance their competitiveness within the growing digital economy, and to help it meet the challenges of the domestic marketplace, as well as to export their catalogs abroad.

As a result, FACTOR undertook an evaluation of its programs and relationships and roles with its sponsors in 2005. The evaluation was conducted on behalf of FACTOR by Ascentia and there was input from 878 people drawn from music and broadcast industries.

"We had been struggling with overhauling programs because we were only getting one year contracts from Heritage," explains Ostertag. "Do you reinvent FACTOR if it may be closed down? Once we had the five year commitment, we started the review process. Then we refocused the organization, and streamlined our programs."

"At most times, FACTOR has been very responsive to the industry's needs, and have listened very carefully," points out Bernie Finkelstein, president of True North Records in Toronto.

"Touring, marketing and promotion funding became more important," says Montreal-based FACTOR Chair, Jim West, also president of Distribution Fusion III, and Justin Time Records. "It used to cost $200 an hour to record, now it's a lot less. And at the same time marketing and promotion costs skyrocketed."

The reorganization was timely. The music industry worldwide began 2007 as a punching bag, in the throes of a slump that appears terminal to many of the people who work in it. Lay-offs have been commonplace throughout the industry—in Canada and elsewhere—as music sales have fallen.

Yet, Canadian independent labels and artists with FACTOR support are finding a more receptive global audience for their catalogs while building a strong brand identity within Canada. As well, confident about their international networking skills, they are increasingly seeking a great international presence.

"FACTOR helps us compete globally," says Peter Cardinali, owner of jazz-styled Alma Records in Toronto. "We've been able to offer support to make international product that competes internationally. It lets us develop product and artists. Anybody I've ever spoken to in any territory elsewhere are very envious that we have something like this."

Many predict a grim picture for Canada's independent sector if FACTOR closed down. "I can't imagine the Canadian music industry surviving without FACTOR," says Rosen.

"FACTOR is as important, if not more important than it's ever been," says Wanagas.

Ostertag agrees, "There's always going to be a place for FACTOR because there is always going to be emerging talent. We're developing the farm team and preparing them for bigger and better things."

DISCUSSION

FACTOR, *The FACTOR Story.*

1. Review the point form highlights and the chart describing FACTOR's delivery of subsidies since it was launched in 1982. Where did the majority of FACTOR's funding come from and where was the majority of it spent over this period?
2. Leblanc describes the difference between multinationals and independents in Canada's recording industry. Summarize these differences in your own words and explain why FACTOR directs some of its subsidies to Canada's independent record labels.
3. The FACTOR story points to the 'trickle down effect' of subsidies. Describe this effect and explain how it might relate to the emergence of 'creative clusters' in the music industry.
4. The history of FACTOR shows how subsidies are now being used to develop international markets for Canadian artists. Wright is critical of this trend because he feels it undermines the distinctiveness of Canadian music. What do you think? Should Canadian artists be subsidized to seek out global success or should they target their music strictly to national audiences? Why or why not?
5. Visit the FACTOR web site at www.factor.ca and click on Approvals. This page allows you to search for grants awarded to individual artists or bands since January 2000. Do a search on Canadian musicians that you are familiar with or ones that are mentioned in the FACTOR story. Which of these artists have received FACTOR funding? Do you think these funding outcomes are making a real contribution to the creation of Canadian music? Why or why not?

Domestic Media Subsidies, Globalization, and New Technologies

Chapter 10

INTRODUCTION

In this final chapter, we consider how domestic subsidies, tax credit programs, and public-private partnerships have been developed to address the challenges of globalization and emerging digital media, especially in the film and television industries. As Grant and Wood (2004) argue in their overview of subsidies, ". . . modern states found ideological and economic reasons to subsidize popular culture aimed at the broadest measure of their citizens." In Canada, rationales for the use of subsidies invoke their importance to the expression of national identity, their role in protecting national interests and generating economic growth in the media industries. Canada is not alone in using direct expenditure and tax expenditure to generate the creation of national culture. Most developed countries, except the US, provide some form of subsidies for cultural production. While this support is not directly linked to political goals, government agencies control access to and distribution of funds. Grant and Wood describe two main types of subsidies. Automatic subsidies are grants provided to media companies from a specific fund based on their performance in the market (e.g., book or album sales, circulation, box office receipts, or viewership). For example, the Canada Periodical Fund, the Book Fund, and the Music Entrepreneur Program at Canadian Heritage all make more or less automatic grants to eligible companies that apply. Discretionary subsidies include loans, equity investment, or cash grant awarded through a competitive process. In this case judgements about the aesthetic merit or commercial viability of specific projects must be made, often through some form of jury process. FACTOR, the Canada Feature Film Fund, and the Canada Council provide discretionary subsidies to artists and cultural producers. The Canada Media Fund (CMF) is a combination of automatic subsidies and discretionary subsidies. The bulk of the Media Fund is allocated to annual 'performance envelopes.' These envelopes are awarded to broadcasters in amounts based on their prior success in supporting Canadian programming and attracting viewers to it. Other components of the Media Fund, such as funds for experimental digital media productions, are awarded on a discretionary basis as assessed by juries. Like FACTOR and the Feature Film Fund, the Media Fund makes equity investments in television programs, and a percentage of any profit made by independent producers must be returned to the Fund.

In the critical analysis for this chapter, Grant and Wood survey the international use of subsidies and trace the history of their implementation in Canadian media industries. They explain how tax expenditures—deductions and credits—act as incentives to encourage private investment in cultural industries without incurring direct costs to governments. Tax expenditures are measured as 'revenue forgone' since the deductions or refundable credits reduce government tax revenues at their source. Tax breaks for investors are politically popular because they do not involve the obvious costs of direct expenditure. Tax credits are especially useful in generating private investment in high budget productions such as television drama and feature film. Grant and Wood assess the effectiveness of tax shelters like the Capital Cost Allowance (CCA) applied to Canadian film investment. Between 1982 and 1995, investors could deduct up to 100 percent of the costs of their investment in a Canadian film from taxable income. This 'tax shelter' vehicle did not produce many quality films however, since the deduction applied whether or not the film made a profit and even if it was never released.

The CCA was replaced in 1995 with the Canadian Film or Video Production Tax Credit (CPTC). The primary objective of the CPTC is "the encouragement of Canadian programming and the development of an active domestic independent production sector" (Nordicity, 2008, i). CPTC allows for a 25 percent refundable tax credit on labour costs, for up to 15 percent of total costs of a film or television production in Canada (Canadian Heritage, 2010a). As Policy Source 17 indicates, the CPTC is available only to eligible Canadian-owned film or video production companies with firm commitments from Canadian television broadcasters or film distributors to show the completed production within two years. Further, in order to qualify for this tax credit program, the film or television production must be in specific genres and must achieve a minimum of six out of ten possible points awarded for Canadian members on the production crew. In addition, key producer-related positions on the production must be held by Canadians. These points are calculated by the Canadian Audio-Visual Certification Office (CAVCO) to ensure that labour costs being claimed under this tax credit policy are actually being paid to Canadian citizens. A 2008 evaluation of the economic impact of the CPTC found that the annual value of tax credits claimed was over $180 million. This is more than the current level of public funding supplied to the Canada Feature Film Fund or to the Canada Media Fund, making CPTC the "federal government's single largest stimulative tool for the film and video production industry" (Nordicity, 2008, iii). The CPTC provides between 8 and 12 percent of the total financing of Canadian production and is a crucial piece in the financing formula for film and television (ibid). Since the independent film and television production industry in Canada is made up of hundreds of small companies with relatively low levels of revenue, federal government tax credits play a central role in their economic survival. Finally, the amount spent on federal tax credits for film and video can be seen as triggering additional financing from other sources, such as other federal or provincial public subsidy programs and private investment. Thus, the overall volume of film and video production in Canada can be linked back to the importance of this tax incentive program.

Policy Source 18 is a brief overview of the Canada Media Fund. As discussed in the previous chapter, the Media Fund is a public-private partnership between the Department of Canadian Heritage and cable and satellite distributors such as Rogers, Shaw, Bell, Cogeco, Videotron, and Telus. These companies are required by the CRTC to contribute a percentage of their annual revenue to the CMF. The rationale for this requirement is that television distributors derive their profits from distributing both Canadian and foreign channels in Canada, but they create very little Canadian content themselves. Their mandated contribution to the Media Fund directs some of these profits back into the production of Canadian television and digital content. The CMF goes primarily to independent television and digital media producers and is the largest public-private subsidy program for any of the media industries in Canada. As described in the overview below, this fund is unique in its process of collecting funds from cable and satellite distributors, allocating the majority of this money to television networks who in turn commit specific amounts to eligible programs made by independent production companies. The Media Fund is a complex set of government interventions in the television industry that attempts to mimic market processes in order to trigger the demand for and supply of Canadian content.

Critical Analysis

Grant, P. S., & Wood, C. (2004). Subsidies (Chapter 13). In *Blockbusters and trade wars: popular culture in a globalized world* (pp. 292–313). Vancouver: Douglas & McIntyre.

Subsidies

By the first weekend of 2003, it was already clear that a pair of diminutive, hairy-footed fugitives had run away with the holiday season box-office. Over twenty-one days, audiences in North America alone paid US$265,467,000 to escape for three bewitching hours into the adventures of Frodo the Ring-bearer and his loyal hobbit sidekick Sam Gamgee. The rapturous reception that greeted *The Two Towers* built on the success a year earlier of the first movie installment based on J. R. R. Tolkien's classic fantasy *The Lord of the Rings*. It was a safe bet that by Christmas 2003, audiences would be lining up for the last episode of the epic trilogy as well.

The five-year production of all three *Rings* episodes—the most expensive film project ever attempted—was an epic of another kind. That it reached the screen filled with images of mountains that in real life tower over the remote South Island of New Zealand was a feat of financial as well as technical wizardry. In addition to featuring live action, computer graphics and a heroic story line, it involved incantations from tax law and a creativity Gandalf himself might admire.

The relevant spells were found in the New Zealand tax code. In effect, they allowed New Line Cinema, a unit of Time Warner, to use money belonging to a New Zealand bank and a German investment fund to finance the high-stakes venture while laying off more than a third of the risk on taxpayers in both countries.

Happily for all, the bet paid off handsomely—but not before the details of the tax sorcery behind the movies' creation came to light, causing an uproar among New Zealand voters, who imagined themselves having to make good a $90 million hole in their government's tax expectations.

Still, the behind-the-lens fellowship of directors, producers, accountants and taxmen illustrates a growing intersection of public and private interests in producing big-screen dramatic feature films, the riskiest and most costly of all cultural products.

State subsidy of culture has a long history. Rome's emperors routinely added statuary, arches and public coliseums to their civic landscapes, either to cultivate their own popularity or to amuse and placate their citizens. Much of the legacy of "high" culture, from the magnificent mosques constructed under India's Mughal or Turkey's Ottoman empires to Shakespeare's *Twelfth Night* and Handel's *Water Music*, was created as a result of the patronage of the governing powers of their day.

In the twentieth century, the motivation for state support shifted. Where once omnipotent rulers ordered up monuments to their own power or personal entertainment that only incidentally enriched the public, modern states found ideological and economic reasons to subsidize popular culture aimed at the broadest measure of their citizens. Some of this was blatantly propagandistic. The stilted "social realism" of the Soviet Union and the People's Republic of China or Wagneresque pretensions of Nazi Germany were true attempts at "command and control" culture.

But since the middle of the last century, all the major democracies have also at one time or another subsidized both high and low culture. They have generally attached few or no overtly political or ideological strings to their aid, although sometimes other conditions have applied. As governments everywhere outside the United States have grappled with the implications for their national identity and cultural creators of the economic realities laid out in the opening chapters of this book, the subsidy tool has become increasingly popular.

In this, New Zealand is far from alone, Australia, Canada, the European Union and most of its member states, most member nations of the Organization for Economic Co-operation and Development (OECD), many Latin American countries and thirty-seven of the U.S. states in addition to the U.S. federal government (through its support for public television), offer some form of public subsidy for the production of filmed entertainment.

Subsidies even have the approval of many sharp critics of other public-policy tools in support of cultural diversity. "If there is a need to make space for Canadian content on television," notes Canadian economist Christopher Maule, who opposes the use of quotas, "there are dispute-free ways of doing it that can make use of subsidies." As Maule notes elsewhere, "neither the GATT nor the WTO prohibit governments from using subsidies as instruments of policy. Only export subsidies and subsidies paid contingent upon using domestic goods are prohibited."

William Stanbury, another fierce critic of measures like content requirements on broadcasters, acknowledges: "There seems to be a reasonable case to be made for subsidizing the production of certain types of TV programs made by Canadians and which have recognizable Canadian themes."

"Subsidies," notes a report to the Australian Broadcasting Authority on the challenge of securing local content in new media, "have the advantage of transparency over quotas. As budgeted transfers, they are more likely than quotas to be the subject of continuing evaluation."

Perhaps it is merely the lure of cheap money, but even Hollywood's arch crusader against every other form of cultural security measure, Motion Picture Association of America president and CEO Jack Valenti, is in favour of subsidies for making movies. "I support the right of sovereign nations to offer enticements to producers," he has said on more than one occasion.

For all that, subsidies for popular culture are no more panaceas, silver bullets or free from unintended consequences than any other measure in the policy tool kit. They pose the difficulty of structuring a process of application and award that will be neutral and transparent. Another problem arises in allocating public support among competing projects, some of which might proceed without help while others perhaps should not proceed at all. Together, those hazards court a third: developing a "culture" shaped more by the pursuit of grants than the pursuit of either artistic or popular merit.

Briton Martin Dale describes something approaching a worst-case outcome in the experience of European film in the decades between 1960 and the mid-1990s. As one European country after another created national funding bureaucracies dominated by intellectual cliques, film auteurs turned increasingly to introspective, self-consciously "cultural" stories and audiences plummeted. "Today," Dale wrote in 1997's *The Movie Game,* "the films that are made are increasingly provincial. There has been an almost total destruction of the cultural fabric of the film industry and this has coincided with massive intervention by the state under the guise of defending the cinema."

Dale's criticism turned out to be somewhat shortsighted. In the next five years, with the support of subsidies, there was a strong resurgence in the popularity of local European films. By 2001, the box-office share of Hollywood films in Europe had dropped from over 80 per cent to 66 per cent. And in France, where subsidies for local films are supplemented by other support measures, the box-office share of U.S. films dropped to only 47 per cent in 2001, while films by French filmmakers were able to garner a box-office share of 42 per cent.

The recent European experience has demonstrated that the combination of subsidies with other support measures can generate films and television programs that get a very positive response from local audiences, although the overall numbers vary year to year. For many countries, however, subsidies represent an unavailable policy choice for the most basic of reasons: they take money. Where citizens must struggle to acquire even basic services, administrations often have higher priorities for scarce resources.

The financial wizardry that allowed the world's biggest media empire to undertake history's most expensive movie project with (mostly) other people's money illustrates how complex the subsidies for the most expensive cultural forms can become.

At the heart of the deal was a provision in the pre-1999 New Zealand tax code that allowed firms not usually involved in show business to buy shares in film-production companies. Those companies were in turn expected to use the money they received for their shares to make a movie in New Zealand. If the movie made a profit, great. If it didn't, the initial company got to write off the cost of its shares—that is, the cost of making the film—against other profits, saving itself the 33 per cent corporate tax it would otherwise have paid on that income.

In this way the mechanism was designed to mitigate the downside of the cultural-goods lottery by delegating some of the risk to the taxpayer. (The mechanism in fact worked very much like "flow-through" shares that some countries, including Canada, have been used to encourage investment in oil and gas exploration, another inherently risky field.) But it was another feature of the law that made it possible for U.S.-based Time Warner to access the tax magic.

Production companies created under the New Zealand law were also allowed to sell their movie, *in advance of actually making it,* to a foreign distributor. Critically, the transaction could close on pre-set terms at a later date, and the money for the sale could change hands later still and over a number of years. Together, the provisions meant that instead of a New Zealand company making a movie "on spec" and then seeking a distributor for it, a foreign studio could engage a New Zealand partner to create a company for the sole purpose of making a movie to order.

Which is exactly what Time Warner's New Line and New Zealand director Peter Jackson did to bring *The Lord of the Rings* to the screen. Most of the money to make the movies came from a New Zealand bank (the rest came from a German investment fund created under that country's own tax-shelter laws). New Line did not have to take possession of the film until it was made (giving it a chance to reject the film if it had been poorly executed) and did not have to make most of its payments until even later, after box-office revenue began to flow. Although the New Zealand bank now stands to recoup, through its stock in the production company, a small share of the three films' eventual profits, if the movies had flopped the bank would have been allowed to write off its entire investment against other income.

Subsidies for popular culture needn't necessarily be that complex. The European Union, for instance, was in 2003 considering a proposal that its otherwise universal value-added (sales) tax (VAT) be reduced or dropped for all cultural products and services. Movie tickets are already exempt from VAT in some European countries. Similarly, some Canadian provinces do not charge this country's equivalent, the goods and services tax (GST), on the sale of books.

Targeted sales and hotel tax exemptions are popular among U.S. states seeking to encourage filmmaking within their borders. According to a survey by the California State Library in 2001, half of all U.S. states exempt some or all purchases made for film-production purposes from state sales tax. Twenty-two offer reduced hotel-room taxes to visiting productions. New York, Texas and Mississippi classify film productions as "manufacturing"—a designation that eliminates sales tax on some costs, such as materials used in set construction.

Ireland offers a variant on this device: it declares any movie for which three quarters or more of the production work occurred on Irish soil a "manufactured product." The benefit of the designation: income earned on the film is taxed at the "manufacturing" rate of 10 per cent, instead of the going corporate tax rate of 24 per cent.

Not all subsidies need be financial. Both the massive U.S. military and the more modest forces of other nations have been known to offer a range of support and assistance to movie productions. Troops of the New Zealand Defence Forces moved earth, planted and tended gardens and helped build sets to create Jackson's screen Hobbiton; three hundred of them appeared in costume in the trilogy's various battle scenes. None received more than their customary soldier's pay for the tour of film duty.

Many state and provincial administrations—and even individual cities such as South Africa's Cape Town—staff full-time bureaus to help visiting film productions find local service providers and camera-friendly filming locations. In France, several regional authorities welcome film productions with free accommodation or local facilities made available gratis. Such support-in-kind is particularly attractive to comparatively cash-strapped jurisdictions.

But aid can be even less direct. Canada's government, for instance, subsidizes a variety of events designed not to increase the *production* of cultural goods but the *visibility* of the country's creators. Those events range from such national cultural awards as the Junos (for recorded music), Genies (movies) and Geminis (television) to subsidized book authors' tours. Lying somewhere between a subsidy for creation and one for promotion is a modest but meaningful amount of aid for Canadian recording artists to make music videos, critical to any contemporary musician's or group's chances of popular success.

In a similar vein, Eurimages, an agency of the Council of Europe, supports thirty-seven cinemas for the exhibition of European movies in nine European countries.

Media +, a similar agency created by the European Union, with a budget of £400 million for 2001–05, supports the development, distribution and exhibition of European audiovisual works and, along with the "Television Without Frontiers" directive, is the main instrument of the European Union's positive audiovisual policy.

Governments in many places, among them Canada, have also contributed to the capital cost of erecting studios and sound stages for filming and invested public funds in the training of audiovisual technical specialists.

More often, however, subsidies are designed to dangle a purely financial carrot in front of a well-defined target.

One straightforward approach entails a sort of top-up bonus designed simply to enrich the market's own reward system. Such arrangements are especially popular in Europe. Spain, France, Belgium and Germany all have one form or another of this kind of subsidy for filmmakers. Under the Spanish scheme, filmmakers get a payment from a state agency worth 15 per cent of their film's first-year box-office receipts in Spain, to a maximum of 50 per cent of the film's production budget. Belgian films made in French qualify for a similar program of "automatic" support proportional to ticket sales. Germany's national Filmforderungsanstalt (FFA) administers what it calls a "success grant" to German producers whose films sell more than 100,000 tickets in German movie houses; amounts range in proportion to the film's popularity from US$98,000 to $1.2 million.

France, the country with the world's richest support framework for filmmaking, predictably has the most highly evolved—or just complicated—"automatic" box-office supplement program. That country's Centre National de la Cinématographie (CNC) maintains a register of every French filmmaker's oeuvre. It also collects a tax of approximately 11 per cent on every cinema ticket sold in France. In a triumph of Gallic bookkeeping, the CNC tracks admissions to each French film and credits an account in each French filmmaker's name for an amount based on a multiple of his or her films' theatre admissions. The multiple varies according to a formula based on the proportion of the films' "French" content (that is, how much of the work was done by French individuals or in France). Producers may take money out of their accounts to finance up to 50 per cent of the production budget of further films, or use the cash expected to flow into the account as a soft form of collateral to borrow production advances from other investors. "The compte de soutien is a massively generous scheme," commented British film-trade magazine Screen Digest, "which effectively means that once a producer has released his or her second film in France, they are set up financially."

Canada operates a subsidy for book publishers loosely based on the same principle. The Book Publishing Industry Development Program (BPIDP—known among its beneficiaries as "Bippydip") is open only to publishers that are predominantly Canadian owned. Other criteria limit it to established companies publishing more than a minimum number of titles annually (the number varies, depending on the genre of book) but below a maximum sales volume and profit margin—effectively targeting smaller houses that focus on distinctive Canadian titles and new authors. The program distributes about C$32 million a year according to a formula that allocates the lion's share of the money to publishers that can demonstrate the highest sales.

More common than such "automatic" subsidies are discretionary programs that contribute public funds in some form of loan, equity investment or straight-up cash grant to film or television productions that must qualify for the support on an individual basis.

The European Union's Media + program provides what amount to semi-forgivable loans of up to £763,000 in the form of cash advances repayable from the "first dollar" of a production's box-office receipts.

Similarly, French producers can get funds from that country's CNC at either the development or production stage of filmmaking. The system of "advances on receipts" was started in 1959 and takes the form of an interest-free loan repayable with the film's receipts or using the automatic support fund discussed earlier. About eighty French films a year are supported in this way.

Britain's government-backed Film Council gives an assortment of cash subsidies. One funds script development. The grant must be repaid—plus a bonus of 50 per cent—only if the script is made into a movie, in which case the fund also expects a percentage of any eventual profits. Two other funds amount to sources of equity investments. They contribute money directly to productions in return for a share of a film's profits, if any.

Portugal's government directs aid to that country's filmmakers through the country's free-to-air broadcasters, reimbursing them for the production costs of domestic made-for-TV movies. Next door in Spain, the Instituto de la Cinematografia y de las Artes Audiovisuales gives comparatively small but non-repayable grants to up to two dozen "new directors or . . . experimental work of remarkable artistic and cultural content" a year.

According to some estimates, a diligent applicant who taps into a combination of Europe-wide and national subsidies can raise as much as 80 per cent of a medium-sized movie budget entirely from public funds.

New Zealand's Film Fund and Film Commission inject lesser amounts of equity into "feature films with *significant New Zealand content.*" The agencies also sometimes make loans against a film's sales or distribution guarantee. They limit aid to "New Zealand filmmakers who have already made one feature film," however, and to one production per filmmaker. NZ On Air, the country's vehicle to support the creation of domestic television fiction, takes the same approach. NZ On Air invests public money on an equity basis in series and television movies that it selects.

Canada subsidizes both film and television through the Canadian Television Fund (CTF), an agency financed with both public money and mandatory contributions from cable and satellite distribution undertakings. The CTF has a hand in a third of all English-language and half of all French-language Canadian TV shows (including a striking 93 per cent of all television drama shot in French). Money is injected into television programs in two ways. One part of the organization invests equity that is recouped only out of a production's profit. Another "tops up" broadcast licence fees for qualifying programs to as much as 35 per cent of production budgets, and is not recouped. The same agency also invests in feature films—typically taking a percentage of revenue from the "first dollar" of a movie's receipts. Over the years, several Canadian provinces have also created funds to make equity investments in films shot within their borders.

The creators of *The Lord of the Rings* tapped into the third major vector of public subsidy: preferential tax provisions. Governments like these mechanisms because they do not involve actual spending, but instead leverage the incentive power of forgone tax revenue. They are often more complex for creators to access than are direct subsidies. And, like subsidies for production infrastructure or cultural awards, their effectiveness can be unclear. But because they rely on deep pools of private capital instead of the limited funds at the disposal of most public granting agencies, they can also generate the large-scale investment required to finance an international blockbuster.

Three models of tax-based incentive are especially popular among investors, producers and governments—although each group gets somewhat different returns from each of those models. One offers a tax write-off tied to a direct investment in a production project. Another offers tax credits linked to some aspect of production, typically labour costs—which may also be refundable and therefore can be treated as anticipated revenue against which to borrow other financing. The last and most common model gives third-party investors a tax incentive for putting their money into investment pools that in turn act as sources of risk capital for filmmakers. The New Zealand scheme that financed *The Lord of the Rings* was an example of the latter.

Canada had a version of the first of these for more than two decades. Introduced in 1974, the "capital cost allowance" allowed investors to write off up to 100 per cent of their investment in a qualifying film production against other income in as little as one year. In effect, the scheme generated a tax benefit equal to slightly more than a quarter of the value of a film budget. The benefit was usually split three ways, among the producer, an outside investor and the middleman who put the two of them together. The allowance died when policy-makers decided other mechanisms would drive more benefits to the actual production.

Similar tax breaks remained available elsewhere. Britain's Inland Revenue let investors in feature films made in that country with production budgets up to US$23 million write off 100 per cent of that cost. Ireland offered a comparable scheme for the deduction of 80 per cent of an investment, capped at 80 per cent of the budget, in a movie for which at least three quarters of the production work took place in Ireland. Australia offered a 100 per cent write-off for investment in a feature, made-for-TV movie or documentary "made substantially in Australia which has significant Australian content." Films made under the terms of a co-production treaty between Australia and another country also qualified for the accelerated write-off.

Canada replaced its capital cost allowance scheme in 1995 with a refundable tax credit calculated on the amount a qualifying film production spent on labour in Canada. Several provinces offer similar tax credits that can be tapped in addition to the federal one, allowing Canadian productions to recoup a varying proportion of their overall budgets, depending on the province.

At least three U.S. states grant subsidies in a comparable form. Minnesota, as of 2001, returned 10 per cent of in-state expenses, to a cap of US$100,000, to visiting feature film, movie-of-the-week or TV series productions. The state billed its "Snowbate" as a "direct counteroffensive" to the Canadian tax credit. Missouri's Production Tax Credit is even richer. It returns 25 per cent of money spent in the state, up to US$250,000, on location budgets above $300,000. Oklahoma also rebates a portion of production spending within its borders. At 15 per cent, the portion rebated is lower than in Missouri, but there is no upper limit to the amount that can be claimed (although the state has earmarked a maximum of $2 million a year for the program).

In 2001, Australia introduced a similar regime. Any film production spending A$15 million or more in the country qualifies for a rebate from the government of

12.5 per cent of defined Australian expenses. As occurs in Canada, Australian states offer additional subsidies. New South Wales, for instance, established a fund that covers up to half the cost of shoots of at least a week's duration in the state, to a ceiling of A$100,000 for shooting in Sydney and A$500,000 for shoots outside the city.

Both the foregoing mechanisms reduce the private investor's risk of putting money into individual productions. The third widely adopted tax-incentive model encourages the creation of venture capital funds dedicated specifically to investing in multiple film productions.

Germany's version of this system allows taxpayers to deduct 100 per cent of their investment from other income in the year the investment is made. The 1999 provision opened a spigot from German wallets into three dozen film-investment funds around the country. The funds are not limited to investing only in German productions—which is how a Hanover-based pool came to share the financing of *The Lord of the Rings* with a New Zealand bank. Canadian studio Lions Gate Films also dipped into the German cash pools for a series of smaller productions.

A French version of this kind of tax-sheltered film-investment pool is known as the Sofica (Sociétés pour le financement du cinéma et de l'audiovisual) system. France's seven Sofica funds collect money from individual and corporate investors and reinvest it—through interest-bearing loans—in film projects the CNC approves. The incentive for individual investors is a 100 per cent tax write-off of investments that can be as much as a quarter of their total income. For both individuals and companies, income from the amount invested is taxed at half the normal rate. Further reducing investors' risk, large French film companies like Canal+ and Gaumont guarantee the investments for as long as eight years.

Creative British financiers have adapted that country's rapid tax write-down of investments in film-production companies to achieve a similar effect. There, what is known as a "sale and lease-back" system allows British investors to reduce their income taxes by risking funds on film productions backed by foreign studios in much the same way that the New Zealand bank did. An additional twist lets them leverage their cash by borrowing more than 80 per cent of the amount they write off against other income.

To access the British system, financial middlemen assemble a pool of investors who each put up, say, £19,000 in cash, and borrow an additional £81,000 each to invest a total of £100,000 in the financing pool. For their £19,000 investment, each investor then gets to shelter £100,000 of other income from taxes. Meanwhile, producers looking for money *sell* their film (or, often, entire slates of films) to the group before shooting begins. At the same time, they secure an agreement to *lease back* the rights to "exploit" the film (collect box-office receipts, distribution revenue or broadcast licence fees) for a period, typically fifteen years. The producers get to keep—and sink into the production—about 14 per cent of the cash they receive. The rest goes into a bank as security for the lease payments to the pool. As those lease payments come into the pool, they go to service the original investors' bank loans. (For their efforts, the financiers who put these deals together also wind up with about 5 per cent of the cash that flows through them.)

Funds from several such schemes may be combined to finance any one production. According to the British Treasury, upwards of £100 million a year flow through such tax shelters into U.K. productions, and observers estimate that as much as 75 per cent of the budget of many British films is tax-subsidized. But only feature films are covered by the scheme; the rules had to be tightened after it was discovered that TV channels were using the system to make soap operas.

As much as trade theorists endorse subsidies for their supposed "transparency," all these mechanisms are as vulnerable to unintended consequences as others designed to remedy market failure in the production of popular culture.

Subsidies may miss the desired target, motivating instead activities that either need no encouragement or court reprisals from trade partners. Subsidies given according to "automatic" formulae risk rewarding the undeserving. Subjective systems court the corruption of the gatekeepers. Then there is the question, never trivial, of where the money will come from.

The last point is especially relevant to less developed nations. "Some argue that subsidy is the more efficient way to promote cultural diversity," remarked Hyungjin Kim of South Korea's International Institute of Cultural Content at a 2001 seminar in Geneva. "However, subsidies also have limited utility. Governments must have money in order to provide subsidies." In practice, many of the countries most vulnerable to foreign domination of their audio-visual markets in particular—South American and Caribbean nations and those in Africa and central Asia—are also the ones with the most limited resources and most pressing humanitarian needs.

But the challenge can confront even wealthy countries. When Canada experienced a burgeoning of new television channels in the 1990s, many of the aspiring ventures promised to air schedules loaded with made-in-Canada programs. Most made those commitments expecting to receive subsidies from the Canadian Television Fund for the anticipated shows. In the event, the fund was heavily oversubscribed for much of the second half of the decade, and the commitments proved harder to fulfill than was anticipated.

Tax breaks possess offsetting advantages and disadvantages on the question of money supply. Politically sensitive finance ministries escape the opprobrium of taking money from one sector of the economy in order to give it away to another. On the other hand, forgone tax revenue is money that is not available to spend for other purposes. Moreover, because the mechanism depends on the decisions of many individual taxpayers, neither the amount forgone nor the amount that will reach the intended beneficiary can easily be forecast with precision. Finally, as appears to be the case in the example of Britain's sale-and-lease-back investment pools, the sums that actually reach the intended target—in this case, film production—may only be a fraction of the amounts that creative accountants manage to shuffle through the tax shelter.

Nonetheless, governments have shown remarkable ingenuity in raising money for targeted cultural subsidies.

Ireland funds its subsidies for film and television production in part from a tax on broadcast ad revenues. France, Germany and Argentina all charge a tax on movie tickets. Germany also levies a tax on the sale and rental of pre-recorded videos. Mexico's president Vicente Fox received a sharp protest note from the Motion Picture Association of America shortly after Mexico began imposing a one-peso levy on every cinema ticket sold in January 2003; the money was to be channeled by the state-backed Mexican Film Institute into local production.

For nearly thirty years, Britain also taxed cinema admissions. The "Eady Plan," named after the cabinet minister who introduced it, directed a portion of cinema box-office receipts to the production in Britain of movies that included many of the early James Bond adventures and Stanley Kubrick's *2001: A Space Odyssey*. The plan was eventually repealed under Margaret Thatcher. Now in the United Kingdom, a portion of receipts from the national lottery is directed into film subsidies, passed on by the nation's Film Council.

Canada raises money for its array of cultural subsidies from a number of sources. Owners of "broadcast distribution undertakings" (better known as cable and satellite distribution systems) are required to pay a portion of their revenues into the Canadian Television Fund. One rationale for this levy is that these businesses profit handsomely from importing inexpensive foreign programs and exhibiting them to Canadian audiences in place of domestic programs that would be more expensive to produce. (Despite these cash flows, the fund early in 2003 blamed limited resources for its inability to finance more than half the proposals before it.) Large media enterprises are expected to commit additional funds as public benefits in order to secure regulatory approval of mergers or acquisitions that would otherwise benefit only shareholders.

Finding the money is one thing. Giving it away again—fairly, efficiently and effectively—raises another distinct set of issues. Prominent among them is a tension that has surfaced repeatedly in these pages, particularly in Chapter 7: the desirability and difficulty of drawing a clear line between two broad categories of cultural product.

Into the first fall works most likely to be failed by the commercial market: distinctively local films or television series that strongly evoke the images and issues, "hopes, fears and dreams" of their place of origin. This is the category of the "visibly" Canadian (or Swedish, Australian or Taiwanese) movie, the one that has only a remote prospect of appealing to audiences unfamiliar with its world.

Into the other group fall those productions generic enough to appeal to wide audiences in many cultures. Science fiction, slapstick animation and special-effects action movies all go in this category.

As Chapter 7 demonstrated, most countries will treat either type of program as national product, provided the creators are nationals of their country and the artistic direction is exercised by local creators. However, when it comes to allocating subsidies, many countries will try to distinguish between the two categories, providing more financial support for culturally distinctive productions likely to have only a domestic audience than they do for generic productions likely to be exported to many foreign audiences.

In making this distinction, these nations recognize that while the culturally distinctive local drama might not get made without public assistance, the internationally generic entertainment probably will. In that case, why should the public contribute its good money to add to the profits of a project that would happen anyway?

The trouble, of course, is that the dividing line between the two categories is seldom bright and clear. *The Lord of the Rings* may convey more about the fictional culture of Middle Earth than it does about New Zealand. But defenders of the decision to let a New Zealand bank plunge tax-exempt dollars into its creation point to the showcase it affords the country's spectacular scenery—and an anticipated surge in tourism as a result. Some film version of the Tolkien epic, which has sold more than 100 million copies in print, might seem to have been inevitable. But "without the tax-incentive support," director Peter Jackson has told fellow Kiwis, *"Lord of the Rings* would not have been made here."

Similarly, television producers like *Degrassi*'s Linda Schuyler speak of the Catch-22 in which they sometimes feel trapped. The desire to reflect and speak to their home audience is in tension with the need to blur strictly domestic references for other markets. Yet, without those foreign sales, it would be financially impossible to put anything on the screen at home at all. They ask whether there is not a legitimate role for public subsidies to make possible a middle way: compensating them for some loss of foreign sales, in order to preserve some greater degree of local reflection.

Trade officials, of course, like to make a clear distinction between domestic and export subsidies in which the latter are potentially actionable under the WTO Agreement on Subsidies and Countervailing Measures if they apply to goods. However, as Chapter 16 will make clear, these provisions are difficult to apply to cultural products. In almost all cases, subsidies for cultural productions apply to the cost of creating the intellectual property in the original master work, efforts that in trade-law terms are considered a service, not a good. Few if any subsidies apply to making copies of the master, the "good" that is actually exported.

Plain in all of this is the difficulty of constructing a subsidy regime that accomplishes all the desired goals in terms of either ends or process. A wide range of formats nonetheless make the attempt.

"We have always had to strike a balance between our cultural mandate and the need to invest in winners," then-executive director of Telefilm Canada, Francois Macerola, said in 1998. "That is a matter of constant discussion." Telefilm's response has been to offer different measures of subsidy for projects that demonstrate different degrees of "Canadian-ness" according to the point-system described in Chapter 7: more money for projects with more "Canadian" points, less for those with fewer.

All of Telefilm Canada's television and film investments are expected to seek at least a measure of commercial success, however, Canada maintains a separate agency, the National Film Board, with a mandate to support clearly experimental films and foster young talent.

A more common approach is for a single agency to provide film subsidies separately to two sets of candidates. The Council of Europe's Eurimages program does this. "Eurimages now awards assistance under two schemes," its Web site explains. "One for films with real circulation potential; one for films reflecting the cultural diversity of European cinema." The former are eligible for more money (a maximum of £763,000) than the latter (£460,000). The European Union (EU) guidelines for national film subsidy programs generally limit state aid for feature productions to 50 per cent of their budget. But that cap may be lifted for what the EU describes as "difficult and low-budget films" (what constitutes a difficult and low-budget movie is for each member state to determine) and for "films produced in a limited linguistic or cultural area."

Similarly, Britain's Film Council has a New Cinema Fund that invests smaller amounts in more experimental films and projects by new filmmakers, and a Premiere Fund with higher ceilings for commercial films that aim at international audiences. Spain, as noted earlier, grants an "automatic" subsidy that rewards films with box-office appeal and gives discretionary aid to "new directors or to experimental works of remarkable artistic and cultural content."

What such distinctions cannot do is duck the difficult and necessarily subjective task of selecting among competing applicants the relative few that will get the green light for funding. Most agencies establish guidelines that typically make reference to the prior experience of senior creative participants in a project, the presence or absence of broadcast or cinema-distribution commitments and the existence of independent private financing. But such factors do not take account of innumerable other relevant but unquantifiable variables. Is there good chemistry among the key creative partners? Have audiences recently been hot or cold towards movies of the proposed genre? Does the plot involve a high risk of unpredictable production costs? (Kids, water shots and animals are three danger signs.) Is the script any good?

In the end, it is always a judgement call. And usually it is made by a panel of "peer" experts, often drawn from the same pool of local film-industry types that contributes most of the candidates for the agency's support. These "experts," inevitably, are only human—and hence fallible. Chapter 4 emphasized that even commercially driven producers have a lamentable track record in predicting audience demand: *nobody knows*. The track record for juries made up of industry peers is no more stellar. Moreover, the potential for cronyism, mutual back-scratching and influence wielded by cliques assembled around particular aesthetic or political views is high. (This again is a phenomenon hardly foreign to Hollywood.)

"When you say you've never heard a word of criticism from producers about Eurimages," remarked French director Jacques Fansten in the early 1990s, "I immediately thought of the story of a Chinese emperor who insisted that he be criticized and then immediately executed anyone who did so."

In Britain in that era, director Mike Figgis charged, the film-funding system was "so inundated with class and snobbery and nepotism that all the talent that is there waiting to be used, waiting to be involved, waiting to be creative . . . is not welcome."

Of Canada's Cable Production Fund (a predecessor to the CTF in the same decade, financed by a levy on cable systems), Toronto media consultant David Ellis fulminated: "It services the old-body network, the players who already have access to capital markets."

That many funding agencies—like the British Film Council, French CNC or Canadian Telefilm—exist at arm's-length from government, does not insulate them from political influence. Chief executives and members of their governing boards often hold their positions at the grace and favour of the government of the day. "The pre-eminent role of political patronage," says Martin Dale in his critique of mid-<\h>>1990s European film financing, "means that commissioning editors, particularly for cinema, are often appointed because of political connections rather than from any prior expertise . . . One film tsar, when attacked by the press for knowing nothing about cinema, used the defence that the previous head knew nothing about cinema either!"

Britain tried to resolve the problem in the second half of the past decade by injecting more than £95 million raised by the state lottery into three organizations with private-sector roots. Policy-makers hoped that the commercial instincts of these "favourite son" companies would prove more astute than the judgment of bureaucratic funding panels. They didn't. Only one of fourteen films the three companies made between 1997 and 2000 turned a profit.

Canada's Telefilm in the same period sought to reduce the discretionary uncertainty in awarding its broadcast licence-fee top-up subsidy for TV productions. Its solution was to grant the awards on a first-come, first-served basis, starting on a certain date each spring (usually the date was April 1—April Fool's Day—an unintended irony occasioned by the start of the federal government's fiscal year). The unhappy result was lineups that formed outside the agency's Toronto offices up to a week in advance of the awards, with better-off applicants hiring place-sitters to keep their spot in line. Worthy projects whose representatives failed to show up in time lost out to more dubious candidates whose eager producers had spent a week camped out in sleeping bags.

Governments and funding agencies continue to search for better ways. Since the mid-1990s, Canada's Telefilm has required applicants to its Television Fund to produce a letter from a Canadian broadcaster committed to airing what they produce. The letter is meant to act as a proxy test for the project's appeal to real audiences. And under new executive director Richard Stursberg, Telefilm restructured its internal operations in 2002, promising Canadian filmmakers a simpler and more straightforward application mechanism with a more standardized commitment of funds. Britain dumped the ill-fated Arts Council that had funded the three hapless favourite sons in the late 1990s in favour of a new Film Council led by experienced director Sir Alan Parker *(Bugsy Malone; Evita)*, although smaller U.K. filmmakers are not entirely happy with the new focus on "safer" films.

Structural subsidies such as tax-credit or tax-shelter systems might seem to avoid the hazards of cronyism that plague funding agencies. But they too can suffer from opaque selection procedures.

Germany's tax-sheltered funds raise enormous amounts of money: an estimated US$1.95 billion in each of 2001 and 2002. "But there is a huge lack of transparency about exactly what and where these funds are," *Screen Digest* commented in a late-2002 survey. "Although an international producer does not need a German co-producer to access the funds, most will find it necessary to consult a local German expert to even find a telephone number for each."

Britain's sale and lease-back system has generated substantial amounts for film production in that country, but it may not be doing much for their exhibition. Nearly 60 per cent of the films made in the United Kingdom in 2000 were not released, the third year running in which the portion of unreleased films climbed. The reason, *Evening Standard* critic Alexander Walker suggested in 2002, might be that so many got made, not on their merits, but so that investors could claim tax breaks. "A producer can put together a syndicate whose individual members take a legitimate tax write-off on the whole that's in excess of their individual investment by 10 or more percent. The producer also pays himself a premium. The film needn't be shown: in fact, it's safer not to risk it. It might turn out to be a hit: the investors would then have to pay tax on their profits."

Canada's tax-credit system for productions that score high on its Canadian-content ratings turned out to be no more watertight in the case of one high-flying and well-regarded Montreal animation house. Cinar Corp. soared in the 1990s on the strength of such popular children's series as *Arthur* and *The Busy World of Richard Scarry*. In 1997, *Hollywood Reporter* listed co-founder Micheline Charest at number 19 in its list of the 50 most powerful women in show business, above Madonna. Then, in late 1999, the company's stock and reputation tumbled to earth together on the disclosure that, among other schemes, the company had paid Canadians to lend their names to scripts written by Americans. With these *prête-noms* standing in for foreign writers, the productions received tax credits available only to "Canadian" scripts.

There is, finally, a risk that adheres to every sort of subsidy. It is the same one that traps generations of the same family and sometimes entire communities in the initiative-destroying grip of welfare dependency. Anticipating exclusion from commercial contention, cinema auteurs turn instead to introverted themes that are of limited interest to anyone but their artistic peers on funding panels.

"The point of a film is to be seen, it's not to massage the ego of the director," asserts *Screen Digest* research director and former Eurimage administrator David Hancock. "French producers until quite recently had so much money going into public funding they haven't really been exposed to a need to make films for the audience."

Some observers find the same symptoms in Canada. "You see the applications that come into the Centre [for Film Studies]," says Wayne Clarkson, director of Canada's preeminent graduate school for moviemaking. "They're all [about] dysfunctional families, demoralizing, despairing, antisocial, angry. You want to pay twelve bucks to see that?"

Mexican B-movie director Guillermo del Toro feels much the same way about the "fossilized" state system that until recently dominated film financing in his country. "Under the old system," del Toro told *The Guardian*, "the state would put [a state-financed movie] on at maybe two or three cinemas and then forget about it. It was tax money so they probably didn't even want it back anyway. When you let in private investors, you're suddenly dealing with people who'll make an effort to recoup their capital."

These criticisms were all too common in the early 1990s. More recently, however, they have faded as more refined subsidy systems in a number of countries increasingly supported a new generation of filmmakers strongly responsive to audiences. Nowhere has the success been more evident than in France, which managed through its generous support systems to achieve a cinema market share for its national films of 42 per cent in 2001, a record unmatched since 1986.

Other European countries also saw their local films enjoy growing box-office success. The most remarkable hit may have been in Finland. A nation with a population of only 5 million, it nonetheless supports production of as many as ten national films a year, subsidizing 60–70 per cent of their costs. In 2002, those few films achieved a domestic box office share of 20 per cent, led by the performance of a feature called *Pahat pojat (Bad Boys),* the third-highest-grossing feature film in Finland's history.

Just as with privately financed films, the audience response to subsidized films is inherently unpredictable. The market share for national films competing with star-driven Hollywood films that cost five or ten times more to produce will inevitably rise and fall. But in the cinema field, the subsidy systems around the world have made a key contribution to diversity in popular culture.

It is certainly true that governments can never create great art. Individuals create great art. But governments have always supported individuals who created great art.

It is equally true that when it comes to popular culture, most people neither expect nor receive great art—from Hollywood any more than from their national arts agency. What they receive may be good. It may just as easily be terrible, uplifting, irritating, boring or fascinating.

But it is important that enough of what people get to read, hear and watch be created by, for and about *them*. And as we have seen with regard to feature films, subsidies—judiciously invested—can do much to accomplish that. The success of Canadian authors, and the pleasure of Canadian readers, is further evidence of the benefit of subsidies.

Canada's book market may be one of the most competitive—and overstocked with titles—anywhere. Big international publishers release in Canada virtually all of the titles they publish in the United States, as well as titles from the United Kingdom and Australia. With "an incredible number of books coming over the U.S. border, plus all the British books, I can't think of a market anywhere that has so much going on," John Neale, president of (German-owned) Doubleday Canada told U.S.-based *Publishers Weekly* in 1998. Yet against that flood of imported titles, including every hot international best seller, Canadian readers in 1995 bought twice as many fiction books written by other Canadians as they had in 1985. Their purchases of Canadian non-fiction grew by 73 per cent in the same period.

"What we believe," Gordon Platt, head of the writing and publishing arm of the Canada Council for the Arts told an interviewer in 2000, "is that for literature to flourish, you have to have a functioning ecosystem."

"By that," commented *The Globe and Mail*'s Sandra Martin, who interviewed him,

he means that the country needs small-circulation literary magazines where beginning writers can test their skills and their imaginations, and literary festivals and readings where they can connect with other writers and perform their works for potential readers. Then you need small publishers, based in local communities, from St. John's to Victoria, that are willing to take risks on emerging writers. The next step is mid-sized publishers to up the ante for writers and to provide them with a larger market. Finally you need major publishers who are able to expose writers to an even higher level of editing and marketing expertise.

To sustain that ecosystem, the Canadian government in 2002 invested less than c$50 million a year—the price of a single low-budget Hollywood movie. From it, the same government reaped taxes, paid by Canadian publishers, of about c$100 million.

Canadian readers and appreciative counterparts around the world harvested the rich works of Alice Munro, Carol Shields, Rohinton Mistry, Michael Ondaatje and hundreds of other talented minds.

Doubling the public's money is not bad. Expanding the human imagination beyond the measure of accountants might well be called truly priceless.

New Zealand's government has since thought twice about leaving its taxpayers open to unlimited liability from some future *Lord of the Rings*. While the cameras were still rolling on that production, New Zealand amended its tax law. The loophole that allowed a Kiwi bank to put up the cash for the world's most expensive movie project snapped shut like the gates of Tolkien's fabled mines of Moria. However, the gates did not stay entirely shut for long. In June 2003, the government announced a less expensive support measure. Producers who chose New Zealand as a location for their big-budget films would be handed back 12.5 per cent of their production expenditure.

DISCUSSION

Peter Grant and Chris Wood, 'Subsidies,' from *Blockbusters and Trade Wars*

1. According to Grant and Wood, subsidies for supporting domestic media content are widely used, allowable under international trade agreements, and more transparent that the use of content quotas. Canada uses both subsidies and quotas. Compare and

contrast the choice of subsidies or quotas in terms of their effectiveness and their political acceptability. If you were to redesign media policy for Canada's television industry, would you choose subsidies, quotas, both, or neither? Why?

2. The authors review the use of subsidies in a number of different countries. Sum up a few of the different approaches that are discussed and explain how these are similar to or different from the Canadian approach to subsidies.

3. Grant and Wood describe three models of tax-based incentives for media industries. In your own words, explain how these models work. Which type of tax incentive was Canada's Capital Cost Allowance and why was it less effective than the refundable tax credit on labour costs in film and video (CPTC) that was developed later?

4. Since the mid-1990s the Canada Television Fund (now the Media Fund) has required that applicants produce a letter from a Canadian broadcaster committed to airing what they produce. Why do Grant and Wood suggest this is important? Do you agree or disagree?

5. Grant and Wood state that 'governments have always supported people who make great art.' How well do you think this statement describes government support for Canada's media industries? Is it more true of some industries rather than others? If so which ones and why?

**Primary Sources: Tax Incentives and Subsidies
for Film, TV, and Digital Media.**
Policy Source 17
Canada. Department of Canadian Heritage. (2010). *CPTC Program Guidelines, Canadian
  Audio-Visual Certification Office.*

Canadian Film or Video Production Tax Credit

3.01 GENERAL DEFINITION

To be eligible for the CPTC, a production must be certified by CAVCO as a "Canadian film or video production". A Canadian film or video production means a film or video production, other than an "excluded production", produced by a prescribed taxable Canadian corporation, and that is either a treaty co-production or a film or video production that meets the requirements of the Income Tax Regulations.

3.02 EXCLUDED PRODUCTION

As set out in subsection 1106(1) of the Regulations, an excluded production is one where:

a. A Part B application has not been submitted within the prescribed application deadline, or a Part B certificate has not been issued by the certification deadline;

b. Except where a production is a treaty co-production, neither the corporation nor another prescribed taxable Canadian corporation related to it is the exclusive worldwide copyright owner of the production, or controls the initial licensing of commercial exploitation of the project;

c. There is no confirmation from a Canadian distributor or CRTC-licensed broadcaster that the production will be shown in Canada within two years of it being completed;

d. The production does not retain a share of revenues, that is acceptable to the Minister of Canadian Heritage, from the exploitation of the production in non-Canadian markets;

e. There is distribution made in Canada, within the 2-year period after completion, by an entity that is not Canadian; or

f. The production falls within the list of genres which are ineligible.

3.03 EXCLUDED GENRES

The following genres of production are not eligible for the CPTC program:

a. news, current events or public affairs programming, or a program that includes weather or market reports;
b. talk show;
c. production in respect of a game, questionnaire or contest (other than a production directed primarily at minors);
d. sports event or activity;
e. gala presentation or an awards show;
f. production that solicits funds;
g. reality television (see surveillance TV);
h. pornography;
i. advertising;
j. production produced primarily for industrial, corporate or institutional purposes;
k. production, other than a documentary, all or substantially all of which consists of stock footage.

More details on each of these categories are available in "Part III—Definitions" of this guide.

3.04 COPYRIGHT OWNERSHIP

The Canadian producer(s) must retain the exclusive worldwide copyright ownership in the production for all commercial exploitation purposes for the 25-year period beginning at the time the production becomes commercially exploitable.

Ownership may be shared in cases where there is a Canadian co-production, a treaty co-production, or through an investment by a prescribed person or another qualified production corporation. As defined in the Income Tax Regulations, a prescribed person includes:

a. a corporation that holds a television, specialty or pay-television broadcasting licence issued by the Canadian Radio-television and Telecommunications Commission;
b. a corporation that holds a broadcast undertaking licence and that provides production funding as a result of a "significant benefits" commitment given to the Canadian Radio-television and Telecommunications Commission;
c. a person to whom paragraph 149(1)(l) of the Act applies and that has a fund that is used to finance Canadian film or video productions;
d. a Canadian government film agency, or
e. in respect of a film or video production, a nonresident person that does not carry on a business in Canada through a permanent establishment in Canada where the person's interest in the production is acquired to comply with the certification requirements of a treaty coproduction twinning arrangement; and

f. a person
   i. to which paragraph 149(1)(*f*) applies,
   ii. that has a fund that is used to finance Canadian film or video productions, all or substantially all of which financing is provided by way of a direct ownership interest in those productions, and
   iii. that, after 1996, has received donations only from persons described in paragraphs (*a*) to (*e*).

The production company must have the right to produce the production, evidenced through a clear chain-of-title. To claim the CPTC, the corporation must also have incurred any claimed labour expenditures. Once the tax credit has been claimed, the copyright may be assigned to a related prescribed taxable Canadian corporation.

3.05 ADMINISTRATION OF OFFICIAL TREATY CO-PRODUCTIONS

CAVCO will certify eligible productions that are official treaty co-productions as recommended by Telefilm Canada. Telefilm's review of a treaty co-production replaces many of the functions of a standard CAVCO review of a domestic production. Note that there are different requirements for supporting documentation and for eligibility.

The Government of Canada has entered into numerous co-production treaties with other countries. Telefilm administers all international agreements governing treaty co-productions. It reviews applications for eligibility of productions as official treaty co-productions, and recommends to the Minister of Canadian Heritage either approval or refusal of the applications. Details regarding Telefilm's policies and requirements are available on its Web site at **www.telefilm.gc.ca.**

Co-productions between Canada and another country are eligible for the CPTC only when co-produced under an official treaty. Treaty co-productions must continue to comply with the requirements outlined in the Income Tax Regulations, unless otherwise specified. A producer must apply directly to CAVCO to obtain a certificate to access the tax credit program. At the Part A review stage, a Preliminary Recommendation is submitted by Telefilm directly to CAVCO. At the Part B review stage, Telefilm sends its Final Recommendation directly to CAVCO.

3.06 RECOGNITION OF OFFICIAL TREATY CO-PRODUCTIONS OUTSIDE OF THE CERTIFICATION PROCESS

A CPTC certificate is used by many Canadian funding programs and regulatory authorities as recognition that a production has been granted official treaty co-production status by the Minister of Canadian Heritage. However, there may be cases where a project is not eligible for the Canadian film or video production tax credit, despite conforming to a treaty in force. This may occur, for instance, where regulatory deadlines were not met for applying to, or being certified under, the CPTC program.

If a production is eligible as an official treaty co-production but does not qualify for a federal tax credit, CAVCO may, upon request by the producer, issue a letter in lieu of a CPTC certificate confirming that the project has achieved official treaty coproduction status. This letter may then be filed with other authorities according to their procedures and requirements. For instance, the CRTC requires that a producer or broadcaster file the letter issued by the Minister (bearing a new identification number) to the CRTC in lieu of the certificate numbers normally issued by CAVCO.

3.07 DOMESTIC CO-PRODUCTIONS

A domestic co-production is one where more than one Canadian production company holds copyright ownership in and incurs expenses in relation to a production. Note that for domestic co-productions, (which generally involve inter-provincial partnerships) CAVCO issues a single certificate number for a production. Each co-producer must claim the relative portion of the tax credit with CRA.

3.08 CO-VENTURES

Co-ventures do not qualify for the Canadian film or video production tax credit.
Co-ventures are defined by the CRTC in Public Notice CRTC 2000–42 and are, generally, international co-productions not included under treaties administered by Telefilm Canada. Co-ventures are productions where, among other things, co-producer functions are performed by non-Canadians, co-producers have equal measures of decisionmaking responsibility on creative elements, and coproducers have responsibilities in the administration of the production budget.

Production Personnel

4.01 PROOF OF CITIZENSHIP

With respect to producer-related or key creative personnel for a production, the term "Canadian" is defined as a person who is, at all relevant times, a Canadian citizen as defined in the *Citizenship Act,* or a permanent resident as defined in the *Immigration and Refugee Protection Act.* An individual performing a producer-related or key creative role for a production must be Canadian at all relevant times. The person must be Canadian by the time he or she begins any duties in relation to the project, and during the remaining course of the production and post-production. An individual with permanent resident status must have this status confirmed before engaging in any activity related to the production.

As part of an application, the production company attests to whether each individual occupying a producer-related or key creative role is Canadian. The applicant must obtain and keep a copy of documentation (such as a birth certificate, permanent resident card, or passport) sufficient to demonstrate that all producers and the key creative positions identified for Canadian content points satisfy the Regulation's definition of

Canadian. CAVCO reserves the right to request a copy of some or all of the documentation from the taxpayer at any time during the application process or during any subsequent audit.

Note that the preceding definition of "Canadian" is different from the definition of "Canadian" referenced within the *Investment Canada Act* used for CAVCO's evaluation of whether a production company is Canadian-controlled.

4.02 KEY CREATIVE PERSONNEL—LIVE ACTION PRODUCTIONS

To be recognized as a Canadian film or video production, a live action production must be allotted a total of at least six points according to the scale below. Points will only be awarded if the person(s) who rendered the services is/are Canadian.

In addition, a production must obtain two of the four points allotted for the director and the screenwriter positions (one of the two positions must be filled by a Canadian). A production must also obtain one of the two points allotted for lead performers (one of these two positions must be filled by a Canadian), other than in circumstances where the production would not have a lead performer, as defined in section 4.05.

Note that there are ten possible key creative points available for a production. In circumstances where all key creative points are not applicable, the total number of available points will be reduced accordingly. For example, where a production has only one lead performer, and all other positions are occupied by Canadians, it will receive 9 out of 9 points.

As stated in the requirements set out in s. 4.05 below, it should be noted that narrators of documentaries are considered to be lead performers.

Live Action Productions

Director	2 points
Screenwriter (see s.4.06)	2 points
Lead performer (see s.4.05)	1 point
2nd Lead performer	1 point
Director of photography	1 point
Art director	1 point
Music composer (see s.4.07)	1 point
Picture editor	1 point

4.03 KEY CREATIVE PERSONNEL—ANIMATION PRODUCTIONS

To be recognized as a Canadian film or video production, an animation production must be allotted a total of at least six points according to the following scale. A point will be allotted only if the person(s) who rendered the services is/are Canadian. In addition, the following conditions must be fulfilled: either the director, or the screenwriter and storyboard supervisor must be Canadian; the lead voice for which the highest or second highest remuneration was payable must be Canadian (other than in circumstances where there are no lead voices or lead performers, as defined in section 4.05); and the key animation must be done in Canada.

Animation Productions

Director	1 point
Screenwriter <u>and</u> storyboard supervisor (see s.4.06)	1 point
Lead voice (see s.4.05)	1 point
Design supervisor (art director)	1 point
Camera operator (in Canada)	1 point
Music composer (see s.4.07)	1 point
Picture editor	1 point

The following points will be allotted if the work is performed solely in Canada.

Layout and background	1 point
Key animation (must be in Canada)	1 point
Assistant animation and in-betweening	1 point

4.04 GENERAL RULES FOR EVALUATING KEY CREATIVE POINTS

a. Regardless of the specific position title given, the head individual(s) for each key creative department will be the individual(s) evaluated for the purposes of awarding the applicable key creative point(s) for a production. For example, for video-based productions, the position of "technical director" or "lighting director" may be equivalent to that of "Director of Photography". As well, the head of the art department often receives the credit "Production Designer".

b. Any individuals grouped under the same position title in a production's credits will be presumed to be performing the same role for the production.

c. No points will be allotted for a Canadian who shares the functions of a key creative position with one or more non-Canadians. Where the functions of a position are carried out by more than one Canadian, only the number of points provided for in the Regulations will be allotted, regardless of the number of individuals named in the credits for this position.

d. For television series or a collection of films, each of the episodes in the series or each of the films in the collection is considered a separate production, for CPTC certification by CAVCO. As such, producers should provide a complete list of individuals occupying all applicable key creative positions for any and all episodes. If key creative positions or locations vary from episode to episode or from film to film in a collection, it is therefore possible that different episodes may receive a different number of points; in these instances, CAVCO accordingly reflects a range of points for the overall cycle of a series.

e. The point awarded for the camera operator position will only be awarded for a Canadian where the work is done in Canada.

f. Where a production consists of both live action elements and animation elements, the production's key creative points will be evaluated according to the criteria of the predominant production type.

4.05 LEAD PERFORMERS

CAVCO will use three criteria to determine which individuals are lead performers in live action and animation productions:

a. remuneration;*
b. billing;
c. time on screen, or, for animation, the length of time that the individual's voice is heard in the production.

A performer is an individual engaged to speak lines of dialogue or mime a scene, or whose performance consists of interpreting a character, even where there is no dialogue. When there is no actor or actress, an individual who performs one of the following functions will be considered equivalent to the lead performer: dancer, singer, specialty act performer, host (a performer who introduces or links segments of a program, such as a master of ceremonies, moderator, quiz master or interviewer), narrator or commentator (a performer engaged to perform narrative material or commentary on- or off-camera), a featured performer or subject in a production within the lifestyle/human interest genre, off-camera performer (a performer other than the narrator or commentator engaged to perform a role in a dramatic work off-camera), or the actor who performs or reads the voice of a character in a film or animated production. Guests on a magazine program, as well as interviewees in or subjects of documentaries are not considered performers for certification purposes.

4.06 SCREENWRITERS

To obtain the points for the position of screenwriter, a production must meet one of the following conditions:

a. Each individual involved in the preparation of the screenplay for the production must be Canadian. This means that all the individuals engaged in developing the screenplay, from the outline or treatment through the various drafts and dialogue polishes to the final shooting script, must be Canadian; or
b. The principal screenwriter must be Canadian and the screenplay for the production must be based on a work authored by a Canadian and published in Canada.

4.07 MUSIC COMPOSER

The point for the function of music composer is allotted only if the music created for the production is original. Note that where original music created for the first cycle of a TV series continues to be used for subsequent cycles of the series (with no new addi-

---

*Note that for the purpose of its evaluation of lead performers or lead voices, CAVCO will consider remuneration, as well as any additional benefits, residuals, travel or living expenses and all similar expenses incurred in relation to an individual.

tional original music by a non-Canadian), the production company may continue to claim the music composer point for later seasons.

4.08 EXCEPTIONS

Where a documentary production does not involve performers or other functions such as art director or music composer, a production may meet the creative services criteria even if the production has not been allotted the minimum six points required and/or has not obtained one of the two points allotted for lead performers. However, all the filled key creative positions must be occupied by Canadians.

For information regarding key creative personnel for treaty co-productions, please consult Telefilm Canada's guidelines on its Website at **www.telefilm.gc.ca.**

4.09 PRODUCER-RELATED PERSONNEL

A "producer" is defined as an individual:

- who controls and is the central decision maker for the production;
- who is directly responsible for the acquisition of the production story or screenplay and the development, creative and financial control and exploitation of the production; and
- who is identified in the production as being the producer.

All positions related to the producer function must be held by Canadians, unless the production is a treaty co-production, or where a request for an exemption for a foreign courtesy credit has been granted by CAVCO. **Note that no exemption will be granted for the functions of producer, co-producer, line producer, or production manager as these positions must be held by Canadians.** For information regarding the producer-related personnel in treaty co-productions, refer to the co-production guidelines issued by Telefilm Canada.'

DISCUSSION

Canadian Film or Video Production Tax Credit, *CPTC Program Guidelines, Canadian Audio-Visual Certification Office.*

1. Several types of film and television productions are listed in the CPTC guidelines as 'excluded productions.' Why are productions that do not have a confirmation of Canadian distribution or Canadian television broadcast ineligible for this tax credit program?
2. The CPTC guidelines list several 'excluded genres' as ineligible for the program. From your reading of this list, what genres can you identify as potentially eligible? Why do you think the tax credit program excludes some genres and supports others?

3. CPTC requires that the copyright for any supported production be retained by the Canadian owner for at least 25 years. Why do you think this provision is in place and what would be the advantages of maintaining the rights to film and video content in Canadian hands?

4. When applying for the CPTC, production companies must identify each of the key production roles according to whether they are held by Canadian citizens or permanent residents. In your own words, describe the CAVCO point system that is used to assign points to key creative personnel. Explain how many points are necessary to qualify for the CPTC and which combination of roles must be occupied by Canadians.

5. What are the eligibility requirements for 'producer-related' roles and production control under CPTC? Why do you think these rules are in place and what is their connection to the development of creative clusters in the Canadian film and video industry?

The Canada Media Fund had its origins in the CRTC's 1994 creation of the Cable Production Fund. Initially, cable companies' contributions to this fund were voluntary and the subsidies awarded from it went primarily to television drama that achieved eight out of ten points on the CAVCO scale (Armstrong, 2010, 254). In 1996, the fund was renamed the Canada Television and Cable Production Fund and was combined with a similar Broadcast Fund administered by Telefilm Canada. Contributions from cable companies became mandatory and were set at 5 percent of their total revenue (ibid). The new fund also received public money through the Department of Canadian Heritage, establishing it as a public-private partnership similar to FACTOR. In 1998 the fund was renamed the Canadian Television Fund and in 2006 its administration was transferred to Telefilm Canada. In 2010, the fund was redesigned in its current incarnation as the Canada Media Fund, absorbing Telefilm's New Media Fund. The CMF includes programs for television development and production, along with requirements that funded projects include 'convergent' content designed for conventional television screening, and multi-platform and interactive programming for digital distribution.

The CMF's current mandate is to champion "the creation and promotion of successful, innovative Canadian content and software applications for current and emerging digital platforms through financial support and industry research ... to connect Canadians to our creative expressions, to each other, and to the world." (CMF, 2012b). In 2011–12 cable and satellite companies contributed $218.2 million to the Media Fund, while the federal government contributed $134.1 million. The fund also included repayments on previous advances and returns on CMF equity investments in profitable productions, at the amount of $10.3 million. Of these combined contributions, $358 million was awarded to Canadian television and digital media projects. The Fund's annual report claims that these subsidies triggered an additional $1.3 billion of media industry activity (ibid). The funding comes from the Convergent Stream or the Experimental Stream, depending on the type of project proposed. Ninety-one percent of the 2011–12 funding went to the Convergent Stream to support Canadian screen-based projects, including television programming and related digital media content. Most importantly, the Media Fund only supports four specific genres of television content that are the most costly to produce and the least likely to be able to compete with imported television in the Canadian market. These genres are drama, documentary, children's and youth programs, and variety and performing arts.

Under the Media Fund model, automatic subsidies are awarded to specific Canadian television networks based on their past performance in supporting

Canadian content and attracting audiences for that content. This network-based subsidy is referred to as the broadcaster's Performance Envelope. A relatively complex formula is applied to each network to measure audience success in terms of total hours tuned for CMF-funded programs, the historic performance of the network in accessing CMF funds, the number of regional productions the network acquires from areas beyond Toronto and Montreal, the amount the network pays to licence productions above the minimum industry threshold, and the amount of the network's digital media investment. These factors are weighted and used to determine how much each broadcaster is allocated from the Convergent Stream. The total amount is assigned to a Performance Envelope which then supports the productions the network has agreed to licence. The envelope is further divided up into amounts for the specific genres that CMF supports, along with a flex amount that permits the broadcaster to move funds between genres as necessary. In 2012–13, for example, CBC's English television network had over $61 million to allocate to various new television programs: $25.6 million to drama, $1.8 million to children's and youth, $2.5 million to documentary, $1.1 to variety and performing arts, and $30.7 million toward flexible funding. By comparison, CTV will have $17.2 million to spend on eligible CMF genres and Global will have $9.7 million (CMF, 2012a). The next two highest Performance Envelopes were awarded to History Television and the Aboriginal Peoples Television Network (APTN).

In the meantime, television and digital media production companies apply separately to the Canada Media Fund to be eligible for these subsidies. In order to even enter into the CMF funding process, the project being proposed by the production company must first of all fall into one of the four genres that CMF supports. Secondly, each production must satisfy the four 'Essential Requirements' across all of these genres as defined by the CMF:

1. The project speaks to Canadians and is primarily intended for a Canadian audience.
2. The project will be certified by the Canadian Audio-Visual Certification Office (CAVCO) and has achieved 10/10 points ...
3. Underlying rights are owned, and significantly and meaningfully developed by Canadians.
4. The project is shot and set primarily in Canada (CMF, 2012d, 8)

Finally, before they apply to the CMF, the production companies must already have a broadcaster licence agreement in hand, indicating that a specific network will acquire the program and screen it within 18 months of completion and distribute the digital media component along with the television episodes (ibid, 12). CMF subsidizes television productions by 'topping up' the licence fee paid by the broadcaster for the program or through equity investment in programs that, if commercially successful, repay income to the Fund. The actual CMF funding is paid to the production company, not the broadcaster. In 2010–11 for example, the television drama series *Republic of Doyle* and *Rick Mercer Report,* documentary program *1812 Revisited,* and children's program *Monster Math Squad,* all received funding under the CBC's Performance Envelope. Global allocated part of its share of CMF funds to *Bomb Girls* and CTV to *Flashpoint,* among others (CMF, 2012c). Apart from the programs that are supported through the automatic envelopes assigned to television networks, the CMF also delivers a number of discretionary subsidies in the areas of experimental digital media production, Aboriginal television, Francophone minority programs outside Quebec, diverse language television, and English point of view documentaries. In these programs, subsidies are discretionary and applications are adjudicated according to social and cultural criteria.

The television programs that are the actual outcomes of CMF funding are produced as a result of partnerships between the CRTC and its requirements for cable and satellite contributors, Department of Canadian Heritage funding support, public and private television networks, and independent television and digital media production companies. As an example of policy implementation, the Canada Media Fund draws upon a complex mix of CRTC expenditure requirements, public and private funding for automatic and discretionary subsidies, and Canadian content quotas for television. The Fund is designed to allow broadcasters some autonomy in acquiring subsidized programs to satisfy their Canadian content requirements, while being rewarded for successfully reaching their audiences with the programs they choose to support. Through this complex mix of different policy tools, Canadian audiences have access to Canadian programs on television and the Internet, while Canadian media producers have the opportunity to create content for national and international television markets.

DISCUSSION

Overview of Canada Media Fund

1. What is the main argument for having cable and satellite distributors support Canadian content production for television? As more people migrate away from watching television on cable or satellite to watching television content on the Internet, do you think these companies will still be able to make significant contributions to the Canada Media Fund? Are there other forms of private contribution to the Fund that could be developed? If so where might they come from?

2. The creation of the CMF's Convergent and Experimental Streams are meant to help foster the creation of new Canadian content for on-line consumption and mobile apps. Do you think this policy tool will succeed in ensuring that Canadians have access to Canadian content on-line? What are some of the risks and benefits of this approach?

3. What four main television genres are supported by the CMF and why? Do you think the allocation of specific amounts of each television network's possible funding to the creation of drama can help create audiences for Canadian television series? Why or why not?

4. Visit the CMF website at www.cmf-fmc.ca and click on 'Funding Results.' Review the files listing quarterly or final funding results for the current year and make a note of any shows or digital content you have seen or heard about. In your opinion, how well do these actual outcomes of CMF support help achieve its stated goal of connecting "Canadians to our creative expressions, to each other, and to the world"?

5. What are the four Essential Requirements that CMF funded projects must meet? Which of these requirements relies simply on identifying the Canadian citizenship of creative personnel and which relies on a subjective assessment of program content? How can you tell if a television program 'speaks to Canadians' and what examples can you think of that fit this description?

References

Armstrong, Robert. (2010). *Broadcasting policy in Canada.* Toronto: University of Toronto Press.

Babe, Robert. (1985). Regulation and incentives, two sides of any policy. In C. Hoskins and S. McFadyen (Eds.), *Canadian broadcasting, the challenge of change.* Edmonton: University of Alberta and ACCESS.

Boggs, Jeff. (2010). An overview of Canada's contemporary book trade in light of (nearly) four decades of policy interventions. *Publishing Research Quarterly 26*(1):24–25.

Canada Council for the Arts. (2007). *The evolution of the Canada Council's support of the arts.* Retrieved from http://www.canadacouncil.ca/aboutus/Background/xp128565418182821011.htm

Canada Media Fund. (2012a). *2012–2013 performance envelope allocations at April 10, 2012.* Retrieved from http://www.cmf-fmc.ca/documents/files/env-admin/allocations/2012-2013-pep-allocations.pdf

———. (2012b). *Canada Media Fund 2011–2012 annual report.* Retrieved from http://ar-ra11-12.cmf-fmc.ca/

———. (2012c). *CMF final 2011–2012 funding results.* Retrieved from http://www.cmf-fmc.ca/documents/files/funded/2011-12/results/2011-12-q4-funding-results.pdf

———. (2012d). *Performance envelope program guidelines 2012–2013.* Retrieved from http://www.cmf-fmc.ca/documents/files/programs/2012-13/guidelines/2012-13_perf_env_guidelines.pdf

Canada. Department of Canadian Heritage. (2000). *Backgrounder, Canada-US agreement on magazines, Foreign Publishers Advertising Services Act.* Retrieved from http://www.pch.gc.ca/pc-ch/org/sectr/ac-ca/pol/magazines/fact-info/magbk1-eng.cfm

———. (2001). *From creators to audience: New policy directions for Canadian sound recording.* Retrieved from http://www.pch.gc.ca/eng/1289312410707/1289312410708

———. (2005). *Sharing Canadian stories: Cultural diversity at home and in the world.* Retrieved from http://www.pch.gc.ca/pc-ch/publctn/raconter-story/index-eng.cfm

———. (2008a). *'Perspective: Publishing' in Intersections: Updates from the cultural landscape. Cultural Affairs Sector 2008–2009 Annual Report.* Retrieved from http://www.pch.gc.ca/pc-ch/org/sectr/ac-ca/pblctns/anl-rpt/2008-2009/ra-ar-eng.pdf

———. (2008b). *Redesigning federal programs for the periodical industry.* Retrieved from http://www.pch.gc.ca/pc-ch/conslttn/fcm-cmf/discussion-eng.pdf

————. (2008c). *Summative evaluation of the book publishing industry development program.* Retrieved from http://www.pch.gc.ca/pgm/em-cr/evaltn/2008/2008-11/bpidp-eng.pdf

————. (2009a). *Government of Canada renews Canada Music Fund and increases investment in digital and international market development.* Retrieved from http://www.pch.gc.ca/eng/1294862453819/1294862453821

————. (2009b). *The government of Canada creates Canada Periodical Fund to better support magazines and community newspapers.* Retrieved from http://www.pch.gc.ca/eng/1294862436162/1294894053366

————. (2010a). *CPTC program guidelines,* Canadian Audio-Visual Certification Office. Retrieved from http://www.pch.gc.ca/DAMAssetPub/DAM-flmVid-flmVid/STAGING/texte-text/cptc_guide_1272631234182_eng.pdf

————. (2010b). *Investing in the future of Canadian books.* Retrieved from http://www.pch.gc.ca/DAMAssetPub/DAM-livres-books/STAGING/texte-text/discuss-paper_1279033118003_eng.pdf?WT.contentAuthority=12.2.1

————. (2012). *2012–2013—Application guide—Support for publishers.* Retrieved from http://www.pch.gc.ca/eng/1322593779110

Canada. Parliament. (1991). *Broadcasting Act.* Retrieved from http://laws-lois.justice.gc.ca/PDF/B-9.01.pdf

Canada. Parliament. House of Commons. Standing Committee on Canadian Heritage. (2003). *Our cultural sovereignty: The second century of Canadian broadcasting* (Lincoln Report). Retrieved from http://www.parl.gc.ca/content/hoc/Committee/372/HERI/Reports/RP1032284/herirp02/herirp02-e.pdf

Canada. Royal Commission on National Development in the Arts, Letters, and Sciences. (1951). *Report of the Royal Commission on National Development in the Arts, Letters, and Sciences 1949–1951.* (Massey Commission). *Radio Broadcasting* (Chapter 18): Ottawa: King's Printer.

Canadian Broadcasting Corporation. (2007). *Public broadcasting in Canada: Time for a new approach.* Submission to the Standing Committee on Canadian Heritage. Retrieved from http://www.cbc.radio-canada.ca/submissions/pdf/Mandate.pdf

Canadian Media Production Association. (2010). Remarks by the Canadian Media Production Association (CMPA) to House of Commons Standing Committee on Canadian Heritage: *Study on the impacts of private television ownership changes and the move towards new viewing platforms.* Retrieved from http://www.cftpa.ca/government_relations/pdfs/CMPA_Remarks_to_Standing_Committee_re_Impact_of_Change_in_Television_Ownership.pdf

Canadian Private Copying Collective. (2011). *Private copying and copyright.* Retrieved from http://www.cpcc.ca/en/the-cpcc/private-copying-and-copyright

Canadian Radio-Television and Telecommunications Commission. (2006). *Broadcasting Public Notice CRTC 2006–158, Commercial Radio Policy 2006.* Retrieved from http://www.crtc.gc.ca/eng/archive/2006/pb2006-158.pdf

————. (2010a). *Broadcasting Regulatory Policy CRTC 2010–167, A group-based approach to the licensing of private television services.* Retrieved from http://crtc.gc.ca/eng/archive/2010/2010-167.pdf

————. (2010b). *Facts and figures: Highlights about Canadian television.* Retrieved from http://www.crtc.gc.ca/eng/cancon/t_facts.htm

———. (2010c). *The MAPL system—defining a Canadian song.* Retrieved from http://www.crtc.gc.ca/eng/info_sht/r1.htm

Canadian Radio-Television and Telecommunications Commission, and Canadian Media Research Inc. (2006). *How many Canadians subscribe to cable TV or satellite TV? Cable TV/DTH subscriber estimates, profile of non-subscribers and special survey results.* Retrieved from http://www.crtc.gc.ca/eng/publications/reports/radio/cmri.pdf

Collins, Richard. (1990). *Culture, communication, national identity: The case of Canadian television.* Toronto: University of Toronto Press.

Dubinski, Lon. (1996). Periodical publishing. In M. Dorland (Ed.). *The cultural industries in Canada.* Toronto: James Lorimer.

Druick, Zoe (2007) *Projecting Canada: Government policy and documentary film at the National Film Board of Canada.* Montreal: McGill-Queen's University Press.

Foote, John. A. (2000). *Federal cultural policy in Canada.* Unpublished manuscript. Published in French as 'La politique culturelle fédérale au Canada.' *Loisir et Société 22*(2).

Freedman, Des. (2008). Introducing media policy. In D. Freedman, *The politics of media policy.* Malden, MA: Polity Press.

Friends of Canadian Broadcasting. (2011). *Presentation to the House of Commons Standing Committee on Canadian Heritage on the mandate and funding of the Canadian Broadcasting Corporation.* Retrieved from http://www.friends.ca/brief/10096

Grant, Peter S., and Chris Wood. (2004). *Blockbusters and trade wars: Popular culture in a globalized world.* Vancouver: Douglas & McIntyre.

Habermas, Jurgen. (2001). The public sphere: an encyclopedia article. In M. G. Durham and D. Kellner (Eds.), *Media and cultural studies key works.* Malden, MA: Blackwell.

Hackett, Robert A., and Steve Anderson. (2011). Democratizing communication policy in Canada: A social movement perspective. *Canadian Journal of Communication 36*(1):161–168.

Krahsinsky, Susan. (18 March 2010). Private broadcasters post first operating loss. *The Globe and Mail.*

LeBlanc, Larry, and FACTOR. (2007). *The FACTOR story: Fostering emerging artists and musical diversity.* Toronto: Foundation to Assist Canadian Talent on Recordings.

Lorimer, Rowland. (1991). Book publishing in English Canada in the context of free trade. *Canadian Journal of Communication* (1), Retrieved from http://www.cjc-online.ca/index.php/journal/article/view/582/488

National Film Board of Canada. (2010). *Emerging and digital media: Opportunities and challenges.* Presentation to the House of Commons Standing Committee on Canadian Heritage, 29 April 2010. Retrieved from http://www.onf-nfb.gc.ca/medias/download/documents/pdf/publications/NFB-ONF_Presentation_10-04-29.pdf

———. (2012). *Our history: The NFB Foundation.* Retrieved from http://www.nfb.ca/historique/about-the-foundation

Nordicity Group Ltd. (2006). *Analysis of government support for Public Broadcasting and other culture in Canada.* Retrieved from http://www.cbc.radio-canada.ca/submissions/crtc/2006/BNPH_2006-5_CBC_RC_Public_Broadcaster_Comparison.pdf

————. (2008). *Economic analysis of the Canadian film or video production tax credit.* Retrieved from http://www.nordicity.com/reports/Economic_Analysis_of_CPTC_final.pdf

Raboy, Marc. (1990). *Missed opportunities: The story of Canada's broadcasting policy.* Montreal, QC, CAN: McGill-Queen's University Press.

Statistics Canada. (2010). *Government expenditures on culture.* Retrieved from http://www.statcan.gc.ca/pub/87f0001x/87f0001x2010001-eng.pdf

Szeman, Imre. (2000). The rhetoric of culture: Some notes on magazines, Canadian culture, and globalization. *Journal of Canadian Studies 35*(3):212–230.

World Trade Organization. (2012). *Canada—Periodicals (DS31).* Retrieved from http://www.wto.org/english/tratop_e/dispu_e/cases_e/1pagesum_e/ds31sum_e.pdf

Wright, Robert A. (2004). Gimme shelter: Cultural protectionism and the Canadian recording industry (Chapter 3). In *Virtual sovereignty: Nationalism, culture, and the Canadian question.* Toronto: Canadian Scholars' Press.